THE SCHULTZ SITE AT GREEN POINT

A Stratified Occupation Area in the Saginaw Valley of Michigan

MEMOIRS OF THE MUSEUM OF ANTHROPOLOGY
UNIVERSITY OF MICHIGAN
NUMBER 4

THE SCHULTZ SITE AT GREEN POINT

A Stratified Occupation Area in the Saginaw Valley of Michigan

Edited and Compiled By
JAMES E. FITTING

CONTRIBUTORS

APRIL L. ALLISON
DAVID S.BROSE
FEL V. BRUNETT
FRED W. FISCHER
JAMES E. FITTING
BARBARA LUXENBERG
ANDREW McCLARY
PETER F. MURRAY
JOHN D. SPETH
GARY A. WRIGHT

ANN ARBOR
1972

PREFACE

The Schultz site is an important site for the understanding of Saginaw Valley prehistory. It also should play a major role in future interpretations of Great Lakes prehistory. The primary value of the Schultz Site report, however, is educational. It has taught a great many of us how little we know about archaeological interpretations. When the site was excavated, we were working with a simple model for archaeological interpretation, essentially involving the description, and, perhaps, stratigraphic placement of the artifacts. It soon became clear that the environmental data produced by our excavations were as significant as the archaeological data. That is why the papers on flora and fauna are placed at the very beginning of the report. The cultural material must be interpreted in the context that these chapters provide. At a later stage of interpretation, many of us became aware of the potential for cross-correlating different types of information; particularly within each living level. I am just as aware as any reader that we have failed to do this adequately. A detailed study of living floor distribution, particularly for the rich Early Woodland floors, is now underway and should partially remedy this weakness at a future date.

Writing a report on a large excavation is always a challenge. One approach is to spend a life time on a single site. An alternative approach is to involve a number of specialists in a "team effort." These specialty reports can be summarized by a single author, or they can be presented by each specialist, as is done in this volume. Each paper in this volume has many excellent features. I am aware, however, that we may not have produced the best possible site report. I do not know if the best possible site report will ever be written.

Field work for this project was supported by NSF Grant GS-86, under the direction of Dr. James B. Griffin. Field work and some aspects of laboratory analysis were supported by NSF-USEP training grants under Griffin's direction. Other phases of laboratory analysis were supported by NSF Grants GS-666 and GS-1486 under my direction.

I should like to thank the many individuals who contributed chapters to this volume for their many hours of work. I should like to acknowledge the aid of my wife, Molly, in editing these papers, the assistance of George Stuber in preparing the many figures, and Millie Smith for typing the final draft of the manuscript. Last, I should like to express my thanks to Dr. James B. Griffin, Director of the University of Michigan Museum of Anthropology, for publishing this volume in the Memoir series of that museum.

J. E. F.
January, 1969

CONTENTS

FIGURES

TABLES

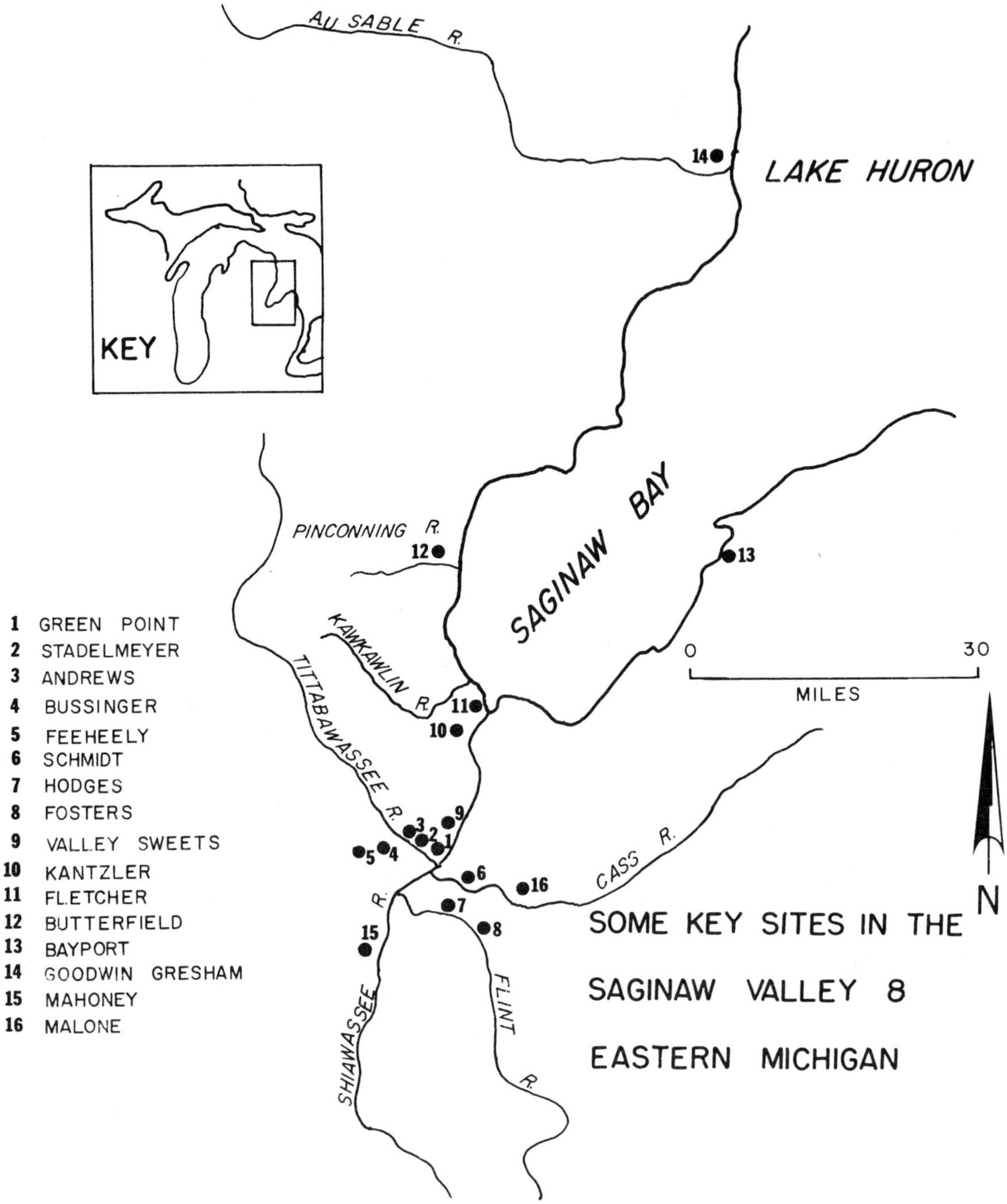
AU SABLE R.
14
LAKE HURON
KEY
SAGINAW BAY
PINCONNING R.
12
13
KAWKAWLIN R.
11
10
TITTABAWASSEE R.
9
3
2
1
5
4
6
16
CASS R.
7
8
15
R.
SHIAWASSEE
FLINT R.
0
30
MILES
N
SOME KEY SITES IN THE
SAGINAW VALLEY 8
EASTERN MICHIGAN
1 GREEN POINT
2 STADELMEYER
3 ANDREWS
4 BUSSINGER
5 FEEHEELY
6 SCHMIDT
7 HODGES
8 FOSTERS
9 VALLEY SWEETS
10 KANTZLER
11 FLETCHER
12 BUTTERFIELD
13 BAYPORT
14 GOODWIN GRESHAM
15 MAHONEY
16 MALONE

Fig. 1.

INTRODUCTION

The Saginaw Valley has long been known for its importance in Michigan prehistory. W.B. Hinsdale, in his study of aboriginal population distribution in the state, estimated that 30 percent of the prehistoric population of Michigan would have lived in this valley. While Hinsdale's estimates might be difficult to validate with our present understanding of patterns of seasonal movement, it does indicate the importance of this region.

Some of the earliest work in Michigan prehistory was carried out in this area, and two of Michigan's best known archaecologist, Harlan I. Smith and Fred Dustin, worked intensively in this rich river valley. This volume is an indirect result of their efforts. A number of Fred Dustin's papers have recently been republished by the Michigan Archaeological Society as a special issue of their journal. Under the heading *Saginaw Valley Archaeology,* these surveys and discussions are essential for understanding the following reports of field work carried out in the valley in the last decade.

The topography of the Saginaw Valley is largely a result of late Pleistocene influences (see Fig. 1). The Saginaw lobe of the Wisconsin ice gouged out the old Huron River Valley to form the present-day Saginaw Bay. The Saginaw lobe melted more rapidly than the general Huron advance, and the area of the Saginaw Valley today owes its smooth topography to these long-dammed waters. As the lake drained, a series of concentric beach ridges were formed in semicircles decreasing in size as they approached the bay. This lake plain slopes gently from 740 feet above sea level to the present level of Lake Huron at 580 feet above sea level. There are few relief features in the area other than the former beach ridges. One of the other principal features is a moraine just below the Schultz site upon which present-day Saginaw is built.

Four main rivers drain an area of slightly over 6,000 square miles. The Flint River has a valley 120 miles long and drains approximately 1,350 square miles of land. The Cass is 75 miles long with a watershed of 920 square miles. These rivers, together with the Shiawassee which drains 1,070 square miles, cover the southern half of the Saginaw Valley. The largest river in the valley is the Tittabawassee which, although it is only 80 miles long, drains 2,600 square miles and furnishes more water to the Saginaw River than the other rivers combined. In addition to the larger watershed, this river carries more water, i.e., .69 cubic feet per second per square mile of watershed, than the other rivers at .50 cubic feet of water per second per square mile of watershed. The Tittabawassee also floods several days later than the other rivers in the valley.

The Flint and Cass flow into the Shiawassee just to the south of the area where the Shiawassee and Tittabawassee join to form the Saginaw. This meeting of the waters, the key location of the aboriginal Saginaw Valley, is at Green Point. Below the present city of Saginaw, the river is sluggish and drops only about one inch per mile until it reaches Saginaw Bay. Strong winds from the bay will cause the water level to rise as far up the river as Green Point.

Precipitation is relatively well distributed throughout the year with a spring maximum. July temperatures average in the low seventies and January temperatures in the low twenties. There is, however, a great deal of variation from day to day. There is an average range of 45 degrees Fahrenheit in both July and January. During the past six years, our field crews have worked through summer temperatures as low as the thirties and as high as 100 degrees Fahrenheit.

The length of the growing season throughout most of the valley is over 140 days. The exception is the weather station at West Branch which reported only 110 days between killing frosts, on an average, for a 30 year period. This West Branch station is located in the northern part of the valley on the central Michigan high plains where soils, vegetation and climate differ from the rest of the valley.

Because of the geological history of the area, there are alternating tracts of clay, sand, and gravel with varying degrees of drainage. This caused a great deal of variation in the presettlement vegetation patterns. Beech-maple would have probably been the climax vegetation in the area if there had been time for a good drainage pattern to develop. As it is, there were many microenvironments, including elements of both northern and southern forest types. Extensive areas of marshland existed along the river in back of the bay and south of the city of Saginaw in the Shiawassee flats. The large stands of pine were located on the sandy Michigan high plains of the upper Tittabawassee.

Much of the area was covered by a mixed forest of hardwoods and conifers. Between small stands of pine, locally called "pine runs," were elm, soft maple, basswood, swamp white oak and black ash. Stands of hardwoods in the valley varied, depending on drainage. On the lake plain were elm, silver maple, black and white ash, basswood and red maple. In the better drained highlands, the hardwoods included beech, sugar maple, hemlock, yellow birch, basswood, oak, hickory, elm and ash.

This is the land in which the prehistoric inhabitants of the valley lived and worked and where Smith, Dustin, ourselves and countless others have lived since, devoting our efforts to the study of the earlier inhabitants. This volume is one of the results of an interest in the area by the Great Lakes Division of the University of Michigan Museum of Anthropology which started with the salvage operations at the Late Archaic Andrews site in 1957 (Papworth, 1967). Mark Papworth and Malcomb Webb, assisted at times by other University of Michigan graduate students, undertook limited survey work in the area between 1957 and 1960. They were particularly interested in Late Archaic sites, and they used Dustin's earlier surveys and collections (which he had given to the University of Michigan Museum of Anthropology before his death) as their guides.

In the summer of 1960 Dr. James B. Griffin obtained funds for actual site excavation on a regular basis, and several sites, most notably the Feeheley site, were tested during that time. University of Michigan field parties returned to the valley for every season between 1960 and 1967. More recent work has been directed toward sites of later time horizons and toward the Saginaw Valley as a buffer area between the Carolinian and Canadian biotic provinces.

Many small sites have been excavated, some reported elsewhere and some which have yet to be fully described. These sites are important, but the site which is the key to the understanding of Saginaw Valley archaeology is the Schultz site, located at Green Point at the very hub of the valley. The following pages are devoted to an analysis of this key site. This is followed by a review of the general patterns of cultural development in the Saginaw Valley.

This volume is not a perfect statement of the prehistory of an area. Extensive work has been carried out in the valley since 1967 by Michigan State University at the Fletcher site, and the past five years has seen a revitalization of the Saginaw Valley Archaeological Society and some very impressive work by nonprofessionals. Our efforts can be considered successful if subsequent workers can draw on them for comparative information, for inspiration, or for interpretive hypotheses with which to argue.

I

EXCAVATIONS AT THE SCHULTZ SITE

James E. Fitting

EARLIER EXCAVATIONS

The Schultz site is located on Green Point, an historic area now within the boundaries of the present-day city of Saginaw. Green Point, according to tradition, is a direct translation of the Chippewa term for the area, *Showskakon.* Fred Dustin felt that this term might be more properly applied to the area across the Tittabawassee from what is commonly called Green Point but bowed to the more standard usage in his own published papers.

A contemporary political description would place it in the southwest quarter of section 2 and the southeast quarter of section 3 of James Township in Saginaw County; an area today owned by Mr. Ruben Schultz of Saginaw. A natural description would place it just to the north of the Tittabawassee River at the point where the Tittabawassee joins the Shiawassee to form the Saginaw River. This is the very "hub" of the Saginaw River Valley.

The earliest account of the archaeological remains in the area dates back to pioneer times. The area was opened for settlement only after the Chippewa Treaty of 1819 arranged by General Lewis Cass. In 1830 there were only 28 white inhabitants in the Saginaw Valley north of Flint. The earliest account of the prehistoric occupation at Green Point which I have so far located is from William R. McCormick's paper, "Mounds and Mound Builders of the Saginaw Valley" in the Michigan Pioneer and Historical Collections.

> Proceeding down the river to the mouth of the Tittabawassee, at a place formerly called Green Point, a favorite camping ground of the indians in olden time, and where they had their corn-fields, quite a distance back from the river on the prairie, contrary to all previous experience, we discovered two very large mounds. I think that I first saw them in 1836. They were sixty-feet long and thirty feet wide by four or five feet high. They are on very low ground and subject every spring to be inundated by the river, and for convenience I shall call them the Green Point mounds. I also saw one after it had been opened, and the whole interior appeared to be of a whitish substence, evidently of decomposed bones, decomposition being more rapid than for the same length of time elsewhere, owing to the lowness of the land and the overflow of the river. What the relic hunters found in these mounds I have never ascertained (McCormick, 1883).

The land on Green Point passed from the government into private hands a few years before McCormick first saw the site. In 1832 Judge Albert Miller purchased land at Green Point and moved to this area in the winter of 1833. He constructed a house and a pen for animals. He planted 30 acres of corn on the prairie area of Green Point in 1833 and wrote bitterly of how it was all lost to the birds.

Harlan I. Smith obtained a small collection from the site while a school boy in Saginaw between 1883 and 1891. He mentioned the Green Point Mounds in connection with the Golson Cache (1894: 2) and located them on his map of Saginaw Valley archaeological sites (1901:8). He also published a picture of the mounds (1901:8) which was later reproduced as a drawing (Smith, 1902) which gave the impression that the wooded area in the background was one of the mounds. Since the mound was clear of vegetation, I would suspect that the picture was not taken until some time around 1900.

Fred Dustin has been one of the main contributors to the study of Saginaw Valley archaeology. Many of his published papers have recently been collected into a single volume (Dustin, 1968). Along with his unpublished papers located at the University of Michigan Museum of Anthropology and in the Michigan Historical Collections, this volume furnishes us with an excellent picture of the archaeology of the Saginaw Valley in general, and Green Point in particular.

His first contact with the mounds, according to an unpublished and undated manuscript entitled "Village Sites," was in 1887, the year in which he came to Saginaw. This is supported by a statement in the *Saginaw Courier-Herald* for December 11, 1910, that he first visited the site 23 years earlier.

Dustin's most vivid description of Green Point can be found in his paper, "Some Ancient Indian Village Sites in Saginaw County, Michigan."

> For the close of this paper, I have reserved an important village site which lies within the corporate limits of the city of Saginaw. It is on the floodplain in the extreme south part of the site on the west side of the Saginaw River and north of the Tittabawassee. Here on this low ground are extensive prehistoric remains extending east and west nearly a mile, and it is quite possible that they extended further to the west, but the land there is still mostly wooded and unbroken so that the arbitrary line of the fence to the west of the abandoned Riverside Mine No. 2 will be taken as its western boundary. Close to the section line between 2 and 3 and from there west to the fence noted, the remains are thick, while east of this section line until we arrive at a point about 1,000 feet east from the junction of the Shiawassee and Tittabawassee Rivers, evidences of primitive cultures are very rare and casual, as far as surface indications are concerned.
>
> The western village site is marked by two large mounds, now nearly leveled by cultivation. For many years, I have made collections in the close vicinity, and near the boundary fence mentioned have occasionally picked up a piece of pottery or a chip of flint, once finding a little pipe . . . . As late as 1900, approximately the entire tract, some of it marsh and covering over a square mile, was wooded except small patches which had been Indian fields or natural prairies (Dustin, 1930: 85-86).

The distinction between 20SA1, the Green Point Village site, and 20SA2, the Green Point Mounds (also a village site), is very clear in Dustin's writing. The difference between the two areas showed up in our own excavation as we shall discuss in more detail.

Dustin described 20SA1 in 1929 in a paper entitled, "Some Ancient Fire-beds in Saginaw County Michigan."

> When the first settlers came to what is now Saginaw, there was a deer lick on the north bank of the Tittabawassee just at its mouth, an ooze of brine coming up from a salt formation at the river's edge. As what we will for convenience call Green Point, was partly prairie land; it was the first pasture into which new comers turned their cows. Hungry for salt, the cattle wallowed in the deer lick and it was only a matter of a few years until aided by the rising waters of spring, a cut was formed running back into the land twenty rods or more (Dustin, 1929*b*:302-03).

I would suspect that Dustin's distinction between 20SA1 and 20SA2 was made, in part, on the basis of the former area being a cleared wet prairie, while the later area was wooded elm flats when he first visited these sites in 1887.

Dustin left descriptions of the mounds. The westernmost mound was 100 feet in diameter and 3.5 feet high. The eastern mounds were 90 feet in diameter and also

3.5 feet high. According to a 1911 manuscript entitled, "Mounds," Dustin trenched both mounds on August 30, 1909, but reported only scattered bone fragments. In another manuscript, dated May 11, 1911, he reported large amounts of skeletal material being plowed up in an area 50 feet west of his westernmost mound. This would place it in the burial area excavated by University of Michigan field parties in 1962 and 1964.

By the late 1920's, the man who owned the mounds became ". . .possessed with the idea that the traditional pot of silver is somewhere hidden on his 300 acres and no longer permits collection . . ."(Dustin, 1929*a*: 75). Subsequent owners of the site have also discouraged collectors and by the late 1950's the site had faded into legend.

In 1959, Mark Papworth and several University of Michigan students visited the site for a day and put in a small test pit somewhere in the area of 20SA1, although from photographs of this pit which I have seen, I would estimate that it was to the north and east of the richer parts of this site. Some chippage, a triangular point and an expanding stemmed projectile point were uncovered at this time, and a cultural sequence was plotted for the site on the basis of these excavations.

In 1960, Malcomb Webb and a crew of six worked at Green Point on July 11 and July 12. They opened three five-by-ten-foot test pits, only one of which was screened. They found no cultural material, no living floors and reached the water table at two and one-half feet below the surface. Records from both the 1959 and 1960 expeditions in the University of Michigan Museum of Anthropology files are not too complete; but from conversations with crew members from that season, it would appear that Webb's excavations were along the Saginaw River well to the north of 20SA1 and more than a mile from 20SA2. It is ironic that the 1959 and 1960 expeditions had literally to drive over the richest areas of both 20SA2 and 20SA1 to get to the areas where they worked.

1962 EXCAVATIONS

On July 22, 1962, Henry T. Wright, a member of the Macomb County Archaeological Survey party, returned to Green Point and obtained permission from the property owner, Mr. Ruben Schultz, to examine the area and make test pits as long as they did not disturb any of the crops. He managed to obtain a large surface collection that day, and on July 24, James Fitting, David Taggart and Henry Wright returned to the site for a more intensive examination of 20SA2. We were able to put in several one-by-one foot test pits between a soy bean and wheat field along what was later to be the East 460 line of the grid system on the site. These pits revealed a burial area, which was covered up since it could not be properly cleared without damaging crops. Another test pit revealed at least a half a foot of cultural material below the plow zone.

On the 27th of July we again returned to the site and put in a test cut along the east wall of the large gully at 20SA1, which was described earlier by Dustin. This cut revealed over seven feet of well-stratified deposits with sparse indications of several occupational levels.

On July 30, the entire Macomb County field crew, consisting of Fitting, Taggart, Henry Wright, Gary Wright, Fred Fischer, and Allan Babb, moved to Saginaw. Between July 31 and August 3, four more profile cuts were opened in the gully at 20SA1. On August 3 the wheat on 20SA2 was cut and we were able to concentrate excavations in that area.

Henry Wright continued work at 20SA1 and was assisted by Sidney Harrison between August 7 and August 24. The work

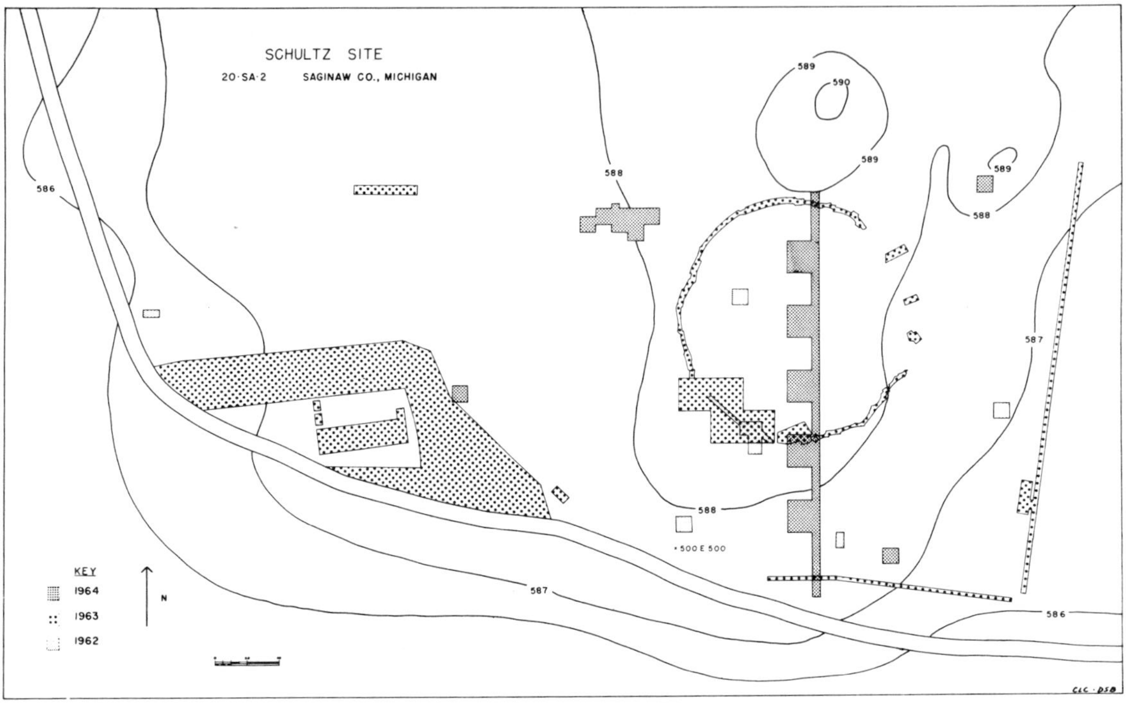

Fig. 2. Excavations at the Schultz site, 1962-1964.

at 20SA1 has been reported by Wright (1964) in another paper.

Because of the initial success of excavations at the Schultz site, Dr. Richard O. Keslin, then Curator of the Great Lakes Division of the University of Michigan Museum of Anthropology and field director of the Division's summer program, called other field crews to the site. The 1962 excavations were assisted at various times between August 7 and August 24 by Richard E. Flanders, G. Richard Peske, Robert Bettarel and Jennifer Rice. Charles E. Cleland and Alan McPherron also spent some time at the site assisting in the excavation.

During the period of August 3 to August 24, a total area of 700 square feet was cleared in six ten-by-ten-foot units and two five-by-five-foot units.

In the grid system of the site these were ten-by-ten-units: 510E550, 580E540, 580E550, 590E540, 590E700, and 650E540. A north to south oriented five-by-ten-foot unit was opened at 500E600 and an east to west five-by-ten-foot unit was opened at the bend of the road into the site and designated Test Pit No. 4 (the earlier test pits between the bean and wheat field were Test Pits No. 1 through No. 3).

During the 1962 excavations a total of 28 hearths, refuse pits, and other cultural disturbances were given feature numbers. The block of excavation units 570E550, 580E540, and 580E550, uncovered a row of six very distinctive post molds running in a generally northwest to southeast direction across these units. These varied between .6 and one foot in diameter and were between two and three feet apart. They formed a pattern suggesting either a large structure or stockade and served as the starting point for the excavations of the following season.

1963 EXCAVATIONS

One of the major problems encountered during the 1962 season was the confusing stratigraphy of the site. Almost every excavation unit or block of units excavated during the 1962 season showed a different depositional sequence with similar cultural materials being recovered from a wide range of depths in various excavation units. Therefore, early in June, before the 1963 field season began, Keslin, assisted by Taggart, Cleland, John Eaton and Martin Wobst, returned to the site and supervised the excavation of several large machine trenches; four running parallel to the river and one running at right angles to the river. These trenches were profiled during that time and they helped to unravel the complex stratigraphy of the site (see Speth, this volume, for the final interpretation).

The main portion of the field season lasted from June 10 to August 17. In addition to Keslin, Taggart, Eaton and Wobst, the field party consisted of Richard Ford, Gary Wright, Susan Doyle, Marilyn Hollander, Joyce Neimi, Diane Foster, Jan Hulett and Howard Lipsum who were assisted at various times during the summer by Rebecca Bahlman, G. Richard Peske, Daniel Higgins, David Griffin and Barry Kent.

Much time was spent in profiling the machine trench, which had been opened prior to the beginning of the season. The main excavations centered around the series of post molds which had been uncovered near the end of the 1962 season.

Fig. 3. Excavations at the Schultz site, 1963.

A series of four contiguous 20-by-20-foot units were opened over the top of the block of units containing the post molds from the 1962 season. These were referred to as 20 by 20 A, B, C, and D. Excluding the areas excavated in 1962, this block of units uncovered, at least to the Middle Woodland level, about 1300 square feet of the site.

This furnished the major source for controlled data from the 1963 season. While profiling the machine trench (Machine Trench No. 6), which ran at right angles to the river, at least 35 square feet more were cleared to the Early Woodland level.

Toward the end of the season, several members of the crew attempted to follow the projected pattern of the post molds. This was done by shoveling off the plow zone and upper levels of the site until the post molds were revealed. This took a great deal of time, and they were almost able to complete the full circle. Very little cultural material was uncovered while this was being done. In one area along the south side of the stockade an additional trench, Trench No. 8, was carefully excavated because of several key features. Of most importance was Feature No. 100, a late Middle Woodland refuse pit with a nearly complete vessel in it, which was located directly over a post mold, indicating that the stockade had been abandoned by the time this pit was dug.

A shell concentration in the northwest corner of the site was stripped for approximately 300 square feet, but only the truncated base of a pit and a very sparse representation of cultural material were present. Excavations in this area contributed little to our knowledge of the site.

Another project undertaken in the 1963 season was the machine stripping of a large area in the southwestern portion of the site. This was done with a road grader. Unfortunately, a misunderstanding arose, and work had to be stopped several times in this area, sometimes for as much as a week at a time. Between frequent work stoppage and irregular participation by crew members in following and clearing behind the grader, the field notes for this area are uneven. There is also some problem in placing this area in the same stratigraphic sequence as the rest of the site, and because of the nature of the excavation and machine stripping, it is impossible to determine the level of origin or true dimensions of most of the features. Therefore, the material from this area will be described, but the excavations could not be placed in the same context as those from the rest of the site.

During the 1963 season, 74 additional features, mostly pits, hearths and artifact concentrations, were uncovered. Twenty-three of these were in the area of machine stripping so only 51 will be included in the feature analysis. The stockade trench uncovered a total of 128 post molds of this structure which was circular and approximately 150 feet in diameter. The main block of excavations had bordered on the southwestern edge of this stockade with most on the outside. We were still uncertain of its function. The excavations so far had seemed to indicate that the densest concentrations of cultural debris were outside the stockade; particularly to the south in the old river channel area. The problem of interpreting this stockade was one of the principal problems posed for the 1964 season.

1964 SEASON

The 1964 season excavation was under the direction of Dr. James E. Fitting, then Curator of the Great Lakes Division of the University of Michigan Museum of Anthropology. The basic field crew consisted of Fitting, Martha Rolingson, Henry Wright, Richard Ford, Karen Ford, Richard Morlan, Michael Clark, David Brose, Elizabeth Stern, Jasmina Stef-

Fig. 4. Excavations at the Schultz site, 1964.

anovic, Diane Foster, Jerry Vanni, Sidney Harrison and Thomas Abler, assisted at times by Andrew Goodman and George Miller. In addition to the Schultz site, satellite excavations were undertaken at the Schmidt site (Harrison, 1966) and the Goodwin-Gresham site (Fitting, Brose, Wright and Dinerstein, 1969) by various crew members at various times during the summer.

The main 1964 excavations at Schultz consisted of a transect of the stockade by a long trench. This was centered around five 20-by-20-foot excavation units separated from each other by 20 feet. These units were eventually joined by a connecting five-foot trench with extensions of 20 and 30 feet on either end to furnish a 230-foot north to south excavation across the entire site. This main unit covered an area of 2,650 square feet, but 150 square feet overlapped with the 1963 post mold trench. Even this was further excavated down to sterile deposits in 1964.

The 20-by-20-foot units were opened at 510E570, located in the old river channel area of the site to the south of the stockade; 550E570, which overlapped the south wall of the stockade; and 590E570 630E570, and 670E570, all located within the stockade. The connecting five-foot units were opened along the East 585 line, and the profile of the site was taken along the East 590 line.

A second major project was the relocation of the burial area around Test Pit No. 2 from the 1962 season. In a preseason visit to the site, Fitting and Ford had located an area of bone concentration in the area of the site where the burials had been uncovered in 1962. They marked the center of this concentration and this

Fig. 5. Excavations at the Schultz site, 1964.

point turned out to be less than .5 feet from Test Pit No. 2. A 20-by-20-foot unit, two 10-by-10-foot units and a 2-by-10-foot extension were opened to reveal a small, plowed down mound with a number of burials. Once again, we were unable to clear the full extent of the burials because of a bean field to the north of the area where we had previously contracted for excavation. In all, 620 square feet were opened in this burial area, although not all of it was excavated down to sterile deposits. The burials had been badly damaged by plowing and grading of the site, and only fragments were recovered, including parts of 7 skulls and the teeth of at least 16 different individuals. From what little was left, they looked like disarticulated secondary burials with piles of skulls, long bones and ribs.

During the final weeks of the summer, we opened three ten-by ten-foot units outside of the stockade in the parts of the site open to us. These were located at 490E630 and 580E360, both in the area of the old river channel, and 720E690 which proved to be basket loaded mound fill.

During the season, the long trench penetrated a low rise directly in back of the stockade, bordering so closely on it as to touch it. This low rise was man-made and quite clearly constructed by basket-loading. The excavation at 720E690 to the east was also basket loaded and a modest rise. By checking old descriptions, we were able to determine that these were the Green Point mounds described by McCormick, Smith and Dustin as they existed after a half century of plowing and, as we later found out, land leveling in the late 1940's. Not only did they correspond to Dustin's location, but the burial area which we excavated in 1964 corresponded to the area where he reported finding human bone in 1910. Dustin saw no rise distinct enough to suggest a burial mound in 1910 and neither did we in 1962. To be truthful, it was only after three years of intensive excavation at the "Green Point mounds" that we were even able to locate the mounds. In the burial area, it was only during excavation that we found basket-loading in this otherwise level area.

Since the burial area was basket loaded, we designated it Mound A; the largest of the mounds in back of the stockade was probably Dustin's westernmost mound and we gave this the designation Mound B. Dustin's easternmost mound was that in the area of 720E690 and we called this Mound C. We made arrangements in 1964 to come back to the site in 1965, after the crops had been removed, to excavate Mound C.

During the summer of 1964, 102 additional features were excavated including pits, hearths and areas of artifact concentration.

1965 EXCAVATIONS

Between August 19 and August 24 of 1965, James Fitting and George L. Miller did an electronic resistivity survey of the Mound B and Mound C areas with a Gossens Geohm. No regular pattern could be observed for Mound B, but we were able to find the approximate limits of Mound C. Excavations were undertaken in this mound between the 21st and 24th by Fitting and Miller, assisted by Dr. Gordon Grosscup of Wayne State University and three students from that university, Burton Barnard, Alan Hugley, and Charna Norman. We were also assisted by Don Foster, Arthur Graves and Harold Thompson of the Saginaw Valley Chapter of the Michigan Archaeological Society.

The mound was initially sectioned by two 5-by-60 foot trenches slightly off center to the northwest. Finally, a 20-by-20-foot unit was opened at the center of the mound working out to the southeast from the point where the two trenches intersected. Since the fill of the mound was virtually sterile, it was not screened. Although some 1,000 square feet were excavated to sterile sands, no burials were uncovered in this mound, and there were only scattered sherds and mica flecks in the fill. One sterile hearth was located beneath the mound and there was a charred log and about 200 bivalve shells beneath the floor in the center of the mound.

The total area excavated between 1962 and 1965, excluding the machine trenching and stripping, was about 6,700 square feet. Of this area, we had good stratigraphic data for about 5,000 square feet, once we excluded areas of mound fill and sterile areas of the site.

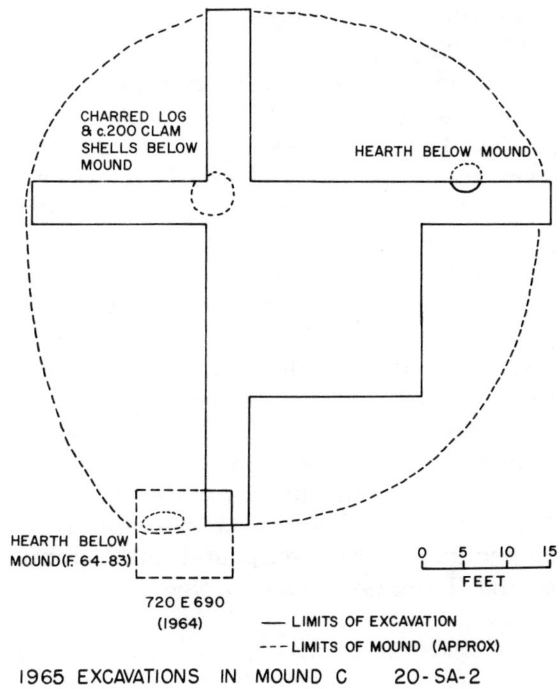

Fig. 6.

FIELD STRATIGRAPHY

The techniques of excavation used for a particular site, particularly the provenience units chosen, are dependent on the type of information you are seeking from the site. The types of information you are seeking are, in turn, dependent on what you expect to find; that is, your preconceived ideas of the depositional or stratigraphic sequence. From a cursory reading of Dustin's fire-bed paper, it was obvious, even before the excavation of the gully trenches, that the deposits on the site were deep. It was also obvious that there was no lack of cultural material and that there was no point in digging just to accumulate artifacts. It was the preconceived idea of the cultural sequence present at the site that determined the excavation techniques of any particular field party. As we learned more about the site, our field technique improved; but even after the 1965 season we still did not have the detail indicated by Speth's geological analysis which was completed only in 1968.

The 1959 expedition to the site was conceived with the idea that certain small, narrow stemmed projectile points found in Fred Dustin's collections from the site were manufactured at an early date. Our excavation suggested that at the Schultz site, these points were most characteristic of the later occupations.

In 1959, the investigators noted the presence of Middle and Late Woodland artifacts and "Middle Archaic" but not Late Archaic projectile points. It was postulated that there was a pre-Lake Nipissing high stage Archaic occupation; that the site was inundated during the Nipissing and Algoma stages and reoccupied during the later post–Lake Algoma period. To quote the field notes:

> Enthusiasm at this typological revelation drove the author to a hurried one day return to Saginaw in the fall (1959). I was able to confirm my suspicion as to the reality of the stratigraphic deposition of the silts at the site and found that there was evidence of occupation during the low stage of the Great Lakes (6500-2000 B.C.) followed by silty lake deposits which were topped by a Woodland occupation level, finally covered by two feet of recent river silt.

It was, in part, this search for Archaic materials that brought us back to the area in the summer of 1962, even after the abortive efforts of 1960. While current interpretations of the site do not exactly support the 1959 interpretations, it was the 1959 interpretations which led to the excavation of the gully trenches in 1962 and led to the excavation of 20SA1, which produced an Early Woodland component seven and one-half feet below the surface of this site.

In 1962, our first concern was with the geological sequence. Our gully trenches revealed a completely different stratigraphic sequence on either side of the gully, possibly because of greater erosion and slump on the western side. The eastern wall profiles suggested the possibility of an early occupation right at the water table and resting on lake deposits. This is what led Henry Wright to further excavation in the area of 20SA1.

We went to work at 20SA2 with this depositional sequence in mind, but the first excavation unit, 510E500, showed an entirely different geological and cultural sequence than any from the gully area. Here we had an upper level just below the plow zone which was more than a foot of dark silt containing Late Woodland cultural material (we learned in this unit that no additional information, only mixed sample, could be gained by screening the plow zone; this zone was thereafter shoveled off before controlled stratigraphic excavation began). Below this was a dense level of Middle Woodland material, and below this was a sparse but thick deposit of a possibly earlier Middle Woodland material taking us down to more than six feet below the surface. This sequence was duplicated in 500E600 with an even more complex stratigraphy in the lower levels.

On the other hand, the central block of units had a very shallow or nonexistant Late Woodland level, a foot or so of sparse Middle Woodland deposits and an Early Woodland level resting on bedded sands as little as three feet below the surface.

In units 590E700 and 650E540, the entire upper portion of this sequence was absent. The deposits directly below the plow zone, except for some obviously truncated pits (from plowing and grading), contained what appeared to be an earlier type of Middle Woodland cultural material.

The 1963 machine trench did much to clear up our picture of the site. The area where the deep units were found at 20 SA 2 was apparently an old river channel which had been operative during the Early Woodland period. This channel cut into the bedded sands of the lake which occupied the area during the Lake Nipissing and Algoma high water stages. The cultural debris in the channel was deposited during the Middle and Late Woodland period.

David Taggart did a field study of the geology of the site in 1963, and his observations largely determined the pattern of excavation followed in 1963 and 1964. He recognized a level of bedded sands which he correlated with lake, or possibly shoreline, deposits which predated 1,000 B.C. Overlying these sands was a level of reduced silts which he referred to as the lower dark silts. These were found along the top of the old levee and contained the Early Woodland cultural material. Taggart correlated the lower bedded silts in the area of the old river channel with the lower dark silts at the rest of the site.

Overlying the lower dark silts were deposits of medium brown oxidized silts; Taggart's brown silt level. They varied in thickness from .6 feet in the northern part of the site to as much as 4 feet in thickness in the old river channel. An apparently earlier type of Middle Woodland cultural material was found in small quantities in this level. In the northern parts of the site, this was the uppermost level that we encountered.

In the central and southern parts of the site there were deposits which Taggart referred to as the upper dark silts and divided in more detail into middle, intermediate and upper dark silt levels. The middle dark silts were believed to be deposited during the later part of the Middle Woodland occupation; the intermediate level was an occupational hiatus with little occupational debris; and the upper dark silts contained Late Woodland material. These subdivisions were most clear in the old river channel. In areas north of the river channel, the upper dark silts were thin or absent. When present, division into the constituent levels was usually impossible.

The 1964 excavations were undertaken following Taggart's depositional sequence, and we tried to make our provenience units correspond to his levels. I emphasize this since the analysis of cultural material is based on the provenience units used in recovery and not on Speth's geological sequence for the site. Speth's later interpretations are more elaborate and more accurate than those which we were using in the field, and there is a very close correlation between the two systems. The main tendency is for the cultural stratigraphic sequence to subsume a number of geological levels which Speth found to be distinct but were not recognized in the field.

To aid in the laboratory analysis of samples, Taggart's levels were given Roman numeral designations with letters added for internal subdivisions. Level I was bedded sands, Level II the lower dark silts, Level III the brown silts and

Level IV the upper dark silts. Four subdivisions were recognized in Level II during the course of excavation. Level II*a* was the transitional area between the bedded sands and the main parts of Level II; Level II*b* was the portion of Level II below the very dense Early Woodland living floor along the old river bank, and Level II*c* was the Early Woodland living floor itself. The bottom of the old river channel which was formed during the Early Woodland period was designated as II*d*. This level produced cultural materials which were stratigraphically earlier than the earliest of the extensive Middle Woodland occupations but probably later than the material on the old river bank.

The brown silts were divided into a lower III*a* member, which contained the earlier of the Middle Woodland occupations, and a III*b* member, essentially a relatively thin yet very dense deposit with many features and large quantities of later Middle Woodland cultural material. The III*b* level was represented most strongly in the old river channel area and occasionally in units right along the old river bank.

The upper dark silts were divided into IV*a*, IV*b*, and IV*c* levels following Taggart's interpretation of middle, intermediate and upper silts. Several of these levels could be grouped together as representative of single time horizons. Levels II*a* through II*c* all could be grouped with the Early Woodland occupation, roughly around 500 B.C. Level II*d* post-dated this time, and the cultural materials probably represented sporadic site utilization some time between 500 B.C. and 100 B.C. Level III*a* contained the early Middle Woodland material, while III*b* and IV*a* contained later Middle Woodland materials. The IV*b* deposits were mixed and possibly redeposited, but those classified as IV*c* and IV were Late Woodland and certainly postdated A.D. 500 and possibly postdated A.D. 900.

During the summers of 1962, 1963, and 1964, different quantities of these different levels were excavated. The volume for the Early Woodland, Transitional, early Middle Woodland, late Middle Woodland, and Late Woodland deposits excavated during each of these three seasons is given in Table 1.

TABLE 1
VOLUME OF OCCUPATIONAL LEVELS
(In Cubic Feet)

Year	Horizon					
	L.W.	L.M.W.	E.M.W.	T(II*d*)	E.W.	Total
1962	165	110	430	135	295	1135
1963	200	0	834	0	635	1669
1964	615	840	2585	830	2170	7040
Total	980	950	3849	965	3100	9844
% of Total	9.9	9.6	39.1	9.8	31.5	

Approximate volume of the Early Woodland (E.W.), Transitional (T), early Middle Woodland (E.M.W.), late Middle Woodland (L.M.W.), and Late Woodland (L.W.) occupational levels at the Schultz site (20SA2) for the 1962, 1963 and 1964 excavations.

THE STOCKADE

One of the major features of the site was the area which we have referred to as the stockade. Part of the pattern was uncovered in 1962 and much more was uncovered during the last few weeks of the 1963 season. The post molds which marked this feature showed up in Level III as light medium brown, circular to eliptical discolorations in the darker brown matrix of this level.

The numbering of these post molds started in the area of the 1962 excavations, and they were traced along the south side of the stockade by a trench and numbered in a counterclockwise direction from one to 49 (Fig. 7). At that point, a gap was left in the numbering system for additional post molds along this line. The numbering started again in 1963 in Unit B with post mold No. 101 and the pattern was traced in a clockwise direction until post mold No. 178 was reached. There were gaps of approximately 45 feet, 25 feet, and 25 feet along the eastern side of this structure, but the pattern was obvious by the end of the season.

A total of 127 post molds were located between two and four feet apart. Approximately one-fifth, 23, were sectioned and

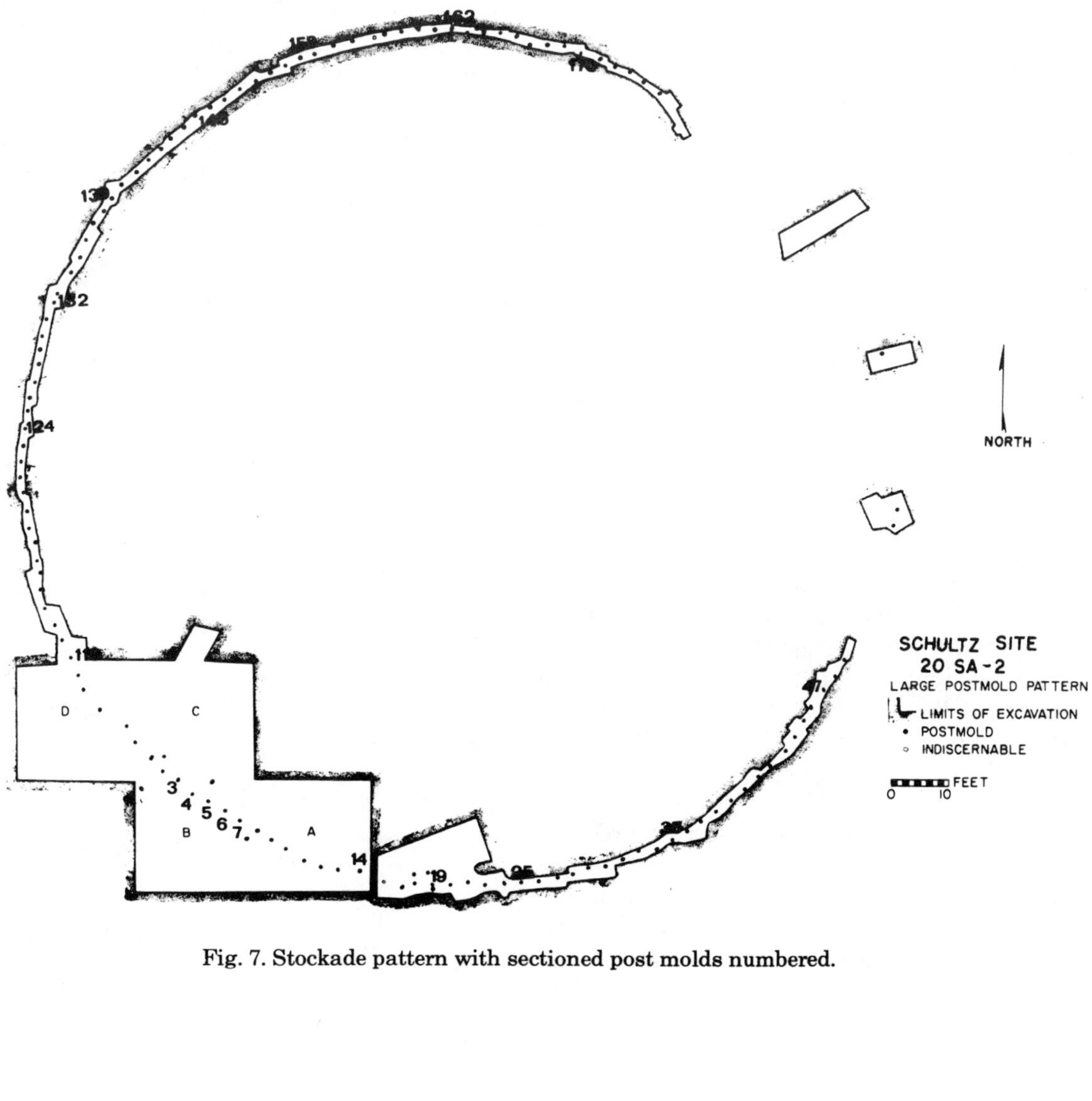

Fig. 7. Stockade pattern with sectioned post molds numbered.

measured in detail. The dimensions for these are given in Table 2. The modal width for these molds was .6 feet and the average width was .71 feet. The average depth was .77 feet, but the modal depth was one foot.

TABLE 2
STOCKADE POST MOLDS
(In Feet)

Post Mold Number	Width	Depth
3	.6	.4
4	.6	.3
5	.6	.5
6	.6	.3
7	.6	.7
14	.7	.6
19	.9	.9
20	.5	.2
25	.6	.4
35	.7	.9
47	.9	1.6
116	.7	1.0
124	.7	1.0
132	.8	.8
136	1.0	1.8
139	.9	1.0
146	.9	1.1
153	.6	.5
160	.9	1.0
162	.7	.3
164	.6	1.2
170	.6	.4
x	.71	.77

See Figure 8.

While excavating at Naomikong Point on Lake Superior during the 1966 season, we uncovered a driven yellow birch post in a sand matrix. This post was apparently associated with the mid-nineteenth century occupation of the site. The mold matched the depth of the post perfectly. In spite of the pointed tip of the post, the mold base was round and was approximately three times the diameter of the post, even allowing for wood shrinkage. While the situation at the two sites is not directly comparable (the Naomikong Point site is located on a sand beach), this can be used as some indication of the nature of the Schultz site posts. First, the fact that the post molds have rounded bases does not mean the posts were rounded. If they followed the Naomikong pattern, the average post diameter would have been about .3, and they would have been driven or set into the ground to a depth of about a foot. These molds could then represent a very small post—one very comparable to a modern fence post. If these were posts of this size, it is unlikely that the stockade was used as a defense structure.

The analogy of fence posts caused a moment of panic when we first learned of Judge Albert Miller's corral for animals constructed at Green Point in the 1830's. However, Judge Miller's farm was in the area of 20SA1, and the timber was not cleared from 20SA2 until some time around 1900. In addition, the stockade was apparently sealed in several places by Level IV deposits, and at least one late Middle Woodland feature, Feature No. 100, was located directly over a post mold.

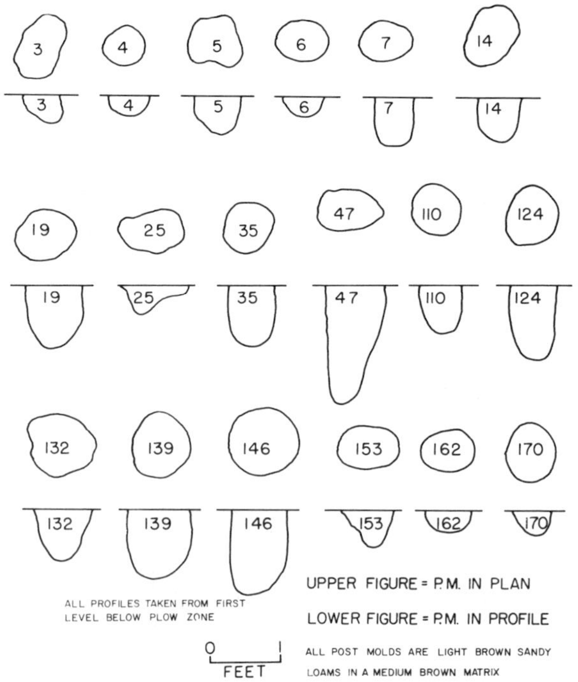

Fig. 8. Plans and profiles of stockade post molds.

Virtually no early nineteenth century historic material was found in the stockade (and very little twentieth century material either) while large quantities were found in parts of 20SA1 and in the area between 20SA1 and 20SA2. The cumulative effect of this evidence was an assurance that the stockade was a prehistoric structure; probably dating to the early Middle Woodland occupation of the site.

We also noted that the post molds, and therefore the posts, were larger in the parts of the site away from the river. The post molds on the northern half of the stockade averaged .76 feet in diameter and .92 feet deep as opposed to .63 feet in diameter and .63 feet deep in the southern half of the structure.

The stockade bordered directly on the central mound and was flanked by the two smaller mounds. The posts appear to have been largest by the mounds and smallest by the old river channel area where the occupational level for the Middle Woodland period would have been lower. The overall effect suggests a relationship between the stockade area and the mounds.

For practical reasons, we found it convenient to divide the site into four main areas: the area of the old river channel; those parts of the levee outside the stockade; those parts of the levee inside the stockade; and the area which we excavated covered by mound fill. The activities performed in different parts of the site, even during the same time periods, varied considerably. Except for the 1965 excavations which were limited to the mound area, the percentage of various site areas varied from season to season. In order to control the differences between various seasons of excavation, the areas in the channel, on the levee, inside the stockade and in the mound areas for the 1962 through 1964 season's are listed in the table below.

FEATURES

Many man-made disturbances were located during the course of excavation at the site which were designated as features. The most significant of these were pits and hearths; but other types of disturbances, such as post molds, particularly dense midden areas and clusters of artifacts on living floors, were also included under this heading. Many items were initially listed as features but were later relegated to other categories: as an example, the first six post molds of the stockade were designated as Feature No.

TABLE 3

AMOUNT OF EXCAVATION IN DIFFERENT AREAS OF THE SITE

(In Square Feet)

Year	Channel	Levee	Stockade	Mound	Total
1962	150	310	240	0	700
Percent	21	44	34	0	
1963	35	880	720	0	1635
Percent	2	54	44	0	
1964	750	380	1745	745	3620
Percent	21	10	48	21	
Total	935	1570	2705	745	5955
Percentage Total	16	26	45	13	

Fig. 9. Burial area (Mound A) at the Schultz site.

22 although they were later given post mold numbers and all subsequent post molds for the stockade were given only post mold numbers (with the exception of Feature No. 64-4 from the 1964 season, which turned out to be post mold No. 164 from the post mold trench of the 1963 season).

During the 1962 and 1963 seasons, 100 features were given separate numbers although three of these incorporated two separate features under a single number. Twenty-four features were in the area of machine stripping, so only 79 out of the 103 features from these seasons were subject to a more detailed examination (Table 4).

During the 1964 season, 102 additional features were uncovered so a total of 181 are listed in Table 4. A separate numbering system was used in 1964, starting with No. 64-1 and running through No. 64-102. Table 4 includes the feature number, the excavation unit in which the feature was found, the probable level in which the feature originated and a brief description of the feature.

These feature descriptions include four types of pits, hearths, post molds, concentrations, portions of the midden and at least one geological feature. This geological feature, No. 64-38, is listed as an area of "raised midden." It looks as though a small anticline, about eight feet in diameter, had been formed in this area. This would have formed after the site was occupied by man, for both Early and Middle Woodland deposits were found in a vertical rather than horizontal profile as we took down level floors in this unit. A similar geological feature was also noted, but not numbered, during the 1963 excavations.

The term "concentration" has been

used to cover clusters of items found on living floors, usually along the interface between II*a* and II*c*. Much of this material was probably associated with the II*c* level. Such concentrations were also associated with living floors in other levels.

The term "midden" is used on the feature list to refer to dense deposits of cultural and organic materials which are found in sheet deposits along with several levels but most commonly in the III*b* level. In fact, this entire level could be subsumed under this heading. The III*b* level had an irregular surface, and excavators working down through the upper dark silts often mistook peaks of these deposits for hearths or pits while excavating in flat levels.

Post molds varied from the stockade

TABLE 4
FEATURES AT 20 SA 2

Feature No.	Excavation Unit	Level	Description
1	510E500	IV*b*	Refuse Pit A
2	580E550	III*a*	Refuse Pit B
3	510E500	IV*b*	Refuse Pit A
4	510E500	III*b*	Refuse Pit B
5	510E500	III*b*	Refuse Pit B
6	580E550	III*a*	Refuse Pit B
7	580E550	III*a*	Refuse Pit B
8	510E500	III*b*	Refuse Pit B
9	590E700	IV*c*	Refuse Pit A
10	580E550	II*c*	Concentration
11	580E550	II*c*	Concentration
12	500E600	IVc	Refuse Pit A
13	590E700	II*c*	Concentration
14	590E570	II*c*	Concentration
15	500E600	IV*b*	Refuse Pit B
16	500E600	IV*b*	Refuse Pit B
17	500E600	III*b*	Refuse Pit B
18	500E600	III*b*	Refuse Pit B
19	570E550	III*a*	Refuse Pit A
20	570E550	(III*a*)	Empty Pit
21	500E600	III*a*	Concentration
22	580E540 plus	III*a*	Post Molds
23	500E600	III*a*	Hearth
24*a*	500E600	III*a*	Hearth
24*b*	500E600	III*a*	Hearth
25	500E600	III*a*	Hearth

TABLE 4 continued

Feature Number	Excavation Unit	Level	Description
26	500E600	III*a*	Concentration
27	500E600	II*d*	Hearth
28	500E600	II*d*	Hearth
29	Machine Trench No.1	III*a*	Refuse Pit B
30	20 x 20 B	IV	Refuse Pit A
31	20 x 20 C	III*a*	Concentration
32	20 x 20 C	III*a*	Hearth
33	20 x 20 C	(III*a*)	Refuse Pit A
34	20 x 20 C	III*a*	Refuse Pit A
35	20 x 20 C	(III*a*)	Refuse Pit A
36	20 x 20 D	III*a*	Refuse Pit A
37	20 x 20 D	III*a*	Refuse Pit A
38	20 x 20 D	III*a*	Hearth
39	20 x 20 D	III*a*	Refuse Pit A
40	20 x 20 B	IV	Refuse Pit A
41	20 x 20 B	III*a*	Refuse Pit A
42a	20 x 20 B	III*a*	Refuse Pit A
42*b*	20 x 20 B	III*a*	Refuse Pit A
43*a*	20 x 20 B	III*a*	Refuse Pit A
43*b*	20 x 20 B	III*a*	Refuse Pit A
44	Machine Trench No. 2	II*c*	Refuse Pit C
45	20 x 20 C	II*c*	Concentration
46	Machine Trench No. 2	III*b*	Refuse Pit B
47	20 x 20 C	II*c*	Concentration
48	20 x 20 D	II*c*	Concentration
49	Machine Trench No. 6	III*b*	Concentration
50	N.W. Shell Conc.	(II*c*)	(Refuse Pit C?)
51	Machine Trench No. 6	III*a*	Midden
52	Machine Trench No. 6	III*b*	Midden
53	20 x 20 D	II*c*	Concentration
54	20 x 20 D	II*c*	Concentration
55	20 x 20 D	II*c*	Concentration
56	Trench No. 7	III*a*	Refuse Pit B

TABLE 4 continued

Feature Number	Excavation Unit	Level	Description
57	Machine Trench No. 6	III*b*	Midden
58	20 x 20 B	II*b*	Concentration
59	20 x 20 B	II*c*	Refuse Pit C
60	20 x 20 B	II*b*	Concentration
61	20 x 20 B	II*b*	Concentration
62	20 x 20 B	II*b*	Concentration
63	20 x 20 B	II*c*	Refuse Pit C
64	20 x 20 B	II*c*	Refuse Pit C
65	20 x 20 B	III*a*	Refuse Pit A
66	20 x 20 B	II*c*	Concentration
67	20 x 20 B	II*c*	Refuse Pit C
68	Machine Trench No. 6	III*b*	Refuse Pit B
69	20 x 20 B	II*c*	Refuse Pit C
70	Trench No. 7	II*d*	Hearth
71	Trench No. 8	III*b*	Refuse Pit B
72	Trench No. 8	III*a*	Refuse Pit A
73	Machine Trench No. 6	III*b*	Refuse Pit B
74	Machine Trench No. 6	III*a*	Refuse Pit B
75-90	Machine Stripping	. . .	. . .
91	Machine Trench No. 6	III*b*	Midden
92-99	Machine Stripping	. . .	. . .
100	Trench No. 8	III*b*	Refuse Pit B
64-1	700E585	III*a*	Hearth
64-2	710E585	III*a*	Hearth
64-3	590E570	IV	Empty Pit
64-4	710E585	III*a*	Stockade Post Mold No. 164
64-5	550E570	IV	Refuse Pit A
64-6	550E570	IV	Refuse Pit A
64-7	590E570	III*a*	Refuse Pit A
64-8	550E570	IV	Animal Burial
64-9	590E570	III*a*	Empty Pit
64-10	510E570	(IV*c*)	Refuse Pit A
64-11	510E570	IV*b*	Concentration
64-12	510E570	IV*b*	Post Mold

TABLE 4 continued

Feature Number	Excavation Unit	Level	Description
64-13	510E570	IV*b*	Empty Pit
64-14	510E570	IV*b*	Refuse Pit B
64-15	510E570	IV*b*	Concentration
64-16	550E570	II*c*	Refuse Pit C
64-17	510E570	IV*a*	Refuse Pit B
64-18	590E570	II*c*	Refuse Pit C
64-19	550E570	III*a*	Empty Pit
64-20	550E570	II*c*	Refuse Pit C
64-21	510E570	III*b*	Concentration
64-22	510E570	III*b*	Concentration
64-23	510E570	III*b*	Concentration
64-24	550E570	IV	Refuse Pit A
64-25	590E570	II*c*	Refuse Pit C
64-26	510E570	III*b*	Midden
64-27	510E570	III*b*	Midden
64-28	590E570	II*c*	Refuse Pit C
64-29	510E570	III*b*	Midden
64-30	590E570	II*c*	Refuse Pit C
64-31	510E570	III*b*	Midden
64-32	510E570	III*b*	Midden
64-33	510E570	III*b*	Midden
64-34	630E570	(III*a*)	Empty Pit
64-35	630E570	III*a*	Empty Pit
64-36	630E570	III*a*	Empty Pit
64-37	630E570	III*a*	Empty Pit
64-38	630E570	II*b* plus	Raised Midden
64-39	510E570	III*b*	Midden
64-64	580E585	(III*a*)	Empty Pit
64-65	570-580E585	III*a*	Empty Pit
64-66	670E570	II*c*	Refuse Pit C
64-67	510E570	(III*a*)	Hearth
64-68	510E570	(III*a*)	Hearth
64-69	670E570	II*c*	Refuse Pit C
64-70	510E570	(III*a*)	Hearth

TABLE 4 continued

Feature Number	Excavation Unit	Level	Description
64-71	510E570	II*d*	Concentration (Natural?)
64-72	510E570	II*d*	Hearth
64-73	690E585	III*a*	Hearth
64-74	510E570	II*d*	Hearth
64-75	540E585	IV	Refuse Pit B
64-76	490E585	IV*c*	Hearth
64-77	690E585	II*c*	Refuse Pit C
64-78	580E360	IV*a*	Refuse Pit A
64-79	580E360	IV*b*	Refuse Pit B
64-80	580E360	III*b*	Refuse Pit B
64-81	490E630	IV*b*	Refuse Pit B
64-82	490E585	III*b*	Hearth
64-83	720E690	III*a*	Refuse Pit B
64-84	530E585	IV	Refuse Pit A
64-85	640E585	II*c*	Refuse Pit C
64-86	490E630	IV*a*	Refuse Pit B
64-87	490E630	III*b*	Hearth
64-88	500E585	III*a*	Hearth
64-89	490E630	III*b*	Hearth
64-90	490E630	III*b*	Hearth
64-91	490E630	III*b*	Hearth
64-92	490E630	III*b*	Hearth
64-93	490E630	III*a*	Hearth
64-94	490E630	III*a*	Hearth
64-95	490E630	III*a*	Hearth
64-96	490E630	III*a*	Refuse Pit A
64-97	490E585	II*d*	Post Mold
64-98	500E585	III*a*	Hearth
64-99	500E585	II*d*	Hearth
64-100	490E630	III*a*	Hearth
64-101	490E630	III*a*	Post Mold
64-102	490E630	II*d*	Hearth

Summary includes excavations between 1962 and 1964, excluding those in the area of Machine Stripping. Level designations in parentheses are probable but not certain levels of origin.

post molds which we discussed earlier to a number of single post molds, some of which appeared to be pits when first observed. Most single post molds in living areas were not given separate feature numbers and were noted only on the square sheets for the levels in which they were found.

The most significant of these features were pits and hearths. Only 122 of the 181 features could be used in this analysis. These were the pits and hearths of fairly certain provenience; those pits which appeared to originate in the IV*b* level were excluded, while those originating in the general IV level were grouped with those from the IV*c* level to form the Late Woodland group.

Type A refuse pits were circular to oval, basin-shaped depressions (Table 5). They were marked by a generally dark fill and the absence of evidence of firing in the pit itself. Some did contain firecracked rock but this was included with the general fill. They usually contained quantities of cultural material, particularly larger sherds and even chipped stone implements. A common field inference was that these were either refuse pits or abandoned storage pits which had been used as refuse pits.

There was a great deal of size variation, as can be seen in Table 5. The north to south dimensions varied from 1 foot to over 5 feet with a mean of 2.3 feet. Their east to west dimensions varied from 1 foot to almost 10 feet with a mean of 2.2 feet. Depths varied from .5 to 1.6 feet with a mean of .8 feet. An attempt was made to find the approximate volume for these pits. We used the formula for a cone although this was only a very rough approximation of the actual pit shapes. First, the north to south and east to west dimensions were averaged; the resulting figure was halved, squared and multiplied by pi. The product of this operation was multiplied by one-third of the depth. The volumes of the pits ranged from .1 cubic feet to over 5 cubic feet. The mean of the volumes for complete pits was 1.1 cubic feet which, in this case, matched the mean volume figure derived from the mean linear measurements.

Type B pits (Table 6) were also round to oval, basin-shaped, and contained a great deal of cultural material. They contained more organic material than Type A pits and also differed from Type A pits in that they contained evidence of burning. This was either in the form of a white ash layer, or a layer of fire-reddened silts, or both. Some contained only a small amount of ash and vast amounts of organic debris, particularly uncharred fish bone. Many were distinctly stratified. Like Type A pits, they usually contained large sherds and occasional chipped stone tools. Field inferences as to function were varied. Some, with the ash layers on the bottom, appear to have been fire pits with refuse dumped on top of the burned areas, while other pits contained ash layers or burned layers at higher levels and were interpreted as refuse pits which were fired later.

The level, location and dimensions for Type B pits are given in Table 6. All of their average dimensions are greater than those of Type A pits with a north to south mean of 2.9 feet, an east to west mean of 2.7 feet and a mean depth of .9 feet. The range of volumes is from .1 cubic feet to over 10 cubic feet with a mean of .75 cubic feet. This is much less than the volume of 1.8 cubic feet suggested from the figure derived from the average measurements. I feel that the latter figure is more reliable.

The difference between the two volume figures is a reflection of the area of the site where these pits were found and the type of sampling that was done in these areas. It is obvious that you will have more incomplete pit measurements in small excavation units than in larger

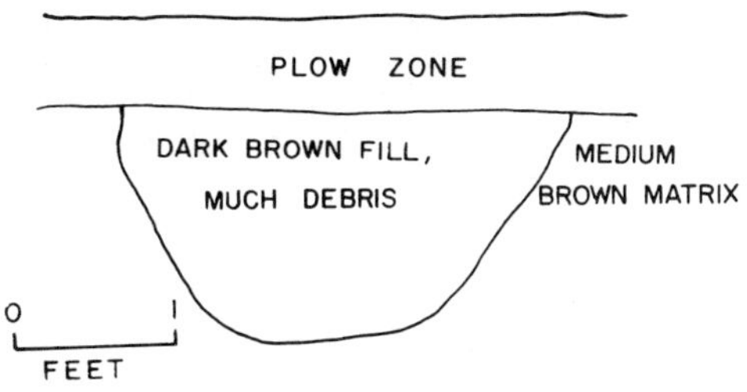

F. 12 PROFILE

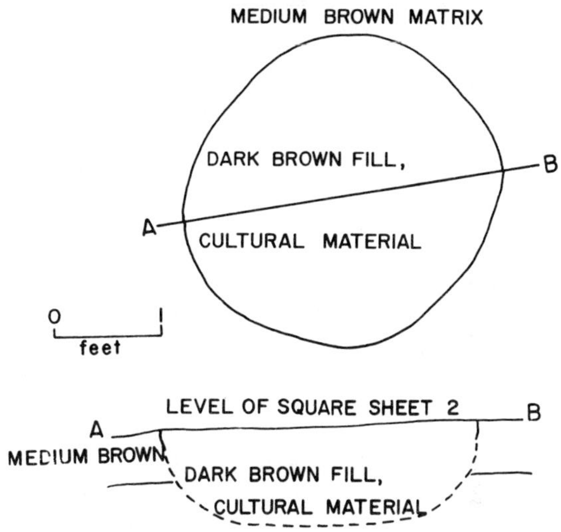

F. 64-5 PLAN & PROFILE

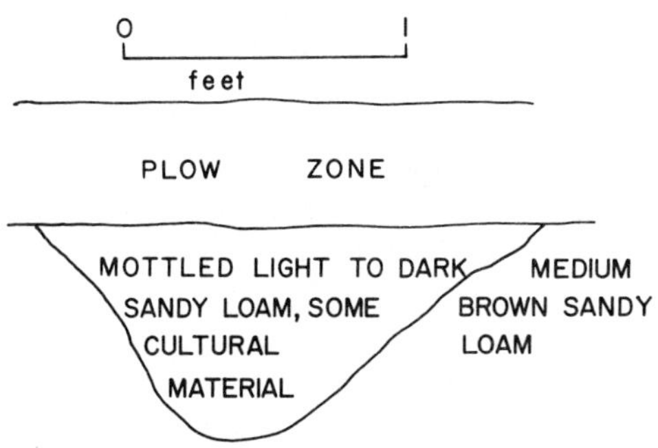

F. 64-24 PROFILE

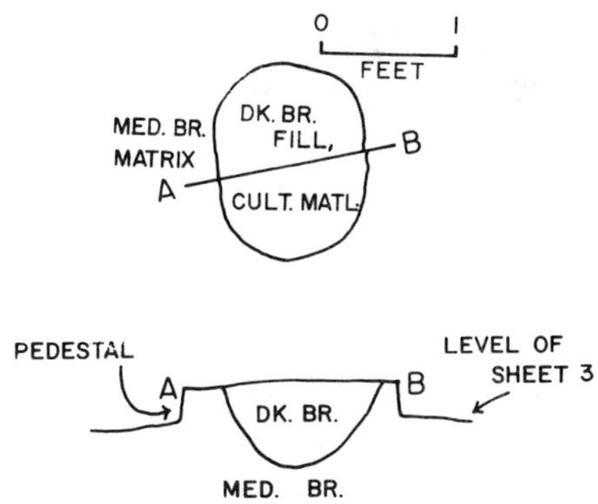

F. 64-45 PLAN & PROFILE

Fig. 10. Type A pits.

TABLE 5
TYPE A PITS

Feature No.	Level	Area of Site	NS	EW	D	Approx. Vol.
1	IV*b*	Channel	(1.8)	2.0	1.0	. . .
3	IV*b*	Channel	3.6	(2.3)	1.3	. . .
9	IV*c*	Levee	3.9	3.5	1.5	5.4
12	IV*c*	Channel	2.8	(1.7)	1.5	. . .
19	III*a*	Levee	1.5	1.5	.4	.1
30	IV	Stockade	2.8	1.8	1.0	1.5
33	III*a*	Stockade	2.4	2.5	.7	1.1
34	III*a*	Stockade	3.5	2.2	.8	.6
35	III*a*	Stockade	2.7	1.3	.9	.9
36	III*a*	Levee	2.4	2.3	.8	1.2
37	III*a*	Levee	1.7	1.3	(.2)	. . .
39	III*a*	Stockade	2.2	1.5	(.4)	. . .
40	IV	Levee	1.9	1.9	.5	.5
41	III*a*	Levee	2.0	2.0	.4	.4
42*a*	III*a*	Levee	2.3	2.6	.7	1.1
42*b*	III*a*	Levee	2.8	1.6	1.0	1.3
43*a*	III*a*	Levee	1.3	1.3	.7	.3
43*b*	III*a*	Levee	1.0	1.1	.5	.1
65	III*a*	Levee	2.0	1.4	.5	.4
72	III*a*	Levee	(1.6)	2.0	.6	. . .
64-5	IV	Levee	2.7	1.9	.9	1.2
64-6	IV	Stockade	1.5	1.0	.7	.2
64-7	(III*a*)	Stockade	(4.2)	9.8	1.0	. . .
64-10	IV*c*	Channel	2.4	2.2	.5	.7
64-24	IV	Stockade	(1.0)	1.6	.8	. . .
64-44	IV	Stockade	1.2	1.8	.6	.4
64-45	III*a*	Stockade	1.2	1.8	1.5	.9
64-46	III*a*	Stockade	1.9	2.0	1.6	1.6
64-55	IV	Stockade	3.2	1.9	.4	.7
64-78	IV*a*	Channel	1.7	1.3	(.2)	. . .
64-84	IV	Levee	1.2	1.6	.6	.1
64-96	III*a*	Channel	4.2	4.5	.9	4.5
Mean			2.3	2.2	.8	1.1*

*Mean Pit Volume derived from mean pit dimensions = 1.1

Note:—North to south (NS), east to west (EW) and depth (D) dimensions are in feet. The approximate volume is given in cubic feet. Measurements in parentheses are incomplete and not used for deriving the means. Levels in parentheses are probable level of origin where data is uncertain.

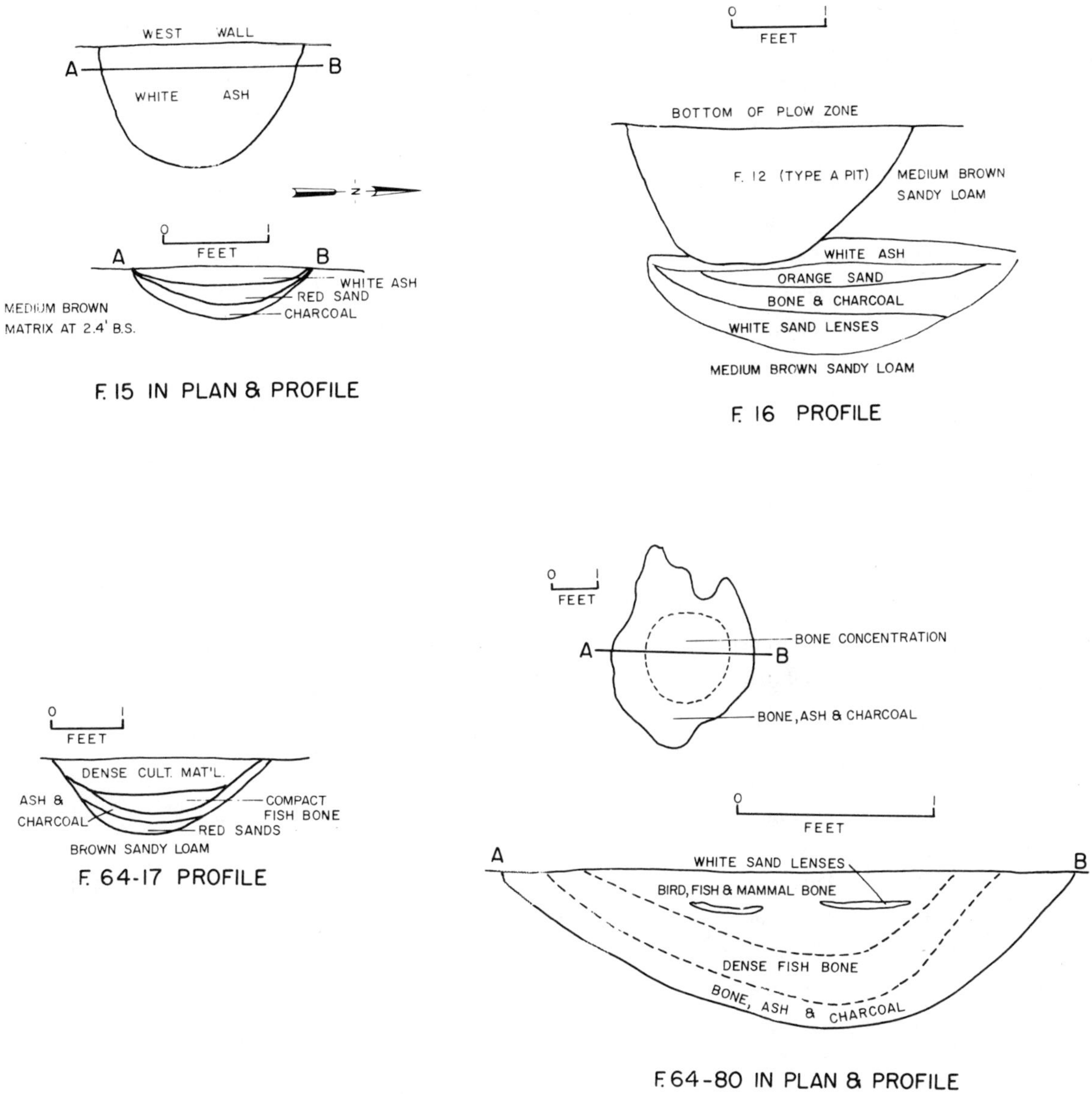

Fig. 11. Type B pits.

TABLE 6
TYPE B PITS

Feature No.	Level	Area of Site	NS	EW	D	Approx. Vol.
2	III*a*	Levee	4.0	5.0	1.3	6.6
4	III*b*	Channel	3.7	2.6	1.4	1.5
5	III*b*	Channel	4.0	(2.5)	1.2	. . .
6	III*a*	Channel	(1.0)	(1.8)	1.0	. . .
7	III*a*	Levee	1.6	1.1	.8	.2
8	III*b*	Channel	1.2	(1.0)	1.0	. . .
15	IV*b*	Channel	1.8	(1.4)	.5	. . .
16	IV*b*	Channel	3.8	(2.2)	1.0	. . .
17	III*b*	Channel	(1.0)	(1.7)	1.0	. . .
18	III*b*	Channel	(1.8)	(1.7)	.8	. . .
29	III*a*	Channel	3.0	3.9	—	. . .
46	III*b*	Channel	1.7	1.1	.5	.3
56	III*a*	Levee	2.3	1.5	.7	.2
68	III*b*	Channel	3.5	2.4	1.8	1.3
71	III*b*	Stockade	(1.5)	1.5	.7	. . .
73	III*b*	Channel	3.2	2.6	.5	1.1
74	III*a*	Channel	2.6	3.6	.5	1.3
100	III*b*	(Over Post Mold)	2.5	2.4	.6	1.0
64-14	IV*b*	Channel	(1.9)	(3.7)	.3	. . .
64-17	IV*a*	Channel	3.3	3.3	.6	1.7
64-43	III*a*	Below Mound A	4.8	2.9	1.2	4.7
64-48	III*a*	Channel	2.0	2.4	.5	.6
64-50	III*a*	Channel	1.3	2.3	.5	.4
64-75	IV	Levee	2.2	2.7	(.6)	. . .
64-79	IV*b*	Channel	2.6	3.0	1.1	2.3
64-80	III*b*	Channel	3.7	2.9	1.2	3.4
64-81	IV*b*	Channel	6.7	6.1	1.0	10.6
64-83	III*a*	Channel	2.8	2.6	.9	1.7
64-86	IV*a*	Channel	.7	.9	.7	.1
Mean			2.9	2.7	.9	.75*

*Mean Pit Volume derived from mean pit dimensions = 1.8

Note:—North to south (NS), east to west (EW) and depth (D) dimensions are in feet. The approximate volume is given in cubic feet. Figures in parentheses are incomplete and not used for deriving means.

units. A 20-by-20-foot excavation unit will include more complete features than a 5-by-10-unit where many features will run to the wall. Type A features were found primarily on the levee and within the stockade, an area on the site which was sampled by eight 20-by-20-foot units as well as several smaller units. The average of pit dimensions includes both large and small pits, and the average volume is the same as the volume determined by the average dimensions.

In the channel area, where Type B pits were most common, we only opened one 20-by-20-foot unit, 510E570. All other sampling was done with smaller units. Therefore, large pits are underrepresented among those pits for which we were able to compute volume. The figure computed from the average dimensions is probably a more accurate reflection of true pit volume for Type B pits. This also suggests that large blocks of contiguous units may give a better picture of the site than randomly placed small units.

Type C pits are very distinctive. They tend to be oval and more straight sided than either Type A or Type B pits. In every instance, the base is marked by a distinct fire-reddened level covered over with a level of ash. The unfired fill of these pits is virtually devoid of cultural or organic material. These appear to have been sunken fire pits which were filled in, possibly by an agency other than man, such as floods.

The dimensions of Type C pits (Table 7) suggest a volume similar to that of Type B pits. The north to south dimensions range from 1.1 to 3 feet with an average of 1.9 feet, while the east to west

Fig. 12. Feature 64-17, A Type B pit.

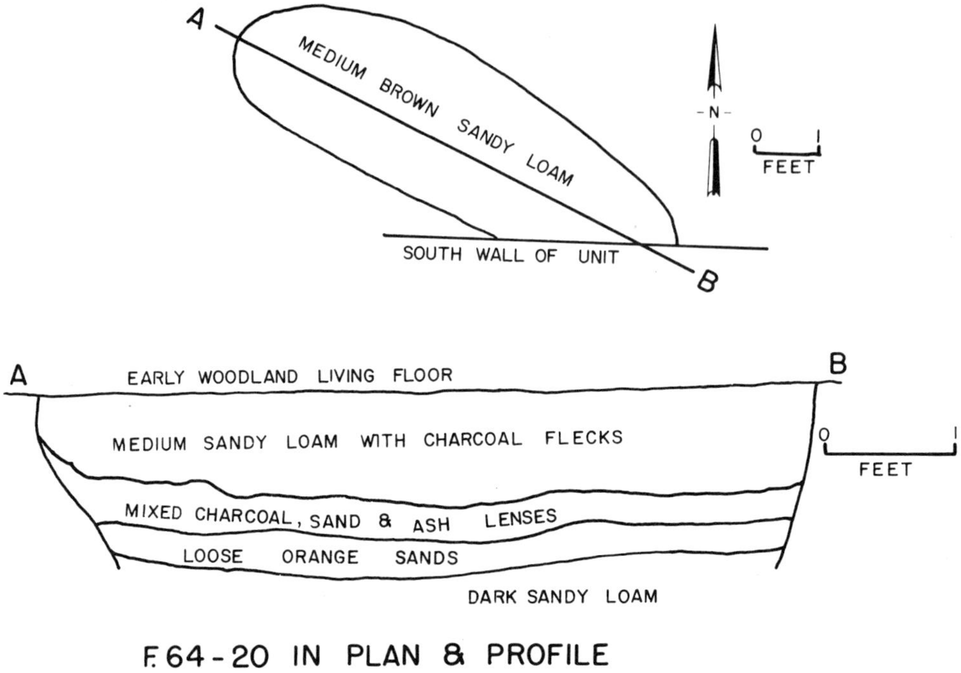

Fig. 13. A type C pit.

dimensions range from 1.3 to 7.2 feet with a mean of 2.7 feet. They are the deepest type of pit, ranging from .6 to 2.5 feet deep with an average depth of 1.2 feet. The approximate volume ranges from .3 cubic feet to 8.8 cubic feet with an average of 2.4 cubic feet. I think that the average volume, in this instance, is overly biased by one very large pit, Feature No. 64-20; and I would accept the approximate volume, based on the average dimensions, of 1.7 cubic feet.

The last group of pits have been referred to as empty pits. They are a group of very regular, circular, basin-shaped depressions with a fill darker than the surrounding soil matrix. Some have a layer of ash toward the bottom, but they all lack any evidence of fire-reddening of the soil. The main characteristic of these pits is the near absence of cultural material. The cultural material that is found is

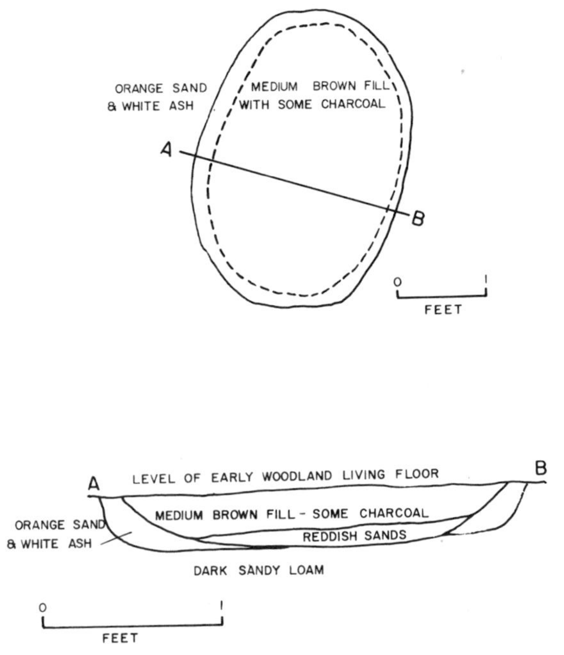

Fig. 14. A type C pit.

TABLE 7
TYPE C PITS

Feature No.	Level	Area of Site	NS	EW	D	Approx. Vol.
44	II*c*	Levee	...	...	...	...
50	II*c*	Levee	...	...	...	...
59	II*b*	Levee	1.8	1.6	2.5	1.9
63	II*c*	Levee	2.2	1.5	1.0	.9
64	II*c*	Levee	(1.0)	2.9	1.3	...
67	II*c*	Levee	1.2	1.7	1.0	.5
69	II*c*	Levee	1.3	6.7	1.4	5.9
64-16	II*c*	Levee	2.5	(1.5)	.5	...
64-18	II*c*	Stockade	2.4	2.8	.8	1.4
64-20	II*c*	Stockade	2.3	7.2	1.8	8.8
64-25	II*c*	Stockade	...	1.8	.9	...
64-28	II*c*	Stockade	(1.5)	1.8	1.2	...
64-30	II*c*	Stockade	1.5	1.3	.6	.3
64-66	II*c*	Stockade	1.9	2.6	1.2	1.6
64-69	II*c*	Stockade	1.1	1.3	1.4	.5
64-77	II*c*	Stockade	3.0	(1.9)	.8	...
64-85	II*c*	Levee	...	...	...	...
Mean			1.9	2.7	1.2	2.4*

*Mean Pit Volume derived from mean pit **dimensions** = 1.7

Note:—North to south (NS), east to west (EW) and depth (D) dimensions are given in feet. The approximate volume is given in cubic feet.Figures in parentheses are incomplete and not used for deriving means.

limited to a few flint chips and some fire-cracked rock. Organic debris is sometimes found in these pits, but ceramics, in particular, are infrequent.

Empty pits are the smallest type of pit (Table 8). Their north to south dimensions range from 1.4 to 3.0 feet with a mean of 2.1 feet. Their east to west dimensions ranged from 1.3 to 3.5 feet with a mean of 2.0 feet. Depths ranged from .3 to 2.3 feet with a mean of .8 feet. The approximate volumes ranged from .2 to 3.3 cubic feet with a mean of 1.2 cubic feet. I think that the approximate volume derived from the average measurements, .9 cubic feet, is a more accurate reflection of the volume of these pits than the mean volume, although the figures are very close.

Hearths were large, oval to circular, shallow depressions with evidence of direct burning on the ground surface. These were sometimes stratified with layers of ash, charcoal and fire-reddened soil. They tended to contain more organic debris than cultural material. There was a great deal of variation in size and shape (Table 9). The north to south dimensions range from .9 to 7.5 feet with a mean of 2.7 feet. East to west dimensions range from .9 to 7.7 feet with a mean of 2.6 feet. They are relatively shallow with depths ranging from .1 to .9 feet with a mean depth of .5 feet.

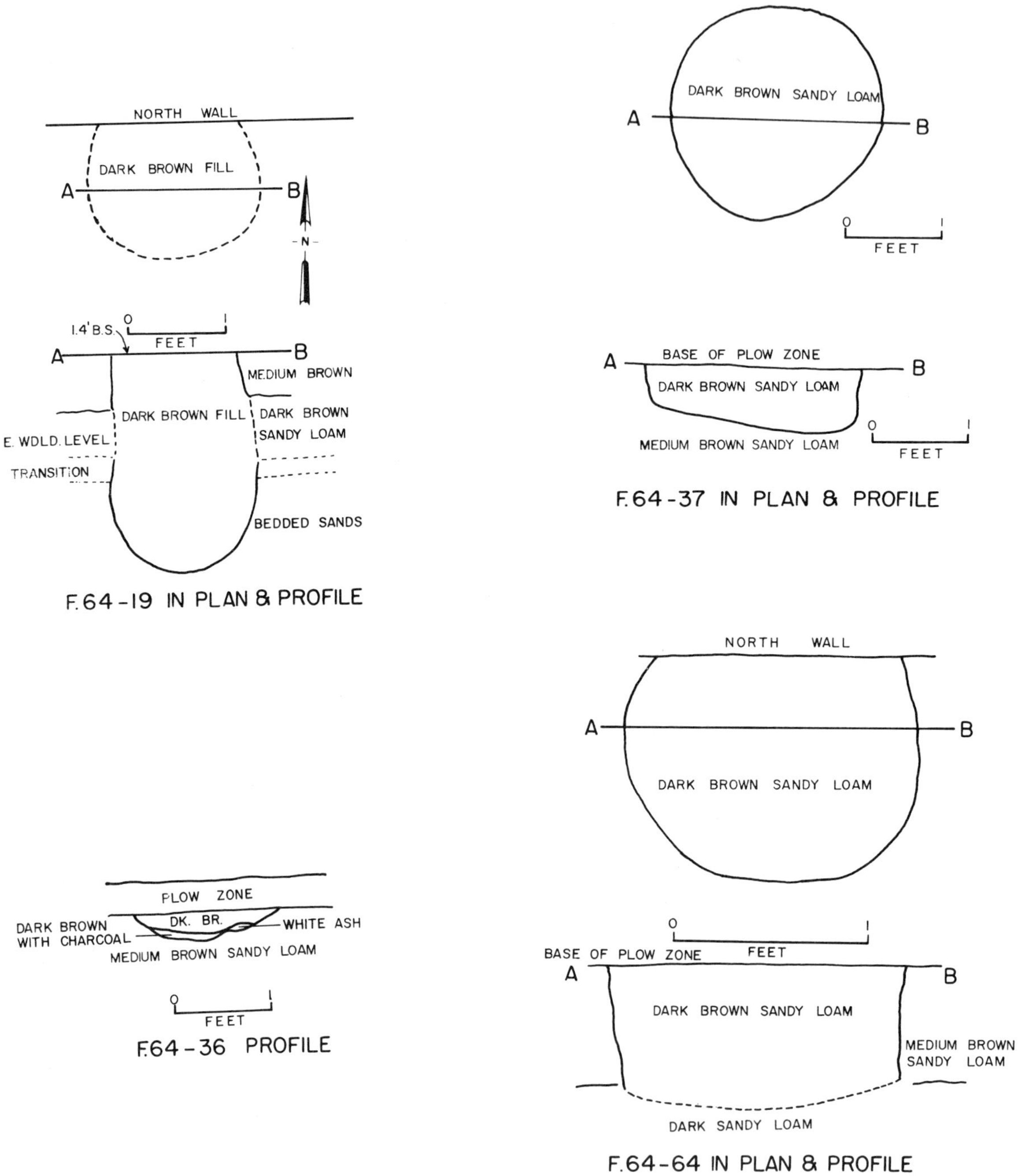

Fig. 15. Empty pits.

TABLE 8
EMPTY PITS

Feature No.	Level	Area of Site	NS	EW	D	Approx. Vol.
20	III*a*	Levee	3.0	3.0	1.4	3.3
64-3	IV	Stockade	2.4	2.5	1.0	1.6
64-9	III*a*	Stockade	2.8	3.4	.8	2.0
64-13	IV*b*	Stockade	(2.5)	(2.3)	.3	. . .
64-19	III*a*	Stockade	(1.6)	1.5	2.3	. . .
64-34	III*a*	Stockade	2.1	1.5	.8	.7
64-35	III*a*	Stockade	2.0	2.0	.7	.7
64-36	III*a*	Stockade	1.6	1.6	.6	.4
64-37	III*a*	Stockade	(1.9)	2.2	.7	. . .
64-41	III*a*	Stockade	(1.2)	1.8	.8	. . .
64-60	III*a*	Stockade	1.6	1.3	.4	.2
64-64	III*a*	Stockade	1.4	1.6	.7	.4
64-65	III*a*	Stockade	2.6	(1.5)	.4	. . .
Mean			2.1	2.0	.8	1.2*

*Mean Pit Volume derived from mean pit dimesions = .9
Note:—North to south (NS), east to west (EW) and depth (D) dimensions are given in feet. The approximate volume is given in cubic feet. Figures in parentheses are incomplete and not used for deriving means.

Average approximate volumes range from .1 cubic feet to 2.9 cubic feet for one of the hearths which is over 7 feet long. The averaged volumes are .6 cubic feet while the approximate volume based on the average dimensions is .9 cubic feet. We might again note that, like Type B pits, most of the hearths were found in the channel where they were cut by small sampling units. Like Type B pits, the approximate volume suggested by the average dimensions is probably more accurate than the average of approximate volumes which is based on the smaller hearths found in the smaller channel units.

Those pits which appeared to have their origin in the IV*b* level were a mixed group containing both Middle and Late Woodland materials and pit types typical of both these horizons. Since their status as a group was ambiguous, they were eliminated for purposes of quantitative comparison. On the other hand, the profile of pits from the general Level IV almost duplicates that from the IV*c* level; these features were grouped to represent the Late Woodland occupation of the site. To get a general picture of the pit and hearth distribution, the 122 pits and hearths of fairly certain provenience were compared on the basis of position of the site and cultural horizon (Table 10), position on the site and feature type (Table 11), and cultural horizon and feature type (Table 12). Our observed and expected values differed in so striking a manner that the original intent of comparing them by Chi-square was abandoned. There are enough observed frequencies of zero alone to cause statistically significant Chi-square values.

TABLE 9
HEARTHS

Feature No.	Level	Area of Site	NS	EW	D	Approx. Vol.
24*a*	III*a*	Channel	(1.0)	(1.1)	.4	. . .
24*b*	III*a*	Channel	2.6	(1.6)	.5	. . .
25	III*a*	Channel	.9	(.6)	.2	. . .
27	II*d*	Channel	2.0	(1.0)	.3	. . .
28	II*d*	Channel	(.8)	1.5	.4	. . .
32	III*a*	Stockade	7.5	4.6	.3	2.9
38	III*a*	Stockade	2.6	2.7	.2	.4
70	II*d*	Channel	(1.7)	7.7	.4	. . .
64-1	III*a*	Mound	1.6	2.4	.1	.1
64-2	III*a*	Mound	(3.0)	(1.0)	.4	. . .
64-51	(III*a*)	Channel	3.3	1.4	.3	.1
64-52	(III*a*)	Channel	. . .	. . .	. . .	. . .
64-53	III*a*	Channel	2.0	(.7)	.3	. . .
64-56	III*a*	Channel	2.5	.9	.4	.3
64-57	(III*a*)	Channel	2.9	1.5	.6	.8
64-58	(III*a*)	Channel	3.8	3.8	.3	1.1
64-59	(III*a*)	Channel	2.5	2.1	.4	.7
64-61	(III*a*)	Channel	1.7	1.5	.5	.3
64-63	(III*a*)	Channel	3.1	(1.5)	.5	. . .
64-67	(III*a*)	Channel	. . .	. . .	. . .	. . .
64-68	(III*a*)	Channel	. . .	. . .	. . .	. . .
64-70	(III*a*)	Channel	. . .	. . .	. . .	. . .
64-72	II*d*	Channel	(2.6)	3.0	.6	. . .
64-73	III*a*	Stockade	1.8	1.9	.4	.4
64-74	II*d*	Channel	. . .	. . .	. . .	. . .
64-76	IV*c*	Channel	1.2	1.1	.2	.1
64-82	III*b*	Channel	4.3	2.9	.5	.6
64-87	III*b*	Channel	2.3	1.2	.4	.3
64-88	III*a*	Channel	1.2	(.9)	.8	. . .
64-89	III*b*	Channel	4.3	(1.5)	.9	. . .
64-90	III*b*	Channel	(2.1)	2.9	.6	. . .
64-91	III*b*	Channel	2.3	(1.5)	.8	. . .
64-92	III*b*	Channel	2.5	1.6	.3	.3
64-93	III*a*	Channel	(1.8)	(1.3)	.3	. . .
64-94	III*a*	Channel	(2.0)	2.0	.8	. . .
64-95	III*a*	Channel	3.1	(1.5)	.8	. . .
64-98	III*a*	Channel	2.7	1.6	.3	.4
64-99	II*d*	Channel	3.3	2.4	.6	1.3
64-100	III*a*	Channel	(1.6)	(1.3)	.6	. . .
64-102	II*d*	Channel	(5.8)	7.0	.4	. . .
	Mean		2.7	2.6	.5	.6*

*Mean Pit Volume derived from pit dimensions =.9

Note:—North to south (NS), east to west (EW) and depth (D) dimensions are given in feet. The approximate volume is given in cubic feet. Measurements in parentheses are incomplete and not used in deriving the means. Levels in parentheses are probable level of origin where data is uncertain.

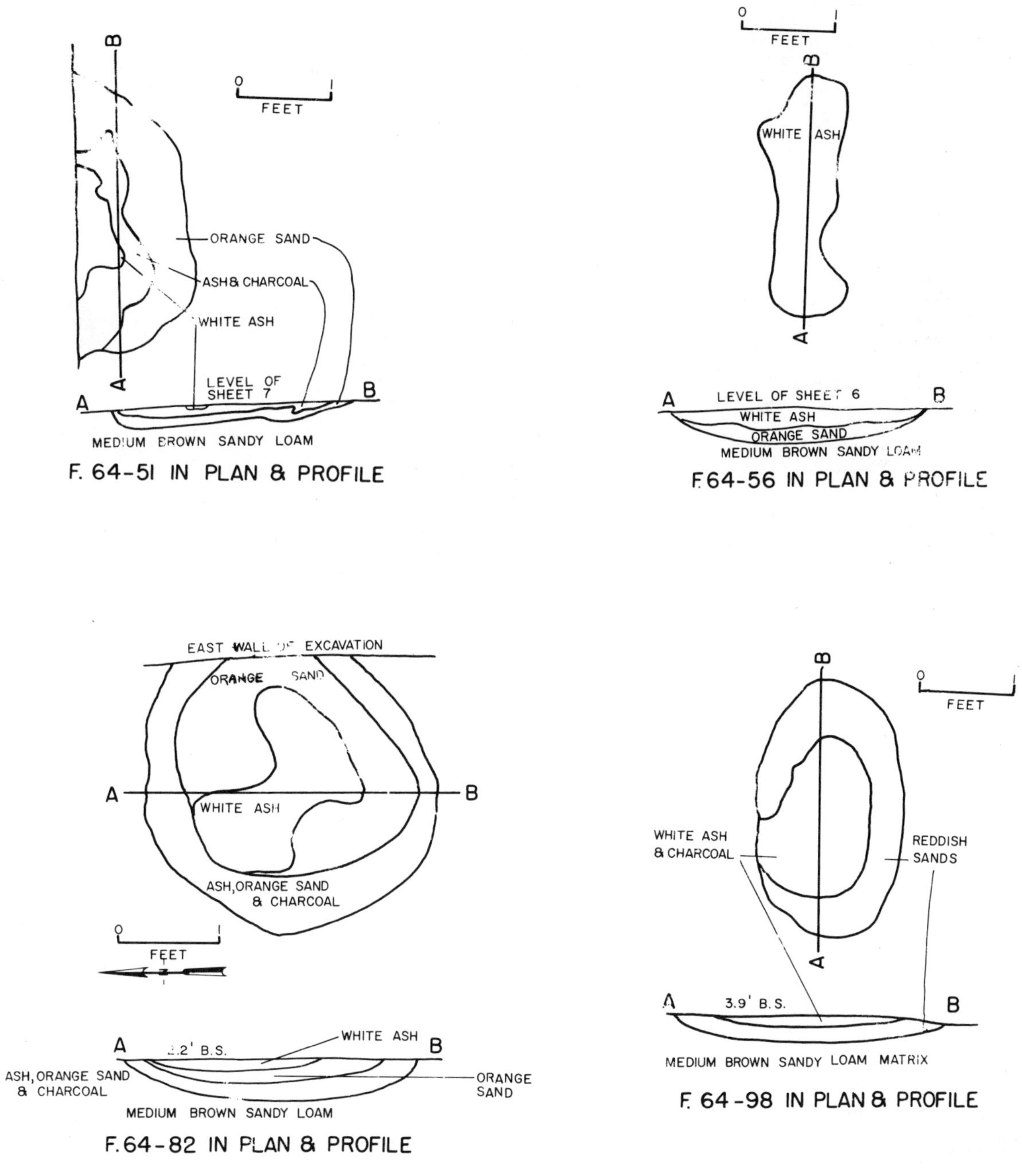

Fig. 16. Hearths.

Fig. 17. Feature 64-2: A hearth, in profile by Stadia rod. (Straw lined pit is from the 1963 post mold trench.)

TABLE 10
HORIZON AND LOCATION
OF FEATURES

Horizon	Area of the Site								Total
	Channel		Levee		Stockade		Mound		
	O	E	O	E	O	E	O	E	
Late Woodland	2	5	5	3	5	3	0	1	12
Late Middle Woodland	19	10	0	5	2	6	0	0	21
Early Middle Woodland	28	30	14	15	20	19	3	1	65
Transitional	7	3	0	2	0	2	0	0	7
Early Woodland	0	8	9	3	8	5	0	1	17
Total	56		28		35		3		122

Observed and expected numbers of features from the Schultz site by site area and cultural horizon.

TABLE 11
FEATURE TYPE AND LOCATION

Feature Type	Area of the Site								Total
	Channel		Levee		Stockade		Mound		
	O	E	O	E	O	E	O	E	
Pit Type A	4	14	14	7	12	9	0	0	30
Pit Type B	17	11	4	5	1	7	1	0	23
Pit Type C	0	8	9	4	8	5	0	0	17
Empty Pit	0	6	1	3	11	3	0	1	12
Hearth	35	17	0	9	3	11	2	3	40
Total	56		28		35		3		122

Observed and expected numbers of features from the Schultz site by feature type and site area.

TABLE 12
FEATURE TYPE AND HORIZON

Feature Type	Horizon										Total
	Late Woodland		Late Middle Woodland		Early Middle Woodland		Transitional		Early Woodland		
	O	E	O	E	O	E	O	E	O	E	
Pit Type A	9	3	3	5	18	16	0	2	0	4	30
Pit Type B	1	2	12	4	10	12	0	1	0	4	23
Pit Type C	0	2	0	3	0	9	0	1	17	2	17
Empty Pit	1	1	0	2	11	6	0	1	0	2	12
Hearth	1	4	6	7	26	22	7	2	0	5	40
Total	12		21		65		7		17		122

Observed and expected numbers of features from the Schultz site by feature type and site area.

Among the more obvious associations are Type C pits and the Early Woodland horizon. *All* Type C pits are Early Woodland and *all* Early Woodland features are Type C pits. It is also striking that all transitional II*d* features are hearths. Almost all of the hearths and Type B pits are found in the channel area, while almost all of the Type A pits and all of the Type C pits and empty pits are found on the levee, either inside or outside of the stockade.

A more detailed examination of this distribution by horizon is necessary for a fuller understanding of these tables. During the Early Woodland occupation, only the levee area of the site was available for habitation, probably because the river was active in the old channel area at the time. The sole feature type was the oval sunken hearth, and there is a suggestion from the distribution on the living floors that these hearths cluster around single post molds. This might indicate that they were associated with a structure of some sort. There are also indications that the Early Woodland occupation of the site took place in late fall and winter. The lack of refuse pits could either be a result of the ground being frozen at the time of occupation or the water table being too high to permit digging of refuse pits. The latter explanation is unlikely since Type C pits are deeper than some of the refuse pits. In relation to the volume of earth excavated for this occupation, nearly 32 percent of the total volume excavated on the site (Table 1), Early Woodland cultural material is sparse and seems to be spread over most of the site. With a light site occupation and extensive dumping of debris there may have been no need for special refuse pits.

The distribution of Early Woodland features on the levee is almost evenly divided between the inside and outside of the stockade, which would indicate that there was no special placement of these features in relation to the stockade. This is logical since other evidence indicates that the stockade was not built until later.

The transitional II*d* occupation seems to have taken place shortly after the Early Woodland occupation. These features are on top of deposits which correspond to the deposits which contain the Early Woodland materials. The volume of excavation in the Transitional area was less than for the Early Woodland levels, only 9.8 percent of the total site volume from areas of fairly certain provenience, but the amount of cultural material recovered was also negligible. While the entire site, in theory, would have been available to these people, only the low-lying channel area was used. All the features here were hearths. This might indicate a series of temporary camps directed toward the use of some swamp resource. The items that these people were after were not available in the higher areas of the site or they would have camped there.

During the early Middle Woodland occupation, the picture became much more complex. All areas of the site were apparently available for occupation and all were occupied. The only areal concentration of features is in the mound area where two early Middle Woodland hearths and a Type B pit were found beneath the mounds. This would indicate that the mounds postdate these features and are either late early Middle Woodland or late Middle Woodland.

Type A and Type B pits are found in about the expected chance numbers in the early Middle Woodland level. There are, of course, no Type C pits with this occupation. There are, however, nearly twice the expected number of empty pits. In fact, all of the empty pits but one (which has been attributed to the Late Woodland occupation) are early Middle Woodland pits, and all but one of these is within the stockade. More than half of the early Middle Woodland features within the stockade are empty pits despite the fact that these constitute less than ten percent of our sample.

Type A pits, which are predominately a Late Woodland feature type, and Type C pits, which are exclusively Early Woodland, are both found in greater than expected numbers within the stockade area, but are both probably unrelated to it. Early Middle Woodland features suggesting economic activities are strikingly absent from the stockade. I would conclude that the stockade itself is an early Middle Woodland structure with living debris and hearths concentrated outside the stockade and empty pits, perhaps of a ceremonial significance, inside of the stockade. The observation that some economic features were found inside of the stockade might indicate that it was built slightly after the initial occupation of the site by these people.

Only two late Middle Woodland features were found outside the channel area, except for the mounds which apparently were also a late Middle Woodland feature. For most of this occupation there was avoidance of both the stockade and the mound area, or so the distribution of living debris would indicate. This could have been because economic activities were centered about the river as in the transitional II*d* occupation. The numbers of specific hearths and the occurrence of other feature types would argue against this as the sole explanation. Another explanation would be that the stockade was either still standing during at least part of this occupation or that the area where the stockade had been was restricted. The occurrence of two late Middle Woodland features inside of the stockade and one directly over a post mold might indicate that this restriction was weakened or abandoned during the final phases of the late Middle Woodland occupation.

The Late Woodland features tend to be found on the levee, both inside and outside of the stockade. They are found in about equal numbers in both areas. This would indicate that the stockade was not interfering with the site occupation pattern at that time; that is, it was gone. The tendency to avoid the channel is also interesting. This could be because of a higher water table or because of a concentration of hunting activities in the upland areas of the site. There is other evidence that this occupation was directed toward hunting of larger forest and forest-prairie edge animals rather than smaller swamp mammals. The actual explanation is probably a combination of these factors along with others which are still obscure.

There is also a strong tendency for Type A pits to be identified with this level. These pits occur in greatest numbers in the early Middle Woodland level and in the Late Woodland level where hunting of large animals is important. In contrast, Type C pits (sunken hearths) and hearths occur in the largest relative numbers in the Early Woodland and transitional II*d* levels where small mammal hunting was more important. Type B pits reach their greatest relative frequency in the late Middle Woodland level when fishing reached its maximum importance.

The relationship between the occupational levels and the density of features might also be used as an indication of the occupational intensity for each horizon represented on the site. The Early Woodland occupation has only .006 features per cubic foot of that deposit and the transitional II*d* feature density is only .007 features per cubic foot of that deposit. This jumps to .017 features per cubic foot for the early Middle Woodland deposits, to .022 features per cubic foot of the late Middle Woodland deposits, and drops again to .016 features per cubic foot of the Late Woodland deposits. In brief, the Early Woodland and Transitional occupations were very low density occupations; the early Middle Woodland and Late Woodland feature density is similar; and the greatest concentration of features occurs during the late Middle Woodland occupation.

II

HISTORIC FLOODS IN THE SAGINAW BASIN

Gary A. Wright

Historic flooding in the Saginaw Basin is undoubtedly due to a number of interrelated causes. Outstanding among these would appear to be: the physiographic features of the Saginaw Valley; the shape of the flood basin; the pattern of discharge streams; reduction of forests; the appearance of surface and tile drains; reclamation projects; accumulated winter snow and ground water; sudden rises in temperature; excessive rainfall or several storms in succession; deeply frozen ground; and thickness of river ice (Frostic, 1918).

The Saginaw River drainage system operates behind and through two barrier moraines: the Bay City and Saginaw moraines. These moraines are effective in impeding the northward movement of water (the Saginaw River) into Saginaw Bay. The Saginaw River proper is formed by the confluence of the Shiawassee and Tittabawasee rivers just south of one of these barrier moraines, the Saginaw moraine, at Green point. The Saginaw moraine has a sea level altitude of approximately 615 feet. The Bay City moraine lies about 600 feet above sea level.

The watershed of the Saginaw River drainage system has been described as resembling a butterfly in shape, with the butterfly's head at the mouth of the Saginaw River at Saginaw Bay and the wings corresponding to the areas drained by the principal tributaries. The northwesterly wing is drained by the Tittabawassee, except for a small portion which is drained by tributaries of the Shiawassee. The southeastern wing is served by the Flint to the southeast, the Cass to the east, and the Shiawassee to the south.

The entire watershed services all or parts of 21 counties. The Tittabawassee, draining the northwestern portion of the basin, flows southward along the Saginaw moraine, joining the Shiawassee to form the Saginaw just prior to the latter river's breaking through the Saginaw moraine. The Cass drains the northern portion of the eastern wing, also following the Saginaw moraine and enters the Shiawassee just prior to the latter's juncture with the Tittabawassee. The Flint serves the southeast portion of the basin and joins the Shiawassee a few miles above the point of the Cass-Shiawassee juncture.

The elevations of the headwaters (sources) of the principal tributaries of the Saginaw are approximately as follows: Tittabawassee, 1000 feet; Shiawassee, 920 feet; Cass, 800 feet; Flint 785 feet; and the Bad, 675 feet (Frostic, 1918: 69). The slope of the Tittabawassee River bottom upstream from Green Point varies from 1.0 to 4.0 feet per mile. The Shiawassee River bottom, upstream from the Shiawassee Flats, has a slope from

2.0 to 5.0 feet per mile. The slope of the Flint river bottom, from its juncture with the Shiawassee, upstream, varies from 2.0 to 4.0 feet per mile. The slope of the Cass river bottom from Cass City downstream to Frankenmuth averages out at 2.5 feet per mile. Upstream in the Sanilac Flats the slope is about 1.0 feet per mile and the same figure is obtained downstream from Frankenmuth. The water surface in the Shiawassee Flats has very little slope, and under normal conditions the water's elevation is only slightly above that of Lake Huron. When the Saginaw's tributaries are experiencing flood conditions, the flats become a large pond or reservoir. From Green Point to the Court Street Bridge in Saginaw, the slope of the Saginaw river bottom is less than .1 foot per mile. The normal surface profile of the Saginaw River, from Green Point to Saginaw Bay, is nearly level. During flood conditions the average water slope may reach 0.5 foot per mile (U.S. Army Corps of Engineers Report, 1957: 17-18).

Topographically, we find that the two barrier moraines and the postglacial geologic history have served in dividing the drainage system further into three smaller basins. The first, the Shiawassee Flats (to which Green Point lies adjacent on the northern edge), lies near the center of the Saginaw Basin. It is a flat, poorly drained area of low-lying swamps (marshes) and marsh grass. An area of one of the old glacial lake beds, it is defined partially by the 595-foot contour, 15 feet above the level of Lake Huron, with its southern flats only 40 miles from this lake (U.S. Army Corps of Engineers Report, 1957:16). This is Frostic's (1918) Upper Basin. Its area is approximately 94 square miles. Between the Upper Basin and the tributary headwaters the land is rolling (undulated) and is characteristically better drained.

Between the Saginaw and Bay City moraines, along the Saginaw River proper, lies Frostic's Middle Basin—the Saginaw Flats. The elevation here varies from 585 to 595 feet. The area is 72 square miles. The Lower Basin, lying along Saginaw Bay, extends below the 585 contour in a narrow strip, varying from 1 to 2 miles wide.

Further lowland areas include the Sanilac Flats along the South Branch of the Cass to the northeast of Marlette. This area lies at an elevation of 768 feet, adjacent to the stream. Along the Flint in its upper reaches there are several low-lying, nearly swampy areas (i.e., the water table normally lies near the surface). There are a large number of inland lakes near the headwaters of the Flint and Shiawassee, but very few near the source of the Cass (U.S. Army Corps of Engineers Report, 1957:16-17). However, these lakes lie generally along the outer borders of the basin, near the divide, and thus help little in drawing water which eventually finds its way into tributary streams. Also, there are no settling basins in the upper valleys which can be used to regulate the discharge of water into the lower valley (Frostic, 1918: 73).

It can be seen that the general shape and positioning of the Shiawassee and Saginaw Flats (Upper and Middle Basins), in collaboration with the narrow discharge openings in the two moraines, have much to do with the regulation of water flow in the Saginaw Basin. Under flood conditions, the narrow opening in the Saginaw moraine retards rapid discharge of water down the Saginaw, with a large back-up occurring in the Shiawassee Flats and low-lying areas (e.g., Green Point) which are inundated. Upon discharge through the Saginaw moraine, the water again expands in the Middle Basin before being discharged through the Bay City moraine and thence into the Lower Basin and finally into Saginaw Bay. However, these narrow openings also serve to retard back-ups from Saginaw Bay, that is, a high rise in the water level caused by strong northeast winds.

Such an occurrence was the main factor in the flood of November 22-23, 1917.

The discharge flow rate of the Saginaw at normal height is estimated at 15,800 feet per second by Frostic (1918:74). The discharge rate at bankfull capacity is tabulated for the Saginaw by the U.S. Army Corps of Engineers at 70,000 cubic feet per second at the Genessee Street Bridge. The elevation of the bankfull stage is 591 feet, corresponding to a Lake Huron stage of elevation at 580 feet (1957: Table 2). The same table gives a rate of 30,000 cubic feet per second at bankfull for Green Point. The flow capacities of all streams, then, are affected by and are dependent upon the stage of water imponded in the Shiawassee Flats and the quantity of water which can be successfully handled by the Saginaw River is similarly affected by the amount of backwater from Saginaw Bay and Lake Huron (U.S. Army Corps of Engineers Report, 1957: 19).

By 1900, through lumbering and forest fires, the Saginaw Valley had lost nearly all of its important forests. It would seem that the mixed deciduous-coniferous forests had served to retain melt water from winter snows, causing a more gradual run-off into discharge streams. The spongelike floors and forest shade would cause slower melting, allowing a more even discharge of water. Frostic (1918) has noted that the Saginaw River was becoming free from ice earlier (by about 10 days) in March since 1900, than it had prior to that time. The above factors may be held accountable for this earlier ice break-up, which indicates that water from melted snow was reaching discharge streams more quickly.

The mixed deciduous-coniferous forest would serve to prevent erosion and sediment loss. There is some reason to believe that from the time of the sixth century B.C. at Green Point until after white contact, destructive floods were rarer than under present conditions.

With depletion of the forests and the corresponding decline of the lumbering industry, much of the land was put to agricultural purposes. The U.S. Army Corps of Engineers Report (1957) states that there were, at that time, 7,359 miles of established county and intercounty drains within the basin, excluding private farm tile and open drains. These "improvements" have caused a considerable amount of water to be channeled into the tributaries—water which normally would have found its way into the ground or eventually into the streams. This hastened run-off has caused severe flood problems downstream.

Reclamation projects in the Shiawassee Flats have reduced the flats' capacity to impond, temporarily, potential flood waters. The Prairie Farm (8,000 acres) and the Little Prairie Farm (3,500 acres) have utilized both pumping stations (for drainage pumps) and levees in order to reclaim and to hold former marsh lands. In the Middle Basin, Frostic (1918) reported another project which had accumulated about 900 acres under a similar procedure. Without the availability of these two basins as natural ponding areas where, during flood conditions, the water would have found a natural reservoir in which to spread before being discharged through the moraines, the flood waters are now forced to find new areas upon which to encroach.

The prime flooding situation occurs after a winter of heavy snows coupled with cold temperatures which do not permit gradual melting. A sudden rise in temperature, often accompanied by heavy rains, causes a large accumulation of water which saturates the ground. Water is then forced to run off into the tributary streams. The streams swell considerably, and the water is held back by the slow discharge through the moraines; lowlands are soon unundated, and severe flooding may follow. The combination of events described above was the main cause of the floods of 1904, 1930, and 1938, for example.

A sudden rise in temperature is often followed by heavy rainstorms. These cause extreme saturation of the ground and immediate run-off into the tributary streams. The major storms for the period of 1895-1948 are found in Table 13.

TABLE 13
PERIODS OF HARD RAINFALL

Date	Inches	Area Affected
1895—Dec. 16-21	2.5	Entire basin
1897—Jan. 2-4	3.0	Entire basin
1904—Mar. 22-25	1.5	Entire basin
1905—June 3-8	2.3	Lower half of basin
1912—Mar. 19-22	4.0	Entire basin
1912—July 19-24	3.0	Entire basin
1913—Mar. 23-27	6.0	Entire basin
1913—Aug. 8-10	4.0	Entire basin
1914—May 10-12	4.0	Southern portion of basin
1914—Aug. 31 - Sept 1	5.2	Outside of basin
1916—Mar. 21-27	2.0	Entire basin
1922—Feb. 19-23	3.0	Northwest portion of basin
1922—June 8-11	3.0	Entire basin
1937—Aug. 31 - Sept. 3	4.0	Northwest portion of basin
1938—Feb. 9-14	3.5	Southern edge of basin
1947—Apr. 4-6	1.5	Entire basin
1948—Mar. 18-19	1.5	Entire basin

Compiled from the U.S. Army Corps of Engineers Report, 1957: 24-25.

Comparing Table 13 with Table 14 we note that eight of these storms produced noteworthy floods in the Saginaw River or its tributaries, seven occurring during February, March or April, and one in May. Further heavy rains produced floods in 1956 (March and May) and in 1962 (March).

Deeply frozen ground causes water to be forced into run-offs, and thence into the tributary streams, rather than being absorbed by the ground. According to Frostic (1918:76), this condition was probably present in most early floods. Winter temperatures in the Saginaw Valley are usually sufficient to produce a deep frost line. Such a deep frost is held partially responsible for the flood of 1904, among others.

Another flood-causing problem arises because the ice in the rivers and the bay breaks up so much more slowly than the snow on the land melts, thus retarding the normal discharge of the snow water into the bay. Ice jams then cause a sudden and excessive increase in water height. Often, ice jams must be dynamited to allow free passage of run-off water. Ice dams have been reported at the confluence of the Tittabawassee and Shiawassee and on the Cass, Flint and Saginaw. This condition was partially responsible for the floods of 1904, 1918, 1920, 1947, 1951, and 1952.

There are little factual data concerning floods prior to 1884. It will be suggested later, however, that the character of these inundations differed from that of those after the destruction of the area forests.

A "Saginaw Emigrant" (Michigan Historical and Pioneer Collections, 1882, 7:270-71) reported in 1823 that the rivers and tributary streams of the Saginaw had a great body of water discharged into them during the spring and autumn freshlets, flooding the lowlands and bayous, although the land (higher) in the vicinity was not overflowed. How long this settler had lived in the area before reporting is not known, but he will be mentioned again.

Possibly the earliest recorded flood in the Saginaw Valley is the note left by Surgeon Pitcher of Fort Saginaw which is related in the *History of Saginaw County* (Leeson, 1881:165). Pitcher says that the winter of 1822-23 had been very cold with much snow and that "when spring came on the rapid solution of it (the snow) caused a great flood in the Tittabawassee and other tributaries of the Saginaw, so that most of the prairie between the post and Green Point was under water."

Judge Albert Miller (1888, 13:378-80) wrote that during late March and early April of 1836, following a winter of heavy snow and heavy spring rains, there was considerable water standing around Crow Island and Cheboyganing Creek. Further, he states that there were two feet of water around his home in Portsmouth and that the water was waist deep on the Quanicassee prairie.

Frostic (1918:73) wrote that due to maximum high water in Saginaw Bay (585 feet) 30,000 to 40,000 acres of land were flooded by backwater in 1838. I have no data for the next 20 years.

The Saginaw News reported that in 1858 there occurred a serious flood with waters spreading as far east as Baum Street. An unusually heavy snow fall is mentioned by *The Saginaw News* for 1864, and this may have led to another flood, but specific data is lacking.

Floods began to be common in the late 1860's and early 1870's, with major floods occurring in 1870, 1871, 1873, 1874 and 1876. The worst of these appear to have been those of 1871 and 1874. In 1874, Cass Street (now Baum), Federal Avenue (German) and Water Street (Tilden) were flooded, as well as the 100 block north of Genesee. These floods ranged from "minor to damaging" as concerned property within Saginaw proper.

In 1884 the flood waters crested at 23.9 feet (flood stage is 19.1 feet). All basements on Genesee from Cass to Warren had water. The water rose 5 feet in six hours on March 26, then rose 15 more inches before cresting. Another major flood is recorded for 1898.

The year 1904 is termed the "spring of high water," with the flood waters cresting on March 29 at 24.9 feet, nearly 6 feet above flood stage. The flood was the worst recorded up to that time in the Saginaw Valley. The winter had seen the heaviest snowfall since 1864, 88.5 inches: December, 20.1 inches; January, 36.8 inches; and February, 31.6 inches. This snowfall was accompanied by an unusually deep frost, allowing little ground absorption. There was an earlier, milder flood due to an early thaw around March 10, with a quick rise of the Flint and Shiawassee at Flint and Owosso. The Saginaw rose 12 inches in 24 hours. This was followed by torrential rains and new snow. With water and ice clogging the sewers, flood waters were forced back into the city.

Table 14 summarizes the floods between 1904 and 1962 including crest points and pertinent remarks as to causes and areas covered by flood waters.

TABLE 14
FLOODING SINCE 1904
(In Feet)

Date	Crest	Remarks
1905, March	20.6	1.5 ft. above flood stage in Saginaw for 8 days
1905, June	19.8	0.7 ft. above flood stage in Saginaw for 8 days
1906, January	19.2	Above flood stage in Saginaw for 2 days
1907, January	20.4	Above flood stage in Saginaw for 7 days
1907, March	19.2	Above flood stage in Saginaw for 2 days
1908, March	22.6	Above flood stage in Saginaw for 22 days
1908, May	20.0	Above flood stage in Saginaw for 4 days
1909, April	19.4	Above flood stage in Saginaw for 2 days
1909, May	22.2	Above flood stage in Saginaw for 8 days
1912, April 9	24.1 ca. 25.0	Crest in Saginaw Crest in Midland
1912, May 21-23	ca. 24.1	Second flood of 1912; heavy cloudburst on May 21 Total rainfall for month, 9.95 in.; 5.71 in. above normal Heavy loss of vegetation
1913, March	21.2	Above flood stage in Saginaw for 4 days
1913, April	20.4	Above flood stage in Saginaw for 3 days
1916, April 1	24.3	Heavy rains throught March Damage estimate: $100,000
1917, Nov. 21-23	24.4(?)	Crest for Saginaw Caused by heavy NE wind off Saginaw Bay; raised lake level ca. 5.0 ft. Probably localized to Bay City—Saginaw area
1918, March 19-28	23.5 18.0	Crest at Saginaw, March 22 Crest at Midland, March 21 Zilwaukee and Carrollton flooded Cause: heavy ice which had to be dynamited out of the Tittabawassee
1919, March 17-20	22.0 23.1	Crest at Midland, March 18 Crest at Saginaw, March 20 Both Tittabawassee and Saginaw reported rising at rate of 2.0 ft. per hour, March 18
1920, March 10-19	20.5	Crest for Saginaw, March 19 On 3/10 rivers frozen solid; Saginaw frozen at mouth of Saginaw River, with 3.0 in. of water on top of ice Slight rains 3/15-16 On 3/16 Tittabawassee ice breaking, with rises at all stations except Bridgeport and Paines
1926, March 23-27	19.9	Crest for Saginaw, March 27 Ice jams dynamited Tributaries falling by 3/27, except Flint
1928, April 6-11	ca. 20.1	Crest for Saginaw, April 9 Tittabawassee principal center of flood conditions—western and southern ends of county inundated, with large areas of Spaulding, Albee, and Tittabawassee Townships under water

TABLE 14 (Continued)

Date	Crest	Remarks
1930, Feb. 24-27	20.7	Crest for Saginaw, 2/27
		Causes: high temperatures (low of 37 on 2/24); 1.56 in. of rain on 2/25; snow, rain and sleet on 2/26
		All area lowlands inundated
		Rain flood at Alma
		Pine flooded at Thames
1938, Feb. 7-14		Entire Saginaw Valley watershed experienced various stages of flood conditions
		Causes: heavy rains, melting snows, high temperatures (ca. 50°), and heavy ice jams
	19.1	Crest for Midland, 2/7
	17.2	Crest for Saginaw—below flood stage though lowlands inundated
		Cass overflowed at Frankenmuth
		Shiawassee flooded lowlands at Chesaning
1942, March	21.0	Crest for Saginaw
1946, March 5-22	22.6	Crest for Midland, 3/8
	21.0	Crest for Saginaw, 3/9
		St. Charles area flooded
		Considerable water standing in low-lying fields in Green Point area; Maple Street impassable south of Merrill Park
		Causes: heavy ice jams, heavy water flows from Tittabawassee and Cass
1947, March 25		Tributaries up—heavy March storm
		Cass ice jams dynamited—extensive flooding
1947, April 4-7		Shiawassee, Flint and Cass overflowed
		St. Charles lowlands inundated by Bad
	19.8	Crest for Saginaw, 4/7
	22.0	Crest for Midland
1948, March 16-27	22.4	Crest for Saginaw, 3/23
		Green Point inundated through Merrill Park
	24.0	Crest for Midland
		Frankenmuth flooded by Cass
		Bad over M-47 at St. Charles
		33,600 tons of topsoil per 24 hours estimated going under Genesee Bridge
1950, March 25-April 6	20.5	Crest for Saginaw, 4/6
	19.7	Crest for Midland
	16.4	Crest for Vassar
	12.3	Crest for Chesaning
		All area lowlands inundated
1951, Feb. 20-23		Ice jams on Shiawassee at Owosso caused overflow onto lowlands
1952, Feb. 5-6		Frankenmuth flooded by Cass—14-16 in. of standing water caused by ice jams
1952, March 13-22		Green Point lowlands inundated by water from Merrill Bridge—not a simple bank overflow
		High rise of Tittabawassee caused by water from Pine and Chippewa—rose 4.0 ft. in 24 hours

TABLE 14 (Continued)

Date	Crest	Remarks
1952, April 14-15		Dozen Green Point homes surrounded by water
	12.0	Crest at Vassar
		Tittabawassee up 7.65 ft. in 24 hours
1954		Frankenmuth flooded by Cass
1956, March 1-21	ca. 25.0	Crest for Midland
	ca. 22.4	Crest for Saginaw
		Cause: heavy spring rains and snow
		Shiawassee drainage possibly not heavily affected
1956, May 7-19		Cause: heavy rains (6.0 in. in 10 days)
		All tributaries affected; Green Point inundated
1959, Feb. 13-26		All lowlands in watershed inundated
		Water 6.0 ft. deep at Green Point
1959, April 2-5		Green Point still under water; most lowlands in basin inundated
1960, March 30-April 7	+20.0	Midland—city and lowlands flooded
	20.9	Crest for Saginaw, 4/2
		20,000 acres inundated south of Saginaw
1962, March 13-24		Cause: spring thaw coupled with new snows and rain
		Lowlands along Cass and Flint flooded
		Little property damage

From the data just presented, it can be seen that the Saginaw Basin experiences four general periods when major flooding occurs: mid-winter (January); late winter-early spring (February, March, April, May); late spring (June freshlets); and late autumn (November). Of these flood times, approximately 95 percent fall into the February-May bracket. The seasonal distribution of floods into the latter category is the result of the various causative factors already discussed: basin morphology, amount of snow, depth of frost line, ice jams, sudden rises in temperature, early rains, and several cultural variables. The January floods are probably due to similar factors, while the June freshlets undoubtedly have their cause in heavy rainfall on already saturated ground. The November flood of 1917, as indicated, was due to high northeasterly winds off Saginaw Bay which caused a back-up of waters and impeded discharge through the barrier moraines.

There appears to have been an increase of (or return to) turbulent flood conditions. These were similar to conditions prior to the earliest recorded occupations of the Green Point sites. Early records tend to show that inundation of the lowlands in and around the Shiawassee and Saginaw Flats (Upper and Middle Basins) were not uncommon. However, it appears that major flood conditions may not have been prevalent until after the influx of white immigrants into the Saginaw Basin. The increasing new population, with its different culture and adaptation to (exploitation of) the basin, seems to have been an important variable in the rise of major flood problems for the valley. The exploitation factors discussed earlier, such as the destruction of the forests, added to the natural conditions, resulted in more than just a possible seasonal inundation of the lowlands and bayous. They were directly responsible for major flood disasters.

In this light, it is interesting to note two early statements about the area. On May 30, 1822, J. L. Cole wrote: "There is a most beautiful flat called Green Point, at the upper extremity of which stands the (Indian) village. The flat is *apparently free from inundation* (emphasis mine) and produces the most luxuriant growth of grass." (1888:474). This would appear to indicate that the lowlands were seldom inundated. However, the statements by Surgeon Pitcher and the "Saginaw Emigrant" (mentioned earlier) indicate something rather different for the Green Point area. Judge Miller's is the earliest account of the Middle Basin. The Emigrant had this to say: After inundation of the bayous in spring and fall, such was the "nature of the soil, however, that immediately upon recession of the water scarcely a trace of the inundation can be seen . . . the alluvial district presents to the eye of the traveler an extensive plain covered with a luxuriant growth of wild grass" (1888:270-71).

One assumption which can be drawn from the evidence is that until a period some time after the turn of the century, little debris (e.g., silts) was carried in the waters and subsequently lost, even when the lowlands were inundated. Thus the grasses were not impeded in their growth and there was little sedimentation build-up. Frostic (1918:71) had this to say: "The rivers of this system are remarkably free from silt. Had the streams been even moderately loaded with sediment, the low marshy lands would have been built up to a higher level long ago." What tests Frostic used to arrive at his statements are not known. However, at present there is a large quantity of silt carried by the streams. *The Saginaw News* for March 19, 1948, states that under the flood conditions at that date, 33,600 tons of topsoil were being carried under the Genesee Street Bridge every 24 hours.

The general conclusion reached here is that the lowlands in the Saginaw drainage basin, particularly in the downstream area, were probably inundated seasonally (spring) for short periods of time. This is evidenced by the geology of 20SA1 which indicates varying conditions of turbulent flooding alternating with more stable conditions from the period of 1000 B.C. to just prior to white contact (H. T. Wright, 1964). However, if it is valid that only a small amount of sediment was carried by the tributary streams, there would be little buildup shown in the geologic record. Further, viewing the late prehistoric geologic record, we would expect quieter current to have prevailed, resulting in a minimum of erosion. With erosion at a minimum and substantial forests we would expect less sedimentation.

It was not until the effects of the new exploitation of the land were fully felt that the return to turbulent flood conditions was experienced. The new cultural practices, coupled with the partial loss of back-up basins, resulted in the loss of topsoil and some subsequent erosion. These, added to the morphological pattern of the basin which is a constant factor, gives us the current flood problem in the Saginaw Basin.

III

GEOLOGY OF THE SCHULTZ SITE

John D. Speth

INTRODUCTION

After the excavations in 1963, Taggart (n.d*b*.) compiled a preliminary statement of the geology of the Schultz site (20SA 2) in which he recognized eight stratigraphic units. This sequence was refined in 1964 by Fitting, who recognized eleven major units. Much of the material presented in other sections of this volume was collected and analyzed prior to the completion of this paper and utilizes a modified form of Fitting's sequence. In the present study, eleven stratigraphic units and a number of subdivisions are recognized. These units, in most cases, correspond closely to those of Fitting. Table 15 gives the correlation of the various stratigraphic sequences used at Schultz site.

TABLE 15
CORRELATION OF STRATIGRAPHIC SEQUENCES USED AT THE SCHULTZ SITE

Taggart Sequence (1963)	Fitting Sequence (1964)	Geologic Units of Present Study (1966)
Plow zone	Plow zone	11
Upper dark silts	IV*c*	10
Intermediate dark silts	IV*b*	9
Middle dark silts	IV*a*	8*c*
	III*b*	8*b*
Brown silts	III*a*	6?, 7, 8*a* (Channel area) 5*a*, 7, 8*a* (Outside channel area)
	II*d* (Occurs in channel only)	5*a*, 5*b*, 6?
Lower dark silts	II*c*	4
	II*b*	3
Gray silts	II*a*	2
Bedded sands	I	1*a*, 1*b*

In 1964, Henry T. Wright sampled three vertical sections in the major north-south trench, at 520E590, 563E590, and 711E590 (Fig. 18). These samples, in conjunction with several radiocarbon dates and a complete sequence of overlapping Kodachrome slides taken of the east wall of the trench by David S. Brose, served as the basis for the discussions which follow.

The color, texture, pH and alkali-soluble organic content were determined for each of the samples collected by Wright. Color was determined by direct comparison of both air-dried and moist samples to a Munsell Soil Color Chart (Munsell Color Company, Inc., Baltimore, Maryland, 1954 edition). The results are tabulated in Table 16. Texture (Fig. 19), based on the Wentworth Grade Scale, was determined in two steps: (1) sands were separated by seiving through U.S. Standard Seive Series screens using the method described by Krumbein and Pettijohn (1938:136-43); (2) clay and silt fractions were determined by the hydrometer method using the procedure outlined by Black, et al., (1965:562-65). The pH of the samples (Fig. 19) was determined using the method described by Black et al., (1965:920-23). The alkali-soluble organic content (Fig. 19) was determined by treating the samples with sodium hydroxide and measuring the color densities of the resultant solutions (Cornwall, 1958:176-78).

Figures 20 through 23 illustrate representative portions of the east wall of the 1964 trench between 490E590 and 720E590.

The stratigraphic and areal placement of the radiocarbon dates from Green Point are summarized in Table 17.

STRATIGRAPHY

Phase I (Units 1*a* and 1*b*)

Unit 1a: Unit 1*a* consists of an undetermined thickness of finely bedded light brownish gray clay, silt and fine sand containing organic matter including unburned twigs and wood fragments. This unit was exposed in a deep test at 563E590. Two radiocarbon dates were obtained from the deposit M-1634 from an elevation of 580 feet which yielded a date of 4250 ± 150 years ago, and M-1633 from elevation of about 581 feet which yielded a date of 5050± 170 years ago. The peculiar inversion of the dates is unexplainable. Both dates, however, represent a late pre-Nipissing time (Hough, 1963:105). The unit probably represents a swamp or near-shore deposit developed late in the transgression of pre-Nipissing lake waters toward the final Nipissing level.

Unit 1b: This unit, exposed completely only at 563E590, consists of about 3.5 feet of light gray, horizontally bedded, oxidized lacustrine sand and silt. The deposit is deeply and irregularly eroded, especially south of 540E590 where a channel developed. The area north of 540E590 lies at an average elevation of about 583 feet and reaches a maximum elevation of nearly 585 feet at 540E590. The lowest point in the channel, at 510E590, lies at an average elevation of about 581 feet. The bottom of the channel slopes up slightly to the south to an elevation of 582 feet at the south end of the trench. The bank situated between 530E590 and 540E590 dips to the south at an angle of about 30 degrees. The south bank of the channel was not exposed in the trench, but it was probably located just south of 490E590. No radiocarbon dates were obtained from Unit 1*b*. The deposit probably represents the final stages of the Nipissing transgression, the Algoma Lake stage, and the final retreat toward the present level of Lake Huron at 580 feet. The retreat of the Algoma was brought about by down-cutting of the St. Clair outlet (Hough, 1963:105). As base level dropped below about 585 feet,

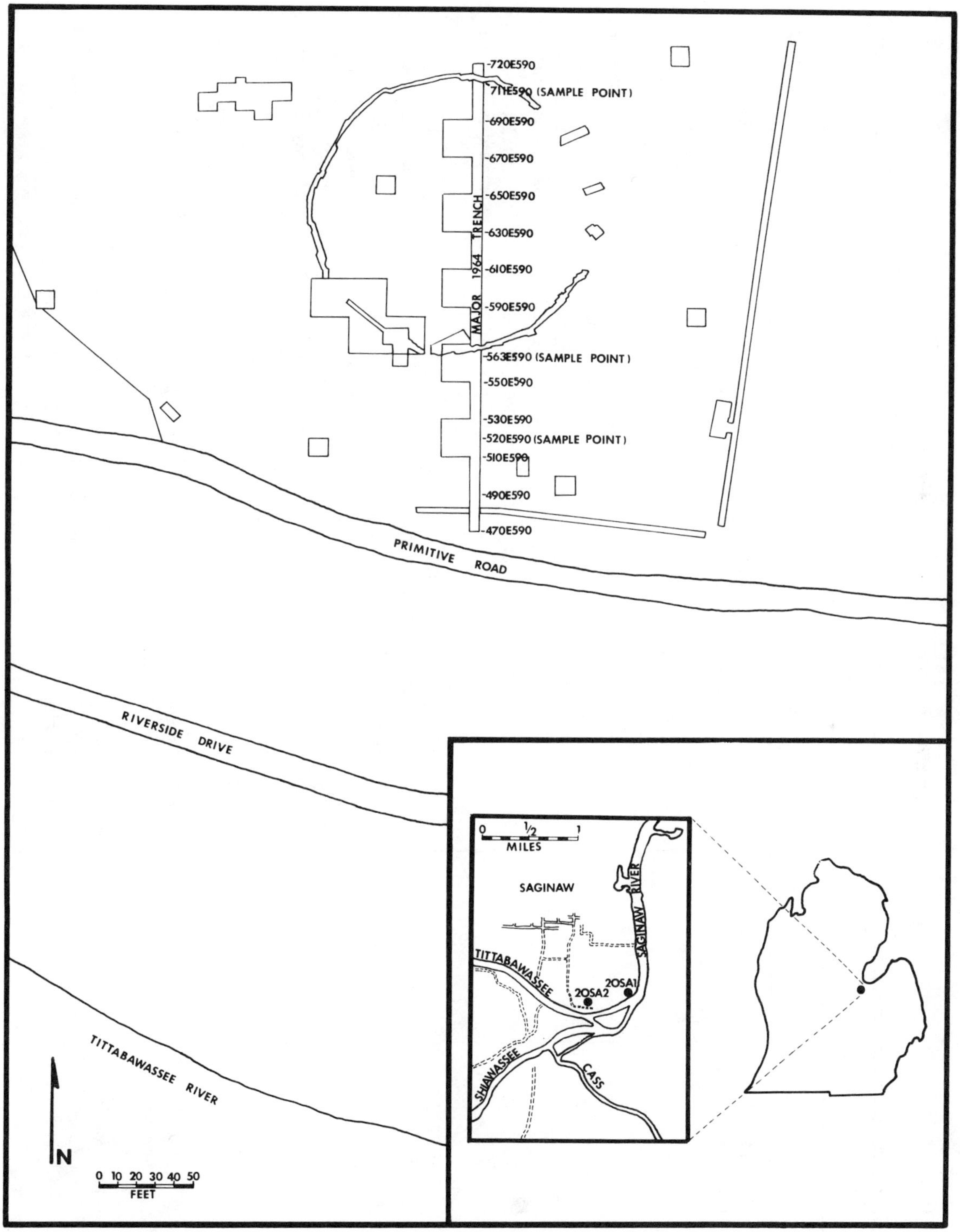

Fig. 18. Location of soil sample sections.

TABLE 16
AIR-DRIED AND MOIST COLORS OF SEDIMENTS AT 20 SA 2

	711E590		563E590		520E590	
Unit	Air-dried	Moist	Air-dried	Moist	Air-dried	Moist
11	10YR4/2 (dk.grayish brown)	10YR2/2 (v. dk. brown)	10YR4/2 (dk.grayish brown)	10YR2/2 (v. dk. brown)	10YR4/1 (dk. gray)	10YR3/1 (v. dk. gray)
10	...	...	...	...	10YR4/1 (dk. gray)	10YR3/1 (v. dk. gray)
9	...	...	...	...	10YR5/2 (grayish brown) w/10YR4/2 FFM mottles	10YR3/2 (v. dk. grayish brown)
8c	...	...	...	...	10YR5/2 (grayish brown)	10YR3/2 (v. dk. grayish brown)
8b	...	...	...	...	10YR6/2 (lt. brownish gray) w/10YR4/2 DCM mottles	10YR4/2 (dk.grayish brown)
8a	10YR5/2 (grayish brown)	10YR3/2 (v.dk.grayish brown)	10YR5/2 (grayish brown)	10YR3/2 (v.dk.grayish brown)	10YR5/2 (grayish brown)	10YR3/2 (v.dk.grayish brown)
7	10YR5/3 (brown)	10YR3/3 (dk.brown)	No Sample	No Sample	10YR5/3 (brown) w/ 10YR4/2 FFM mottles	10YR3/3 (dk. brown)
6	...	...	...	...	10YR5/2 (grayish brown) w/10YR4/1 DMC mottles	10YR3/2 (v.dk.grayish brown)
5b	...	...	...	...	10YR5/2 (grayish brown) w/10YR4/2 DCM mottles	10YR3/2 (v. dk. grayish brown)
5a	10YR5/3 (brown)	10YR3/3 (dk.brown)	10YR5/3 (brown) w/ 10YR4/1DFM mottles	10YR3/2 (v.dk.grayish brown)	10YR6/2 (lt.brownish gray)w/7.5YR6/6 DMC mottles	10YR4/3 (dk. brown)
4	10YR5/3 (brown) w/ 10YR4/1 DCM mottles	10YR3/2 (v.dk.grayish brown)	10YR4/2 (dk. grayish brown) w/10YR5/3 FCM mottles	10YR2/2 (v.dk. brown)	7.5YR5/6(strong brown)w/10YR6/1 DMC and 10YR8/2 DMF mottles	10YR3/4 (dk. yellowish brown)

TABLE 16 (Continued)

	711E590		563E590		520E590	
Unit	Air-dried	Moist	Air-dried	Moist	Air-dried	Moist
3	10YR4/1 (dk. gray)	10YR2/2 (v.dk. brown)	10YR4/2 (dk. grayish brown)	10YR2/2 (v. dk. brown)	No Sample	No Sample
2	10YR6/2(lt. brown-ish gray)w/10YR4/2 FCF mottles	10YR5/3 (brown)	10YR6/3 (pale brown) w/10YR5/2 DCM mottles	10YR5/3 (brown)	10YR6/1 (gray) w/ 7.5YR5/6 DFM mottles	10YR5/3 (brown)
1b	10YR7/2 (lt. gray)	10YR5/3 (brown)	10YR7/2 (lt. gray)	10YR5/3 (brown)	10YR7/2 (lt. gray)	10YR5/2 (grayish brown)
1a	No Sample	No Sample	10YR6/2(lt. brown-ish gray) w/ organic matter	10YR5/2 (grayish brown)	No Sample	No Sample

Note:—Mottles—Described according to Munsell color, contract, abundance and size (Soil Survey Manual, 1951:192); contrast (F faint, D distinct, P prominent); abundance (F few, C common, M many); size (F fine, M medium, C coarse). Dotted line—unit probably not present in section. No Sample—unit present in section but not exposed in excavation or no samples collected.

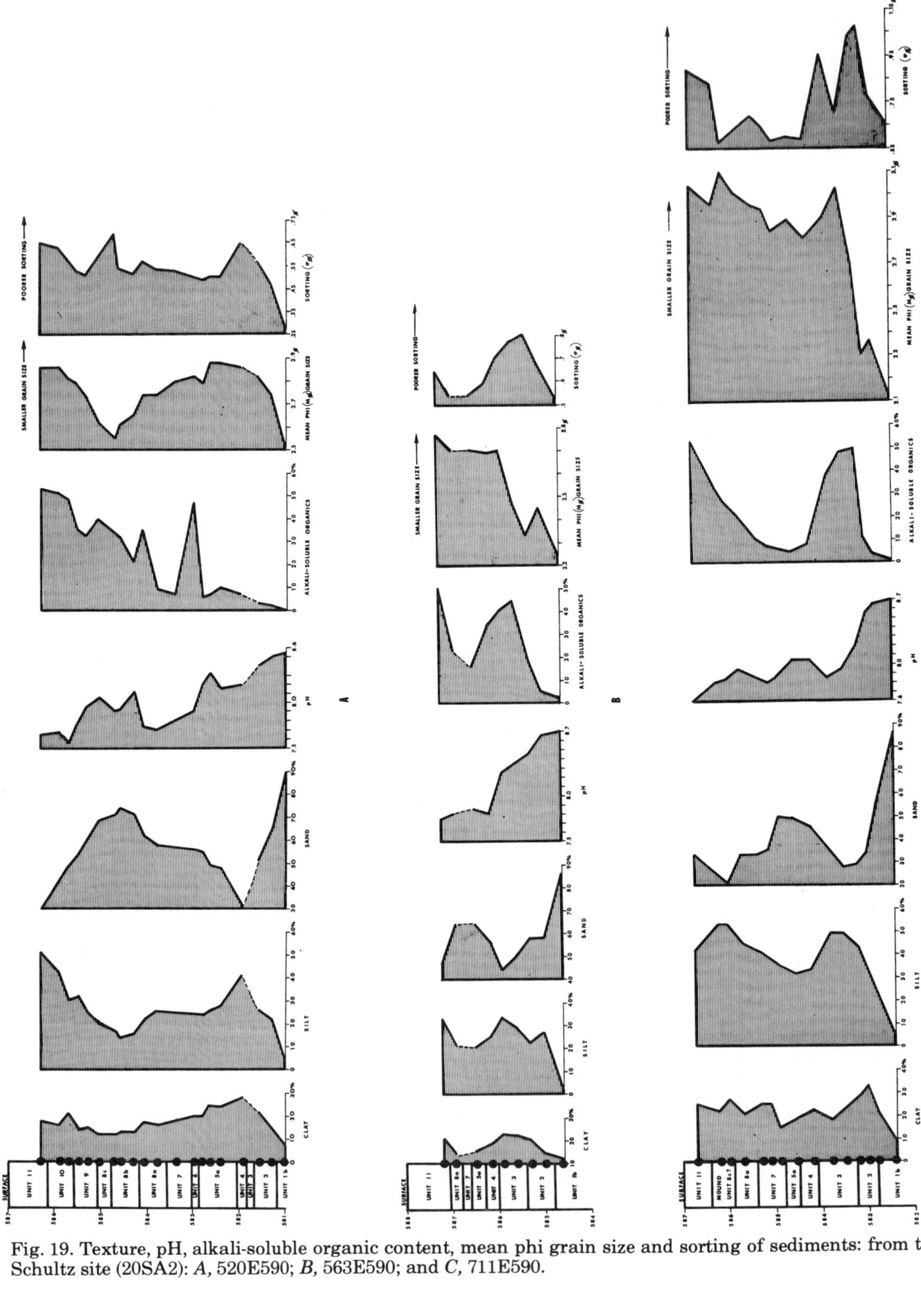

Fig. 19. Texture, pH, alkali-soluble organic content, mean phi grain size and sorting of sediments: from the Schultz site (20SA2): *A*, 520E590; *B*, 563E590; and *C*, 711E590.

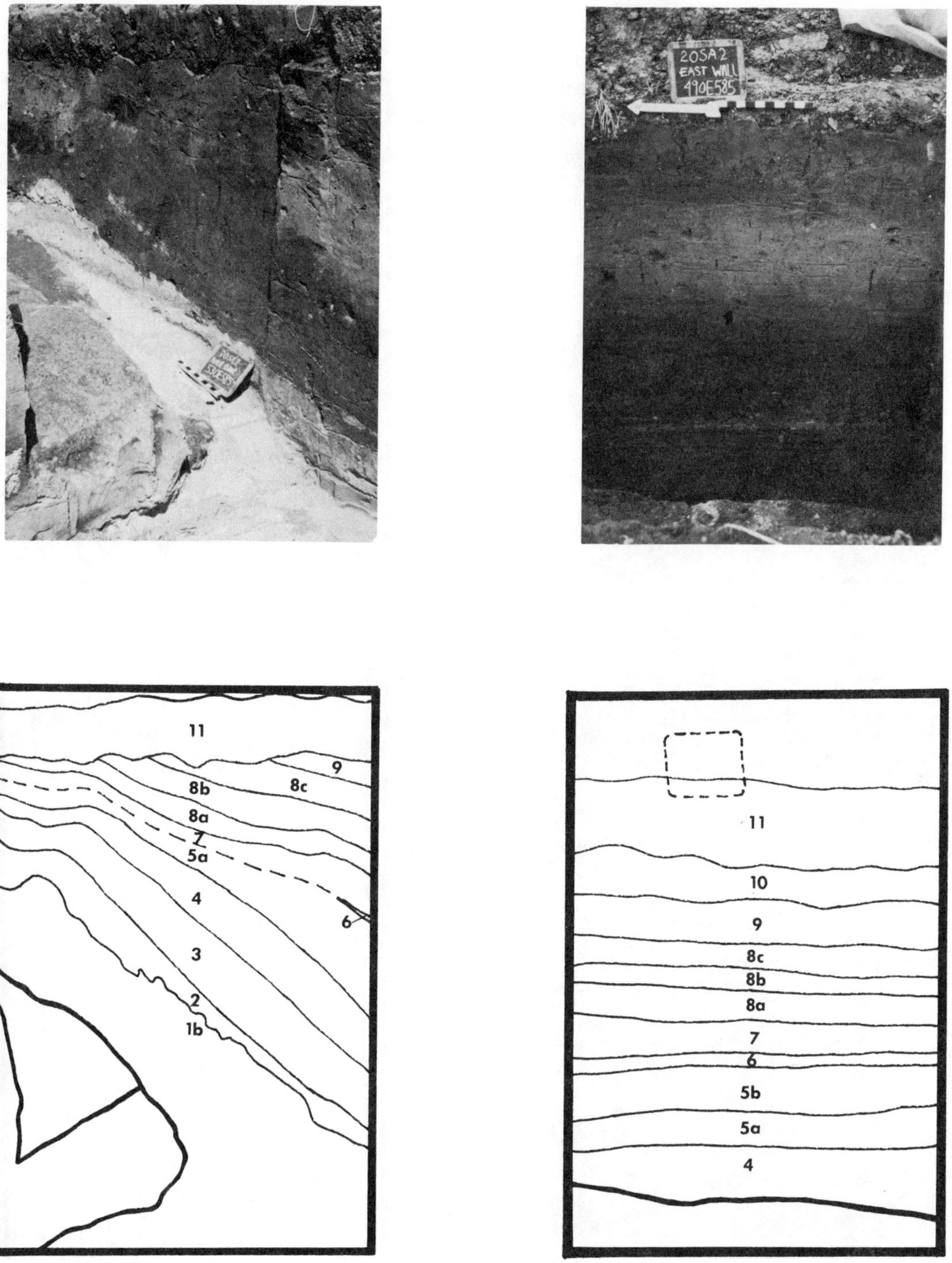

A B

Fig. 20. East wall of 1964 Trench; Schultz sitz (20SA2): *A*, channel bank and levee area between 528-535E590; *B*, south end of trench between 490-495E590. North arrow is one foot long. Ignore lines engraved directly on sections.

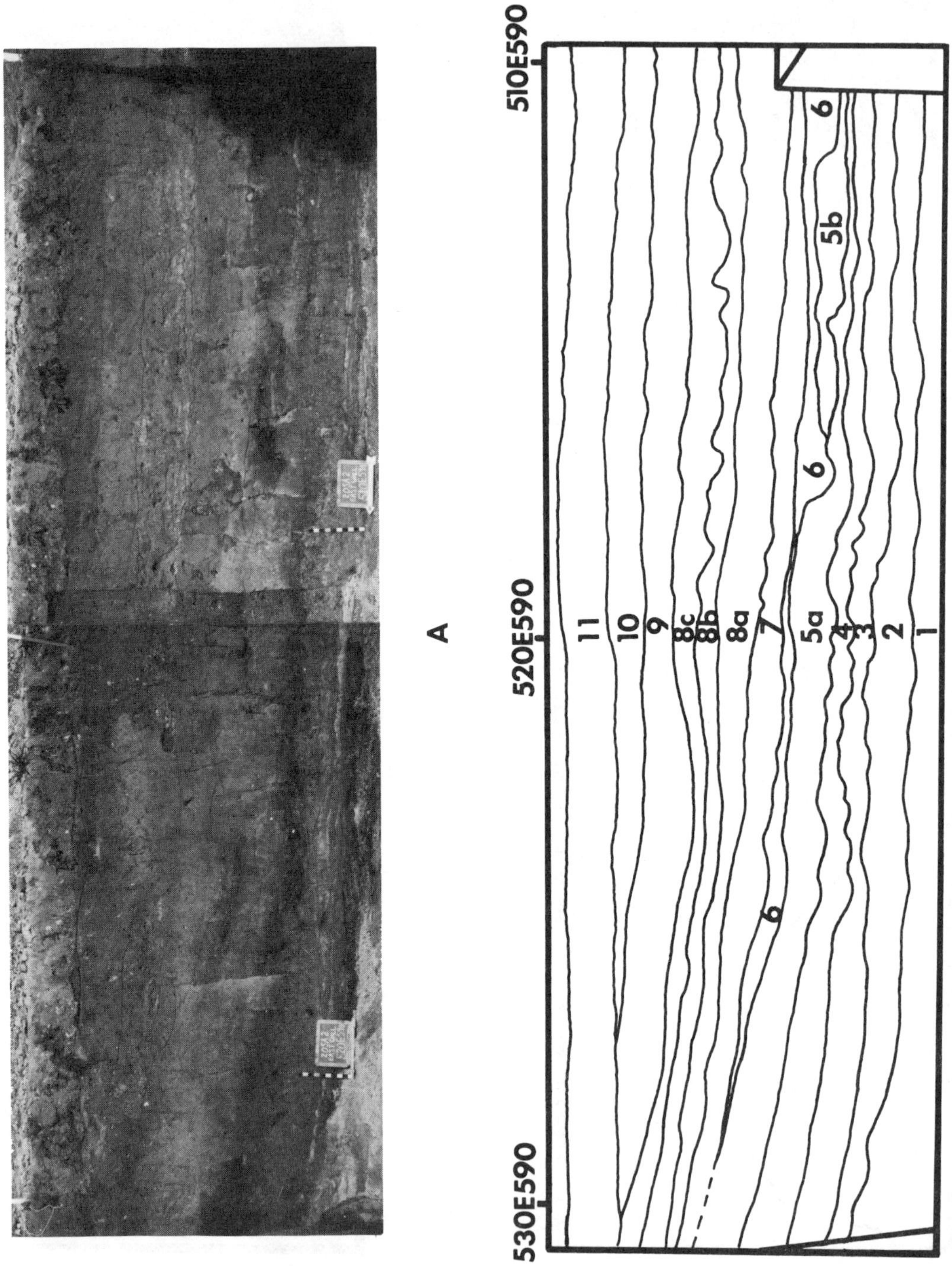

Fig. 21. East wall of 1964 Trench, Schultz site (20SA2): *A, B,* Channel area between 510-530E590. North arrow is one foot long.

TABLE 17
STRATIGRAPHIC AND AREAL PLACEMENT OF RADIOCARBON DATES

Sample	Date	Site	Feature	Location	Stratigraphic Placement	Reference
M-1648	AD 1180±100	20 SA 2	64-75	543-546E587-590	Unit 10	3
M-1647	AD 450±200	20 SA 2	64-17	516-521E575-579	Upper Unit 9	3
M-1646	AD 310±120	20 SA 2	64-21	513-517E577-580	Upper Unit 8*c*	3
M-1644	AD 380±120	20 SA 2	64-74	510-512E586-590	Upper Unit 6	3
M-1432	BC 530±120	20 SA 1	6	305E650	Stratum VI, Zone II	1
M-1525	BC 530±150	20 SA 2	62	20 X 20 B	Upper Unit 4	2
M-1524	BC 540±130	20 SA 2	48	20 X 20 D	Upper Unit 4	2
M-1633	BC 3100±170	20 SA 2	Deep Test	563E590	Unit 1*a*	4
M-1634	BC 2300±150	20 SA 2	Deep Test	563E590	Unit 1*a*	4

References: 1, Crane and Griffin (1965); 2, Crane and Griffin (1966); 3, Crane and Griffin (in press); 4, Crane and Griffin (unpublished).

the highest elevation of Unit 1*b* preserved at the site, the deposits were eroded by the initial stages of the modern drainage system (Phase I/II Disconformity). The termination of this period of erosion may be estimated. There is no evidence at 20 SA 2 of repeated entrenchment and deposition prior to the depositional sequence of Phase II which would indicate prolonged stands and subsequent retreats of the post-Algoma lake level. Deposition of Phase II probably did not begin until near the termination of the Algoma retreat, after the lake had reached a relatively stable base level at or slightly above 580 feet. According to Hough (1963:105), this occurred about 2500 years ago. This date is supported by the 530 B.C. Early Woodland occupation at 20 SA 1 at an elevation of 581 feet (Wright, 1964:18; Griffin, 1965:664). Modern lake level was certainly reached prior to 2000 years ago, the date suggested by Wayne and Zumberge (1965: 80). Thus, the disconformity separating Unit1*b* and Unit 2 may be assigned a tentative terminal date of about 550 B.C.

Phase I/II Disconformity

Phase II (Units 2, 3, and 4)

Unit 2: Unit 2 is separated from Unit 1*b* by an erosional disconformity. Lower Unit 2 consists of light grayish brown sandy loam; upper Unit 2 consists of mottled, dark grayish brown sandy loam in the north grading into mottled gray sandy clay loam in the south. The unit ranges in thickness from about 0.4 feet in the north to 0.7 feet in the channel. The proportion of sand-sized clastics in lower Unit 2, as in the underlying lake sediments, is high throughout the site. In upper Unit 2, however, the proportion of sand remains high in the south but decreases sharply in the north. Numerous sand lenses slope up out of the channel onto the bank forming a levee with its crest coincident with the crest of the bank left by the erosion of Unit 1*b*. Thus, Unit 2 marks the initiation of floodplain and levee development at the Schultz site.

Unit 3: Unit 3 conformably overlies Unit 2 and consists of dark gray to dark grayish brown sandy loam and sandy clay loam north of the channel area. No

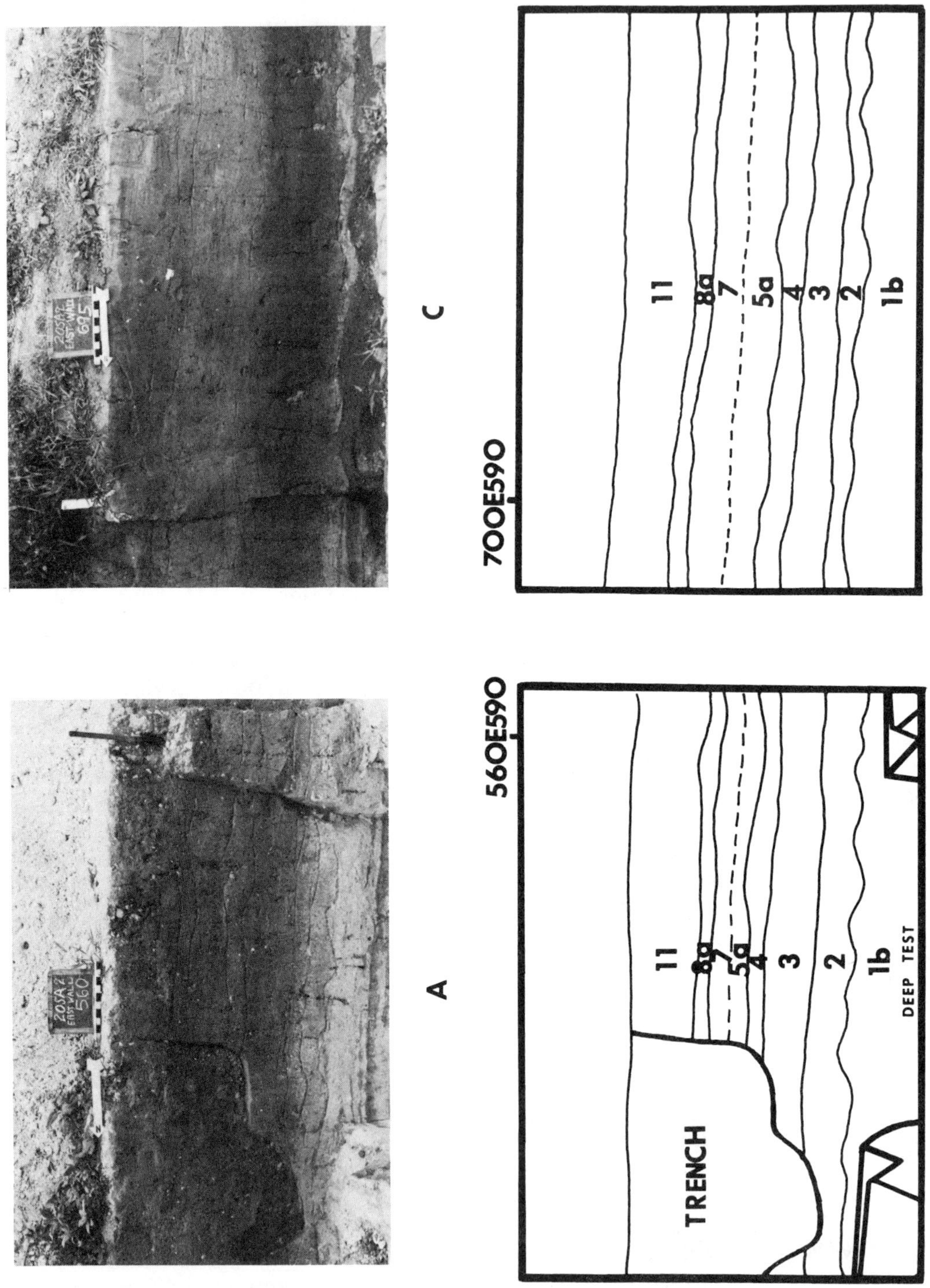

Fig. 22. East wall of 1964 Trench, Schultz site (20SA2): *A, B,* area north of levee between 560-567E590; *C, D,* northern end of trench between 694-701E590. North arrow is one foot long.

C

A

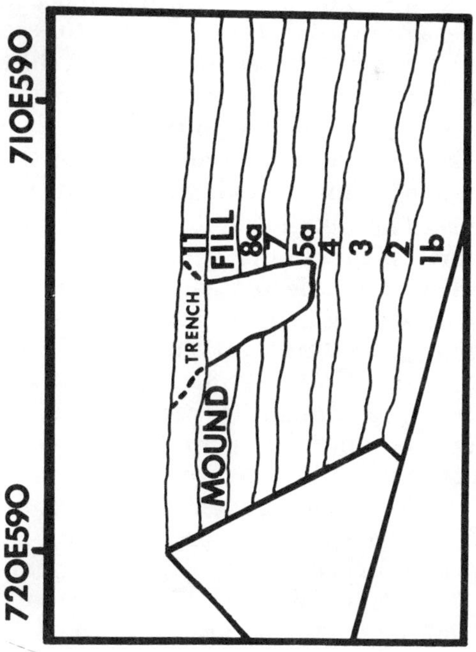

B

Fig. 23. East wall of 1964 Trench; Schultz site (20SA2): *A, B,* northernmost end of trench between 709-720E590; *C,* General view of trench north of channel area between 580E590 and 720E590.

samples were collected at 520E590; however, the unit closely resembles Unit 4, for which samples were collected in gross texture, color and distribution. Unit 3 ranges in thickness from about 0.8 feet in the north to less than 0.3 feet in the south. Unit 3, outside of the channel area, shows a sharp increase in alkali-soluble organic content (Table 19) which suggests prolonged periods of ponded water or swampy conditions at the site. The unit has a distinctly undulating surface in the channel, probably the result of slump from the bank during Unit 4 time. No radiocarbon dates were obtained from the unit. Small traces of cultural material were found in upper Unit 3 in the north which may represent a limited terminal Archaic or Early Woodland occupation (Fitting, this volume).

Unit 4: Unit 4 conformably overlies Unit 3 and consists of grayish brown to dark grayish brown loam in the north, grading into mottled strong brown clay loam in the channel. The unit ranges in thickness from 0.4 feet in the north to less than 0.2 feet in the south. Unit 4, like Unit 3, has an undulating surface in the channel. Apparently during late Unit 4 time the bank slumped, compressing the deposits of Unit 3 and Unit 4 in the channel. The alkali-soluble organic content north of the channel remains high in lower Unit 4 but decreases rapidly in upper Unit 4 suggesting a marked decline in swampy conditions at the site. Within the channel, Unit 4 is strongly mottled or gleyed, perhaps the result of alternating wet and dry periods. The first definite human occupation of the site, Early Woodland, characterized by Schultz ware, occurred in uppermost Unit 4. Two radiocarbon dates, 2490±130 years ago (M-1524) and 2480±150 years ago (M-1525), from 20SA2, and a third, 2480 ±120 years ago (M-1432) from a similar cultural context at 20SA1, indicate an average terminal date for Unit 4 of about 530 B.C. Occupation was restricted to the slightly elevated area north of the channel at 20SA2 at an elevation of 584.5 feet. This was not the case at 20SA1. During the Early Woodland period, occupation occurred at an elevation as low as 581 feet on a small knoll or ridge within a swampy or marshy area (Wright, 1964:18). There is some evidence of a seasonal alternation between the drier elevated areas of 20SA2 and the lower, swampy conditions of 20SA1 (Cleland, 1966: 59).

Phase III (Units 5*a*, 5*b*, 6 and 7)

Unit 5a: Unit 5*a* conformably overlies the Early Woodland level and consists of brown loam in the north grading into strongly mottled, light brownish gray sandy clay loam in the channel and finally grading into lenses of sand and clay south of 510E590. The unit ranges in thickness from 0.3 feet in the north to 0.8 feet at 520E590 thinning to less than 0.2 feet at 510E590. No radiocarbon dates were obtained from this unit. Unit 5*a* marks both a slight shift of the channel to the south, establishing the new north bank between 515E590 and 510E590, and a decrease in width and depth of the channel. Alkali-soluble organic matter continues to decrease in the north but increases slightly at 520E590, suggesting that swampy conditions became restricted almost entirely to the channel area. The trend of the channel during Unit 5*a* time was from northwest to southeast.

Unit 5b: This unit extends only as far north as 515E590 and, therefore, was not included in the sections sampled by Wright. Samples were obtained, however, by Fitting at 500E590; the results of the chemical and mechanical analyses have been included in Table 19. The unit consists of mottled, grayish brown loam ranging in thickness from a maximum of 0.5 feet at 510E590 to less than 0.3 feet south of 505E590. Unit 5*b* represents a channel filling or accretion developed late in Unit 5*a* time.

Unit 6: Unit 6 is a relatively thin and somewhat irregular zone of mottled grayish brown sandy loam with flecks of charcoal and a few well-preserved pits and hearths originating in upper Unit 6. The unit is present only in the channel area pinching out north of 530E590 and thinning to the south to less than 0.1 foot by 495E590. Unit 6 represents a thin humic zone mixed with occupational debris developed on the damp channel filling (Unit 5*b*) and on the adjacent low areas of Unit 5*a*. Unit 6, characterized by Shiawassee ware, marks the first occupation in the channel. A radiocarbon date of A.D. 380±120 (M-1644) was obtained from a feature originating in uppermost Unit 6. The date is suspect, however, and may be several hundred years too late. The date suggests a late Middle Woodland cultural placement of the same order of magnitude as the A.D. 310 date (M-1646) from upper Unit 8*c* in Phase IV which is some two feet higher in the sequence and which is clearly associated with late Middle Woodland Green Point ware. In addition, Phase III and Phase IV are separated by an erosional disconformity. Unit 6 predates the appearance of the Havana-like Tittabawassee ware which is found primarily in Unit 8*a* and perhaps in Unit 7. The only dated occurrences of Havana-like ceramics in the Michigan area, to my knowledge, occur at the Norton Mounds in southwestern Michigan (Flanders, 1965) and at the Porte des Morts site on the Door Peninsula of Wisconsin (Mason, 1966). At Norton four dates have been obtained: M-1488 from the burial pit of Mound H provided a date of A.D. 160±120; M-1489 from the same context provided a date of A.D. 1000±100; M-1490 from ash at the base of the cap of Mound H provided a date of A.D. 100±100; and M-1493 from a fire pit on the original ground level west of the burial pit in Mound C provided a date of 10 B.C.±120. Griffin (Crane and Griffin, 1966:261) considers three of the dates acceptable; he believes M-1489 to be *ca.* 900 years too late. Mason (1966:125) reports a date of A.D. 160±100 (I-888) from the Porte des Morts site in association with North Bay ceramics. Mason (1966:121) indicates that the North Bay ceramics show close affinities with Illinois Hopewell; and, of particular interest, he notes that several of the North Bay ceramic types ". . . seem to be northern relatives of what in central Illinois is called Havana ware." If one uses the Norton Mound and Porte des Morts site dates as a tentative estimate of the age of Havana-like material in the Upper Great Lakes area, than Unit 8*a* (with Tittabawassee ware) should span the period between about 10 B.C. and A.D. 160, and Unit 6 (with Shiawassee ware) should date somewhat earlier.

The suspect date (M-1644) was run on charred walnut and butternut shells which frequently contained remnants of the nutmeat. Photographs of vertical sections through the feature show at least two rodent burrows leading directly from the pit up into Unit 8*b* and probably into Unit 8*c*. It seems likely, therefore, that the dated material was derived from the major late Middle Woodland midden and carried by rodents into the underlying feature. Almost all of the features in Unit 6 and Unit 7 were disturbed in this manner.

Unit 7: Unit 7 consists of 0.6 feet of lightly mottled brown sandy loam in the north, grading into 0.5 feet of fine lensed sand in the channel area and finally grading into 0.2 feet of grayish brown sandy clay loam south of 511E590. No sample was obtained from Unit 7 at 563E590. Unit 7 overlies Unit 5*a* in the north and Unit 6 in the channel area. South of 511E590, Unit 7 contains at least three very thin dark humic zones (about 0.05 feet in thickness) similar in nature to Unit 6; several pits and hearths originate in these zones. The occupational debris is characterized by Shiawassee ware and perhaps some Tittabawassee ware in the upper part of the unit. The deposits of Unit 7, as well as Unit 6 in the channel area, represent a series of short, perhaps seasonal, occupations alternating with periods of flooding and channel filling. The area to the north seems to have been less affected by flooding, and occupation there may have been continuous throughout Unit 7 time. No radiocarbon dates were obtained. The actual channel shifted somewhat to the south and southwest of its position in Unit 5*a*-5*b* time but still trended from northwest to southeast. Unit 7 was subsequently eroded, removing virtually all of the deposit southwest of 510E570 and deeply eroding the unit between 511E590 and 540E590.

Phase III/IV Disconformity
Phase IV (Units 8*a*, 8*b*, 8*c*, and 9)

Unit 8a: Unit 8*a* disconformably overlies Unit 7. The unit consists of grayish brown loam and sandy loam ranging in thickness from 0.4 feet in the north to 0.6 feet in the channel area. Some midden development occurred in Unit 8*a* north of 540E590. The midden appears to have been reworked to a large extent and washed into the channel. No features were found in the channel area. The deposits of Unit 8*a* thicken to the southwest, filling the Unit 7 channel. No channel existed within the immediate area of the site after Unit 7 or early Unit 8*a* time. Unit 8*a* was deeply eroded at the crest of the original bank at the close of Phase IV making correlation between the channel area and similar deposits in the north somewhat tenuous (see Table 20). No radiocarbon dates were obtained. On the basis of the occurrence of Tittabawassee ware in Unit 8*a*, a tentative age for the deposit of approximately 10 B.C. to A.D. 160 has been suggested (see above).

Unit 8b: Unit 8*b* consists of a thick zone of sand lenses and mottled grayish brown sandy loam. In uppermost Unit 8*b* on the slope and crest of the bank, the deposits are interspersed with charcoal, fish and mammal bones, and late Middle Woodland Green Point ceramics. The unit averages 0.6 feet in thickness. On the crest of the bank Unit 8*b* is deeply eroded; north of the channel area the unit is preserved only in small patches. South of 510E590 the midden debris and organic content diminish rapidly, but the unit remains approximately the same thickness. Much of the cultural debris on the slope of the bank appears to have been washed from the crest; occasional waterworn sherds are mentioned in the field notes. No features were found in the channel area. No radiocarbon dates were obtained.

Unit 8c: Unit 8*c* consists of grayish brown sandy loam and fine sand lenses interspersed with large quantities of cultural material. The unit averages 0.3 feet in thickness between 535E590 and 510E590; to the south the unit thins rapidly and virtually disappears south of 495E590. The deposit has been almost completely eroded from the crest of the bank. Midden material characterized by Green Point ware is especially heavy in middle to upper Unit 8*c*. Well-preserved features occur throughout the channel area. A radiocarbon date of A.D. 310±120 (M-1646) was obtained from a feature in upper Unit 8*c*.

Unit 9: Unit 9 consists of lightly mottled grayish brown sandy loam averaging 0.5 feet in thickness in the channel area. The unit pinches out or has been eroded away north of 535E590. Midden debris is light in lower Unit 9 and virtually absent in upper Unit 9. Much of Unit 9 appears to have been derived from the erosion of the bank and other elevated areas of the site.

In places on the crest of the bank, erosion removed all of the Phase IV deposits, exposing the upper part of Unit 7. A radio-carbon date of A.D. 450±200 (M-1647) was obtained from a feature situated in upper Unit 9.

Phase IV/V Disconformity
Phase V (Units 10 and 11)

Unit 10: Unit 10 disconformably overlies Unit 8*a* or occasionally small patches of Unit 9 in the north and Unit 7 or Unit 8*a* at the crest of the bank; the unit paraconformably overlies Unit 9 in the channel area. Unit 10 consists of dark gray loam. Modern plowing has disturbed the upper part of the deposit throughout the site. What remains of Unit 10 averages 0.6 feet in thickness in the channel and less than 0.2 feet in irregular patches in the north. A radiocarbon date of A.D. 1180±100 (M-1648), in association with Late Woodland ceramics, was obtained from a feature which intruded directly into Unit 7 near the crest of the bank.

Unit 11: Unit 11 represents the modern plow zone. The unit, a dark grayish brown to dark gray silt loam, averages 0.8 feet in thickness and consists of a mixture of the deposits of late Phase III, Phase IV and Phase V.

FLOODING ACTIVITY AT THE SCHULTZ SITE

The flooding activity at Green Point has undoubtedly had a significant influence on the cultural activities at the Schultz site effecting available habitable and cultivable land, the types and abundance of mammals, local vegetation, molluscs, and so on. Flooding activity also reflects local and regional environmental factors such as precipitation, temperature, surface runoff, sediment availability, ice jams and fluctuations in lake level.

Several approaches can be used to obtain some indication of the general fluctuations in flooding which have occurred at the Schultz site and perhaps to distinguish between local and regional causes. These include: evaluation of the stratigraphic evidence at 20SA2; comparison of the stratigraphy of 20SA2 to that of 20SA1, which is situated directly on the levee of the Tittabawassee River; calculation of the changes in mean grain size and in sorting of the sand-sized clastics at 20SA2.

Stratigraphic Evidence of Flooding Activity at Schultz Site

During Phase II at 20SA2—well north of the area of levee development—nearly 1.0 foot of sediment was deposited in the estimated 20 years between the end of Phase I/II erosion (550 B.C.) and the Early Woodland occupation (530 B.C.). Deposition was most rapid during the early part of Phase II (Unit 2) when large quantities of sand were washed from areas of Unit 1*b* with slightly higher relief into adjacent depressions. North of the channel area during Unit 3 and Unit 4 time, the proportion of sand decreased sharply while the proportions of silt and clay and of alkali-soluble organic matter (Table 19) increased, suggesting that during most of Phase II deposition was for more gradual, probably in ponded far low-moving water in backswamps. The Early Woodland occupation of the area north of the channel in upper Unit 4 indicates that by the close of Phase II the swamps were present only during part of the year, probably disappearing by late summer and reappearing in the flooding season in the spring.

During Phase III the flooding activity at the Schultz site continued to decrease. The channel shrank and shifted to the south, restricting sedimentation to a great extent to minor levee development and channel-filling within the original channel area. Organic content dropped to its minimum values north of the channel area during Phase III, suggesting a significant reduction in the backswamps. Also during Unit 6 and Unit 7 time several occupations occurred for the first time in the channel area. The lowland deposits of early Phase III are strongly mottled or gleyed and relatively high in organics, suggesting that the channel area at this time was subject to alternate periods of dry and moist conditions. By upper Phase III gleying ceased; the channel area may have become relatively dry throughout the year.

During early Phase IV (Unit 8*a* and Unit 8*b*) flooding increased considerably. Occupation ceased entirely within the channel area. The organic content of the sediments increased sharply suggesting an increase in swampy conditions. Some midden development occurred on the crest of the bank during early Unit 8*a* time and late Unit 8*b* time; much of the cultural material appears to have been reworked and washed into the channel. Several waterworn sherds were recovered in Unit 8*b*. Although no channel existed within the immediate area of the site during Unit 8*b* time, the proportion of coarse clastics increased sharply. One prominent zone of sand lenses, averaging nearly 0.3 feet in thickness, could be traced from the crest of the bank into the south wall of the trench.

During Unit 8*c* time flooding again decreased. Heavy midden development and numerous well-preserved features occurred for the first time within the channel. The midden shows no evidence of reworking. The intensity of the occupation within the channel suggests that the site may have become drier than at any previous time.

During Unit 9 time some occupation continued within the channel. The deposits were derived to a large extent from the erosion of the crest of the bank rather than from midden development or from overbank deposition from the channel to the south. Thus flooding activity was probably lower than during Unit 8*c* time.

During Phase V the organic content and silt and clay proportions rose to values similar to those of Unit 3 and Unit 4, suggesting a return to relatively intense seasonal flooding with deposition occurring in slow-moving or ponded water in backswamps.

Correlation of 20SA2 and 20SA1

The stratigraphy of 20SA1 has been outlined briefly by Wright (1964). More detailed data are available in the unpublished field notes (Wright, n.d.). Excavation unit 305E650 was the most thoroughly discussed unit and has been used here as the basis for the correlation. Table 18 gives the tentative correlation between the two sites.

The sequence at 20SA1 begins with a series of basal lake sands (Zone I) overlain by marsh deposits (Zone II and Zone III). A small transitory channel meandering through the marsh developed a low sand ridge which was occupied around 530 B.C. There is no evidence of a major river at 20SA1 prior to or during the Early Woodland occupation. Immediately after this period, however, rapid levee development began at 20SA1 (Zone IV and Zone V) while at 20SA2 (Phase III) the channel which had already been in existence for some time shrank and began to shift to the south (Unit 5*a*). By the close of Phase III, the channel no longer existed at 20SA2. It appears that during early Phase III either lake level dropped slightly or a threshold was opened, perhaps at the Port Huron moraine, draining the swamps at 20SA1 and rerouting the drainage to the south around 20SA2 via the modern Tittabawassee channel.

TABLE 18
CORRELATION OF THE STRATIGRAPHY OF (A) 20SA2 AND (B) 20SA1

Unit	Thick-ness (Feet)	Approximate Cultural Placement
11	0.9	Recent
10	0.5	Late Woodland
9	0.5	Late Middle Woodland
8*c*	0.3	Late Middle Woodland
8*b*	0.6	Late Middle Woodland
8*a*	0.6	Middle Woodland
7	0.5	?
6	0.2	?
5*b* 5*a*	0.8	?
4	0.2	Early Woodland
3	0.2	?
2	0.5	?
1*b*	?	?
1*a*	?	?

Zone	Thick-ness (Feet)	Zone Description (Based On Wright, n.d.)
X	0.7	Recent flood deposits, plow zone, etc.; historic material
IX	1.1	Reduced sandy loam, dark gray, homogeneous with occasional sand lenses, thicker and darker in back-swamp area, lenses dip down foreslope of levee to at least 581 feet; Late Woodland ceramics
Disconformity		
VIII	0.5	Extensive lensed fine sand, pale brown to brown, mainly on levee crest and backslope, lenses do not occur below 584.5 feet, superface on crest of levee irregular and truncated; some Middle Woodland ceramics
VII	0.3	Humic sandy loam, pale brown to dark grayish brown, fine lensed sand in upper VII; midden material on levee and in backswamp, Middle Woodland ceramics
Disconformity		
VI	1.9	Oxidized sandy loam, light yellowish brown to brown, homogeneous, sand lenses in lower VI, superface ir-regular and truncated, small channels transversing levee in lower VI
V	0.7	Grossly stratified loam and sand, light grayish brown to brown on levee to dark grayish brown in backswamp, heavy sand lenses on foreslope of levee; no ceramics
IV	0.5	Fine clay, light grayish brown to pale brown, small lenses of fine sand on foreslope, first evidence of levee development at 20SA1; no ceramics
III	0.6	Finely lensed sand, clay and loam, light gray to gray, horizontally bedded, lenses form east-west trending ridge in marshy area; Early Woodland occupation on ridge, C-14 dated at 530 B.C.
II	0.7	Fine carbonaceous clay, light gray to light grayish brown, thin lenses of unburned organic matter tenta-tively identified as grasses, reeds, etc.; no ceramics
Disconformity		
I	1.4	Basal sands, pale brown to light gray, coarse, well-sorted, superface dips slightly to southeast.

The levee deposits of Zone V at 20SA1 are overlain by a bed of homogeneous oxidized loams with sand lenses at the base (Zone VI). The superface of the zone is irregular and, in places, truncated by erosion. Zone VI corresponds closely to middle and upper Phase III at 20SA2 (Unit 6 and Unit 7) and suggests a period of steadily decreasing flooding terminated by a period of erosion probably equivalent to the Phase III/IV Disconformity at 20SA2.

After the period of erosion, a limited Middle Woodland midden developed on the backslope of the levee (Zone VII). Occasional sand lenses developed on the foreslope. Zone VII is probably equivalent to early Phase IV (Unit 8*a*).

In Zone VIII occupation virtually ceased at the site and levee development increased sharply. Deposition occurred primarily on the crest of the levee and in the backswamp area; lenses belonging to this zone do not occur below 584.5 feet on the foreslope. This zone corresponds closely to the high flooding peak during early to middle Phase IV (Unit 8*a* and Unit 8*b*) at 20SA2. As flooding increased, occupation probably shifted to the drier elevated area north of the channel at 20SA2; and, at the peak of Phase IV flooding, Green Point may have been completely abandoned. There is some evidence recorded in the field notes of a period of erosion after Zone VIII at 20SA1. The superface of the zone, as in Zone VI, is irregular and on the crest of the levee erosion has in places truncated Zone VIII and the underlying midden deposit. The period of erosion may be equivalent to Unit 9 and to the Phase IV/V Disconformity.

Zone IX consists of dark fine-grained humic sediments and marks a period of renewed flooding activity and heavy backswamp development at 20SA1. Sand lenses developed on the levee and could be traced in patches down the foreslope to an elevation of about 581 feet. They were subsequently partially stripped away by active flooding during the historic period. The zone contains occasional Late Woodland materials. Wright (n.d.) interprets the zone as a period of flooding with prolonged stands of ponded water. Zone IX probably corresponds to early Phase V (Unit 10) at 20SA2 or perhaps to an earlier phase of the Late Woodland for which deposits were not recognized at 20SA2.

The Late Woodland period was followed by a resurgence of active levee development (Zone X). The deposits contain historic materials. Zone X probably reflects, in part, an increase in runoff and erosion resulting from modern lumbering and agricultural activities within the drainage basin. At 20SA2, deposits equivalent to Zone X were not observed and have probably been incorporated in the plow zone.

Mean Phi Grain Size and Sorting Coefficients

The mean phi grain size (MΦ) and the sorting coefficients (So) have been calculated for the sand-sized clastics following the procedure described by Krumbein and Pettijohn (1938:242-50). The results for the three sections sampled by Wright are given in Figure 19.

In all three sections grain size decreases rapidly (mean phi values increase) with the initiation of floodplain development. By upper Unit 2 the largest mean grain size values (smallest MΦ values) occur at 563E590 which is situated within or slightly north of the area of major levee development. Highest grain size values continue at 563E590 at least through Unit 8*a*, the last unit prior to the plow zone preserved in the two northern sections. At both 563E590 and 711E590 grain size remains relatively constant from upper Unit 3 throughout the remainder of

Phase III. At 520E590, however, grain size increases in uppermost Unit 5*a* and then levels off in Unit 6 and Unit 7. This appears to reflect the proximity of 520E590 during late Unit 5*a* and Unit 5*b* time to the development of a small secondary levee on the bank of the greatly reduced and southward-shifted channel. The secondary levee is located approximately between 525E590 and 515E590 (see Table 22). In Unit 8*a*, after the Phase III/IV Disconformity, grain size again increases. In Unit 8*b* grain size increases tremendously, reaching a peak in upper Unit 8*b*. As pointed out in the discussion of the stratigraphy, no channel existed in the immediate site area after Unit 7 time. Thus the sharp increase in coarser clastics suggests the resurgence of flooding (noted above from other evidence) during Phase IV from a channel located to the south of the site and probably from the modern Tittabawassee River. In all three sections grain size decreases in Phase V, returning to values similar to those of the latter part of Phase II.

In all three sections sorting is best in the lake sediments. With the initiation of flood-plain development in Unit 2, sorting becomes poorer (Φ increases) and remains relatively poor throughout the remainder of the sequence (average 0.56 Φ). At 520E590 there are three peaks of poorest sorting (each attaining values of about 0.65 Φ). They occur in Unit 4 (Phase II), upper Unit 8*b* (Phase IV) and in Unit 10 and Unit 11 (Phase V). Although the other sections (563E590 and 711E590) do not include the relevant portions of Phase IV; they do show peaks of poorest sorting in Phase II and Phase V (Fig. 19*b* and 19*c*). The three peaks of poorest sorting coincide closely with the periods of most active flooding at Green Point already indicated in other discussions.

Three periods of active flooding (Phase II, early to middle Phase IV and Phase V) and two relatively stable periods (Phase III and upper Phase IV) have been postulated at the Schultz site in the above discussions. Ascribing particular environmental causes to these periods and distinguishing between local and regional causes is extremely difficult with the limited evidence available. Environmental changes which would result in increased or decreased flooding at Green Point may be restricted entirely to the Saginaw drainage basin. These might include local changes in rainfall, snowfall, thaws, sediment availability, ice jams, etc. Regional changes in rainfall, snowfall, and so on, if of sufficient magnitude and duration, would alter the level of Lake Huron and hence the base level of the Saginaw drainage system. Local and regional changes can counteract each other; for example, a lowering of lake level accompanied by a particularly heavy ice jam in the mouth of the Saginaw.

The Phase I/II Disconformity developed in response to dropping base level during the final retreatal stages from the Algoma lake stage. In Phase II, when lake level had reached an elevation of about 581 feet, the retreat of the lake either halted or, more likely, slowed sufficiently for floodplain development to begin at 20SA2. During this period the eastern part of Green Point was a marsh. The decrease in size and southward shift of the channel during Phase III and the simultaneous disappearance of the marsh at 20SA1 suggest a slight renewal or continuation of lake retreat (regional base level change) or, less likely, the opening of a threshold in the Port Huron moraine (local base level change). Regional base level lowering might have been in response to regional climatic changes or to continued downcutting of the St. Clair outlet; the latter would place the end of the Algoma retreat at the close of Unit 5*b* time rather than at the end of Phase I/II erosion. The Phase III Disconformity and its equivalent disconformity at 20SA1 apparently represent a period of erosion of the elevated levee areas in response to the lowered base level. The elevation of the lake at this time is not known, but it may have been somewhat below 580 feet.

The renewal of flooding activity at Green Point during Phase IV suggests a change of regional significance. The sediments deposited during Phase IV are distinctly different from those of Phase II and Phase V (see Fig. 19) which are strikingly similar to each other. As noted above, lake level during Phase II was at or slightly below 581 feet. Lake level was at approximately the same level during Phase V. This is indicated at 20SA1 by the sand lenses of Zone IX on the foreslope of the levee which dip down to an elevation of at least 581 feet. In contrast, the deposits of Zone VIII at 20SA1, which are equivalent to the peak of Phase IV flooding at 20SA2, do not appear below an elevation of about 584.5 feet. Their absence below this level may be due, in part, to the subsequent Phase IV/V erosion. But the sand lenses show little or no downward dip toward the foreslope of the levee. This suggests that the river was at an elevation of about 585 feet or higher during the peak of Phase IV flooding. The deposits which mark the peak of flooding at 20SA2 consist of prominent sand lenses and form the bulk of lower to middle Unit 8*b*.

The exact duration of the *peak* flooding period is not known but it was probably less than 150 years, the interval between the estimated end of the Tittabawassee occupation (Unit 8*a*) and the end of the major late Middle Woodland midden (Unit 8*c*). The duration of the flooding period is critical for distinguishing between short-term local causes and prolonged regional causes. Wolman and Leopold (1957:97) list examples of the thickness of sediment deposited on floodplains by major floods. The figures ranged from a low of 0.008 feet to a maximum of 0.114 feet with an average of about 0.07 feet per flood. They were not able to specify exactly the recurrence intervals of these major floods; that is, ". . . the average interval of time within which a flood of a given magnitude will be equaled or exceeded but once" (Leopold, *et al.* 1964:65-66). One certainly exceeded a 100-year flood and the others probably had intervals of similar magnitude. The average thickness of sediment deposited by *peak* Phase IV flooding at 20SA2, far from the area of levee development at 20SA1 and continuous over a considerable distance at 20SA2, was about 0.30 feet; this figure is nearly two and one-half times greater than the maximum value cited by Wolman and Leopold (1957:97) and over four times greater than the average. Floods of sufficient magnitude to produce this thickness of sediment would very likely have a recurrence interval greatly exceeding the 150 year maximum duration of Phase IV flooding. Thus, the deposits are probably not the result of overbank deposition; and they are not due, therefore, to short-term fluctuations in river level in response to local causes such as ice jams, seasonal increases in snowfall, or the like.

This suggests that the deposits owe their origin, rather, to a prolonged rise in mean lake level in response to regional climatic changes. As already noted, the level of the river rose to at least 584.5 feet and probably higher, completely inundating 20SA1. The deposits can be traced up the slope of the channel bank at 20SA2 to an elevation of 586 feet where they are completely destroyed by plowing; thus, at the peak of Phase IV flooding even the elevated area at

20SA2 may have been inundated. The maximum elevation of the encroaching lake cannot be determined, but it reached at least 586 feet. Peak lake level may not have been maintained for more than 50 to 100 years; but the trend of rising base level may have spanned a period of 200 to 300 years or more.

A survey of the literature was made in the hope of locating sites close to the shores of Lake Michigan and Lake Huron south of the Algoma hinge line with sufficient geological data to test the hypothesis of an elevated mean lake level during the Middle Woodland period. The survey was rather discouraging. Only three sites, all reported by Mason (1966, 1967), were found which were in the correct physical setting and which had an adequate discussion of the geology. All three sites, Heins Creek, Mero and Porte des Morts, had raised gravel beaches clearly associated with the Middle Woodland period. The sites are located on the Door Peninsula of Wisconsin south of the Nipissing hinge line (Hough, 1958:136) and presumably well south of the Algoma hinge line. At Mero a gravel beach was found interstratified between two cultural levels containing Middle Woodland North Bay ceramics; the beach reached an inshore elevation of about 585.5 to 586 feet, above present lake level (Mason, 1966:39). Highly waterworn North Bay sherds attributed to the occupation level beneath the beach were recovered from the gravels. A radiocarbon date of A.D. 160 ± 100 (I-888) was obtained from similar North Bay ceramics underlying the beach deposits at the Porte des Morts site (Mason, 1966:125; 1967:327). The evidence from the Door Peninsula agrees well with the flooding evidence from Green Point: a rise of mean lake level reaching an elevation of at least 586 feet around A.D. 200.

Thus, early to middle Phase IV (Unit 8*a* and Unit 8*b*) was probably a relatively wet period which began about the time of Christ and which culminated with a high lake level shortly after A.D. 160. Unfortunately, with the available data, it is impossible to specify the particular climatic factors responsible for the increase in moisture. The increase might be the result of higher precipitation or a reduction in evaporation in response to lower temperatures or a combination of both.

Phase IV flooding at Green Point was followed by a period of increasing stability during the late Middle Woodland period and finally by a period of erosion which began around A.D. 450. The decrease in flooding activity and finally the period of erosion probably represent an adjustment to dropping base level in response to new regional climatic changes. This period was probably drier than the preceding period, but again the particular climatic factors responsible for the change, such as temperature and precipitation, cannot be specified. The level to which the lake dropped is not known but was probably below 580 feet.

In Phase V, again apparently in response to regional climatic changes, lake level rose, reestablishing seasonal flooding similar to that which occurred in later Phase II and similar perhaps to that which occurs today at Green Point. Phase V appears to have been wetter than late Phase IV but probably drier than early to middle Phase IV.

A gravel beach attributable to the Late Woodland period is reported by McPherron (1967) at the Juntunen site on Bois Blanc Island in the Straits of Mackinac. The beach, at a maximum inshore elevation of about 590 feet, is interstratified between two Late Woodland occupations. The beach deposits attain a thickness of about 1.5 feet and contain waterworn sherds. The earlier occupation level dips down toward the lake to an elevation of about 586 feet or lower and has been radiocarbon dated at A.D. 825 ± 150 (M-1142, Crane and Griffin, 1961:110). The later occupation dips down to an elevation of 588 feet and has been radiocarbon dated at A.D. 900 ± 150 (M-1141, Crane and Griffin, *ibid*).

Powers (1962) postulates a rate of uplift for Bois Blanc Island of about eight inches per century. At the time of deposition, therefore, the earlier occupation would have been at or below 578 feet; the beach deposits somewhere between 582 and 583 feet, and the later occupation extending no lower than 581 feet.

The beach at Juntunen suggests a rise of lake level beginning sometime prior to A.D. 800 reaching its maximum elevation during the ninth century and retreating again some unknown amount by the early tenth century. The total rise in base level was somewhat greater than five or six feet and began at an elevation below modern lake level. Peak lake level was probably maintained for only about 50 to 100 years; but the trend of rising base level, as in the Middle Woodland case, may have spanned a period of 200 to 300 years.

Jelinek and Fitting (1963) measured the Beta activity of fishbone by stratigraphic levels from several excavation units at the Juntunen site. In almost every case they obtained an S-shaped curve with low radioactivity at the base of the section, followed by an increase in activity to a peak between A.D. 800 and A.D. 900, then a decrease to a low during the eleventh century and finally an increase in activity after A.D. 1100. The authors suggested several possible reasons which might account for the observed differences in Beta activity. These included: (1) differences in the radioactivity of the soil of the various levels; (2) differences in the amount of radioactivity accumulated during the lifetime of the fish; and (3) differences in the amount of soil moisture. The authors concluded that the latter is the most probable, in which case the Beta activity at the site, as a reflection of the amount of soil moisture, may indicate climatic conditions subsequent to burial. The earliest peak in radioactivity coincides well with the rise in lake level indicated by the beach. The subsequent decrease in radioactivity corresponds to the retreat in lake level from the beach and suggests that base level continued to drop throughout the eleventh century. In addition, the Beta activity suggests that this period may have been as dry as that prior to the ninth century. This dry period is followed by a period of relative wetness beginning around the end of the eleventh century. It is this last wet period, rather than the wet period of the ninth century, which is apparently represented by the Late Woodland deposits at 20SA2. The deposits of the earlier Late Woodland wet period may have been stripped away by erosion during the tenth and eleventh centuries or they may have been largely destroyed, as most of the Late Woodland deposits were, by recent plowing activity. Perhaps they can be distinguished in future sediment studies using a smaller sampling interval.

The Juntunen data, therefore, add additional support to the low lake level beginning in the fifth century A.D. postulated at the Schultz site (Phase IV/V Disconformity). In addition, the radioactivity data have suggested that the Late Woodland "wet" phase may actually consist of at least two wet periods and an intervening dry period, the first wet period spanning the eighth and ninth centuries and second occurring after the eleventh century.

CONCLUSIONS

In the above discussions, evidence has

been presented in an attempt to delineate the major changes in flooding activity which have occurred at Green Point during the past 2500 years. An attempt was also made to determine whether the fluctuations were the result of changes in local or in regional environmental factors.

Unfortunately, with the limited available data, it was not possible to specify the changes of particular climatic elements such as temperature or precipitation which brought about the changes in regional "wetness" or "dryness."

It cannot be overemphasized that the conclusions reached in this paper are *tentative*. No attempt will be made to correlate these results to the more theoretical climatic schemes for the Great Lakes Region (see for example Griffin, 1960, 1961; Baerreis and Bryson, 1965; Cleland, 1966) because, at present, there is very little adequate comparative data from other sites of this time period.

It is hoped that in future excavations in the area, especially of sites along the shores of Lake Michigan and Lake Huron and along the lower reaches of rivers which flow into these lakes, greater interest will be devoted to the problems of environmental reconstruction. In this way the sequence of regional climatic changes in the upper Great Lakes during the late prehistoric period can be clarified.

IV

PLANT REMAINS

April L. Allison

The plant remains from the Schultz site under consideration were recovered by hand excavation during the 1964 field season. All charred plant remains from square 510E570 and from all 1964 features were analyzed. In all, 784.35 grams of charred plant remains were recovered from these areas of the site.

SQUARE 510E570

The plant remains of square 510E570 consist of charred nutshell and seeds, wood charcoal, and uncharred berries. The presence of bone, coprolites, and flint chips is recorded in Tables 19 and 20, but like the uncharred berries, is neither totalled nor used in calculating percentages for comparative purposes. Nutshell was the most common category of food plant remains in square 510E570, comprising 23 percent by mass of the material analyzed. Ordered from most frequent to least frequent, the nutshell represented butternut (*Juglans cinerea*), walnut (*Juglans nigra*), hickory (*Carya* sp.), nutmeat, hazelnut (*Corylus* sp.), and acorn (*Quercus* sp.). Seeds represent only .1 percent of the entire sample. These seeds included one corn kernel (*Zea mays*) from the plow zone, seven unidentified, uncharred berries, one goosefoot (*Chenopodium* sp.) seed, one hackberry (*Celtis* sp.) seed, one cherry (?) (*Prunus* sp.) seed, and one unidentified seed. Wood charcoal comprised 77 percent of the remains. The wood charcoal was not identified as to species represented. The remaining .4 percent of the total consisted of unidentified material.

Analysis of the charred plant remains from the midden of square 510E570 of the Schultz site indicates a decrease in the percentage of nutshell through time. As can be seen in Table 20, the earliest excavation group, the transitional (II*d*) occupation, shows the highest (90 percent) percentage of nutshell. In excavation group III*a*, the strata above II*d*, the percentage of nutshell drops drastically to 63 percent of plant remains from the group. Again in III*b*, the lower of the Late Middle Woodland excavation groups, there is a significant drop in the percentage of nutshell, this time to 12 percent. After this spectacular reduction in the percentage of nutshell we see a general, but uneven, trend toward a reduction in the percentage of nutshell through time. From 12 percent the percentage rises to 24 percent in excavation group IV*a*, the upper strata of Late Middle Woodland. The percentage then declines to a low of

TABLE 19
CHARRED PLANT REMAINS—510E570
(In Grams)

	S-2	IV*c*	IV*b*	IV*a*	III*b*	III*a*	II	Total
NUTSHELL								
Walnut	.1	1.2	.2	1.75	20.9	20.0	3.05	47.2
Butternut	1.5	1.3	1.8	1.35	17.25	41.3	6.7	71.2
Hickory	. . .	.85	.4	.5	12.25	2.05	.8	16.85
Acorn	. . .	. . .	. . .	. . .	.1	. . .	. . .	.1
Hazelnut	. . .	.4	. . .	. . .	.15	. . .	. . .	.55
Nutmeat	.2	. . .	. . .	. . .	1.1	.1	. . .	1.3
Unidentified	. . .	. . .	.05	.05	.2	.5	.4	1.2
Total	1.8	3.75	2.45	3.65	51.95	63.95	10.95	138.5
WOOD CHARCOAL	11.9	17.9	28.0	11.45	366.55	37.15	.05	474.0
SEEDS								
Zea mays	.1	. . .	. . .	. . .	. . .	. . .	. . .	.1
Prunus	. . .	.1	. . .	. . .	. . .	. . .	. . .	.1
Chenopodium	. . .	. . .	. . .	. . .	.1	. . .	. . .	.1
Uncharred berries	.1	.1	. . .	. . .	.1	.1	. . .	.4
Celtis	. . .	. . .	. . .	. . .	.1	. . .	. . .	.1
Unidentified	. . .	.1	. . .	. . .	. . .	. . .	. . .	.1
Total	.1	.2	. . .	. . .	.2	. . .	. . .	.5
MISC. bone and coprolites	.2	2.25	2.3	6.3	71.4	12.55	1.15	96.15
Flint and stone	. . .	. . .	. . .	. . .	. . .	.8	. . .	.8
Unidentified	. . .	. . .	.45	. . .	1.15	.6	.1	2.3
Total	. . .	. . .	.45	. . .	1.15	.6	.1	2.3
TOTAL	13.8	21.85	30.9	15.1	419.85	101.7	12.1	615.3

.*x* = not totalled

8 percent in excavation group IV*b*, the lower strata of Late Woodland. In the upper strata of Late Woodland, excavation group IV*c*, the percentage of nutshell rises to 17 percent. Finally, between the surface of the site and square sheet 2 (a disturbed area), nutshell comprises 13 percent of the recovered plant remains.

No seeds appear until excavation group III*b* (Late Middle Woodland, where one *Chenopodium* and one hackberry seed were recovered. Excavation group IV*a* yielded one *Prunus* and one unidentified seed, while the single corn kernel was located between the surface and square sheet 2, a false plow zone caused by recent erosion on this part of the site.

TABLE 20
Charred Plant Remains—510E570
(In Percents)

	S-2	IV*c*	IV*b*	IV*a*	III*b*	III*a*	II	Total
NUTSHELL								
Walnut	.7	5.5	.6	11.6	5.0	19.7	25.2	7.7
Butternut	10.9	5.9	5.8	8.9	4.1	40.6	55.4	11.6
Hickory	...	3.9	1.3	3.3	2.9	2.0	6.6	2.7
Acorn	...	...	...	...	.02	...	...	.02
Hazelnut	...	1.9	...	...	.04	...	...	.09
Nutmeat	1.5	...	...	...	.3	.1	...	.2
Unidentified	...	...	.2	.3	.05	.5	3.3	.2
Total	13.1	17.2	7.9	24.1	12.41	62.9	89.9	22.51
WOOD CHARCOAL	86.2	82.0	90.6	75.8	87.3	36.5	8.7	77.0
SEEDS								
Zea mays	.7	...	...	...	...	...	...	.02
Prunus	...	.5	...	...	...	...	...	.02
Chenopodium	...	...	...	...	.02	...	...	.02
Celtis	...	...	...	...	.02	...	...	.02
Unidentified	...	.5	...	...	...	...	...	.02
Total	.7	1.0	...	...	.04	...	...	.1
UNIDENTIFIED	...	...	1.5	...	.3	.6	.8	.4
TOTAL	100.0	100.2	100.0	99.9	100.0	100.0	100.0	100.1

As can also be seen from Table 19, there is no significant variation through time in the relative frequency of utilization of the three major nut species. The line depicting walnut most closely parallels the fluctuations of total percentage of nutshell, and the line depicting hickory remains at the most stable level throughout time. Although the percentage of butternut dips slightly below that of walnut during the Late Middle Woodland, butternut is generally the predominant nutshell present.

This data could perhaps suggest a degree of climatic stability through time, whereas the increased utilization of a given taxa at the expense of another might have suggested a climatic shift (provided, of course, that the two taxa occurred under significantly different climatic conditions). This interpretation is offered as a suggestion rather than an established fact since alternative explanations are plausible.

The abrupt decline in nutshell from the Transitional and Early Middle Woodland strata more strongly suggests a shift in the subsistence pattern than a climatic change, since there is a quantitative, rather than qualitative change in the taxa represented. If such a shift to a new subsistence base occurred, the fact that the new food left no charred remains must be accounted for. There are at least three possible explanations. The absence could be due to differential preservation of the plant remains from the two subsistence bases. An extreme example of this would be a shift to a reliance on greens (an unlikely possibility since greens are available in spring and have too low a caloric content to provide a possible subsistence base). A second possibility is a shift to a source of food which may be preservable, but is difficult to recover with the techniques utilized. An example of this might be small seeds which, unless found in a compact mass, might not be noticed by the excavator unless a structured program ensured that a set proportion of excavation units be subjected to flotation or fine screening, even though no plant remains were conspicuously visible in each unit. One more possibility is that the new subsistence base could be more likely to be totally consumed than, for example, a walnut. A seed is often ground up and totally consumed, leaving as refuse no more than a bit of chaff, at most. If we were forced to pypothesize nut consumption at the Schultz site only upon the incidence of charred remains of the edible portion of the nut, rather than upon the refuse of nutshell, we would have to conclude that the Schultz site inhabitants had eliminated the necessity of eating—in all of square 510E570 only 1.3 grams of nutmeat were found.

Of course, these three factors are not mutually exclusive. Small seeds can be more fragile and less likely to be preserved than nutshell, more easily overlooked by excavators, and more completely consumed than a nut. Corn agriculture would fit the first category—it is less likely to be preserved intact than nutshell—but it does not fit the second or third category, since the cob is left after consumption of the kernels.

FEATURES

Tables 21 and 22, representing the percentage of nutshell from all features which were analyzed, do not show the clear-cut decline in the percentage of nutshell through time which can be seen in Table 20. The features in these tables include all forty features excavated in 1964 which yielded plant remains and consists of square 510E570 and all other relevant squares. Several reasons may be given for favoring the interpretation provided by Table 20. The features in Table 21 and 22 include a variety of functional categories ranging from storage pits to a dog burial. The sample (169.05 grams) was significantly smaller than that taken from square 510E570 (615.3 grams), yet it represented a much greater geographical area. Another significant reason for rejecting this data is that it combines data from two functionally specific areas from the site.

STOCKADE

Tables 21 and 22 record the percentage of nutshell represented in the features of each excavation group within the ring of post molds delineating the stockade and compare these percentages with those of features lying outside the stockade. The comparison is striking. Within the stockade the percentage of nutshell found in features is negligible, never reaching 20 per cent of a given excavation group. The percentage of nutshell found in features outside the stockade is consistently greater, reaching a maximum of 71 percent in one excavation group.

We are still dealing only with 169 grams of material, and the validity of the exact percentage in any given stratigraphic unit may be challenged due to the small quantum of plant remains per relevant excavation group ($169 \div 8 =$ an average of only 21 grams of plant re-

TABLE 21
CHARRED PLANT REMAINS—FEATURES WITHIN STOCKADE
(In Grams and Percents)

	IV		III*a*		II*c*		Total	
NUTSHELL								
Walnut	.1	(.4)	. . .		. . .		.1	(.2)
Butternut	.5	(2.1)	. . .		. . .		.5	(1.1)
Hickory	.1	(.4)	1.3	(14.4)	. . .		1.4	(3.1)
Acorn	. . .		. . .		. . .		. . .	
Hazelnut	. . .		. . .		. . .		. . .	
Nutmeat	. . .		. . .		. . .		. . .	
Unidentified	. . .		. . .		. . .		. . .	
Total	.7	(2.9)	1.3	(14.4)	. . .		2.0	(4.4)
WOOD CHARCOAL	22.6	(96.2)	7.4	(82.2)	12.7	(100.0)	42.7	(94.5)
SEEDS								
Zea mays	. . .		. . .		. . .		. . .	
Prunus	. . .		. . .		. . .		. . .	
Chenopodium					. . .		. . .	
Celtis	. . .		. . .		. . .		. . .	
Unidentified	.1	(.4)	.1	(1.1)	. . .		.2	(.4)
Total	.1	(.4)	.1	(1.1)	. . .		.2	(.4)
UNIDENTIFIED	.1	(.4)	.2	(2.2)	. . .		.3	(.7)
TOTAL	23.5	(99.9)	9.0	(99.9)	12.7	(100.0)	45.2	(100.0)

( ) = percentage of level

mains per relevant excavation group). However, the significance of the results shown in the bipartite division between features lying outside the stockade and those lying inside the stockade cannot be denied. Ignoring the stratigraphic-chronological divisions completely, 34 percent of the plant remains from all features lying outside the stockade consists of nutshell as opposed to only 4 percent of all plant remains from features within the stockade.

This data strongly suggests a functional differentiation between these two general areas of the site, the area of general occupation lying outside the stockade. The exact function of the stockade cannot, of course, be determined from this data, but it is suggested that there was little or no domestic activity occurring within it.

METHODS OF QUANTIFICATION

Developing an accurate method for making meaningful quantitative comparisons between plant remains of different taxa and/or different strata has been somewhat difficult. At this point I should acknowledge a total lack in knowl-

TABLE 22
CHARRED PLANT REMAINS—FEATURES OUTSIDE STOCKADE
(In Grams and Percents)

	IV	III*b*	III*a*	II*d*	II*c*	Total
NUTSHELL						
Walnut	.05 (.5)	1.5 (13.5)	4.6 (5.0)	...	...	6.15
Butternut	.4 (3.7)	3.9 (34.9)	17.65 (19.1)	.5 (71.4)	...	22.45
Hickory	...	1.6 (14.3)	5.55 (6.0)	...	...	7.15
Acorn	...	...	...	...	.1 (1.2)	.1
Hazelnut	...	...	...	...	...	...
Nutmeat	...	...	...	...	...	...
Unidentified	...	...	3.15 (3.4)	...	...	3.15
Total	.45 (4.2)	7.0 (62.7)	30.95 (33.5)	.5 (71.4)	.1 (1.2)	39.00
WOOD CHARCOAL	10.4 (95.9)	2.55 (22.9)	60.9 (65.9)	.2 (28.6)	8.2 (98.8)	82.25
SEEDS						
Zea mays	...	...	...	...	...	...
Prunus	...	...	...	...	...	...
Chenopodium	...	...	...	...	...	...
Celtis	...	.1 (.9)	...	...	...	.1 (.9)
Unidentified	...	.2 (1.8)	...	...	...	.2 (1.8)
Total	...	.3 (2.7)	...	...	...	.3 (2.7)
UNIDENTIFIED	...	1.3 (11.7)	.5 (.5)	...	...	1.8
TOTAL	10.85 (100.1)	11.15 (100.0)	92.35 (99.9)	.7 (100.0)	8.3 (100.0)	123.35

edge of statistical methods. Within the unit, the small size of the nutshell fragments made it impossible to quantify in terms of the number of nuts. Since the number of fragments was not a good indicator, the fragments being of such variable size, the mass was finally used as the basis for comparison. There are serious drawbacks to the utility of this measurement for comparisons between species. For example, charred hickory nutshell is more dense than charred acorn shell, besides the obvious fact that surrounding any given hickory nutmeat there is a greater quantity of nutshell than is found surrounding an acorn nutmeat.

Perhaps the only accurate way of quantifying these remains is to make a substantial collection of wild-growing hickory, walnut, and other relevant nut species, char these, and calculate from a fairly large quantity of the charred whole nuts the average mass represented by one nut. Then, more important to a final analysis, calculate from this data the mass of nutshell of each species which must be present in order for the analyst to be able to assume that a given mass of nutmeats is represented in the sample (hypothetical example: 5 grams of hickory nutshell recovered might possibly indicate the utilization of 1 gram of nutmeat). If this data were carefully collected and measured for each relevant taxa of food plant, the results would be useful for the analysis of plant remains from any archaeological site in the same general environmental zone and would provide comparable data between sites—something which now is nonexistent.

With this thought in mind, and because it is the only basis for comparison even within the site at the present time, the mass in grams was used as the basis for calculation. When further study is made, my results can then be easily converted to the probable weight in nutmeats. That done, it will then be possible to begin considering relative caloric intake and more sophisticated topics. A much more accurate indication of the importance of various plant foods to aboriginal subsistence will then be possible.

In attempting to make comparisons between strata there were more difficulties to be dealt with. The amount in grams of any given taxa was not directly comparable between strata, since the number of samples analyzed varied greatly between strata. Since masses were not directly comparable, it was necessary to convert the number of grams of a plant remain into the percentage of the total plant remains analyzed from that strata. Although this method is adequate, it obscures the fact that some of the percentages—those from strata yielding large samples—are necessarily more accurate than those which are calculated from small samples. It is also impossible to note absolutes, as opposed to relative, decline between strata in the total amount of plant remains or within any taxa.

The only way seen to improve upon the method of comparison finally used is to alter excavation techniques in regard to the recovery of plant remains. To obtain data that can be used for accurate comparative purposes between strata or between regions of a site and, eventually, between sites, it would be necessary to have a structured method for selection and recovery of remains built into the excavation program. Although the exact methodology must be left to someone with a knowledge of statistical methods, this would include the fine screening or flotation of soil from a prearranged number of soil samples of equal size taken from an excavation unit or group of units. The location of the samples to be intensively treated for extraction of plant remains would be determined by use of a table of random numbers or other acceptable statistical method. Cultural midden and features would be treated separately, but with the same technique.

The use of a recovery method such as this would reduce the subjectivity implicit in recovery of only those plant remains which are of sufficient size, or occur in sufficient concentration, to be noticed by the excavator while in the field. With a consistent selection of samples it would be possible to recognize more accurately an absolute change in the quantity of plant remains between strata and between areas of the site. The measurement in grams could be used directly as the basis for comparison, giving immediate indication of both relative and absolute change in the quantity of plant remains between strata and between areas of the site. Finally, more complete and representative data would emerge from a recovery method such as suggested above which would not only give a far more exact picture of subsistence practices within one site, but would also provide data which were easily comparable to data from other sites which had utilized the same recovery techniques.

After presenting the above suggestions, it is necessary to refute one implication of such a method. It is not meant to imply that, for example, if the excavator uncovers a storage pit containing a solid mass of charred plant remains, and this pit is not one selected by the table of random numbers for recovery of plant remains, that he should ignore these remains and make no attempt to recover or identify them. The method was suggested as a technique for obtaining additional data, not as an excuse for ignoring obvious data—which would occur if the method was too rigorously applied. In such a case, the data from the statistically controlled samples and the data recovered by the excavator in the traditional fashion should be analyzed in separate but complementary ways, and both should contribute to the final interpretation of subsistence activities on the site.

PLANT FOOD UTILIZATION AND SITE ENVIRONMENT

An extensive analysis of changes in environment throughout the occupation of the Schultz site will not be attempted on the basis of food plant remains. We can make the very basic assumption that an element of deciduous forest was present in the site area throughout the site occupation. Completion by Fel Brunett of the identification of the wood charcoal from the site will yield a more complete qualitative picture of the vegetation surrounding the site area, although it will not be useful for quantitative analysis of the surrounding environment because of cultural selection of firewood.

The following summarizes data relevant to environment favored by each food plant, ethnobotanical uses made of the foods, and their season of availability. Data below are from Yarnell (1964).

acorn (*Quercus* sp.)—"Acorns available in September to November (later on the ground). All Algonkians used all available species and removed tannin from acorns by soaking in hot wood ash lye water [p. 70]. Oaks grow in a variety of habitats, but most of those growing in the Saginaw area (primarily the red, white, and bur oaks) have a tendency to grown in moist to damp or even wet soils" (p. 27).

butternut (*Juglans cinerea*)—"Nuts available in October, good crop every two or three years . . . stored for winter. Grows . . . in low, rich woods, riverbanks, and low hillsides." (pp. 67-68).

hazelnut (*Corylus* sp)—"Nuts available in August to September. . . stored for winter. . . Grows . . . in thickets, along stream banks, and on borders of woods" (p. 6). The hazelnuts can be gathered by hand from the bushes when ripe (U.S. Dept. of Agriculture, 1948:152).

hickory (*Carya* sp.)—"Nuts available in Ocotber . . . stored for winter" (p. 68). C. *ovata* grows "in rich woods, bottoms, and slopes" (p. 68) and C. *cordiformis* grows "in wet to dry woods, stream banks, and swamps" (p. 69).

walnut (*Juglans nigra*)—"Nuts available in October; good crop irregular. Grows . . . in rich woods" (p. 61).

goosefoot (*Chenopodium* sp.)—"Seeds available in autumn to early winter. Grows . . . in cultivated and waste ground" (p. 70).

hackberry (*Celtis occidentalis*)—"Berries available in autumn; good crop most years . . . Grows . . . in rich, moist, well-drained soil, gravelly and rocky hillsides and riverbanks; very shade tolerant" (p. 72).

cherry (?) (*Prunus* sp.)—"Berries available in August to September; good crop every year . . . dried for winter. Grows . . . in rich, moist soil, dry gravelly or sandy soils, dry woods, and fence rows" (p. 62).

SUMMARY

Analysis of food plant remains from the Schultz site suggests at least an autumn occupation, probably extending through the winter. The three most common plant foods—butternut, walnut, and hickory—are all available in October. This data does not preclude a spring or early summer occupation, but there is no support for such a hypothesis.

Environmental change, if any occured, apparently was not sufficient to alter the nature of the available food plants. Although there is a significant change in frequency in nutshell throughout time, there was no qualitative change in the nut species utilized.

The change in the percentage of nutshell from each excavation group changed drastically through time, as shown below:

Period	*Level*	*Percentage*
Transitional	II*d*	89.9
Early Middle Woodland	III*a*	62.9
Late Middle Woodland	III*b*	12.4
	IV*a*	24.1
Late Woodland	IV*b*	7.9
	IV*c*	17.2

This change is interpreted as indicating a shift in subsistence base during Early Middle Woodland and completed by Late Middle Woodland. Possible reasons for the absence of remains from the plant food which replaced a reliance upon nuts include (1) differential preservation, (2) need for revised recovery techniques, and (3) more total consumption of the new plant food.

A functional difference between the area of the site lying inside the ring of postmolds designating a "stockade" was noticed in analysis of plant remains from features both inside and outside the stockade. Within the stockade only 4 percent of the plant remains consisted of nutshell; whereas outside of the stockade 34 percent of plant remains from features consisted of nutshell. Apparently the area inside the stockade was not used for domestic purposes as was the area outside of this structure.

It is admitted that valid criticisms can be made of the comparative methods used in this analysis, and suggestions for future improvement are incorporated in the body of the paper. Until new recovery techniques can be implemented in the field, final analysis must remain on an elementary and inaccurate level.

V

WOOD FROM SCHULTZ AND OTHER PREHISTORIC SITES IN THE GREAT LAKES AREA

Fel V. Brunett

Wood has been tied to cultural activities throughout the prehistory of man in the Great Lakes Basin. Griffin (Jennings and Norbeck, 1964:225) reconstructs the technology of the Fluted Blade Hunters as including small amounts of wood working, the ability to produce fire and to cross streams on logs or other more sophisticated crafts. During the contact period 10,000 years later, European missionaries recorded the existence of fortified villages constructed of wood and bark sheltering, use of bowls, spoons, baskets, mortars and pestles, sleds, bows, shields, and other objects of wood. Time horizons for these technological advances must be recovered from the archaeological record, but because wood artifacts are rare and require biological interpretation, little work has been done with them.

WOOD PRESERVATION

Because wood is organic its preservation is rare. Spores of saprophytic fungi occurring by the thousands in each cubic centimeter of forest soil attack either the lignin or cellulose content of wood where minimal amounts of moisture and oxygen exist. The alteration of the substrate or protection from oxygen or water is required for preservation.

Almost all wood from archaeological sites excavated in the Great Lakes Basin exists because its organic composition has been rendered useless to fungi. Charcoal is the largest division under this category, resulting from incomplete oxidation of wood. It is a common hearth bi-product and a source of carbon for dating. The age relationship of the wood to the site must be determined for correct interpretations. Center wood from mature trees in the basin may be from two hundred to three hundred years earlier than the site. Curvature of the annular rings is the index to age in large specimens, with those with least arc being most nearly contemporaneous with the site. Where a variety of specimen diameters are available, those with axes of small diameter produce the best dates. If wood from large axes is used, selection of exterior material is desirable.

Great care must be taken to select wood from archaeological context since natural forest fires create huge amounts of charcoal which can be concentrated and covered by silt-carrying runoff water in low spots and which exists in stump holes where subsurface burning has created *in situ* charred wood especially in the resinous species. Charcoal from roots can usually be recognized in the field by careful investigation of the exterior surface; remnants of decayed wood that was not carbonized because of the cooling effect of the moist soil on the outside should be noticeable. Natural fires have probably covered all areas of the basin at least once every five hundred years in prehistoric times and possibly much more frequently.

Charcoal is destroyed naturally by water, absorbed in its porous structure, expanding as it freezes. Hearths with concentrations of minute carbon particles were probably exposed to freezing over long periods of time while those with good charcoal preservation would indicate protection. Patterns of surface snow retention may be reflected by the condition of charcoal near the surface. In porous soils the small particles are sometimes leached into lower soil horizons and may contaminate carbon selected from lower features.

Analysis of charcoal from hearths may give invalid statistics concerning fuel composition because of different heats of combustion for different species of wood. Resinous woods are poor producers of charcoal, as smelters of iron have pointed out in their selection of nonresinous species for the kilns. The highly combustible resin aids in burning the species containing it to ash. This is particularly true of red pine (*Pinus rosinosa* Ait.).

Analysis of twenty-one hearths from the Schultz site (20SA2) in Saginaw County, Michigan, demonstrate the existence of a mixed deciduous forest throughout the Woodland cultural period. Hemlock appears in the earliest levels and, except for an indetermined conifer in the Middle Woodland period, no other conifers were found. Three hypotheses can be made to explain this: (1) no conifers were available; (2) conifers were available but not acceptable to wood users; (3) coniferous wood was used and completely oxidized in the process. Since white pine existed there historically and probably came as a subclimax following each major fire, one would expect to find it in hearths. Perhaps hypothesis 2 or 3 is the explanation. An analysis of represented vegetation is presented in Table 23.

Carbonized wood chips from under Mound F at the Norton Mounds site (20KT1) appear to have been chopped from four to eight inch diameter poles of black walnut, hickory, hackberry, and American elm. They were found in an occupation zone with Naples dentate stamped sherds (Flanders, 1965:292). This is the only known occurrence of preserved wood chips in the Great Lakes Basin. Since such materials definitely tie a particular species to the occupation period, they are of value to the environmental archaeologist.

Oxides of metals, especially copper, are toxic to fungi and when concentrated in organic material act as preservatives. Wood buried in close association with copper absorbs the oxides and is preserved in its natural state.

The Bussinger site (20SA194) supplied two mineralized spear shaft tips preserved in Middle Woodland conical copper points from Burial 36. Both are red maple (*Acer rubrum* L.) saplings pointed with a knifelike object to fit the interior contour of the points. The diameter is approximately one centimeter at the base in each specimen. The length of the shaft could not be determined since no part of the shaft outside of the points remained.

Because of low temperature and lack of sufficient oxygen, wood is preserved under water especially where silt has been deposited over it. With the development of scuba gear, lakes and streams adjacent to sites should become archaeological units, adding greatly to the nearly nonexistent record of wood artifacts. Two dugout canoes have been raised from the Manistee River, Michigan, and no known extensive search has been made for others. In lake basins such

TABLE 23
WOOD FROM SCHULTZ

Tree	Cultural Period			
	Early Woodland	Early Middle Woodland	Middle Middle Woodland	Late Middle Woodland to Late Woodland
Acer sp. Maple	X	X		
Betula alleghaniensis Britton Yellow Birch		X		X
Carya glabra Sweet Pignut hickory				X
C. laciniosa Loud. Shellbark hickory			X	X
C. ovata K. Koch Shagbark hickory	X	X	X	X
Castanea dentata Borkh. Chestnut		X	X	X
Celtis occidentallis L. Hackberry		X	X	X
Fagus grandifolia Ehrh. American beech				X
Fraxinus americana L. White ash	X	X	X	X
F. nigra Marsh. Black ash	X		X	X
Juglans nigra L. Black walnut		X	X	X
Morus rubra L. Red mulberry		X		
Nyssa sylvatica Marsh. Black gum				X
Ostrya virginiana K. Koch Eastern hop-hornbeam	X			X
Populus tremuloides Michx. Quaking aspen	X			X
Quercus alba L. White oak		X		X
Q. bicolor Willd. Swamp white oak		X		X
Q. macrocarpa Michx. Bur oak		X		
Q. rubra L. Northern red oak	X	X		X
Tsuga canadensis Carr. Eastern Hemlock	X			X
Ulmus rubra Muhl. Slippery elm			X	X
U. americana L. American elm		X	X	X

as the Great Lakes which are currently higher than in earlier occupation periods, inundated sites should yield wood artifacts, especially if they were covered shortly after occupation and were not destroyed by fire. Small nonresinous wood artifacts would probably not survive more than five years out of water. Larger nonresinous specimens and those containing resin could be expected to last from ten to fifty years or longer depending on the species represented. Bacterial destruction in the aquatic environment is a factor for study, especially if new bacteria are introduced for pollution abatement. Flooded stream beds caused by the rising water level of the lakes covered river valleys with silt and water, preserving possible archaeological sites. Location of such sites would, unfortunately, be extremely difficult.

Wood deposited in a water-free area is protected from fungi, resulting in its preservation. In the eastern United States most known prehistoric wood artifacts have been preserved in this manner in dry rock shelters. Few shelters of this type exist in the Great Lakes Basin because of regional geology. One, at Burnt Bluff on Michigan's Garden Peninsula along the northern shore of Lake Michigan, has been excavated by the University of Michigan Museum of Anthropology. Four problematic wood artifacts were found, one of birch and three of northern white-cedar (*Thuja occidentalis* L.). The subsistence base at the site was primarily fishing and the artifacts may represent fishing paraphernalia (Donald Janzen: Personal Communication).

WOOD IDENTIFICATION

Botanical identification is based on comparison of the unknown to the known. This procedure is used for wood. The transverse scheme of structure is compared to patterns in known samples, and the specimen is considered part of the species with which it best correlates. "Type" models are established for all plants and must contain the defining characteristics which are reproductive parts mainly because of their low degree of variability. Woody plant "type" specimens do not generally contain typical wood material. If wood is to be identified, such specimens must be obtained and circulated for comparison. The least variable structures must be pointed out so that samples from poor as well as rich growth zones will be identified as the same species. A variety of photographs of transverse sections of the current economic species is available and illustrates specific similarity. About seventy species from the Great Lakes Basin are available, leaving two hundred woody plants—all shrubs—to prepare and photograph. Since color and weight vary according to preservation, the information available from a good black and white photograph is adequate for comparison and should be inexpensive enough for mass availability. The alternative to mass dispersal of type photographs and individual interpretation is a center for wood identification built around a bank of computerized "type" patterns where photographs and perhaps eventually direct projections from the microscope into the system can be compared impartially with wood patterns from wide geographical areas.

VI

FAUNAL REMAINS

Babara Luxenberg

The 1964 UMMA excavations at the Schultz site in Saginaw County, Michigan, uncovered a large amount of bone refuse, most of which was excessively fragmentary and therefore unidentifiable. (For an account of earlier animal bone see Cleland, 1966:117-44.) There was a total of 280,715 bone fragments found, of which only 14,883 were identifiable as to species. On the basis of bone structure, the unidentifiable material was sorted into fish, mammal, bird, and turtle. Table 24 shows the relative abundance of each type of bone by provenience unit. There were no articulated bones, and only in the smaller birds and mammals were whole limb bones found, these being comparatively rare. Butchering techniques plus deterioration probably account for the condition of the bone refuse. Rib and vertebral identifications were, for the most part, not attempted.

The excavation units represent four areas of the site: the channel area, the levee above the channel, the southwest levee (represented in this sample by one lone unit), and the mounds at the north end of the site. The channel and levee were the best sampled. The faunal sample is not a random one, though it probably is representative of the animals hunted. All worked bone was analyzed separately by Peter Murray (this volume). Human bone occurred only in burials in the mound area. The present report does not include the burials themselves, but rather faunal material found in the units excavated in the mound area. This material, due to lack of stratigraphic control, has been lumped into the category "Mound Fill" (see Table 24).

Analysis of bone in its stratigraphic context is much more meaningful than analysis by excavation unit in a site such as Schultz, in which there was occupation over a long time period. The various levels of the excavation units were assigned stratigraphic levels by Fitting (this volume). The levels used are II*b* and II*c* which are definite Early Woodland occupations; II*d* which is probably intermediate but is included with Early Woodland in this analysis; III*a*, III*b*, and IV*a* which are Middle Woodland occupations; and IV*b* and IV*c* which are Late Woodland occupations. The Late Woodland occupations could not be differentiated from each other in some places due to plowzone mixing. Material found in these areas has been placed in category IV and analyzed separately from the Late Woodland materials which could be assigned more specific provenience.

The minimum number of individuals represented by the identifiable bone material was calculated according to

TABLE 24
ANIMAL BONE BY UNIT
(1964 Season)

	Unidentifiable				Identifiable				
Provenience Units	Mammal	Bird	Turtle	Fish	Mammal	Bird	Turtle	Fish	Total
Channel—									
490E585(5x20)	6002	21	417	11,101	217	1	23	687	18,469
490E630(10x10)	7120	15	305	13,418	223	4	16	1047	22,148
510E570(20x20)	44,735	117	3333	136,376	1548	29	156	10,048	196,342
Levee—									
530E585(5x20)	1266	0	97	1940	59	0	7	231	3600
550E570(20x20)	3294	14	166	3840	144	1	10	447	7916
570E585(5x20)	431	1	20	184	42	0	1	37	716
590E570(20x20)	3528	2	124	1624	199	0	12	250	5739
610E585(5x20)	1308	2	31	823	112	0	2	82	2360
630E570(20x20)	1266	2	29	179	58	0	15	35	1584
650E585(5x20)	259	0	1	0	22	0	0	0	282
670E570(20x20)	4510	8	169	1120	234	2	1	148	6192
690E585(5x20)	660	0	16	176	22	0	2	35	911
Southwest Levee—									
580E360(10x10)	3557	10	146	7106	104	0	32	960	11,915
Mound Fill	128	33	183	1819	180	17	20	205	2585
Total	78,064	225	5037	179,706	3164	54	297	14,212	280,759

stratigraphic levels. Within each level, minimal counts of individuals were tabulated for each of four areas within the site (channel, southwest levee, levees inside and outside the stockade) in an attempt to determine differential usage of areas through time. A group of adjacent, or even noncontiguous, excavation units may represent the same utilization area of the site, and the number of individuals therein may be significant. The number of individuals was not tabulated for each separate excavation unit since adjacent units may have bone fragments from one individual and the total count thus determined would be too high. Due to lack of stratigraphic control, the number of individuals in the mound fill units could only be estimated and cannot be compared with counts from the other areas.

The most frequently-occurring bone in each species was used to determine the number of individuals represented. Calculations took into account age, size, and laterality (sex difference, for the most part, not being ascertainable in this faunal sample). This worked well for the mammal, bird, and turtle bone. The fish were more of a problem. Specifically, the gar were represented only by hundreds of scales and a very few pterygoid fragments, the sturgeon by hundreds of tiny skull fragments. The number of individuals represented by these and the amount of meat they contributed to the diet had to be estimated and are probably too conservative.

There was some bone whose stratigraphic provenience could not be determined due to indistinct stratigraphy and/or plowzone mixing. Such bone was included in Tables 24 and 25, according to its excavation unit, but was not included in the rest of the analysis which is based on stratigraphic provenience. Thus the amount of material included in Tables 24 and 25 is greater than that in Table 26.

MAMMALS

There were 81,224 fragments of mammal bone, only 3,160 of which were identifiable as to species. Fragmentation was extreme, but the majority of the pieces, on the basis of bone structure, shape, and size, seemed to be from the long bones of animals in the deer, bear, and elk size range. These bones were probably split for marrow. Only nineteen mammalian species were represented, and of these, the three small rodent species (bog lemming, meadow vole, and pine vole) may have been intrusive or their presence independent of human activity.

Over half of the identifiable mammal bone, and almost two-thirds of the number of individuals, were animals living in or dependent upon an aquatic habitat. The muskrat is a semiaquatic marsh-dweller, and its abundance at the Schultz site suggests extensive marshland near the site. Beaver also are found in abundance, indicating that not too far from the site, or on the levee itself, there were woods providing raw materials for the construction of dams and lodges. Conifers are seldom touched by beavers, so the deciduous element must have been substantial enough to support a fairly large beaver population. The otter is found along good-sized watercourses such as the Saginaw and Tittabawassee rivers. It is very secretive in its habits and correspondingly hard to catch, and it comprises, indeed, a very small percentage of the total mammal bone. Mink are always found near the water. The raccoon inhabits forested regions, doing most of its foraging in streams and lakes.

Open woodland species were not as common in the bone refuse, comprising only one-third of the number of individuals. However, due to their much greater size, these animals contributed six times as much meat as those from aquatic habitats. The deer and elk are most common in open woodland areas, though they are both extremely wide-ranging. Skunk are found near human occupations in wooded areas. Woodchucks and bobcats are also found in sparsely wooded areas.

Animals from densely forested habitats made up a very small part of the sample. Bears are found in dense, usually coniferous, forests. Thick stands of spruce are the home of the little pine marten and the fisher. Though the porcupine prefers coniferous stands, it is found in deciduous forests if they are dense. There is thus no real indication of heavy coniferous forestation near Schultz. The wooded areas near the site must have been predominantly deciduous and fairly open. Most of the species identified are found in the region today, with the exception of those whose pelts have been highly sought after.

There is evidence, from the differential representation of the elements of the deer skeleton that it was butchered fairly completely at the kill site and only certain parts were brought back for food. There are almost no ribs and vertebrae, other than the atlas and axis, indicating that the limbs and head were severed off the trunk, which was left at the kill site. There were many scapula and pelvic fragments; possibly the limbs were severed at these points. The foreleg and hindleg elements were just about equal in representation; probably neither was a preferred food item. Both the distal and proximal ends of the metapodials are severed off the shaft and both are pres-

TABLE 25
NUMBER OF BONES, SPECIES AND PROVENIENCE UNITS

	Provenience														
FISH	490E585 (5x20)	490E630 (10x10)	510E570 (20x20)	530E585 (5x20)	550E570 (20x20)	570E585 (5x20)	590E570 (20x20)	610E585 (5x20)	630E570 (20x20)	650E585 (5x20)	670E570 (20x20)	690E585 (5x20)	580E360 (10x10)	Mound Fill	Total
Walleye	259	369	4,639	53	165	18	61	6	5	...	32	13	396	133	6,149
Drum	136	152	2,674	62	99	11	50	28	5	...	31	6	160	14	3,428
Sturgeon	155	396	1,537	89	155	3	110	34	9	...	71	14	268	37	2,878
Gar	71	75	245	16	9	...	10	1	...	...	1	1	60	3	492
Bullhead	2	3	390	...	3	...	...	3	...	...	...	...	12	2	415
Channel catfish	46	24	205	8	1	1	15	9	15	...	11	...	31	12	378
Bowfin	14	17	131	3	13	3	2	1	1	...	2	...	18	2	207
Catfish	...	...	98	...	...	...	2	...	...	...	...	...	2	...	102
Northern pike	1	...	51	...	2	...	...	...	...	...	...	1	1	...	56
Largemouth bass	...	6	26	...	...	...	...	...	...	...	...	...	3	...	35
Perch	2	2	20	...	...	1	...	...	...	...	...	...	5	...	30
Sucker	1	1	15	...	...	...	...	...	...	...	...	...	2	...	19
Lake trout	...	2	11	...	...	...	...	...	...	...	...	...	1	2	16
Smallmouth bass	...	...	6	...	...	...	...	...	...	...	...	...	1	...	7
Subtotal fish	687	1,047	10,048	231	447	37	250	82	35	...	148	35	960	205	14,212
MAMMAL															
Muskrat	90	66	752	19	72	7	125	90	34	1	125	6	47	43	1,477
Deer	99	120	546	25	38	18	43	9	13	10	72	9	32	38	1,072
Beaver	10	27	81	4	16	12	23	5	9	11	24	3	2	27	254
Raccoon	2	1	62	4	9	1	1	1	...	...	2	...	12	3	103
Elk	...	2	11	4	1	...	1	...	...	...	...	3	3	44	69
Bear	6	2	23	3	...	2	2	1	...	...	2	1	5	14	61
Dog	3	1	33	...	2	2	1	1	1	...	...	...	2	...	46
Otter	6	3	8	...	1	...	...	...	...	...	...	...	...	2	20
Meadow vole	...	...	6	...	...	...	...	1	...	...	...	...	...	4	11

TABLE 25 (continued)

MAMMAL (cont.)	Provenience 490E585 (5x20)	490E630 (10x10)	510E570 (20x20)	530E585 (5x20)	550E570 (20x20)	570E585 (5x20)	590E570 (20x20)	610E585 (5x20)	630E570 (20x20)	650E585 (5x20)	670E570 (20x20)	690E585 (5x20)	580E360 (10x10)	Mound Fill	Total
Mink	...	...	6	...	...	...	...	3	...	...	1	...	...	...	10
Porcupine	...	...	1	...	5	...	3	...	...	...	...	...	...	...	9
Fisher	1	1	7	...	...	...	...	...	...	...	...	...	...	...	9
Woodchuck	...	...	5	...	...	...	...	1	...	...	...	...	1	...	7
Wolf	...	...	1	...	...	...	...	...	...	...	3	...	...	...	4
Marten	...	...	...	...	...	...	...	...	1	...	...	...	...	2	3
Skunk	...	...	2	...	...	...	...	...	...	...	...	...	...	1	3
Bobcat	...	...	2	...	...	...	...	...	...	...	...	...	...	...	2
Pine vole	...	...	1	...	...	...	...	...	...	...	...	...	...	...	1
Bog lemming	...	...	1	...	...	...	...	...	...	...	...	...	...	...	1
Subtotal mammals	217	223	1,548	59	144	42	199	112	58	22	234	22	104	180	3,164
BIRD															
Duck	...	1	2	...	...	...	...	...	...	...	1	...	...	14	18
Blue-winged teal	1	1	7	...	...	...	...	...	...	...	...	...	...	...	9
Hooded merganser	...	...	5	...	...	...	...	...	...	...	...	...	...	1	6
Common mallard	...	...	4	...	...	...	...	...	...	...	...	...	...	1	5
American bittern	...	...	4	...	...	...	...	...	...	...	...	...	...	...	4
Crow	...	...	2	...	...	...	...	...	...	...	...	...	...	...	2
Sandhill crane	...	1	1	...	...	...	...	...	...	...	...	...	...	...	2
Great blue heron	...	...	...	...	1	...	...	...	...	...	1	...	...	...	2
Turkey	1	1	...	...	...	...	...	...	...	...	...	...	...	...	2
Common loon	...	...	1	...	...	...	...	...	...	...	...	...	...	...	1
Common snipe	...	...	1	...	...	...	...	...	...	...	...	...	...	...	1

TABLE 25 (continued)

BIRD (cont.)	490E585 (5x20)	490E630 (10x10)	510E570 (20x20)	530E585 (5x20)	550E570 (20x20)	570E585 (5x20)	590E570 (20x20)	610E585 (5x20)	630E570 (20x20)	650E585 (5x20)	670E570 (20x20)	690E585 (5x20)	580E360 (10x10)	Mound Fill	Total
Canada goose	...	...	1	...	...	...	...	...	...	...	...	...	...	...	1
Passenger pigeon	...	...	1	...	...	...	...	...	...	...	...	...	...	...	1
Subtotal bird	2	4	29	...	1	...	...	...	...	...	2	...	...	16	54
TURTLE															
Soft-shell turtle	6	10	114	5	6	1	7	2	14	...	1	...	24	7	197
Snapping turtle	12	5	25	2	3	...	4	...	1	...	...	...	6	13	71
Blanding's turtle	2	1	11	...	1	...	1	...	...	...	...	2	...	...	18
Map turtle	3	...	4	...	...	...	...	...	...	...	...	...	...	...	7
Painted turtle	...	...	1	...	...	...	...	...	...	...	...	...	2	...	3
Pond slider	...	...	1	...	...	...	...	...	...	...	...	...	...	...	1
Subtotal turtle	23	16	156	7	10	1	12	2	15	...	1	2	32	20	297
TOTALS	929	1,290	11,781	297	602	80	461	196	108	22	385	59	1,096	421	17,727

TABLE 26
NUMBER OF BONES, SPECIES AND STRATIGRAPHIC LEVEL

Species	Stratigraphic Level									
	II*b*	II*c*	II*d*	III*a*	III*b*	IV*a*	IV*b*	IV*c*	IV	Total
Sturgeon	4	4	8	664	1,945	446	134	363	330	3,898
Deer	4	35	10	270	368	97	47	55	113	999
Drum	2	5	2	296	1,203	298	99	118	187	2,210
Muskrat	2	10	4	322	417	122	67	135	297	1,376
Raccoon	2	4	...	28	40	17	2	4	7	104
Beaver	1	31	...	86	27	8	11	41	37	242
Soft-shell turtle	...	17	...	50	93	10	4	3	15	192
Walleyed pike	...	15	4	756	3,746	743	239	261	227	5,991
Channel catfish	...	4	1	84	185	34	5	7	19	339
Bullhead	...	1	...	16	251	100	1	13	3	385
Otter	...	1	...	2	8	1	4	2	...	18
Blanding's turtle	...	1	...	7	6	...	...	...	1	15
Painted turtle	...	1	...	...	...	1	1	...	...	3
Longnose gar	...	...	3	120	161	88	22	57	15	466
Bowfin	...	...	1	26	112	30	3	11	19	202
Snapping turtle	...	...	...	30	20	3	...	1	5	59
Catfish	...	...	...	19	73	1	...	7	...	100
Elk	...	...	...	11	...	...	2	...	4	17
Bear	...	...	...	8	15	7	8	1	3	42
Dog	...	...	...	6	27	3	3	...	3	42
Perch	...	...	...	4	16	13	1	3	1	38
Largemouth bass	...	...	...	4	26	2	3	...	...	35
Northern pike	...	...	...	3	33	13	...	4	2	55
Wolf	...	...	...	3	...	...	...	...	2	5
Lake trout	...	...	...	2	7	5	...	...	...	14
Fisher	...	...	...	2	4	...	...	2	...	8
Blue-winged teal	...	...	...	2	6	...	...	...	...	8
Map turtle	...	...	...	2	2	3	...	...	...	7
Sucker	...	...	...	1	13	1	...	3	...	18
Mink	...	...	...	1	1	...	1	3	4	10
Woodchuck	...	...	...	1	2	2	2	1	...	8
Meadow vole	...	...	...	1	3	2	...	...	...	6
American bittern	...	...	...	1	1	1	...	1	...	4
Great blue heron	...	...	...	1	...	...	...	...	1	2
Sandhill crane	...	...	...	1	1	...	...	...	...	2
Turkey	...	...	...	1	1	...	...	...	...	2

TABLE 26 (continued)

	Stratigraphic Level									
Species	II*b*	II*c*	II*d*	III*a*	III*b*	IV*a*	IV*b*	IV*c*	IV	Total
Marten	...	...	...	1	...	...	...	...	...	1
Hooded merganser	...	...	...	...	4	...	...	1	...	5
Smallmouth bass	...	...	...	...	3	2	...	1	...	6
Duck	...	...	...	...	3	...	...	...	1	4
Common mallard	...	...	...	...	2	1	...	1	...	4
Crow	...	...	...	...	2	...	...	...	...	2
Bobcat	...	...	...	...	2	...	...	...	...	2
Porcupine	...	...	...	...	1	...	...	...	3	4
Bog lemming	...	...	...	...	1	...	...	...	...	1
Common snipe	...	...	...	...	1	...	...	...	...	1
Common loon	...	...	...	...	1	...	...	...	...	1
Passenger pigeon	...	...	...	...	1	...	...	...	...	1
Canada goose	...	...	...	...	...	1	...	...	...	1
Skunk	...	...	...	...	...	...	...	2	...	2
Pine vole	...	...	...	...	...	...	...	1	...	1
Pond slider	...	...	...	...	...	...	...	1	...	1
TOTALS	15	129	33	2,832	8,834	2,055	659	1,103	1,299	16,959

ent in equal numbers. It is possible that, because of their straightness, the shafts were being used to make bone tools. Alternately, they were just being split for marrow, as were the other long bones.

Though the sample of the other big game animals, bear and elk, is not nearly so complete, there also seems to be differential representation of skeletal elements. With few exceptions, only teeth and distal limb elements are represented, indicating that, like the deer, butchering was at the kill site and only limbs and jaws were brought back to camp. It is thus possible that the larger game animals were hunted on long trips away from the site during the colder months when the local fauna was unavailable.

All other animals have fairly equal distribution of elements. The dog was probably also used for food because its bones were in the refuse along with all other bones and because there were butchering marks on the long bones. The dog could have been domesticated, but its scarcity at the site would indicate that it was not.

FISH

Thirteen species of fish were identified from the 14,172 identifiable fish bone fragments. These were, for the most part, fragments of skull or jaw, though scales were the single most important element in identifying the longnose gar. There were 179,706 pieces of unidentifiable fish bone, most of which were small, poorly-preserved fish vertebrae and spines. The most abundant fish was the walleye, both in number of bones and number of individuals. While walleye are most common in large lakes and rivers, they migrate long distances inland in the early spring to spawn on shallow water shoals. They are not easy fish to catch, and their abundance at Schultz indicates they were present in large masses during the spawning time.

The rock sturgeon and the drum were the next most abundant fish. The drum is a bottom-dweller and prefers a silty, somewhat turbulent habitat. Though today this fish is not considered a food fish of any merit, it was evidently eaten with relish by the Indians, considering that drum is such a large percentage (one-fifth) of the sample. The rock sturgeon comprises about one-fifth of the sample. It is not generally found in an inland river except in the late spring and early summer when it spawns in shallower areas.

The longnose gar, channel catfish, and bullhead all compose about three percent each of the fish sample. The gar is found in quiet, warm waters. The bullhead is also found in quiet, silty, shallow waters; it can often be found in waters which are too muddy to support other food fish. The channel cat is found in more rapidly-moving waters.

The bowfin is another fish that prefers a quiet, muddy bottom and profuse vegetation. This species and the remaining six species each are only one percent or less of the sample. The northern pike is not particularly common anywhere except in its optimal environment: clear water and abundant vegetation. It does, however, spawn in marshy areas in the spring. Suckers and redhorses, though quite common in the Great Lakes drainage at the present time, were represented by a very few bones in the Schultz sample. Since they make excellent eating, this would suggest that they were not as abundant in the past as they are now. The two basses are found in different environments, the largemouth bass preferring weedy, muddy bottoms and the smallmouth bass preferring clear, cool waters. Both the lake trout and yellow perch are found predominantly in deep, clear, cool lake waters but move inland to spawn in shallower waters in the spring.

There are thus two major sources of fish represented in the Schultz sample. Some of the fishes are basically lake fishes which probably only moved inland to spawn in the spring and early summer. These fish include the sturgeon, walleye, channel catfish, suckers, yellow perch, and smallmouth bass, with the lake trout spawning inland in the fall. These fish prefer clear, weed-free waters. Other species, which probably were found year-round in the Saginaw River, prefer shallow, fairly quiet, somewhat turbid water with a fair amount of aquatic vegetation. The bowfin, drum, bullhead, and largemouth bass are representatives of this group.

Thus it seems that the Saginaw River then was not too different from today, having a fairly slow current with much material in suspension and a good deal of aquatic vegetation. It was probably only during the spawning season that the fish preferring clear, rapidly-moving water made their way into the river. Personal accounts of the early settlers in the Saginaw Valley give a good description of the vast numbers of spawning fish in the flooded areas of the Shiawassee and Tittabawassee during the spring. Thus, it does not seem implausible that the greatest amount of fish represented should be from this source while local fish are not so strongly represented.

BIRD

There were a total of 279 bird bones, 54 of which were identifiable as to genus or species. This is less than .09 percent of the total bone refuse. Most of the species are found in aquatic environments. The heron and bittern are fish-eaters and waders. The loons, geese, mallards, and ducks are all water-loving. The crane lives in a marshy habitat. The remaining four species, the turkey, passenger pigeon, snipe, and crow which are represented by only five bones, are forest dwellers. Of the game birds there is only one representative, the turkey. When hunting in the woods, the Indians were interested in larger game: deer, bear, elk. When they hunted near the site, fish, aquatic mammals, and turtles were of greater importance. It seems that birds were not considered a significant food source and were hunted only incidentally, if at all. Only two of the bird bones were charred and none of them had any evidence of butchering marks. This does not preclude the possibility of birds having been used for food, but it does mean that if they were, they were probably boiled whole until the meat could easily be stripped from the bone and no marks would remain. It can be argued that birds were more important than is indicated by their representation in the archaeological record because bird bone is so fragile and easily destroyed. However, fish bone, which is even more fragile than bird, has a higher percent composition of the bone refuse than any other class of animal.

Only 36 bird bones could be placed in stratigraphic context. This is because a large amount of the bone came from the burial mound area at the north end of the site. The presence of such a large quantity of bird bone in this area indicates that birds may have had some ceremonial significance as opposed to economic importance. The greatest concentration of bird bone was in the channel area, which appears to have been a refuse area and possibly also a butchering area, conveniently adjacent to the river and swamps, where fish and small aquatic mammals were brought for cleaning and butchering. This would explain the dominance of bone in this area for all classes of animals.

Normally the presence of bird bone is taken to indicate summer occupations. The heron, American bittern, blue-winged teal, sandhill crane, and passenger pigeon (before it became extinct) do occur in lower Michigan predominantly during the summer and are found only very rarely in the winter. However, the Canada goose, mallard, loon, hooded merganser, snipe, and the crow can and do winter-over in the Saginaw Valley under today's climatic regime. The turkey was a year-round resident before it was so intensively hunted that it became locally extinct.

TURTLE

There were 5,037 pieces of unidentifiable turtle bone, mostly consisting of tiny pieces of carapace and plastron. From the 297 identifiable pieces, six species of turtle were found. All six turtles are thoroughly aquatic, though Blanding's turtle will wander about on land. The map turtle prefers a riverine environment, but the eastern spiny soft-shell can live in quiet water if there are sand or mud bars. As the eastern spiny soft-shell comprises over two-thirds of the identifiable turtle bone, it seems safe to assume that there was a slow current near shore with some development of sand and mud bars and a faster current offshore. The snapping turtle will live in any body of water, even in brackish, stagnant places. The painted turtle prefers shallow water where vegetation is profuse and the bottom is soft and muddy. The pond slider, represented by only one carapace fragment, is not found as far north as Michigan at the present time. A difference of one or two degrees in the mean annual temperature would probably make the difference in its distribution, but a climatic interpretation on the basis of one fragment of bone is not valid. Another possible interpretation is that the presence of that fragment shows contact with peoples to the south during that time period.

Turtles were undoubtedly used for food, but their importance as a source of raw material for making bowls may have equalled or surpassed their importance as a food item. All worked and decorated turtle carapaces were analyzed with the other worked bone (see Murray, this volume). The unworked pieces found were fragmented in the extreme. There were butchering marks on the proximal ends of only two femurs. There was very little charring of either limb or shell fragments. Possibly the turtles were boiled whole in a stew pot rather than dismembered and roasted on an open fire.

Two-thirds of all identifiable turtle came from the channel area, another indication that this was a refuse and/or slaughtering area and that turtles were caught along with the fish, perhaps in nets, and killed in the channel area. The snapping turtle, supposedly the most delectable of turtles, only composed one-fourth of the sample. Possibly it was not as abundant as the soft-shell, and undoubtedly it was harder to catch. All turtles hibernate during the winter, and therefore are harder to catch at that time. Their presence is thus taken as supporting evidence for warm weather occupations. The map turtle is slower to go into hibernation than the other species but, as he is only represented by seven bones, this does not by itself indicate a fall occupation.

EARLY WOODLAND

The levee area above the channel was the only place bone refuse was found for Early Woodland levels II*b* and II*c*, the channel being the only place where bone was found for the II*d* occupations. During this latter period at Schultz, the channel was possibly a butchering area for fish and mammals from the marshy lowlands; with the exception of one deer, only fish and muskrat are found there.

There were five mammal species (deer, muskrat, raccoon, beaver, otter), four of them small, aquatically-oriented animals. The seven species of fish also indicate that the area surrounding the site was important in hunting. With the exception of the bullhead, all the fish are two pounds or heavier, which may indicate spearing or harpooning as the method of fishing. Of the fish species, the bowfin, longnose gar, bullhead, and drum are found year-round in the area. The sturgeon, walleye, and channel catfish ascend the Saginaw River to spawn in the spring, and their presence indicates that at least some of the occupations were during the spring or early summer. Sturgeon is present in all three Early Woodland levels, but walleye and channel catfish are only in II*c* and II*d*.

During the whole Early Woodland period, the greatest dependence was upon deer as a food source. Seventy-five percent of the usable pounds of meat are deer (see Table 27). Such figures can at best only be approximate because they are based on (*a*) a minimal count of individuals which may be low if a species is under-represented in the archaeological record and (*b*) a live weight per individual which is only an approximation of the average weight per individual in the species' population at that time. The dressed weight, or usable pounds per individual, is probably more accurate in that it represents the maximum amount of edible meat for a species. This means the Indians probably were not using more, though it is conceivable that they were using less if food was abundant and they could be selective in what they used, discarding the rest. White (1953) was used as the major source for

TABLE 27
IMPORTANCE OF FOOD SPECIES

Species	STRATIGRAPHIC LEVEL																		
	II*b*		II*c*		II*d*		III*a*		III*b*		IV*a*		IV*b*		IV*c*		IV		Total
	No.	Pounds	No.	Pounds	No.	Pounds	No.	Pounds	No.	Pounds	No.	Pounds	No.	Pounds	No.	Pounds	No.	Pounds	Pounds
Sturgeon	1	24	1	24	2	48	57	1,368	137	3,288	40	960	9	216	28	672	26	624	7,224.0
Deer	2	200	3	300	1	100	18	1,800	18	1,800	7	700	3	300	3	300	9	900	6,400.0
Drum	2	6	3	9	1	3	38	122	98	314	38	122	32	96	13	39	59	177	888.0
Muskrat	1	2	3	6	1	2	29	61	26	55	9	19	6	12	8	17	24	50	224.0
Raccoon	1	17.5	2	35		...	6	105	4	70	2	35	2	35	1	17.5	2	35	350.0
Beaver	1	31.5	3	94.5		...	8	252	3	94.5	1	31.5	2	63	3	94.5	4	126	787.5
Soft-shell turtle		...	2	12		...	7	42	8	48	2	12	2	12	1	6	2	12	144.0
Walleyed pike		...	3	17	1	5.5	131	734	518	2,901	157	879	59	330	52	291	55	308	5,465.5
Channel catfish		...	2	6.5	1	3	12	38	28	90	5	16	2	6.5	2	6.5	4	13	179.5
Bullhead		...	1	0.5		...	4	2	35	17.5	18	9	1	0.5	3	1.5	1	0.5	31.5
Otter		...	1	12.5		...	1	12.5	2	25	1	12.5	1	12.5	1	12.5		...	87.5
Blanding's turtle		...	1	1.0		...	2	2.0	2	2.0		...		...		...	1	1.0	6.0
Painted turtle		...	1	0.5		...		...		...	1	0.5	1	0.5		...		...	1.5
Longnose gar		...		...	1	1.5	12	19	15	24	6	9.5	3	5	3	5	2	3	67.0
Bowfin		...		...	1	2	6	12	26	52	5	10	2	4	2	4	3	6	90.0

TABLE 27 (continued)

Species	Stratigraphic Level: II*b*		II*c*		II*d*		III*a*		III*b*		IV*a*		IV*b*		IV*c*		IV		Total Pounds
	No.	Pounds	No.	Pounds	No.	Pounds	No.	Pounds	No.	Pounds	No.	Pounds	No.	Pounds	No.	Pounds	No.	Pounds	
Snapping turtle	. . .		. . .		. . .		7	42	3	18	1	6	. . .		1	6	1	6	78.0
Elk	. . .		. . .		. . .		4	1,400	. . .		. . .		2	700	. . .		2	700	2,800.0
Bear	. . .		. . .		. . .		3	630	2	420	2	420	2	420	1	210	1	210	2,310.0
Dog	. . .		. . .		. . .		2	30	3	45	1	15	2	30	. . .		2	30	150.0
Perch	. . .		. . .		. . .		2	1.0	9	3.5	4	1.5	1	0.5	2	1.0	1	0.5	8.0
Largemouth bass	. . .		. . .		. . .		1	2.0	7	14	2	4	2	4	. . .		. . .		24.0
Northern pike	. . .		. . .		. . .		2	5	13	31	3	7	. . .		2	5	1	2.5	50.5
Wolf	. . .		. . .		. . .		2	60			. . .		. . .		. . .		1	30	90.0
Lake trout	. . .		. . .		. . .		1	14.5	1	14.5	2	29	. . .		. . .		. . .		58.0
Fisher	. . .		. . .		. . .		1	5	1	5	. . .		. . .		1	5	. . .		15.0
Blue-winged teal	. . .		. . .		. . .		1	0.5	2	1.0	. . .		. . .		. . .		. . .		1.5
Map turtle	. . .		. . .		. . .		1	0.5	1	0.5	1	0.5	. . .		. . .		. . .		1.5
Mink	. . .		. . .		. . .		1	1.5	1	1.5	. . .		1	1.5	2	3.0	1	1.5	9.0
Woodchuck	. . .		. . .		. . .		1	5.5	1	5.5	1	5.5	1	5.5	1	5.5	. . .		27.5
American bittern	. . .		. . .		. . .		1	4.0	1	4.0	1	4.0	. . .		1	4.0	. . .		16.0
Great blue heron	. . .		. . .		. . .		1	5	. . .		. . .		. . .		. . .		1	5	10.0

TABLE 27 (continued)

Species	Stratigraphic Level																		
	II*b*		II*c*		II*d*		III*a*		III*b*		IV*a*		IV*b*		IV*c*		IV		Total
	No.	Pounds	No.	Pounds	No.	Pounds	No.	Pounds	No.	Pounds	No.	Pounds	No.	Pounds	No.	Pounds	No.	Pounds	Pounds
Sandhill crane		...		...		...	1	8.5	1	8.5		...		...		...		...	17.0
Turkey		...		...		...	1	8.5	1	8.5		...		...		...		...	17.0
Marten		...		...		...	1	2.0		...		...		...		...		...	2.0
Hooded merganser		...		...		...		...	1	2.0		...		...	1	2.0		...	4.0
Smallmouth bass		...		...		...		...	2	3.0	1	1.5		...	1	1.5		...	6.0
Common mallard		...		...		...		...	1	2.0	1	2.0		...	1	2.0		...	6.0
Crow		...		...		...		...	1	2.0		...		...		...		...	2.0
Bobcat		...		...		...		...	1	15		...		...		...		...	15.0
Porcupine		...		...		...		...	1	10		...		...		...	1	10	20.0
Common loon		...		...		...		...	1	3.5		...		...		...		...	3.5
Passenger pigeon		...		...		...		...	1	0.5		...		...		...		...	0.5
Canada goose		...		...		...		...		...	1	5.5		...		...		...	5.5
Skunk		...		...		...		...		...		...		...	1	5		...	5.0
Pond slider		...		...		...		...		...		...		...	1	1.0		...	1.0
Total weight		281.0		518.5		165.0		6,795.0		9,399.5		3,317.5		2,254.5		1,717.5		3,251.0	27,699.5
Percent of Total Meat		1.0		1.9		0.9		24.5		33.8		11.9		8.1		6.2		11.7	...

live and dressed weights. In many instances those figures are at the maximum end of the species' range at the present time (William H. Burt, personal communication). The amount of meat contributed to the diet by the various species should therefore be taken for what it is, an estimate. It is useful in that it allows comparison of the relative amount of meat contributed by each species. It attempts to deal, in a quantitative way, with the size differences in the different kinds of animals hunted. Thus, this method is a tool toward determining which animals were most important in the diet.

There was no bird bone found in any Early Woodland area. Turtle was sparse, and virtually all of it came from the southwest levee area in level II*c*. The presence of the soft-shell turtle indicates a shallow marshy area at the edge of the river, at least for this period. There are four individuals, which strongly suggests some summer occupations at this level. The lack of turtle and bird in II*b* and II*d* may mean these were winter occupations.

The information as to what season(s) the site was occupied during Early Woodland times seems nebulous and contradictory; the seasonal indicators are not conclusive for any of the three levels. This could mean there were occasional occupations in different seasons of the year, but this can only be a tentative hypothesis. On the basis of my sample, a climatic interpretation cannot be made. Key species are simply absent. In another sample from the Schultz site, the UMMA excavations in 1962 and 1963, such species as marten, fisher, and bear were identified (Cleland, 1966). These species suggest a climate slightly cooler than that of the present, while my sample does not lend itself to such a hypothesis. The difference can be explained because neither of the samples was a random one. This is an illustration of the differences which can arise when interpretations must be based on small samples.

MIDDLE WOODLAND

During Middle Woodland times, a stockade was built on the levee above the channel area. The channel area was utilized throughout the entire period and showed the greatest concentration of bone material, number of individuals, and diversity of species. The southwest levee showed evidence of use for the whole period but the density of bone refuse was much less than that of the channel. Practically all bone refuse on the levee occurs in III*a* levels, and even here is much less than the amount found on the channel at this time. In the ceramic distribution and in the distribution of edible molluscs, there was an avoidance of the area inside the stockade, a seemingly conscious attempt to keep debris out of the stockade area. The density of faunal material is four times as great immediately outside the stockade as within it, thus corroborating this avoidance pattern. On the basis of the total amount of faunal debris and the number of individuals, the debris in the channel was four times as dense as on the levee outside of the stockade and eight times as dense as that within the stockade.

The three Middle Woodland levels, III*a*, III*b*, and IV*a*, show basically similar faunal assemblages, and the major food species appear in all levels. The only significant difference is that there are ten species of birds in III*b* as compared with five for III*a* and three for IV*a*. This possibly indicates longer periods of warm weather occupation or more occupations. However, as Table 27 shows, in terms of both number of individuals and in amount of dressed meat obtainable from these birds, their presence has no dietary significance compared to all other food animals. Another possibility is that the birds were prized for their plumage or bones. In this event, however, there would have been concentration on one or a few individuals. The most likely explanation is that III*b* occupations were the most intense, and therefore we have a better sample of the refuse of those occupations.

Of the twelve avian species in the Middle Woodland levels, only the turkey and crow are deciduous woodland species. The ducks, geese, loons, mallards, cranes, bitterns, heron, and even the snipe are aquatic birds, most of them preferring a marshy environment. As the turkey and crow only occur in III*a* and III*b*, it is possible that there was a local clearing of forested areas by IV*a*, but so few bones are concerned that it is not wise to do more than hazard a guess. The heron, American bittern, duck, crane, and passenger pigeon are only found in the Saginaw Valley in the warmer months of the year, and their presence shows at least some summer occupations for each level.

Throughout all three levels it can be seen that birds and turtles contribute less than two percent of the total meat poundage. It would seem that they were insignificant as food species, though both groups were undoubtedly abundant in the marshes and rivers near Green Point. This indicates hunting selectivity, probably based on the abundance of other game which would provide more protein and calories for the amount of energy expended. It is possible that the projected poundage from turtles is low, for it is calculated solely from unworked bone. In his analysis of Schultz worked bone, Murray (this volume) found that forty-one percent of the bone artifacts were from freshwater turtles. Since the percentage of usable meat on a turtle is so low, turtles were more likely caught for their shell than for their meat. All species found in Middle Woodland levels are river or marsh dwellers, and the Saginaw Valley is well within their present range of distribution. There are no exotic species that might have been imported as trade items.

The hunting of large game animals was of great importance in Middle Woodland subsistence patterns, as evidenced by the amount of meat provided by deer, elk, and bear (see Table 27). However, as a class, mammals declined in importance through Middle Woodland times. They provided almost two-thirds of the usable meat in III*a*, less than one-third in III*b*, and just over one-third in IV*a*. Though deer were probably abundant all year round, the large amount of antler recovered indicates fall-winter hunting. Smaller aquatic mammals such as beaver, muskrat, and raccoon were also extensively hunted. The majority of the nonaquatic species are those of a deciduous woodland or forest, but in III*a* and III*b* there was an element of animals preferring fairly dense, coniferous forests: bear, porcupine, fisher. Bear was also present in IV*a*; this is not surprising because many times its preferred habitat can be described as cosmopolitan, the scavenging being good near human activity. Cleland (1966:143) has postulated a Middle Woodland trend toward more open forests and greater amounts of woodland area. If this change was real, it was probably local in nature, as evidenced by the abundance of deciduous and coniferous forest species, and possibly was the result of a shift in the river's course. The bear, elk, fisher, wolf, and porcupine are no longer found in the area due to (1) movement of the mixed deciduous-coniferous forest belt further north and (2) virtual extinction of the bear, elk, and wolf in the area by white settlers.

Hunting techniques for deer can be reconstructed to some extent. Stalking methods were undoubtedly used, but probably not to a great extent. The population curve would be bimodal (the oldest and youngest deer being killed more frequently) if stalking were the major hunting technique. At Schultz, though the material is fragmentary, it seemed that there were immature, mature, and old individuals equally represented. There is thus a strong possibility that deer drives, or some similar method, were used. This would be a less selective hunting technique, and the individuals caught would have a normal age distribution. The explorer, Samuel de Champlain, described a Huron deer drive in October, 1615, in which one hundred and twenty deer were captured. Though this is, of course, much later in time than the Schultz Middle Woodland occupations, and though it describes an area further north, Champlain's account does give a vivid description of what was probably a similar method of hunting. The following passage is quoted from his account (Taylor, 1965:10):

> . . . September, 1615, (he) crossed Lake Ontario, and then followed course of river through Pigeon, Buckbarn, Deer, Clear, and Rice Lakes, Ontario.
>
> The cleared portion of these regions is quite pleasant. Hunting deer and bear here is quite common, and for the sake of the experience we had a hunt and captured quite a good number as we journeyed down. To do this four of (or?) five hundred savages placed themselves in line in the woods, until they reached certain points which jut out into the river; then marching in their order with bow and arrow in their hands, shouting and making a great noise to frighten the animals, they keep on until they come to the end of the point. In this way all the animals that are between the point and the hunters are compelled to throw themselves into the water, unless they pass through the line at the mercy of the arrows which are shot at them by hunters. Meanwhile, the savages posted in the canoes, ranged on purpose along the edge of the shore, easily draw near the stags and other animals, hunted and harried and very terrified.
>
> October, 1615, traveled up Napanee or Salmon River to Lake Loughborough and thence to a spot some 10 leagues distant toward Lake Simcoe where they 'waited for the capture of deer.'
>
> When this was made they went into the woods near a little grove of firs where they made a triangular enclosure, closed on two sides, open on one. This enclosure was made of great wooden stakes eight or nine feet in height, joined close together, and the length of each side was nearly fifteen hundred paces. At the extremity of this triangle there is a little enclosure, getting narrower the farther it goes, and partly covered with branches, with only one opening five feet wide, about the width of an average gate, by which the deer were to enter. They did so well that in less then ten days their enclosure was ready. Meanwhile, other savages went to catch fish, such as trout and pike of enormous size, of which we had no lack.
>
> When everything was completed, they set out half an hour before daybreak to go into the woods about half a league from their enclosure, keeping about eighty paces apart, each having two sticks which they strike together, walking slowly in that formation until they reach their enclosure. The deer, hearing this noise, flee before them until they reach the enclosure into which the savages force them to enter. Then the latter gradually coming together towards the opening of their triangle, the deer steal along the said palisades until they reach the extremity, whither the savages pursue them hotly with bow and arrow in hand, ready to shoot. And when the savages reach the extremity of their said triangle, they begin to shout and imitate the cry of wolves, whereof there are many that devour deer. The deer hearing this terrifying noise, are forced to enter the retreat by the small opening, whither they are very hotly pursued with arrows, and when they have entered, they are easily caught in this retreat, which is so well enclosed and barricaded that they can never get out of it. I assure you one takes a peculiar pleasure in this mode of hunting which took place every second day, and they did so well that in the thirty-eight days that we were there, they captured one hundred and twenty deer, with which they made good cheer, keeping the fat for the winter and using it as we do butter, and a little meat which they carry home for the feasts. They have other devices for catching deer, such as traps wherewith they cause the death of many.

Fish show a marked increase in importance as a food group from level III*a* to III*b*. The amount of meat they provided jumps from around one-third of the total in III*a* to over two-thirds in III*b*. This can only mean a shift in hunting emphasis and possibly a change in occupation patterns. That this change is not due merely to the greater size of the sample is corroborated by a similar percentage in IV*a* (sixty-one percent of the total is fish). The range in size of the fish species indicates fishing with nets or weirs which would take in all sizes indiscriminately from a thirty-pound sturgeon to a tiny half pound yellow perch, though fishing with spears was probably practiced. The wide variety and abundance of lake fish as well as river species indicates fishing was most intense during the spring spawning period. The lake trout is the only fall spawner. Its presence at all Middle Woodland levels can only indicate fall occupations for these levels; the lake trout would not have been found this far inland except during its spawning time. Locally, at least, the Tittabawassee River was silty-bottomed and probably somewhat weedy near shore, as evidenced by the three turtle species—soft-shell turtle, snapping turtle, and painted turtle—and four fish species—drum, bullhead, bowfin, and largemouth bass—all of which prefer this habitat. The other fish, found where the water is more clear and the bottom more sandy or gravelly, are the species which are generally present in the Saginaw Basin only during the spring spawning period. The abundance of such species shows the importance of exploitation of fish resources at this one time of the year.

Throughout the three levels, the channel area had by far the greatest amount of bone material on the site, both in numbers of fragments and in minimal numbers of individuals. This area was a natural place to dump and prepare fish, muskrat, turtles, etc., caught in the swamps and rivers. But all other types of vertebrate remains were found in this area. The channel thus seems to have been used as a refuse area, though possibly also a butchering and/or processing area for most of the game caught.

LATE WOODLAND

Level IV*b*, if it represents true occupations and not erosional deposition, would seem to show a shift to dependence on big game animals as the major source of meat: deer, bear, and elk contributed the greatest amount of meat of all food animals. However, if it was reworked, older material, the more fragile fish and bird bone would be destroyed and so would the bones of smaller mammals. Remaining would be precisely those bones which are most common in the IV*b* refuse: fairly dense, strong bones of the larger mammals. In occupation level IV*c*, fish were without question the most important source of meat. The category IV, as mentioned earlier, probably includes material from both Late Woodland periods, but it cannot be assigned to either, due to mixed stratigraphy. The relative dependence on fish and on mammals is thus not precisely known. As IV was found in units only on the levee, the high proportion of mammal may be because most of the fish refuse was out in the channel. Table 27, showing the composite of Late Woodland species and poundage, also obscures the dependence on fish in IV*c*.

There are three species of bird in IV*c*. The American bittern is the only one which would definitely be found in the Saginaw Valley only in warm weather. Turtles are also present in the level, indicating some warm weather occupations. The presence of one carapace fragment of the pond slider turtle (not found at the present as far north as the Saginaw Valley) does not necessarily mean there was a climatic warping at that time. There is no supporting evidence for such a change in the climate.

There are strong elements of deciduous and woodland mammalian fauna, such vegetational cover probably being near the site. Exploitation of the marsh area surrounding the site does not seem as

TABLE 28
BONE FRAGMENTS BY LEVEL

Class	IIb		IIc		IId		IIIa		IIIb		IVa		IVb		IVc		IV	
	No. of Bones	Percent of Level	No. of Bones	Percent of Level	No. of Bones	Percent of Level	No. of Bones	Percent of Level	No. of Bones	Percent of Level	No. of Bones	Percent of Level	No. of Bones	Percent of Level	No. of Bones	Percent of Level	No. of Bones	Percent of Level
Bird	...		...		...		6	0.2	23	0.2	3	0.2	...		3	0.2	2	0.2
Turtle	...		19	14.8	...		89	3.1	121	1.4	17	0.8	5	0.8	5	0.5	21	1.6
Mammal	9	.60	81	62.7	14	42.4	742	26.3	916	10.4	259	12.6	147	22.3	247	22.4	473	36.4
Fish	6	.40	29	22.5	19	57.6	1,975	70.4	7,774	88.0	1,776	86.4	507	76.9	848	76.9	803	61.8
Totals	15		129		33		2,832		8,838		2,055		659		1,103		1,299	

Stratigraphic Level

TABLE 29
INDIVIDUALS BY LEVEL

Class	IIb		IIc		IId		IIIa		IIIb		IVa		IVb		IVc		IV	
	No.	Percent of Total	No.	Percent of Total	No.	Percent of Total	No.	Percent of Total	No.	Percent of Total	No.	Percent of Total	No.	Percent of Total	No.	Percent of Total	No.	Percent of Total
Bird	...		...		...		5	1.4	9	0.9	3	1.0	...		3	2.2	1	0.5
Turtle	...		4	15.4	...		17	4.6	14	1.4	5	1.6	3	2.2	3	2.2	4	2.0
Mammal	5	62.5	12	46.1	2	22.2	77	21.1	63	6.5	24	7.7	22	16.2	22	16.2	47	23.0
Fish	3	37.5	10	38.5	7	77.8	266	72.9	889	91.2	281	89.7	111	81.6	108	79.4	152	74.5
Totals	8		26		9		365		975		313		136		136		204	

Stratigraphic Level

TABLE 30
MEAT BY LEVEL

Class	Stratigraphic Level																	
	II*b*		II*c*		II*d*		III*a*		III*b*		IV*a*		IV*b*		IV*c*		IV	
	Total lb.	Percent of Level	Total lb.	Percent of Level	Total lb.	Percent of Level	Total lb.	Percent of Level	Total lb.	Percent of Level	Total lb.	Percent of Level	Total lb.	Percent of Level	Total lb.	Percent of Level	Total lb.	Percent of Level
Bird	. . .		. . .		. . .		26.5	0.4	32.0	0.3	11.5	0.3	. . .		8.0	0.5	5.0	0.2
Turtle	. . .		13.5	2.6	. . .		86.5	1.3	68.5	0.7	19.0	0.6	12.5	0.6	13.0	0.7	19.0	0.6
Mammal	251.0	89.3	448.0	86.4	102.0	61.8	4369.5	64.2	2546.5	27.2	1225.0	37.1	1579.5	70.0	670.0	39.0	1992.5	64.3
Fish	30.0	10.7	57.0	11.0	63.0	38.2	2317.5	34.1	6752.5	71.8	2048.5	62.0	662.5	29.4	1026.5	59.8	1134.5	34.9
Totals	281.0		518.5		165.0		6800.0		9399.5		3304.0		2254.5		1717.5		3151.0	

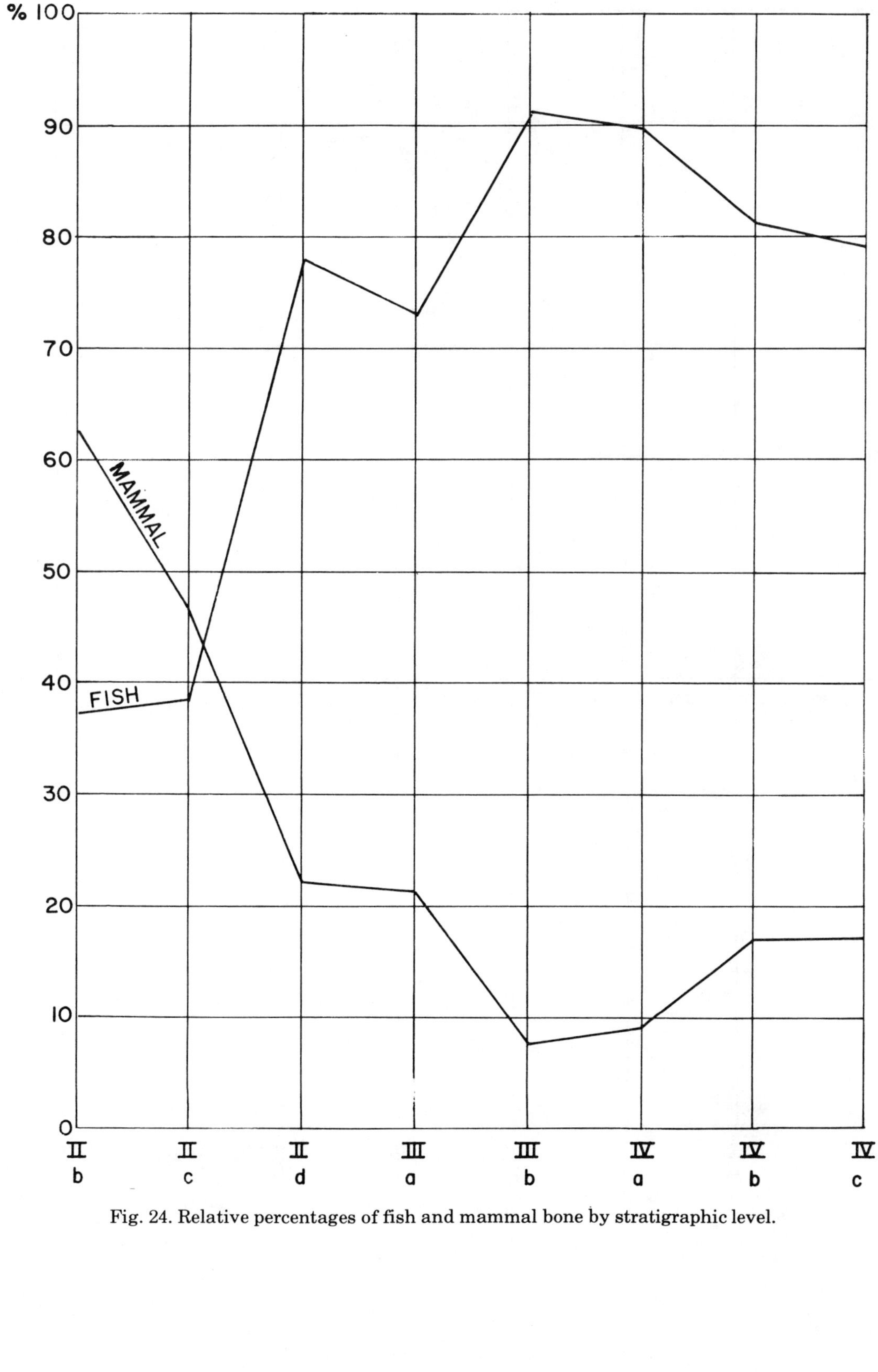

Fig. 24. Relative percentages of fish and mammal bone by stratigraphic level.

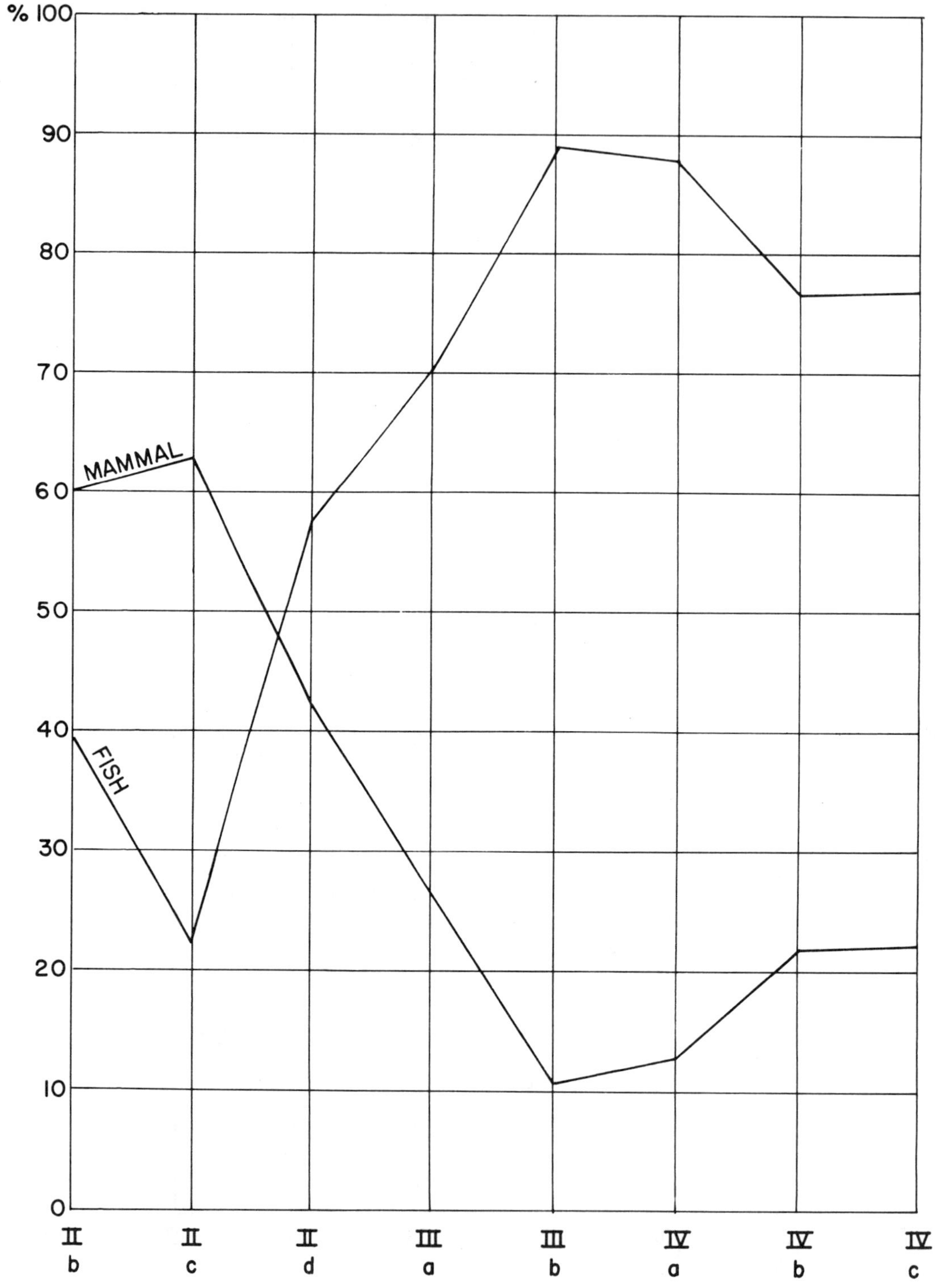

Fig. 25. Relative percentages of individual fish and mammals by stratigraphic level.

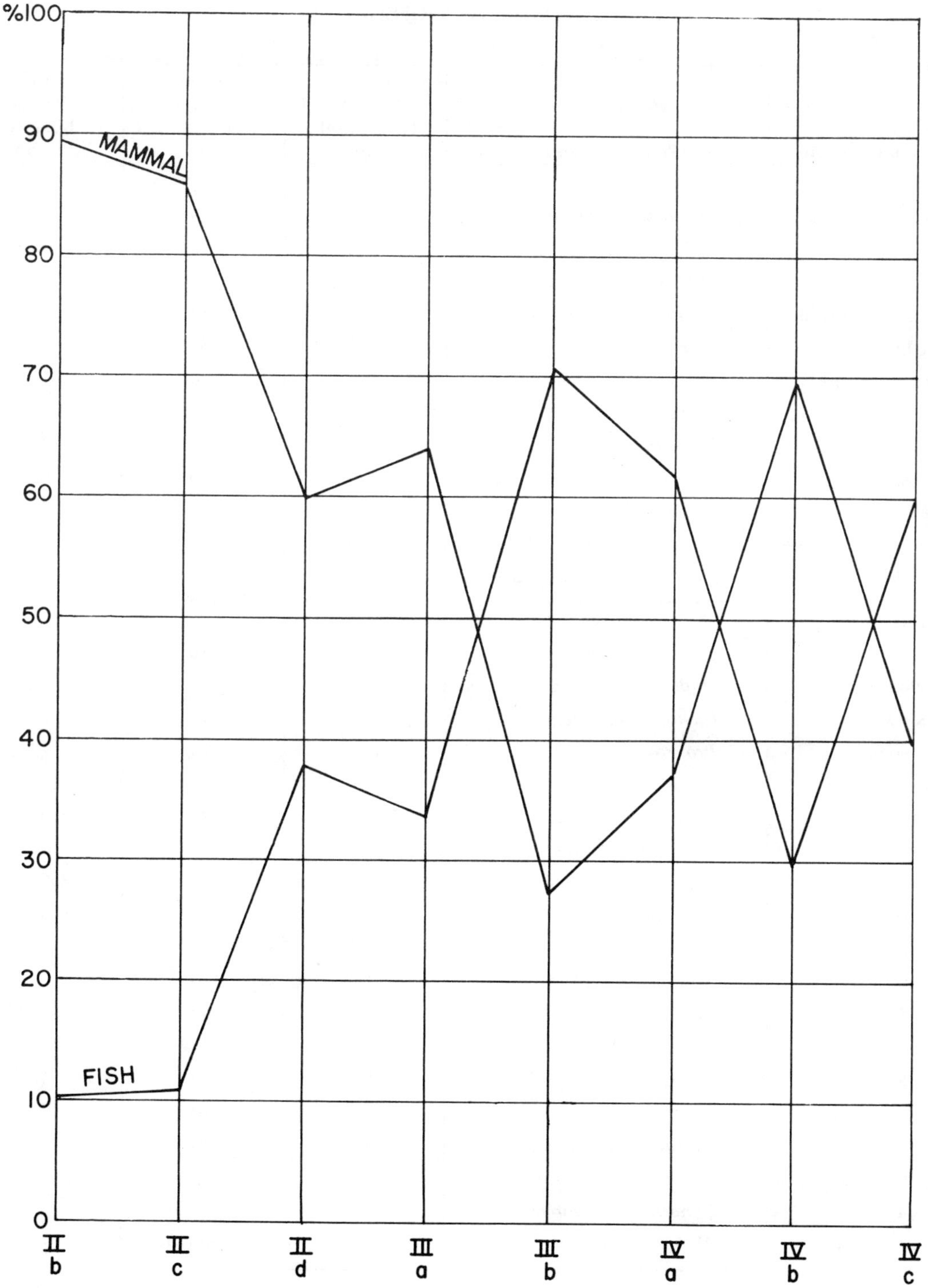

Fig. 26. Relative meat weights of fish and mammals by stratigraphic level.

TABLE 31
SPECIES IDENTIFIED AT THE SCHULTZ SITE

Common Name	Scientific Name	Average Weight/ Individual (Pounds)	Percent of Usable Meat	Pounds Usable Meat/ Individual
FISH				
Sturgeon	*Acipenser fulrescens*	30	80	24
Drum	*Aplodinotus grunniens*	3.7	80	3.0
Walleyed pike	*Stizostedion vitreum*	7	80	5.6
Channel catfish	*Ictalurus punctatus*	4	80	3.2
Bullhead	*Ictalurus* sp.	0.75	80	0.6
Longnose gar	*Lepisosteus osseus*	2	80	1.6
Bowfin	*Amia calva*	2.5	80	2.0
Lake trout	*Salvelinus namayoush*	18	80	14.4
Northern pike	*Esox lucius*	3.0	80	2.4
Yellow perch	*Perca flavescens*	0.5	80	0.4
Largemouth bass	*Micropterus salmoides*	2.5	80	2.0
Smallmouth bass	*Micropterus dolomieui*	2.0	80	1.6
MAMMAL				
Deer	*Odocoileus virginianus*	200	50	100
Muskrat	*Ondatra zibethica*	3	70	2.1
Beaver	*Castor canadensis*	45	70	31.5
Raccoon	*Procyon lotor*	25	70	17.5
Otter	*Lutra canadensis*	18	70	12.6
Bear	*Ursus americanus*	300	70	210
Dog	*Canis familiaris*	30	50	15
Elk	*Cervus caradensis*	700	50	350
Woodchuck	*Marmota monax*	8	70	5.6
Fisher	*Martes pennanti*	7	70	4.9
Marten	*Martes americana*	1.8	70	1.3
Wolf	*Canis lupus*	60	50	30
Bobcat	*Lynx* sp.	30	50	15
Mink	*Mustela vison*	1.8	70	1.3
Skunk	*Mephitis mephitis*	7	70	5
Porcupine	*Erethizon dorsatum*	15	70	10
Pine mouse	*Pitymys pinetorum*		Not a food species	
Bog lemming	*Synaptomys cooperi*		Not a food species	
Meadow vole	*Microtus pennsylvanicus*		Not a food species	

TABLE 31 (continued)
SPECIES IDENTIFIED AT THE SCHULTZ SITE

Common Name	Scientific Name	Average Weight/ Individual (Pounds)	Percent of Usable Meat	Pounds Usable Meat/ Individual
TURTLE				
Soft-shell turtle	*Trionyx spinifer*	30	20	6
Painted turtle	*Chrysemys picta*	2	20	0.4
Blanding's turtle	*Emydoidea blandingi*	4	20	0.8
Snapping turtle	*Chelydra serpentina*	30	20	6
Map turtle	*Graptemys geographica*	3	20	0.6
Pond Slider	*Pseudemys scripta*	6	20	1.2
BIRD				
Blue-winged teal	*Anas discors*	0.8	70	0.6
Common mallard	*Anas platyrhyncos*	2.8	70	2.0
Hooded merganser	*Lophodytes cucullatus*	3.0	70	2.1
American bittern	*Botaurus lentiginosus*	6.0	70	4.2
Crow	*Corvus brachyrhyncos*	3.0	70	2.1
Sandhill crane	*Grus canadensis*	12	70	8.5
Turkey	*Meleagris gallopavo*	12	70	8.5
Great blue heron	*Ardea herodias*	7	70	5.0
Common snipe	*Capella gallinago*	0.3	70	0.2
Common loon	*Gavia immer*	5	70	3.5
Passenger pigeon	*Ectopistes migratorius*	1.0	70	0.7
Canada goose	*Branta canadensis*	8	70	5.6

intense during IV*c* as during the Middle Woodland levels. Distribution of refuse on the site was also somewhat different than in the Middle Woodland times. The channel units showed the greatest concentration of fish bone. Turtle bone was concentrated up on the levee. Mammal bone was most common on the levee area though there was a fair amount in the channel area. The selective presence of fish in the channel units lends support to the idea of the channel as a processing area for the fish catches. It seems, though, that utilization of the channel area, whether for refuse or for processing meat, was not as great as during Middle Woodland times.

The wide size range of the fish caught again indicates fishing with nonselective fishing techniques such as nets or weir traps. The fish species are evenly divided between spring-spawning lake fish and species found year-round in the Green Point area. But the total poundage of lake fish is almost twenty times that of local fish, and almost twice that of the larger mammals. The Middle Woodland pattern of exploiting the spring runs of the lake fish seems to have been true of IV*c* occupations, too, because there was a primary dependence on these fish. The faunal material for this period suggests the site, at this time, was a spring-early summer camp where many people gathered to take advantage of the spring spawning runs.

VII

THE MOLLUSC FAUNA

David S. Brose

The University of Michigan Museum of Anthropology excavations at the Schultz site yielded over 16,000 identifiable molluscan remains of 41 species in good stratigraphic context. These molluscs were identified and counted by stratigraphic level and by feature. To avoid the error of counting fragmented specimens more than once, only a pair of identifiable hinge and beak portions of bivalve shells or the *unbilicus* to *operculum* portion of the gastropods (where present) were considered single individuals. While the resultant minimum number is certainly far below the total number of molluscs recovered from the excavations, the relative frequencies of each species represented should remain the same and any "random sampling error" introduced through this procedure will be ignored.

The analysis of snails present in archaeological sites is not a new phenomenon. In paleontology the use of molluscs as index fossils is well known, and efforts have been made in archaeological site reports to use the molluscs recovered as an index of time (e.g. Ral el Kelb, Lebanon), climate (e.g., Boyleston Street, Massachusetts; Lindenmier site, Colorado) or both. Often what seem to be overly general statements about climate or environment have been made on the basis of insufficient data (Lambert, 1952). It is hoped that this paper can avoid these mistakes.

In describing the molluscs from any archaeological site, there are two distinct methods by which to interpret the data. The first is analysis of the cultural selection for or against any particular species of mollusc at the site. The second major aspect of faunal interpretation is to attempt an environmental reconstruction of the site area through time. It is clear that these two aspects will be closely related and may often be inseparable. This does not mean that they are equivalent. The cultural vectors may result in the presence of locally nonextant species at a site as well as the exclusion of many prevalent ones, thus producing an inaccurate picture of the environment of the site unless these cultural factors can be recognized and adjustments made for them. At the Schultz site the first step we took was to discover those species which were imported onto the site for food. To accomplish this, the identifiable species from the general excavations were separated from those which had been recovered from fire pits, hearth areas, refuse pits and similar cultural features within the site. When this had been accomplished, it was clear that 13 species (Table 32) had produced over 54.7 percent of the molluscs from such features. These same 13 species represented only slightly over 14 per-

TABLE 32
FOOD ASSOCIATED SPECIES

Scientific Name	Common Name
Amblema costata	Three-ridge, wash board
Elliptio dilatatus	Spike, lady finger
Fusconaia flava	Pig toe
Pleurobema cordatum	Flat nigger head
Quadrulla pustulosa	Pimple back, warty-back
Cyclonaias tuberculata	Purple warty-back
Lasmigona costata	Fluted shell
Strophitus rugosus	Squaw foot
Lampsilus siliquoidea	Fat mucket
Ligumia (recta) latissima	Black sand-shell
Sphaerium sulcatum	Fingernail clam
Sphaerium rhombodium	Fingernail clam
Sphaerium striatum	Fingernail clam

cent of the total molluscs from the site. These molluscs, tentatively identified as "Food Species," gave the following counts within features:

1962 - 147

1963 - 330

1964 - 268

This made a total of 745 for these 13 species out of the 1,361 molluscs of all species recovered from such features. The relationship of these species to definite cultural areas of food preparation or discard seemed to be a highly significant one. The statistical test shown in Table 33 strongly indicates that the observed association was not due to chance. The difference in the relative composition of the mollusc groups in features and on the rest of the site is clearly seen in Figure 32 where the only significant differences occur in the species tentatively identified as those imported for food. Of these 13 species, over 80 percent of those not found in features which indicate definite use as food were found to occur in large midden deposits. In light of these data, as well as of the fact that many of these species found together in single features do not occur in similar natural environments, I have felt it safest to assume that these species are present as the result of cultural activity and are thus not to be treated with all other shell from the site when making environmental reconstructions.

The question of aboriginal utilization of terrestrial gastropods for food has often been raised by archaeologists. Where the answer has been affirmative the evidence advanced has often consisted of the high frequencies of land snail shells found in the midden deposits (Braidwood and Howe, 1960; Baker, 1941:53); ethnographic reports of such a dietary trait are scanty at best. Excavations on a late nineteenth century refuse area at Fort Mackinac, Mackinac Island, Michigan (20MK17), have yielded remains of *Anguispira alternata*, the most common terrestrial gastropod, in

TABLE 33
FOOD SPECIES AND FEATURES

Molluscs	O/E Food Species	O/E Other Mollusc Species	Total
From entire site	227/2, 763	12,465/11,975	14,738
From features described	745/255	616/126	1,361
Total	3,018	13,081	16,099/16,099
x^2=3933.3	df = 1	p>.0001	ϕ = .496

Pearsons C = .44 where upper limit = .707. This indicates a very strong relationship between the Food Species and the fire pits with charcoal and/or ash, and hearth areas.

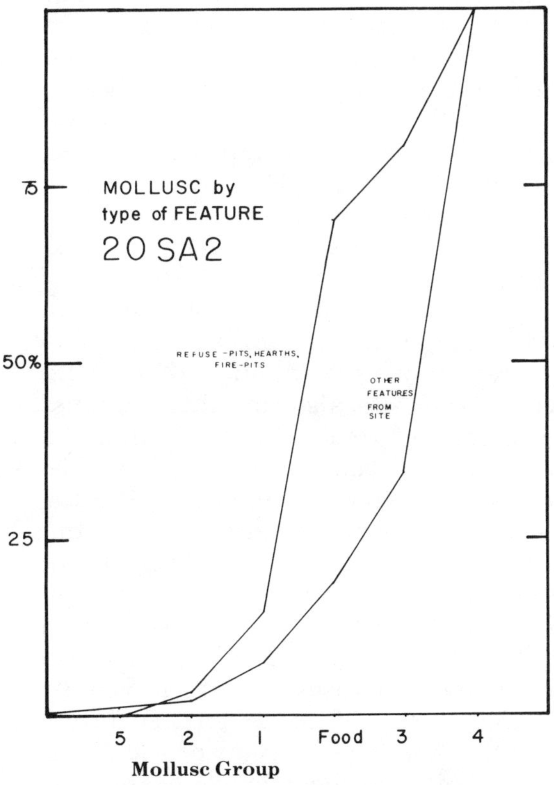

Fig. 27. Mollusc groups and features.

frequencies which, at some levels, surpass by 350 percent frequencies of this species in culturally sterile levels of equal volume on the site (Brose, 1967). This can in no way be taken to indicate that these snails were a food resource for the post-Civil War United States Army, but rather serves to show the attraction the decomposing organic material present in such refuse areas exerts on the omnivorous land species. At the Schultz site, the relative frequencies of the 10 terrestrial gastropod species which are found within features or in living areas reflect quite closely the relative frequencies of these species on the site as a whole for their level. This is not the case with the "food species" as has been indicated above. It seems clear that at the Schultz site the terrestrial gastropods are present in midden areas as scavengers. Their use as food resources is an untenable hypothesis.

Among those species considered as food species the *Sphaeriidae* represent quite a small mussel. Their occurrence in relatively large colonies on sand bottoms of permanent, shallow, slow streams may have made their collection worthwhile (Goodrich, 1932; Herrington, 1962). Most were recovered from two large features, both of which contained dense masses of sand and burned fish bone (Features 64-17, 64-42), and it is possible that these molluscs were carried into the site inadvertently. Since they may not have been intentionally collected, it has seemed safest to exclude them from consider-

TABLE 34
MOLLUSCS BY LEVEL

Preferred Environment	Early Woodland	Middle Woodland	Late Woodland
6 Species: Slow large rivers or still waters in rivers or lakes with stagnant water or much decaying vegetation, sand or mud bottom	242	609	129
4 Species: Swift streams or large well-moving clearer rivers with sand or gravel bottom	686	857	349

From: Baker, 1928; Van der Schalie, 1938, 1948; Allen, 1923; Goodrich, 1932; Ortmann, 1924.

ation in the next section of this paper.

Within the remaining species of food mussels, changes in the frequencies are clearly seen over time. This is noticeable in molluscs recovered from the excavations of all areas except the burial mounds themselves. Table 34 shows the changes within the food molluscs by cultural levels. It is clear from this table that the increased use of mussels for food noted in the Middle Woodland levels comes from the increased exploitation of resources available in slow drainage areas. At Early Woodland levels such an area seems to have been present on the site itself in the form of a slough or a cut-off channel of the Tittabawassee River, but this condition does not exist at later periods (Speth, this volume). During Middle Woodland times these mussels would have been available in the Shiawassee Flats, an area of poor drainage immediately to the southwest of the site across the Tittabawassee River. In the Early Woodland levels, attention was apparently directed to the swifter, more accessible drainage patterns of the Saginaw, Tittabawassee or Cass rivers to the north and east.

In terms of edibility there is no seasonality for mussels. They are digestible throughout the year. They are also rather strongly flavored. No evidence of fire scorching was noted on any of the mussel shells recovered from the Schultz site. This would indicate that these mussels were not roasted. At several Illinois sites (e.g. Havana; Baker, *et al.,* 1941:54-55) possible remains of small earthen ovens were encountered indicating that shellfish may have been baked. No such evidence is present at the Schultz site. Personal experience leads me to believe that they were not consumed raw as they are nearly unpalatable when uncooked. The high degree of association with cooking areas at this site also mitigates against this method of consumption. Boiling the shellfish is possible, but inadvisable. The loss of water, shrinkage of the tissues, and overall toughening of the meat which results from this latter method of cooking renders the animal " . . . as tough as shoe leather" (Van der Schalie, 1960:1). I would assume that the mussels recovered at the Schultz site were steamed in green vegetation below the fire. The location of the shells near fire pits and hearths would seem to support this assumption. This aboriginal method of shellfish preparation is well documented for the eastern Woodland Indians at the time of white contact (Underhill, 1953:57ff).

While there are no exact data on the amount of meat available from a fresh-water mussel, experiments conducted by

Fred Dustin during the summer of 1933, have indicated that an average "muckett" (*Lampsilus siliquoidea*) or "Three-Ridge" (*Amblema costata*) weighs 3 to 5 ounces with the animal inside. After being cleaned these same mussel shells weighed from 2 and 1/3 to 2 and 2/3 ounces (Dustin, Unpublished Journals: 1887-1933). Thus there would seem to be from 1/3 to 2/3 ounces of available meat in an average mussel. It should be noted that the two species on which Dustin's observations were based are the largest of those species identified as food resources at the Schultz site. If these data are correct, then the ratio of shell weight to weight of available meat is about 8 to 1. In a study of much smaller shellfish on the California coast (*Mytilus* and *Macoma* spp.), Cook has indicated an average shell weight of 17.3 grams and an average weight of available meat of 1.06 grams (Cook, 1959:51). This is a ratio of about 12 to 1. Few species of mussel recovered from the Schultz site excavations were as large as the two reported on by Dustin, and shells from those two species at the Schultz site averaged only 3.15 ounces or 89.3025 grams. A representative sample of 290 pairs of valves of the 10 species of mussels present at the Schultz site and identified as food resources produced an average weight of 36.11 grams for a pair of bivalve shells. This sample collection reflected the relative frequencies of occurrence of the respective species at the site. The *Sphaeridae* were not included in this sample. By assuming that the ratio of average weight of meat to weight of freshwater bivalve shell is 1 to 11, the average pair of mussel shell valves at the Schultz site represents about 3.28 grams of available meat or about 0.236 grams of animal protein. This meat would have a negligible vitamin content but would provide an excellent supplement of basic amino acids to a diet low in easily assimilated protein such as one depending on much vegetal food (Rose, cited in Cook, 1959:52). It is clear that if the molluscan resources formed an important dietary supplement to the inhabitants of the Schultz site, not all of them were processed or consumed at excavated portions of the site. Vastly greater amounts of animal protein were available as vertebrate remains (Cleland, 1966; Luxenberg, this volume).

The general intensification of molluscan food resources in Middle Woodland levels is also noteworthy. This sharply decreases in Late Woodland levels. In this respect one must bear in mind the smaller volume of both Early and Late Woodland levels at the site. This also seems to show that the Middle Woodland levels indicate the period of most intensive occupation despite the short time involved. This may be, in part, dependent on the newly utilized molluscan resources.

All of the mollusca used as food at the Schultz site are obtainable year-round. Studies have indicated that there is no "season" for mussels. They do not migrate into deeper water in winter, to return to the shoals with spring (Van der Schalie, 1938:75ff). They do, however, burrow into the bottom to a depth slightly less than the length of their siphons (about 3 cm) and become quite inactive until the water returns to a temperature of over 10 degrees centigrade. During the winter and early spring, the water currents tend to cover them with a thin layer of silt which makes them almost invisible (Van der Schalie, 1938:77). Since the few extant accounts of aboriginal shellfish collection seem to indicate that actual wading about in the water was required (Volney Jones, personal communication), the general difficulty of locating beds of

TABLE 35
MOLLUSCA RECOVERED FROM 20SA2
(1962, 1963, 1964)

Mollusca	Number
Mussels	
Amblema costata (Raf.)	1403
Elliptio dilatatus (Raf.)	784
Fusconia flava (Raf.)	403
Pleurobema (cordatum) coccineum (Conrad)	22
Quadrilla pustulosa (Lea)	92
Lasmigona costata (Raf.)	43
Strophitus rugosis (Swain.)	23
Lampsilus siliquoidea (L)	85
Obovaria subrotunda (Raf.)	2
Ligumia (recta) latissima (Raf.)	14
Actinonais carinata (Barnes)	1
Sphaerium sulcatum	21
Sphaerium rhombodium	85
Sphaerium striatum	40
Total	3018
Gastropods	
Valvata tricarinata (Say)	9
Pleurocera acuta (Raf.) *Goniobasis liviscens* (Menke)	1051
Campeloma decisum (Say)	844
Amnicola lustrica (Pilsbry)	358
Somatogyrus subglobulosis (Say)	9
Amnicola limosa (Say)	62
Pomatiopsis lapidaria (Say)	74
Stagnicola palustris (Say)	19
Lymnea columella (Say)	2
Helisoma anceps (Conrad)	61
Helisoma trivolvis (Say)	288
Helisoma companulatum (Say)	34
Stenotrema monodon (Rackett)	241
Mesodon thyroidus (Say)	481
Triodopsis albolabris (Say)	1579
Triodopsis multilineata (Say)	81
Retinella rhoadis (Pilsbry)	2
Anguispira alternata (Say)	7244
Anguispira (solitaria) kochii (Say)	68
Discus (cronkhitei) anthonyi (Pilsbry)	39
Helicodiscus parallelus (Say)	68
Haplotrema concavum (Say)	89
Succinea ovalis (Say)	361
Mesomphix (omphalina) cuprea (Say)	6
Busycon perversa	?
Marginella sp.	1
Total	16,089

mussels as well as the water temperature itself would argue that most mussel collecting was probably done between April and November.

Several species of mussels similar to those recovered in the excavations at the Schultz site were reported to occur in large quantities in the Saginaw-Shiawassee-Tittabawassee drainage prior to industrial pollution. Dustin's notes of his summers spent clamming off Green Point frequently mention collection of good numbers of "Natsua Muckett" *(Ligumia nasuta),* "Floater" *(Anodonta grandis),* "White Heel-Splitter" (*Lasmigoma complanata),* "Kidney Shell" (*Ptychobranchus fasciolaris*), "Angel Wing" (*Proptera alata*), "Rainbow Shell" (*Micromya iris* [*villosa*]), "Elk Toe" (*Alasmidonta marginata*), and "Paper Shell" (*Leptodea fragilis*). These were also commercially taken from various localities of the Shiawassee or Tittabawassee or Saginaw rivers (Dustin, Unpublished Journals: 1887-1933). Of these *L. nasuta* is commonly a Great Lakes species only rarely coming as far upstream as Green Point. The others are still common in unpolluted areas of this drainage system (Van der Schalie: personal communication). They were certainly present at the time of aboriginal occupation of the site. Of these seven available species of mussels, present but not utilized by the aboriginal population, four species, *Lasmigona complanata, Anodonta grandis, Leptodea fragilis* and *Proptera alata* were also available but unutilized at the Hopewellian McGraw site in Ohio (Stansbery, 1965:121-22). Of these species not used as food at the Schultz site *Proptera alata, Lasmigona complanata, Anodonta grandis, Leptodea fragilis* and *Ptychobranchus fasciolaris* were also all present in the Mississippi-Illinois drainage system (Parmalee, 1959:64; Baker, 1928; Van der Schalie, personal communication). There seems to have been selection against these same species for use as food, in spite of a general reliance on shellfish, at the Havana site (McGregor, 1952:54). At the Norton Mound site (Flanders, 1965), and in the Muskegon River series of sites investigated by E. J. Prahl in the summers of 1964-1965 (Prahl, personal communication) these several species were not utilized as food although they were present in the Grand River-Muskegon River drainage systems (Van der Schalie, 1948).

At the Manker site, the Snyders site, and the Pool and Irving Village sites in Illinois, freshwater bivalves formed a significant part of the aboriginal diet (McGregor, 1958:172). In spite of this, in the Manker, Snyders, and Pool sites not a single individual of either *Proptera alata, Anodonta grandis, Lasmigona complanata, Ptychobranchus fasciolaris, Micromya iris,* or *Leptodea fragilis* were found in village debris (McGregor, 1958: 162-63). At the Irving site, which McGregor feels is a rather late Hopewell in the Illinois area (McGregor, 1958:22, 29-30), *Anodonta grandis* accounted for 6 percent of early mussel remains and 6.8 percent of later ones. *Lasmigona complanata* and *Micromya iris* were both present at later levels of the Irving site, but totaled less than 0.3 percent. *Proptera alata* had a frequency of occurrence of from 1.5 to 2.6 percent at the Irving site, but this may be a factor of the Mississippian elements present there (McGregor, 1958:133). At the Irving site there is no areal provenience given for shell. A very early Hopewell site in the Illinois area, the Clear Lake Mound and Village site, has also produced *Anondonta grandis, Leptodea fragilis,* and *Lasmigona complanata* in the village debris (Schoenbeck, 1943:81) and fragments of *Proptera alata* from within the mounds (Baker, in Cole and Deuel 1937:267-70). At several Illinois Hopewell sites such as the Knight Mounds *Proptera alata* has been found as cut shell grave goods within the mounds (Flanders, 1965). In these areas, pre-, post-, and non-Hopewell village sites and mounds such as Dickson Camp, Whitenah Village, the Morton Mounds, and the Ogden-Fettie focus, have produced *Proptera alata, Anodonta grandis,* and *Lasmigona complanata* from village refuse and mound fill (Baker, in Cole and Deuel, 1937:267-68). *Proptera alata* and *Andonta* spp. were also recovered from the Steuben site, which is a rather late date Hopewell site. None of the other species indicated above were present (Morse, 1963:115-25).

As far as I can determine, there is no report in the literature of any individual of the species *Proptera alata, Anodonta grandis, Lasmigona complanta,* or *Leptodea fragilis* in an association that would indicate it was being used as food by a Middle Hopewellian population. At least one of these species (*Proptera*) would seem to have had some use as a raw material for the manufacture of artifacts used in mortuary complexes. The possibility of a Hopewell-related cultural avoidance of certain readily available freshwater mussel species for food would seem to be worthy of further investigation.

During the 1963 season, the excavations revealed the presence of a pattern of post molds in a circle with a diameter of 150 feet. The 1964 excavations further defined this pattern and intensive excavation both within and without this feature was undertaken. All features were noted in their relation to this post mold circle which has been designated as a stockade. Midden deposits and general areal analysis have supported the original stratigraphic interpretation that this stockade is a feature of the Middle Woodland levels. An analysis of the molluscs recovered from features which have been identified as hearths, fire pits or refuse pits with ash and/or charcoal has also reinforced this contention. The molluscs have been grouped by preferred habitat and arranged in terms of environmental location, with the exception of the 13 food species (Table 32) which have been treated as a separate unit. The frequency of occurrence of each of these groups has been analyzed by its stratigraphic position in terms of cultural level and in terms of its relationship to the circular post mold pattern. The results of this analysis are presented in a cumulative graph (Fig. 28). From this presentation it is clear that there is no significant difference in molluscs found within features at non-Middle Woodland levels which can be correlated with the post mold pattern. This would indicate that at both Early and Late Woodland levels the stockade had no

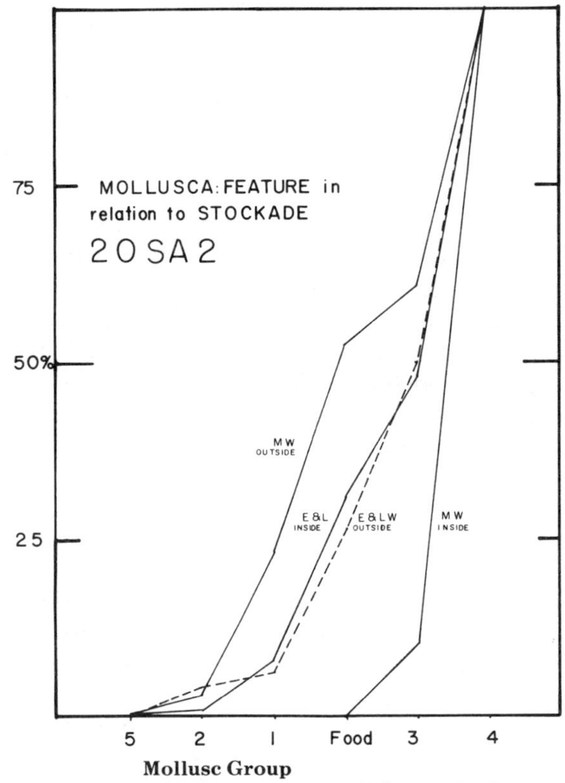

Fig. 28. Mollusc groups and the stockade.

significance for the distribution of molluscs. There is a wide divergence in molluscs found in similar features at Middle Woodland levels. The Middle Woodland features within the post mold pattern show a complete absence of all but terrestrial gastropods (and less than 10 percent of those were aquatic gastropods which live on vegetation on the banks of a large river and could have been introduced into the area by flooding). Those Middle Woodland features outside of the postmold pattern show a similar frequency of these naturally introduced groups, but also show a much higher frequency of occurrence for the food species than any other area or feature of the entire site. It is also interesting to note that while nearly 300 specimens of mollusca were identified from Middle Woodland features, less than 15 percent of these were from areas inside the stockade whereas in both Early and Late Woodland features, of over 350 specimens identified, over 40 percent occurred inside the post mold pattern. Further, while the Middle Woodland levels were nearly three times thicker than both Early and Late Woodland levels combined, they produced less than 25 percent of all molluscs recovered from within the post mold pattern. The conclusions to be drawn from these analyses are that there is some selection against the presence of any mollusc within the post mold pattern in Middle Woodland levels. In spite of an increased use of molluscs as food in Middle Woodland levels, there is very strong selection against these food species being introduced within an extant structure represented by the post mold pattern at the Middle Woodland levels.

Other than for use as food, the Schultz site has produced several examples of cultural selectivity of molluscs. Several artifacts were recovered which seem to have ornamental and/or ceremonial significance.* From the western mound at the Schultz site a multiple secondary burial was excavated from Middle Woodland levels. Among the grave goods were 33 drilled columella beads probably cut from *Busycon perversa* (Fig. 29, 6). A single long (7 cm) drilled columella bead (Fig. 29, 4) and a large fragment of a *B. perversa* shell were found on the surface to the south of this mound. These were common trade items in Hopewell burials in the Illinois area and were imported from the Gulf Coast, probably through several intermediaries. Also present with this burial were several cruder beads of the same style (Fig. 29, 2), cut from the hinge region of a local river mussel (probably *A. costata*). The ceramics from this burial indicate that it was late in the Middle Woodland period. The utilization of local resources for the production of ersatz prestige trade items may indicate a breakdown in existing communications at this period. At other areas of the site three cut columella beads of *B. perversa* were found within the stockade at Middle Woodland levels (Fig. 29, 5). A cut or ground shell bead of *Marginella* sp. (Fig. 29, 1) was found in a late Middle Woodland or possibly early Late Woodland level as was a single shell effigy claw (Fig. 29, 3) probably cut from the inner surface of a local river mussel. No other items of worked shell were present at the Schultz site.

Within the prepared floor of the western burial mound a single specimen of *Actinonais carinata* (Barnes) was recovered and two individuals of *Obovarias subrotunda* were noted within the mound fill itself. Both of these mussels are typically found in a large swift river mouth on a sand or gravel bottom or on an estuary in the Great Lakes. Neither occurred anywhere else at the site. The exact significance of these data is

*Editors Note: Additional shell artifacts were analyzed by Peter Murray and are included in his report in this volume.

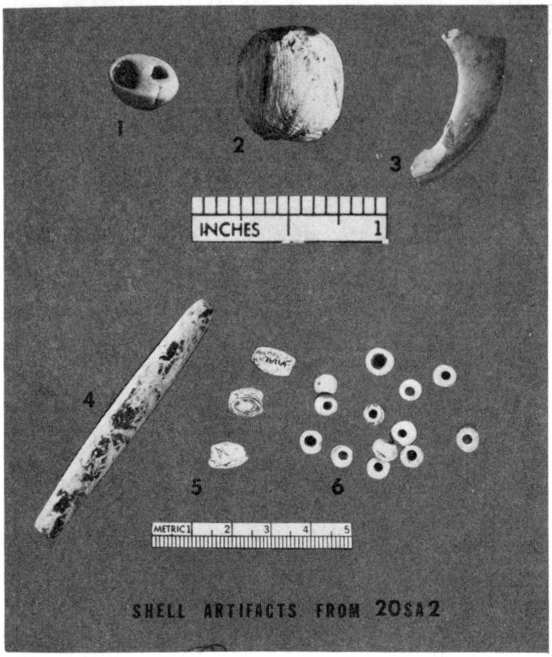

Fig. 29.

uncertain; but it could be that the sand for the prepared floors of the mound was obtained from the Saginaw river channel itself or perhaps even the Bay rather than from a nearby location. The importance of this will depend on whether it is an isolated occurrence or not. The data is far too insufficient to make any suggestions beyond those tentatively proposed. An equally possible and somewhat more probable explanation is that these represent subfossil remains which occupied the shallows of the Saginaw embayment of Lake Algoma. These shells could easily have been incorporated into the Algoma sands which were used to form prepared floors for these mounds. If this is true, these shells could have come from the immediate site area although from a depth of several feet (Speth, this volume).

During the late summer of 1965 a small field party, under the direction of Dr. James E. Fitting, excavated the easternmost mound at the Schultz site. Below the prepared sand floor at the center of the mound, a feature (F. No. 65-1) was encountered. This feature consisted of burned earth, charred wood, charcoal, ash, and mollusc shells (Table 36). Of 193 individuals identified, 177 or 91.7 percent were freshwater bivalves, 82 percent of which were *Amblema costata*. There were two species of aquatic gastropod represented by one individual each, and 14 terrestrial gastropods. The mussel shells were counted by pairs of valves, although it should be stressed that they were not so recovered. Many of the bivalve shells appeared to have been opened and the animal removed prior to deposition. The small frequency of the omnivorous terrestrial gastropods indicates that the mussel shells did not remain uncovered for any great length of time, but that they were not immediately covered by the prepared sand floor. In general, the frequency of the respective species reflects Middle Woodland frequencies more closely than either Early or Late Woodland.

In analysis of the molluscs found at the Schultz site for a reconstruction of the environment, those species discussed above have not been included. All other molluscs recovered from the 1964 season (and from those units of the 1962 and 1963 excavations where adequate control was kept) have been used. Initially, the entire site had been divided into three zones. The southern areas of the site which showed stratigraphic evidence of early incorporation into the river channel were designated Zone I. The areas within the post mold pattern were designated as Zone III. All other excavated areas were designated as Zone II. Zone III showed a smaller amount of shell at Middle Woodland levels which is probably culturally determined as has been noted above. Zone I showed a slightly higher frequency of aquatic gastropods which would be expected from the closer prox-

TABLE 36
MOLLUSCAN REMAINS FROM 20SA2
(1965 Season)

Location	Mollusca	Number
Mound Fill	*Anguispira alternata*	41
	Triodopsis multilineata	5
	Amblema costata	86
	Fusconia flava	12
	Cyclonaias tuberculata	6
	Lampsilus siliquoidea	2
Sub-floor concentration (F. No. 65-1)	*Anguispira alternata*	9
	Triodopsis albolabris	3
	Triodopsis multilineata	1
	Lymnea columella	1
	Stagnicola palustris	1
	Amblema costata	145
	Elliptio dilatatus	14
	Fusconia flava	9
	Cyclonaias tuberculata	6
	Lampsilus siliquoidea	2
	Quadrula pustulosa	1
Total		344

imity of the river. In general the analysis of the molluscs at the site showed no significant differences between zones. In order to produce a general picture of the environment of the site as a whole occupational area, changing through time, all areal zoning has been ignored and no material recovered from features possibly associated with food preparation or refuse has been included. What we are left with are changes in the relative frequencies of different mollusc groups recovered from non-midden floors and culturally sterile areas throughout the entire site.

The molluscs used for this reconstruction comprised 24 species (excluding the 17 species which have been culturally introduced) and have been grouped into five environmental zones based on preferred habitat. The various groups are listed below:

Group 1: Aquatic gastropods occurring along banks or on vegetation in water of slow rivers or streams with slow to moderate current a few feet in depth, or in river fed lakes.
- *Valvata tricarinata* (Say)
- *Goniobasis livescens* (Say)
- *Somatogyrus* sp.
- *Amnicola lustrica* (Pilsbry)
- *Lymnea columella* (Say)
- *Helisoma campanulatum* (Say)

Group 2: Aquatic gastropods occurring in marshes, swamps, sloughs, or shallow ponded water, generally under 1.5 feet in depth and always with decaying vegetation, generally muddy bottoms.
- *Amnicola limosa* (Say)
- *Pomatiopsis lapidaria* (Say) (amphibious)
- *Lymnaea* (Staginicola) *palustris* (Say)
- *Helisoma trivolvis* (Say)

Group 3: Aquatic gastropods occurring in small, relatively swift streams or creeks. Generally shallow water with *Helisoma* in pools.
- *Campeloma decisum* (Say)
- *Helisoma anceps* (Conrad)

Group 4: Terrestrial gastropods occurring in damp deciduous forests (generally river valleys) of elm and hickory.

Stenotrema monodon (Rackett)
Mesodon thyroidus (Say)
Triodopsis albolabris (Say)
T. multilineata (Say)
Anguispira alternata (Say)
A. solitaria (Say)
Discus cronkhitei anthonyi (Pilsbry)
Helicodiscus parallelus (Say)
Haplotrema concavum (Say)
Mesomphix cuprea (Say)

Group 5: Terrestrial gastropods occurring in dry shady deciduous forests with maple and oak, or beechmaple.

Retinella rhoadsi (Pilsbry)
Succinea ovalis (Say) (within the drier forests near streams or upland swamps)

(After Baker, 1928, 1939; Pilsbry, 1939, 1940, 1946, 1948; Goodrich, 1932; Burch, 1962; Tuttle, Clayton and Laird, 1964).

I have proceeded on the assumption that those gastropods recovered from areas of the site which are not, or were not at the time of deposition, stream or river bank, were carried into the area by seasonal flooding. Some of this flooding did not quickly evaporate or run off, thus leaving pools of water standing in topographic depressions for several weeks or even months. These are generally represented by small concentrations of aquatic gastropods and an absence of those bivalves which would be expected if these areas were permanent drainage features. The preferred habitat of many of these aquatic gastropods is rather specific as to stream size and flow as well as bottom conditions. This has enabled me to deduce the local drainage systems generally extant at the time of deposition. In this respect I have had to assume that small creeks and streams were as liable to flood action as the major river system. In the absence of entrenched stream beds this is a tenable hypothesis. Unfortunately, while flooding of the larger rivers has been documented, the smaller tributaries have been generally ignored (Wright, this volume).

Like most other investigators attempting an environmental reconstruction, I have assumed that the habitat preferences of the terrestrial gastropods recovered from the excavations has not changed in the last several thousand years (Cheatum and Allen, 1966:42). The habitat preference of many of the more common terrestrial gastropod species is generally known (Van der Schalie, 1947:174-75), but exact data on individual ranges and movements or initiation of new colonies is lacking (Boycott, 1929:221-24). Species which are generally forest dwellers are suspected to cross rather broad stretches of inhospitable territory to attain preferred ecological zones with a relatively high frequency (Van der Schalie: personal communication). Since most species feed on decaying vegetation, food is seldom so scarce as to be an important factor in localizing new colonies. However, the terrrestrial gastropods found in the highest frequencies at the Schultz site (*A. alternata, T. albolabris, S. ovalis*) are omnivorous and would be drawn from the nearby forest to any clearing where there was a significantly great amount of organic decomposition. If the activity of these species is assumed to be more or less constant, and if the degree of organic decomposition is also assumed to remain the same for any level of the site, the presence of such species will indicate the nature of forest cover and proximity to the site area.

The frequency of occurrence of the species with different tolerance for moisture and temperature conditions has been used to create some sort of index to determine climatic conditions contemporary with the deposition of levels within the site. This information may, of course, reflect merely microenvironmental conditions. A surer control would have been to use the bivalves to determine stream flow conditions as well as temperature and limpidity of water. The

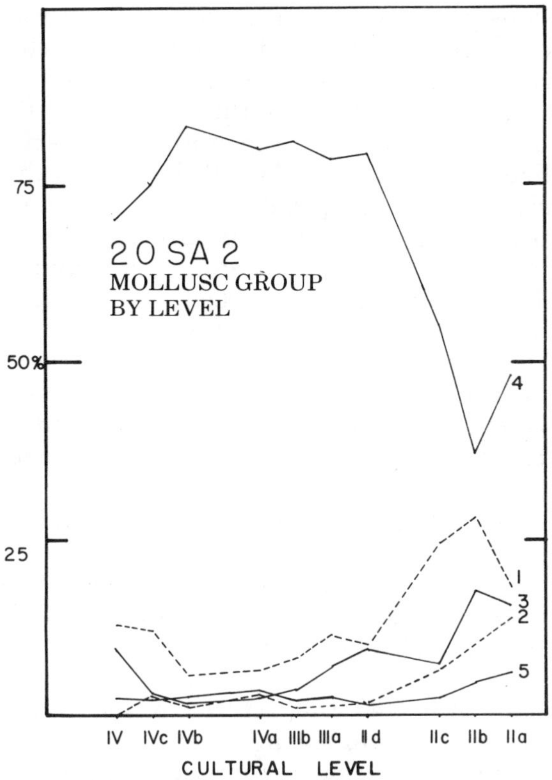

Fig. 30. Occurrence of mollusc groups by cultural levels.

cultural selectivity of these molluscs has destroyed this possibility. The following environmental picture is based, therefore, on gastropods alone. These groups have been arranged by their frequency of occurrence within each cultural level (as defined by Fitting, 1964), and the results of this have been shown in a graph (Fig. 30). This graph shows the relative frequency of each environmental group for each level, that is, the changes in the composition of the molluscan fauna over time. In this manner, the general environment of the site area may be reconstructed.

Level II*a*: This level represents a stratigraphic transition prior to the Early Woodland occupations of the site. There seems to be little forest cover in the immediate site area. The climate may be somewhat drier and cooler in general than at present. There are small swift creeks in the general area, but the site itself, and especially its southern areas, represent the bank of a slough or stagnant water condition with seasonal overflow.

Level II*b*: This level represents an arbitrarily limited Early Woodland occupation. The cover of deciduous forest seems to be less in evidence than at the earlier level, and drainage patterns seem to have improved but with poor runoff to most small streams. There is some decrease of swampy conditions at the site. Flooding from the larger rivers seems frequent. Climate may be somewhat damper.

Level II*c*: This level represents an intensive Early Woodland occupation at the site. There is an increase of deciduous forest cover on the site itself. The climate seems to be more moist although the swampy environment is little in evidence. Minor drainage patterns show a decrease and the Tittabawassee River seems to be moving to the south away from the site. Flooding is less frequent at this level. Lower Level II*c* has been dated at 530 BC ± 150 (M-1524) and 540 BC ± 130 (M-1525).

Level II*d*: This level seems to represent a cultural hiatus at the site. There is a great increase of hickory and elm forest at the site with the climate quite similar to present conditions. Minor drainage patterns continue to decrease in the site area. The major river system shows some decrease in flooding, but there are areas of the site where ponded water stands seasonally.

Level III*a*: This level represents the early Middle Woodland occupation at the site. The heavy deciduous forest cover seems to decrease in the site area itself but not much beyond the occupation areas. Climate seems to be slightly damper than present and perhaps slightly warmer.

Level III*b*: This level is the intensive middle Middle Woodland occupation. There is a slight increase of deciduous forest cover beyond the immediate site area. Most minor drainage patterns seem increased, but the Tittabawassee-Saginaw rivers seem to show somewhat less frequent flooding. Climate is probably slightly damper than present. There is a major decrease of deciduous forest on the site itself.

Level IV*a*: This level is an arbitrarily limited late Middle Woodland occupation of the site. While forest cover continues to decrease at the site itself, the presence of *A. alternata* and *H. parallelus* indicate that heavy deciduous forest cover exists in the area. Climate may be considerably drier and *Mesomphix* indicates it was certainly much cooler than earlier levels. There is no evidence for any minor drainage pattern within the site area. The major rivers seem to evidence considerably less flooding. A feature from the upper part of the level is dated A.D. 380 ± 100 (M-1841).

Level IV*b*: This level is arbitrarily limited and represents the transition to Late Woodland. It should date *ca.* A.D. 500-600. Heavy deciduous forest cover at the site as well as in the general area. Climate may be slightly drier than present. There are no minor drainage patterns or ponded water at the site. The major rivers seem to show a slight increase in flooding.

Level IV*c*: This level represents the Late Woodland period at the site and should date *ca.* A.D. 600-1000. At this level the deciduous forest cover shows a marked decrease on the site itself. There is an increase of minor drainage pattern within the site area, and the major rivers show evidence of frequent flooding. There seem to be some areas of the site where ponded water stood seasonally. The climate may be slightly warmer than present and is certainly much damper than earlier levels.

Level 5 general: This level represents the surface and plow zone at the site. It seems to show an increase in forest cover and improved drainage patterns, but this level is so disturbed by recent agricultural activity that any environmental inferences seem unwise.

It should be kept in mind that molluscs may reflect changes in the environment that would not affect the human population of the area. Often molluscs are merely indicative of a microclimate which may be at variance with general conditions. In spite of these limitations, it is interesting to note that the trend to drier climatic conditions in Levels III*b* and IV*a* would agree with a general climatic deterioration described by Griffin for the end of Middle Woodland times (Griffin, 1961*a*:154). The postulated periods of milder climate for Middle Woodland, 200 B.C.—A.D. 300, and Late Woodland post-A.D. 1000 (Griffin 1961*a*:153, 154) are also reflected in the data from the Schultz site.

At the Schultz site, analysis of the molluscs recovered from three years' excavations has revealed a picture of the natural environment of the site and several cultural activities of the inhabitants. In general one could say that at no time do the molluscs indicate a prairie or prarie-like environment. At all levels of the site there occur large numbers of terrestrial gastropods which inhabit deciduous forests. The climatic changes postulated do not seem to have been of sufficient magnitude to create a natural open grassland of any signficant size anywhere near the site prior to A.D. 1200, after which the stratigraphy is too distrubed to be of much value in environmental reconstruction. One may speculate that the cooler drier period following the Middle Woodland occupation of the site was contributory to both the postulated breakdown in trade and the collection of shellfish from areas to the southwest of the site. This climatic variation may also have initiated the return to the larger deeper rivers of the north and east as the principle location for mussels. Of the 41 species which have been identified from this site, 13 species have been interpreted as food resources and two species have been interpreted as trade items. With the exception of the last two species *(Busycon perversa* and *Marginella* sp.) all of the remaining species are presently thought to occur in Saginaw County, although due to pollution of the Tittabawassee River, many of the mussels are no longer present at the site area.

ACKNOWLEDGEMENTS

Support for much of the analysis was through NSF-USEP Grants GE-2782 and GE-6226. I was aided in specific identification by Earl J. Prahl and David Rupp. David Rupp also assisted in the species-level correlations. I am especially grateful to Professor Henry Van der Schalie of the Zoology Department, University of Michigan, who gave every possible assistance and read the manuscript.

VIII

NOTES ON SOME LATE MIDDLE WOODLAND COPROLITES

Andrew McClary

The last several years have seen increasing interest in recovering evidence of human parasites from fecal material associated with archaeological sites. To date, evidence of parasites has been obtained from the intestinal contents of mummies from Peru, East Prussia and Denmark; coprolites from Peru, Israel and the southwest United States; cesspits from England; and cultural soils from Poland (Callen and Cameron, 1960; Pike, 1967; Pike and Biddle, 1966; Samuels, 1965).

The following description covers portions of what appeared to be twenty coprolites recovered from the Late Middle Woodland level in the channel area at the Schultz site. It is the first analysis of coprolites from the Michigan area.

METHODS

Recovered material took the form of fragments which were varied in shape, and generally small, normally ranging in weight from a fraction of a gram to a few grams, although one large fragment (coprolite No. 18) weighed 13 grams. Coprolites were generally hard and dessicated, such that a scalpel was needed to break them open. Although variation occurred, color was normally dark brown to tan externally, several shades lighter internally. With the exception of one coprolite, texture resembled hardened soil. One coprolite (No. 18) differed from others in that it was largely composed of a coarse matted plantlike material. To date, no entirely satisfactory method of distinguishing human from nonhuman coprolites has been developed. The rather small size of the coprolite fragments and the one fragment with a heavy inclusion of matted material suggested dog coprolites, an assumption reinforced by microscopic findings, as indicated later.

Coprolite fragments were examined as follows: After records of weight, texture, and so forth were made, fragments were gently broken apart with a scalpel and probe. With one or two exceptions. fragments contained numerous embedded objects such as bits of bone and shell. These were removed and stored dry for later examination. The disassociated coprolite fragments were then immersed in a rehydrating solution, so as to soften them and aid in separating any parasite eggs from surrounding material. Two rehydrating solutions were tried; trisodium phosphate as used by Callen and Cameron (Callen and Cameron, 1960) and EDTA (ethylenedinitrilo tetraacetic acid disodium salt) as used by Samuels (Samuels, 1965). The latter solution was used for the major portion of the study. Fragments were placed in rehydrating solution, placed in a refrigerator for at least 72 hours, and agitated on occasion so as to further dissociate them. After rehydration the coprolite material, now in sediment form, was washed free of rehydrating solution, and repeated wet mounts made for microscopic examination. During this process, a few samples of sediment from each coprolite were mounted in glycerine jelly so as to form a semi-permanent record. Early in the examination stage, attempts were made to recover parasites from sedimented material by use of the zinc sulfate floatation method (Faust and Russell, 1964). After several coprolites had yielded negative results this procedure was discontinued.

RESULTS AND DISCUSSION

Macroscopic observations

Coprolites yielded numerous bone fragments. These were typically unidentifiable, although one recognizable fish vertebra was recovered from one coprolite. Other macroscopic objects included fish scales, shell, bits of plant tissue, and what appeared to be carbonized material.

Microscopic observations

Objects of an obvious organic nature occurred with surprising infrequency on prepared slides. A typical slide (with a preparation area of 22 by 50 mm) would show only ten to twenty such objects. Most common were pollen grains and spores of various kinds. A variety of other objects occurred in lower frequency. Some examples of microscopic objects encountered are shown in Figure 31.

In one coprolite (No. 14) an object strongly suggestive of a taeniid egg was observed* (Fig. 32). The taeniids (Phylum Plathelminthes, class Cestoidea, family Taeniidae) typically have a life cycle involving two hosts. The adult or "tapeworm" stage of the parasite inhabits the intestine of a vertebrate "definitive host" where it produces large numbers of eggs which pass from the definitive host with fecal matter. If these eggs are ingested by a second species of vertebrate called the "intermediate host," they will develop into a larval stage and become inactive within the intermediate host's tissues. If these tissues are then eaten by a vertebrate capable of being a definitive host, the parasite becomes active and develops into an adult tapeworm, thus completing the cycle.

Assuming that the object from coprolite 14 is indeed a taeniid egg, this would suggest that the Schultz site coprolites are from a dog or dogs, as the only two species of taeniid in which the egg laying stage occurs in man require the pig or domestic cattle as intermediate hosts. A number of taeniids are found in dogs. Of these, one, *Echinococcus granulosus*, can cause a serious human health problem, and will thus be considered further. A sylvatic cycle of this parasite is known to exist in northern North America, involving wolves and other carnivores as definitive hosts and moose, elk, deer or other herbivores as intermediate hosts (Miller, 1953; Magath, 1954; Meltzer, et al., 1956; Sweatman and Williams, 1963). Through eating herbivore offal, domestic dogs can "break into" this cycle as definitive hosts (Miller, 1953; Magath, 1954). If infected dogs then associate with humans under unhygenic conditions, the latter may ingest the eggs and become intermediate hosts. Methods of transmittal to man from the dog can be through food or water containing eggs, through soiled clothing, or simply by means of hand contact with the pelts of infected dogs (Miller, 1953; Magath, 1954; Rausch, 1952). Once ingested by man, *E. granulosus* eggs develop into larval forms which pass via the blood stream into the lungs, liver, or other organs, after which they transform into "hydatid

*I am indebted to Drs. E. O. Callen and Eugene Meerovitch of McGill University, Toronto, for aid in making tentative parasite identifications.

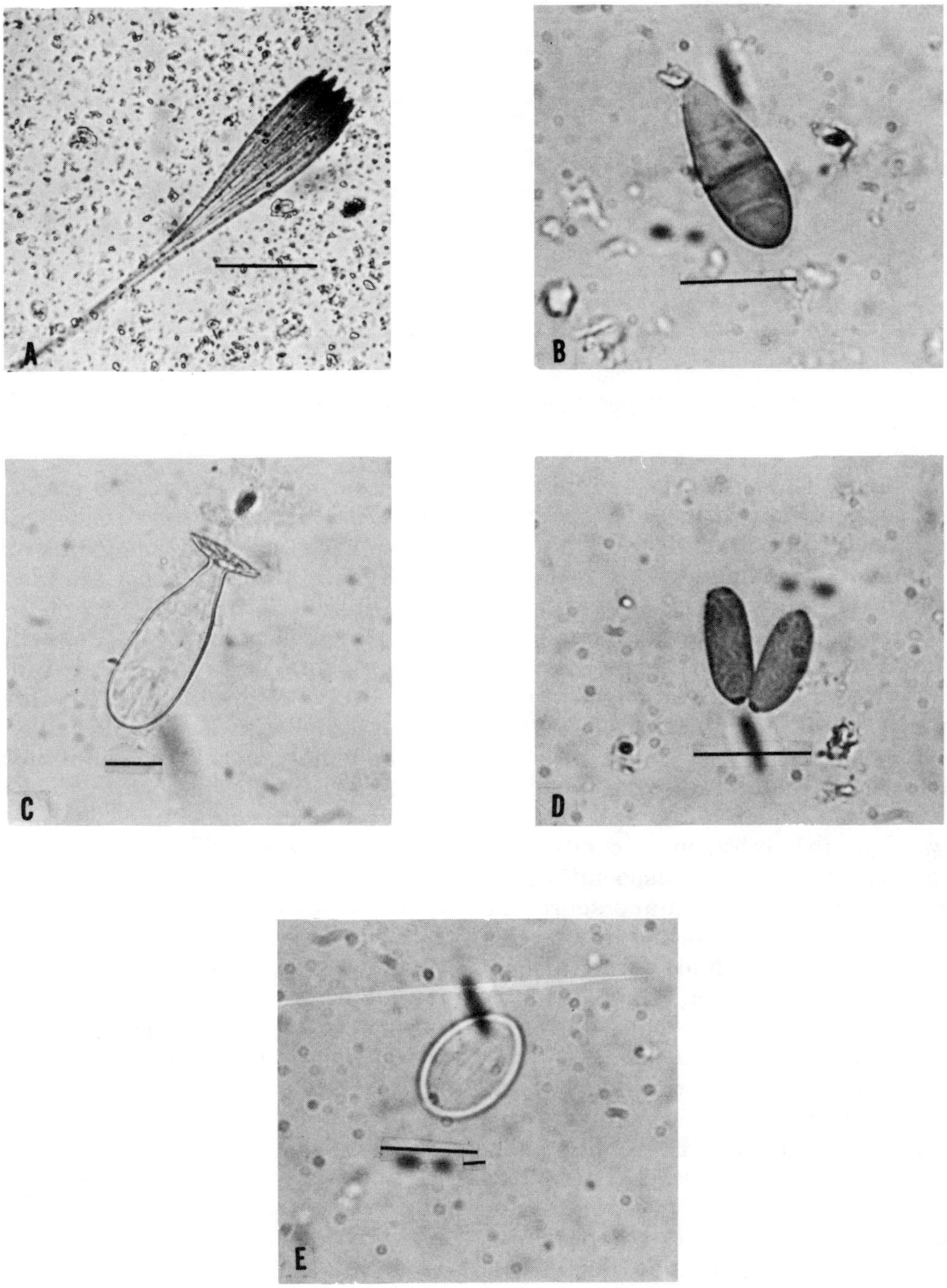

Fig. 31. Microscopic objects in Schultz coprolites.

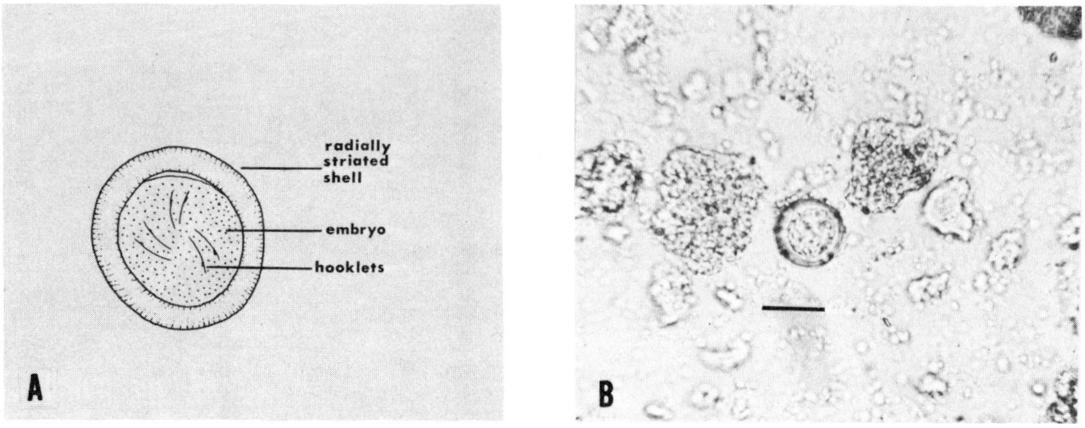

Fig. 32. Taenid eggs in Coprolite No. 14.

cysts," liquid filled vesicles containing numerous embryo worms. These cysts enlarge slowly, and after 10 or more years may reach tremendous size (Faust and Russell, 1964). In early stages of infection, symptoms of hydatid disease are commonly absent. Later stages may be characterized by allergic reactions, gastro-intestinal and respiratory symptoms (Rausch, 1952).

Incidence of hydatid disease is high today among Canadian Indians. This is partly due to unhygenic conditions, and partly to the close association of Indian with dog. The primary source of infection is apparently the sylvatic cycle, with dogs receiving their parasite load from this source (Miller, 1953; Meltzer et al., 1956; Rausch, 1952; Poole, 1957).

Assuming that *E. granulosus* was present in North America prior to contact, it can be argued that the occupants of the Schultz site would have been likely candidates for hydatid disease. This view is supported by the presence at the site of the species necessary to complete the cycle (dog, elk, deer) and by the probability that among people such as occupied the Schultz site, hygenic conditions conducive to egg transmittal would be likely to exist.

In coprolite 8, several objects suggestive of *Diphyllobothrim latum* eggs were found (Fig. 33). Diphyllobothrids (phylum Plathyhelminthes, class Cestoides, family Diphyllobothriidae) include several species which occur in the dog. Of these, *Diphyllobothrium latum* is also found in man. As with the taeniids, the life cycle of diphyllobothrids also involves more than one host, but is somewhat more complex. The adult tapeworm, *D. latum,* which can measure up to 10 meters in length, inhabits the intestines of fish-eating mammals, including the dog, fox, mink, bear and man. Eggs passing from the intestine of this definitive host will, if they reach water, hatch into a swimming "coracidum" larval stage. If this larva is eaten by a copepod, it will further develop into a "procercoid" larva. If the infected copepod is in turn eaten by a fish, such as the perch or northern pike, the larva will develop into a "sparagnum" stage. If the fish is then eaten raw or semicooked by one of the earlier mentioned mammals, the larva will develop into an adult tapeworm, thus completing the cycle (Magath and Essex, 1931; Wardle, 1935; Vik, 1964).

Symptoms of diphyllobothriasis, or fish tapeworm disease, include abdominal dis-

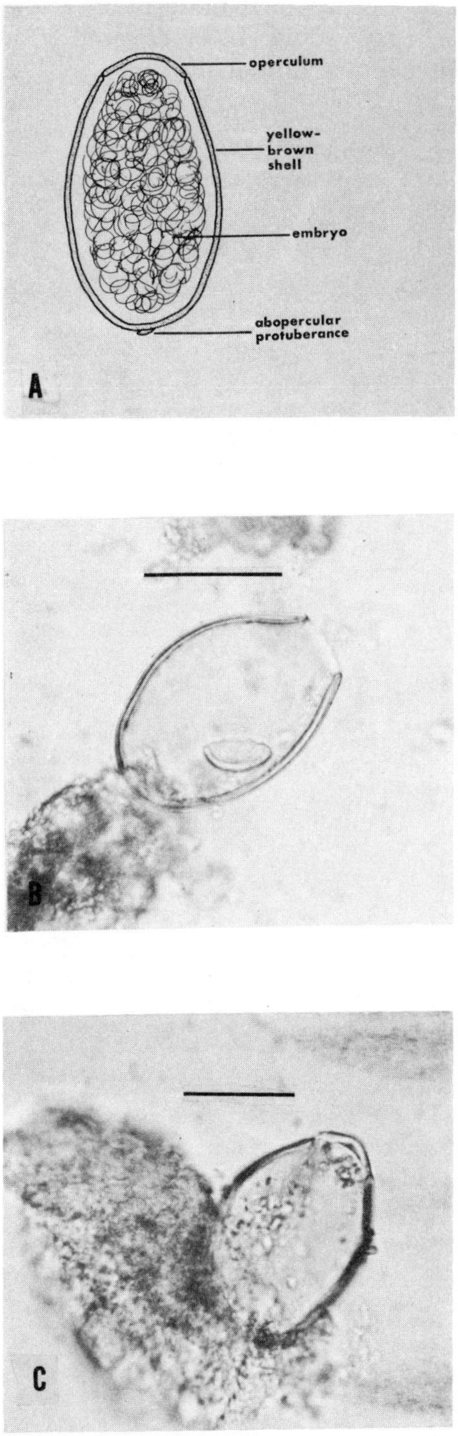

Fig. 33. Possible *Diphyllobothrium lutum eggs.*

comfort, nausea, loss of appetite, and anemia (Wardle, 1935; Saunders, 1949).

Today, the fish tapeworm is found among those native groups in Canada and Alaska utilizing fish in their diet (Fournelle et al., 1948; Saunders, 1949; Brown, et al., 1950; Wolfgang, 1954).

Most parasitologists have accepted *D. latum* as an exotic species, most probably introduced from Europe with Scandinavian immigrants, who brought with them a tradition of eating undercooked fish (Magath and Essex, 1931; Vergeer, 1929, 1930). Certain aspects of the parasite's life cycle, however, have led some parasitologists to argue that *D. latum* is either indigenous, or that two races exist here, one indigenous, the other introduced (Wardle, 1935; Cameron, 1945). In support of the view that *D. latum* was present in North America prior to contact is the identification of possible fish tapeworm eggs of unidentified species from precontact Peru (Callen and Cameron, 1960), nineteenth century reports of the fish tapeworm in man in Canada (Wardle, 1935:17), and the fact that Indian herbal lists contained vermifuges, implying recognition of large intestinal worms such as *D. latum* (Densmore, 1926; Smith, 1932).

As was argued with *E. granulosus,* should *D. latum* have been in North America prior to contact, the Schultz site occupants would seem to have been likely candidates as carriers of the parasite. Perch and pike, fish commonly involved in the life cycle, were found at the site, and it seems reasonable to infer that Schultz site occupants occasionally ate fish in a raw or partially cooked condition, particularly as this custom still exists among Indians of North America (Saunders, 1949).

As indicated earlier, the dog harbors several species of taeniid parasites. Since in this group it is not possible to carry identification to species level on the basis of eggs alone, it is possible that the observed eggs, if such they are, belong to a species other than *E. granulosus.* To confirm the presence of this parasite in precontact North America, it would be necessary to find preserved tissue belonging to one of the intermediate host species, and to recover the cyst stage from this tissue. The presence of *D. latum* would be confirmed if more readily identifiable eggs could be recovered from coprolites of precontact sites.

ACKNOWLEDGEMENT

This work was aided by a grant from the Michigan State University ALL University Research Fund.

IX

SCHULTZ SITE CERAMICS

Fred W. Fischer

PREFACE

This paper is concerned with the typological description and stratigraphic and areal analysis of the Schultz site ceramics. Section one describes the methodology of the study. Sections two through four present a chronologically ordered, general descriptive statement of certain ceramic attributes present at the Schultz site. The physical distribution of each of the wares and types is discussed, and some chronological and cultural interpretation is offered. Finally, some previously published material is examined in order to learn something of the generic relationships of the Schultz site ceramics. Section five deals with several miscellaneous small groups of sherds that are present at the Schultz site. Detailed discussion of these small, often heterogeneous, samples seems tenuous and unwarranted.

Anyone interested in more detailed descriptive information and distribution data should also refer to the Appendix A. Formal ceramic descriptions are given in Appendix AA, and the charts in Appendix AB offer detailed distribution information.

It is my pleasure to note here my appreciation to the following people for assistance in this study. Dr. James B. Griffin extended advice that was helpful in formulating both my approach to the analysis and its presentation. Constant reference has been made to relevant work on ceramics carried out by Dr. Griffin. The project was under the direction of Dr. James E. Fitting whose composit stratigraphic correlation is the basis for my stratigraphic analysis. Mr. John Speth and Mr. David Brose suggested several of the geological and cultural interpretations that I have used here. My wife, Dianne K. Fischer, offered several suggestions regarding analytical methodology and helped me in the preparation and editing of the typescript. Finally, a number of Museum Techniques students, Undergraduate Research Participants, and Undergraduate Science Education Participants undertook the frequently onerous tasks of washing, cataloging, and sorting the Schultz site material. These students also aided in the preliminary ceramic analysis.

METHODOLOGY

General

It was apparent early in the 1962 season that at least three archaeological components were represented at the Schultz site. It was also obvious that various elements had correlates in published ceramic assemblages outside the Saginaw Valley. After washing, numbering, and cataloging, the sherds were sorted into groups of rim sherds, decorated body sherds, and undecorated body sherds. Certain key attributes, common to both the Schultz site ceramics and better known assemblages in Illinois, Indiana, Ohio, and other areas of Michigan, were used as guides in sorting the 18,716 Schultz site sherds into groups corresponding to the major occupations of the site.

Typological Analysis

A basic typological analysis was made using rim sherds, since this body of material presents the greatest attribute variety. Care was taken to group two or more rim sherds from a single vessel in an attempt to work with minimal vessels. It should be noted, however, that the total number of rims may be considerably greater than the total number of vessels represented due to rim variations present on individual vessels. Technological, morphological, decorative, and metric variations were noted for the entire group of rim sherds, and a punched card system was devised for recording the attributes of each rim sherd.

It was hoped that the resulting punched card data would give us an objective basis for setting up ceramic types through the clustering of dependent ceramic attributes. The system permitted the recording of the presence (or absence) of 31 nonparametric technological, morphological, and decorative attributes. In addition, average sherd thickness was recorded to the nearest 0.5 millimeters. Five by eight inch McBee Keysort (KD 585 B) punched cards were used.

Use of the punched cards in formulating the typology proved unsatisfactory for several reasons. About ten students were involved in recording the information to be punched. I often felt that it was necessary to refer back to the sherds themselves in order to check the accuracy of the information. This entailed a cumbersome search and reordering of sherds and cards after many of the pulls. It was realized too late that the ceramic material, particularly that of the Middle Woodland period, exhibited much subtle variation. Thus, the attributes punched proved insufficient in number and, often, too general in character to obtain significant results. In the end, the punched cards were little used, and the final typology presented here is the result of a more conventional but less objective analysis: the grouping of sherds of similar appearance.

The following characteristics were analyzed in constructing the typology; observations on technology include method of manufacture, paste, temper, texture, interior and exterior surface finish, and interior, exterior, and core colors. Morphological observations include lip form, rim form, rim attitude, rim modification, body form, and, where possible, base form. Decoration observations include a study of technique (incising, rocker stamping, etc.), motif, and placement. Metric information is utilized where this seems appropriate.

The body sherds of several sherd groups can be specifically identified. For instance, it is possible to identify the body sherds of Schultz Thick, Shiawassee Plain, Shiawassee Cordmarked on the basis of paste and thickness. Several decorative treatments occur in only one type or subtype, and sherds bearing these particular decorative treatments are therefore identifiable. All non-rimsherds were size sorted before typing and tabulation by use of a one-half inch wire mesh. Only the sherds not passing this mesh were used in the analysis. Thus, although the typological descriptions rest primarily upon the observations made on rim material, some of the information in the formal descriptions of Appendix AA is derived from non-rim material.

Taxonomy

The largest ceramic units referred to in this paper correspond directly to the major culture periods represented at the Schultz site: Early Woodland, Middle Woodland and Late Woodland. These period designations, however, do not necessarily imply a discreet ceramic reality in the typology, for certainly we can see transitions within one period that carry over into the succeeding period. The period designations, then, are used only for convenient general reference. The basic unit of ceramic description here is the *type*. The type consists of a series of sherds sharing one or more attributes which serve to distinguish that series of sherds from other sherds. The type implies some spatial or temporal integrity. This integrity is usually demonstrated by a specific type's unique position in the site.

Where specific variation within the type seems to warrant it, the type is divided into two or more *subtypes*. Some of these subtypes exhibit chronological or areal differences within the type sample at the Schultz site; others do not. Subtypes of a single type share several attributes and are assumed to be culturally related.

A *ware*, as the term is used below, occupies a loose position between the type and the period designation. Types within a ware are physically similar and, therefore, thought to be related. The degree of similarity and implied relationship between the types in a single ware or from one ware group to another may vary considerably. Thus, like types, no two wares have equal analytic value.

Typology

The analysis and classification described above has resulted in the formulation of a typology composed of sixteen types in eight ware groups representing three gross culture periods. Five of the types have been further broken down into fifteen subtypes. Table 37 outlines the Schultz site ceramic typology.

Several sherd groups that are discussed in section two and Appendix AB are omitted in Table 37. Plain body sherds (7187), cordmarked and smoothed body sherds (962), and scraped body sherds (369) are deleted because their exact ware placement is undetermined. Forty-four sherds comprising five sherd groups are omitted because the sample size is deemed inadequate for typological placement. These five groups are simple stamped sherds (13), miniature vessel rim sherds (13), miscellaneous unclassified rim sherds (10), shell-tempered plain sherds (6), and cordwrapped stick impressed body sherds (2).

Finally, the 3187 sherds classed as indeterminant are also omitted from Table 37. These sherds are discussed briefly in section two.

Distribution Analysis

University of Michigan field crews worked at the Schultz site in 1962, 1963, and 1964. Several subsequent visits have been made by small University of Michigan parties. This work has resulted in the recovery of archaeological material from a large number of excavation units, unit levels, structural features, and surface areas. The pottery of 607 provenience units was analyzed during the course of this study. Table 38 presents a simplified breakdown of the ceramic samples of the several provenience classes.

Two types of distribution analysis were undertaken. First, the various wares, types, and subtypes were plotted against the excavation unit levels in order to obtain a relative ceramic sequence beyond that suggested by comparisons with as-

TABLE 37
SCHULTZ SITE CERAMIC TYPOLOGY

Period	Ware	Type	Subtype	Sample
Early Woodland	Schultz	Thick		360
	Shiawassee	Cordmarked		208
		Plain		84
		Incised		31
Middle Woodland	Tittabawassee	Dentate Stamped[1]		164
		Cordwrapped Stick Stamped		78
		Plain Noded		49
	Green Point	Rocker Stamped[2]	Plain Oblique Left	153
			Plain Vertical	102
			Plain Horizontal	50
			Dentate	25
		Incised	Crosshatched[3]	79
			Horizontal	10
			Vertical	13
			Dentate Tool[4]	8
		Plain		38
		Brushed		19
		Miscellaneous[5]		450
		Ruben Linear Cord Impressed	Plain Interior[6]	22
			Striated Interior[7]	25
?	Unnamed	Plain	Straight Rim	65
			Excurved Rim	43
Late Woodland	Unnamed	Cordmarked[8]	Undecorated Rim	62
			Noded	19
			Cordwrapped Stick Imp. Lip	17
	Saginaw	Thin Cordmarked		707
	Unnamed	Textile Impressed		33

[1]Includes 21 sherds that exhibit Tittabawassee Dentate Stamped incising only.
[2]Figures do not include 2203 rocker stamped body sherds.
[3]Figure does not include 22 crosshatched body sherds.
[4]Figure does not include 61 dentate tool incised body sherds.
[5]329 incised and 121 punctated body sherds. Specific type indeterminate.
[6]Figure does not include 134 plain interior, linear cord impressed body sherds.
[7]Figure does not include 32 striated interior, linear cord impressed body sherds.
[8]Figures do not include 1601 cordmarked body sherds.

semblages from other areas. Second, the horizontal areal distribution of each ceramic unit was considered in an attempt to further define the nature of each ware, type, and subtype.

The exact provenience of a small amount of material from the excavation units is in question and, thus, unsuitable for stratigraphic analysis. Several units having a single excavation level are not

TABLE 38
SCHULTZ SITE PROVENIENCE CLASSES
AND SHERD SAMPLES

Provenience Class	Number		Sample
Excavation units	67		14,518
Total provenience units		415	
Features	145		3808
Total provenience units		187	
Surface areas		5	390
Total		607	18,716

used in this phase of the study. Feature material is treated separately because of the difficulty of assigning much of this material to its proper vertical position. All of the sherd material was considered in the areal analysis. Due to the fact that surface collections were made in terms of very general areas of the site, these sherds are not treated. Table 39 indicates the sample sizes of the distribution analyses.

TABLE 39
SCHULTZ SITE DISTRIBUTION
STUDY SAMPLES

Study	Sample	
Stratigraphic analysis	13,770	
Areal analysis of excavated sherds	18,326	
Excavation units		14,518
Features		3808
Surface sherds, not analyzed	390	

Stratigraphic Analysis (Table 42)

A number of individual excavation units are useful in establishing relative temporal positions for certain ceramic types. Unit 510E570, a twenty-foot square with 3561 sherds, is most important in this regard, especially since an intensive stratigraphic study has been carried out on this unit (Speth, this volume). Two other units produced over a thousand sherds each. Naturally, not all of the excavation units are comparable, either in terms of culture content or excavation level. In the field, arbitrary cuts of varying depths were resorted to, where natural and cultural stratigraphic breaks were absent or could not be discerned.

Some method for relating the various excavation units is needed in order to obtain really adequate samples for several type and subtype comparisons. James Fitting has worked out a general stratigraphic-cultural sequence for the Schultz site based primarily on soil variations. Thirty-three excavation units with a total of 10,304 sherds are adaptable to Dr. Fitting's correlation (Table 40). This system is the mainstay of the stratigraphic analysis.

Areal Analysis
(Appendix AB)

A total of 13,488 sherds were used in the final ceramic areal distribution analysis at the Schultz site. The investigated portion of the site was divided into fifteen 100-foot squares. Using the original datum of 1962 as a reference point, this grid system extends from 250 feet east on the west to 750 feet east on the east. It extends from 450 feet north on the south to 750 feet north on the north. The resulting fifteen 100 foot squares are designated by the letters "A", "B", and "C" from north to south, and with the numbers one through five from west to east. Thus, the grid "block" furthest to the northeast is designated Block A-5, the second from the north and third from the west is Block B-3, etc.

The total area tested within each of the different blocks and, therefore, the resulting sherd samples vary considerably. To the west, Blocks A-1, A-2, and C-1

TABLE 40
SCHULTZ SITE GENERALIZED STRATIGRAPHIC SEQUENCE AND SHERD SAMPLES

Vertical provenience	I	IIa	IIb	IIc	IId	IIIa	IIIb	IVa	IVb	IVc	IV Undif.
Sherd Sample		5	84	348	61	2668	2128	2128	717	1063	2022
Period	Early Woodland				Middle Woodland			Late Woodland			

were not investigated by excavation. To the east, Blocks A-5, B-5, and C-5 were investigated primarily by means of a trenching machine in order to obtain a north-south stratigraphic profile. Few sherds were collected in the operation. Table 41, below, lists each of the 100-foot grid blocks and records the total utilized sherd sample of each.

TABLE 41
SCHULTZ SITE AREAL
DISTRIBUTION SAMPLES

(Number of sherds and percent of total sample)

Block	1	2	3	4	5
A	0	2 0.1	317 2.3	256 1.9	20 0.2
B	3727 27.7	582 4.3	1825 13.4	1077 7.9	82 0.6
C	1 0.1	266 2.0	436 3.2	4897 36.5	0

EARLY WOODLAND

General

Two Early Woodland wares are recognized at the Schultz site. Schultz ware consists of a single type, Schultz Thick (Fig. 34). This exterior-interior cordmarked ceramic is clearly the earliest pottery at the Schultz site and, very probably, in southeastern Michigan. The later Shiawassee ware is made up of three types. The two wares exhibit certain technological similarities, but diverge in specific characteristics. Both Schultz ware and Shiawassee ware are rather crudely constructed and finished. As the name implies, Schultz Thick is notable for its thickness (rim sherds average about 9.0 mm). Shiawassee ware is also relatively thick, but less so than the earlier ceramic. The paste of both wares is coarse and contains abundant tempering material. Shiawassee ware is demonstrably later than Schultz Thick and comes into use before the Middle Woodland Tittabawassee ware.

Schultz Thick, General

The sandy paste Schultz Thick is characterized by wide-mouth jars (or deep bowls) with the greatest diameter occurring at or immediately below the lip. The body tapers toward a small flat base (Fig. 34E) and some few vessels are very slightly constricted at the orifice. Elongate and ovoid riveted and applique lugs facilitated handling (Fig. 34C, D). The jars appear to have been about 30 centimeters deep and 20 to 25 centimeters in diameter. About 60 percent of the rims have flattened lips and the remainder are rounded. Both lip forms can occur on the same vessel. The lips are frequently cordmarked.

The exterior and interior surfaces of Schultz Thick are undulating as if hand finished. The exterior, and usually the interior, surface is cordmarked with a coarse cord. A single body sherd has two narrow rectilinear incised lines that converge at an acute angle. No other

Fig. 34. Schultz thick: *A* and *D*, rim sherds; *C* and *D*, lugs; *E*, basal sherd. (UMMA Neg. No. 94-21).

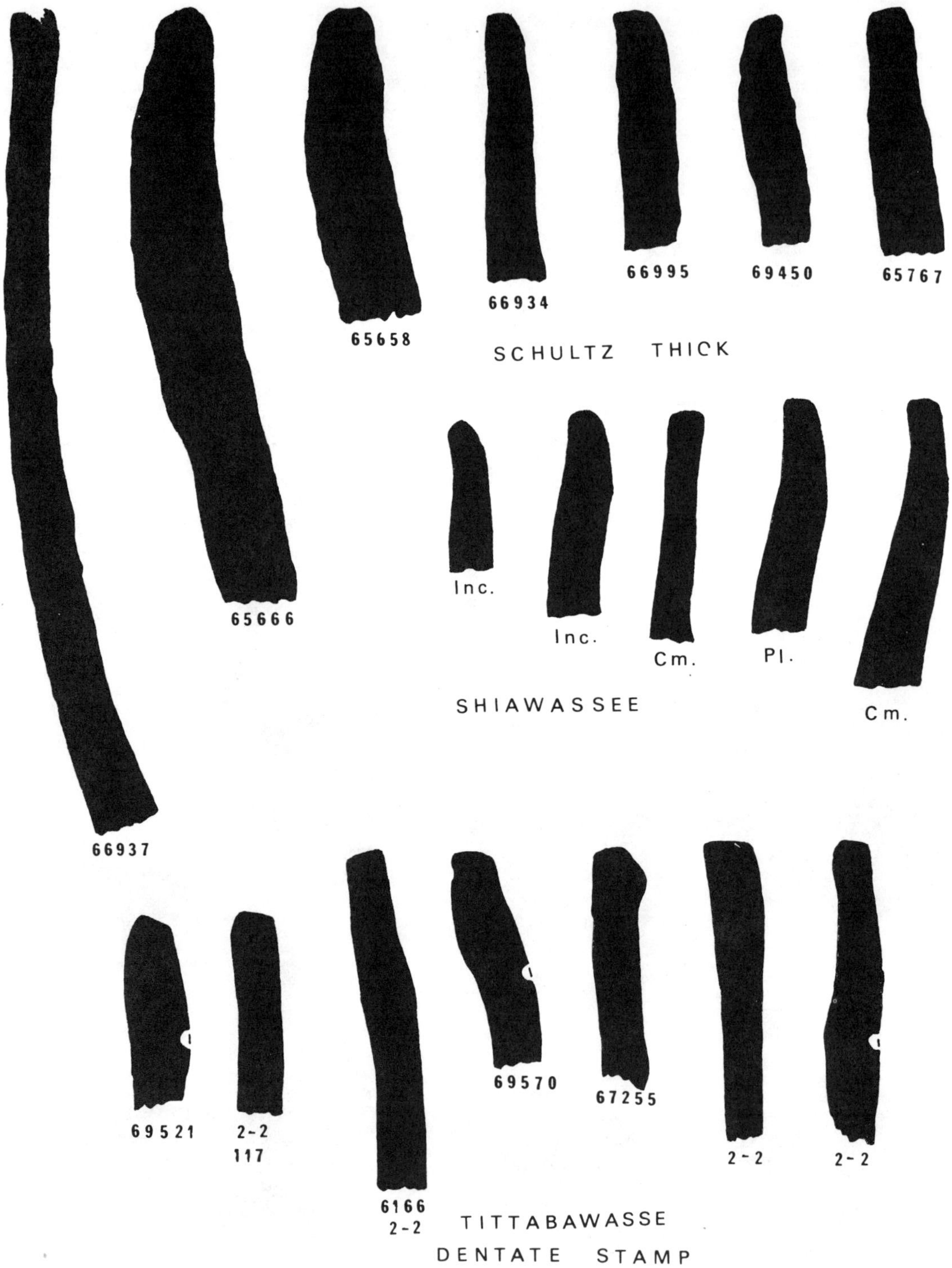

Fig. 35. Schultz site rim profiles. The interior is to the right.

decoration is observed in the Schultz site sample.

Schultz Thick, Stratigraphic Distribution

The stratigraphic position of Schultz Thick clearly indicates that it is the earliest ceramic at the site. The vertical position is so clear-cut that one would suspect that there was almost certainly a hiatus in occupation between the Schultz Thick phase and the succeeding Shiawassee phase. Analysis of the areal distribution, below, bears out this suspicion.

The composit stratigraphic correlation (Table 42) indicates that 134 (55.4%) of the plotted total 241 Schultz Thick sherds are from level II*c* and that 78 sherds (32.6%) were found in the III*a* level. The paucity of Schultz Thick sherds in the II*d* level is due to the fact that this natural stratigraphic unit is not represented in the north-central portion of the site, the area of the site where Schultz Thick occurs with greatest frequency. Only 27.7 percent of the 235 plotted Shiawassee ware sherds are from below the III*a* level. This compares with 61.2 percent of the Schultz Thick sherds.

Schultz Thick, Areal Distribution

Schultz Thick is found primarily in the northeastern portion of the area investigated (Appendix AB). One hundred fifty-five (46.6%) of the 333 plotted Schultz Thick sherds are from Block B-3, 96 (28.8%) from Block B-4, 31 (9.3%) from Block A-4, and 22 (6.6%) from Block B-5. This distribution takes on meaning when compared with the areal composit chart for the 13,488 plotted Schultz site sherds (Table 42). Although these four blocks account for the 91.3 percent of the Schultz Thick sample, they produced only 23.8 percent of all of the plotted Schultz site sherds.

Schultz Thick, Distribution Discussion

It is of interest to note that the Schultz Thick habitation area conforms to the north bank of the now-buried former channel of the Tittabawassee River. This old channel bank, located near the north edge of Blocks C-4 and C-5, was discovered during the excavation of Unit 510E570 and Trench 2. Eighty-two percent of the Schultz Thick sherds come from the blocks adjacent to the north edge of the channel (Blocks B-3, B-4, and B-5). The blocks immediately to the south (C-3, C-4, and C-5), presumably within the old river channel, produced only 2.4 percent of the Schultz Thick sherds. Of the sherds of the subsequent Shiawassee ware phase 65.7 percent are from blocks within the old channel. There seems to be little doubt that the habitation area during the Schultz Thick phase of the Early Woodland period was along the north bank of the old Tittabawassee River channel. If this channel had been stable for any duration, there may well have been a hospitable natural levee in the area of occupation. There also seems little doubt that some time must have elapsed between the Schultz Thick phase and the subsequent Shiawassee ware phase reoccupation—enough time, at least, for the channel to shift south, fill, and stabilize.

A cursory examination of the Schultz Thick distribution might suggest that the large circular palisaded structure in the north-central portion of the site is to be assigned to the Schultz Thick phase. Some 41 percent of the Schultz Thick sherds come from within this structure. An examination of the sherd counts for individual excavation units, however, indicates that this is not the case. While it is true that Block C-3, partially within the impressive structure, produced 46.6 percent of the Schultz Thick sherds, the majority of these (105 sherds or 67.8 percent of the Block C-3 sherds) came from two twenty-foot square units, Units B and D, which are almost entirely outside of the structure.

TABLE 42
COMPOSIT STRATIGRAPHIC DISTRIBUTION

Ceramic	Stratigraphic Levels									
	IV Undif.	IV*c*	IV*b*	IV*a*	III*b*	III*a*	II*d*	II*c*	II*b*	II*a*
Schultz Thick	15	...	...	...	...	78	5	134	8	1
Shiawassee - All Types	7	...	4	2	...	157	34	25	6	...
Shiawassee Cordmarked	6	...	2	2	...	91	15	25	5	...
Shiawassee Plain	...	...	2	...	...	47	12	...	1	...
Shiawassee Incised	1	...	...	...	...	19	7	...	...	...
Tittabawassee - All Types	28	8	13	19	11	69	1	4	7	...
Tittabawassee Dentate Stick	22	5	11	12	4	52	1	3	5	...
Tittabawassee Cordwr. St. Sta.	2	2	2	6	6	6	...	...	...	...
Tittabawassee Plain Noded	4	1	...	1	1	11	...	1	2	...
Green Point - All Types	282	65	78	246	502	489	1	28	11	...
Green Point Roc. St., Plain	24	8	4	19	52	39	...	...	...	...
Roc. St., Plain, body	158	28	34	96	295	297	1	11	4	...
Green Point Roc. St., Dentate	3	...	...	3	3	...	...	1	...	...
Roc. St., Dentate, body	15	4	...	19	15	31	...	6	2	...
Green Point Incised, Crosshatched	4	2	1	5	3	15	...	...	...	...
Incised, Crosshatched, body	...	1	...	4	3	3	...	...	...	...
Green Point Incised, misc.	36	11	18	46	57	52	...	4	2	...
Green Point Plain	2	1	...	4	5	1	...	2	1	...
Green Point Brushed	2	1	...	...	2	2	...	...	...	...
Brushed (zoned), body	...	...	1	...	...	1	...	...	...	...
Green Point undif. incised, body	28	7	15	40	44	42	...	3	2	...
Green Point undif. punct., body	10	2	5	10	23	6	...	1	...	...
Ruben Lin. Cord Imp., Plain Int.	22	7	18	11	16	11	...	2	...	...
Ruben Lin. Cord Imp., Stria. Int.	8	1	7	3	5	1	...	2	...	...
Plain straight rim	7	1	1	4	12	3	...	1	2	...
Plain excurved rim	2	1	4	6	3	...	...	2	1	...
Cordmarked undecorated rim	8	9	4	3	5	9	...	1	...	...
Cordmarked noded	...	...	2	1	...	2	...	...	...	...
Cordmarked cordwr. st. imp. lip	2	3	...	...	...	1	...	...	...	...
Saginaw Thin Cordmarked	144	297	70	2	...	28	...	2	...	...
Textile Impressed	12	3	4	...	...	5	...	...	...	...
Simple Stamped	5	4	1	1	...	1	...	...	...	...
Cordmarked undecorated, body	335	217	85	71	48	204	2	32	10	...
Cordmarked incised, body	4	7	4	10	2	3	...	...	...	...
Cordmarked punctated, body	3	4	2	...	1	...	...	...	...	...

TABLE 42 continued

Ceramic	Stratigraphic Levels									
	IV Undif.	IV*c*	IV*b*	IV*a*	III*b*	III*a*	II*d*	II*c*	II*b*	II*a*
Plain undecorated, body	637	195	212	588	1052	928	2	44	22	4
Scraped, body	38	16	34	37	33	34	2	...	1	...
Cordmarked and smoothed, body	104	43	29	55	54	148	1	14	7	...
Plain shell tempered	1	...	...	...	...	...	...	...	...	...
Indeterminate	385	180	159	215	405	534	13	60	11	...

Schultz Thick, Relationships

Sherds in the University of Michigan collections indicate that Schultz Thick is present at a number of sites in southern Michigan. In the Saginaw Valley, Schultz Thick is present at the Frazier site (20SA9) and at the Bussinger site (20SA194). To the west, this type was noted at the Spoonville site (20OT1) and at the Moccasin Bluff site (20BE26). Several Schultz Thick sherds, including a heavy riveted lug handle, were noted in a small collection from the Brems site (Indian Hill) in Stark County, Indiana.

Schultz Thick is the Michigan equivalent of Marion Thick (Helman, 1950:4-5; Griffin, 1952:98). Such Early Woodland types as Fayette Thick of Kentucky and southern Ohio (Griffin, 1943:667-72; 1945:221-22) and Vinette I of New York (Ritchie and McNeish, 1949:100 and 119) are closely related, if not areal variations of the same ceramic. Orrin Shane has recently described a closely related ceramic, Leimbach Thick, from several sites in north-central Ohio (1967*b*:106-09). Less than two percent of the Leimbach Thick sherds are cordmarked on the interior.

Schultz Thick is the regional representative of a widespread Early Woodland ceramic tradition in the central-eastern and northeastern United States. This tradition includes Marion Thick of Indiana, Fayette Thick of Kentucky and southern Ohio, Leimbach Thick of northern Ohio, and Vinette I of New York. Although widespread in space, all of these types are really quite similar in form and technology. The entire group of types can be characterized as a fairly homogeneous generalized utilitarian ceramic.

Shiawassee Ware, General

Like most of the local ceramics, the clay of the Shiawassee ware contains an appreciable amount of sand. The paste of this Early Woodland ware is distinctive, however, in that the proportion of silt in the clay is high. This gives many of the Shiawassee ware sherds a chalky texture.

The Schultz site sample of Shiawassee ware does not present much information on vessel form. A moderately large widemouth jar is suggested. The bussinger site (20SA194), about four miles west of Schultz site, has produced a large sample of this ware and formal type description should come from this site. Two Shiawassee Incised sherds from the Bussinger site appear to be from flat (or flattened) base vessels. Rims are slightly excurved or, less frequently, straight.

Three types of Shiawassee Ware are recognized at the Schultz site. Shiawassee Cordmarked, (Fig. 36), representing 64.4 percent of the Shiawassee sample, is carelessly impressed on the exterior sur-

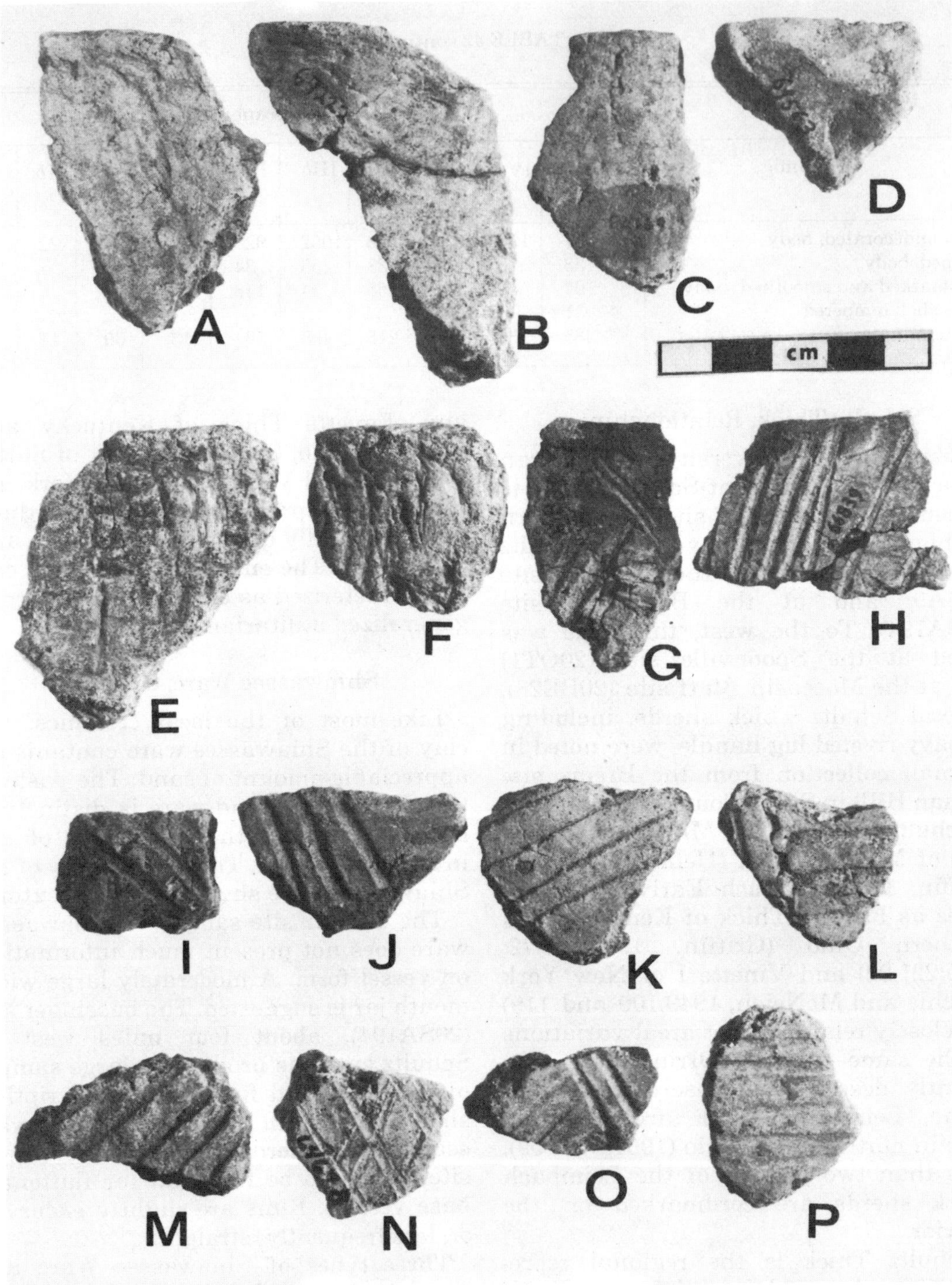

Fig. 36. Shiawassee Ware: *A-D,* Shiawassee Plain; *E-F,* Shiawassee Cordmarked; *G-P,* Shiawassee Incised. (UMMA Neg. No. 94-1-1).

face with coarse loosely twisted cord. Subsequent smoothing has largely obliterated the impressions on about one-quarter of the sherds. Shiawassee Plain (Fig. 36) accounts for 26 percent of the ware. It is carelessly smoothed on the exterior and interior. Thirty-one sherds of Shiawassee Incised (Fig. 36 G-P) make up the remaining 9.6 percent of the Shiawassee ware sample. Of these, all but one, a cordmarked sherd, exhibit a plain surface finish. However, of the 64 Shiawassee Incised sherds examined from the Bussinger site, 23 have a cordmarked surface and 4 are scraped. The relatively broad narrow incisions of this type usually form groups of parallel lines which abutt, at right or acute angles, against a similar set of parallel lines. The incising is generally carelessly executed. All of this incising at the Schultz site is rectilinear in form; however, at the Bussinger site 4.6 percent of the Shiawassee Incised is curvilinear. One incised rim sherd from Bussinger site has a punched exterior node about two centimeters below the lip. The nature of the Shiawassee Incised sample from both Schultz site and Bussinger site precludes any description of decoration motif or placement.

Shiawassee Ware, Stratigraphic Distribution

Reference to the composit stratigraphic distribution (Table 42) indicates that Level III*a* produced 157 (66.9%) of the 235 plotted Shiawassee ware sherds. Only 27.6 percent of the sherds of this ware group are from below this level. This is well above the level of maximum occurrence of the earlier Schultz Thick. Although 69 (43.1%) of the 160 plotted Tittabawassee ware sherds occur in Level III*a*, only 12 sherds (7.5%) come from below that level. Similarly, in unit 510E570 where both Shiawassee ware and Tittabawassee ware are well represented (Table 43), the level of maximum occurrence of the former ware is below that of Tittabawassee. This clearly indicates that the Shiawassee material is earlier than the Tittabawassee ware phase of the Middle Woodland period.

Shiawassee Ware, Areal Distribution

There is a marked concentration of the Shiawassee ceramics toward the southeastern portion of the tested area (Appendix AB). Block C-4 yielded 196 (63.5%) of the 309 plotted Shiawassee ware sherds. Compare this with the composit plot (Table 41; Appendix AB) in which only 36.5 percent of the total plotted sherds occur in this block. Block C-4 is south of the north bank of the former channel of the Tittabawassee River described above, and well south of the area in which the Schultz Thick material is found. This would clearly seem to support the argument that there was a hiatus of some duration between the Schultz Thick phase and the Shiawassee ware phase.

It should also be noted that there are marked differences between the areal distribution of Shiawassee ware and the subsequent Tittabawassee material. The occurrence of the latter ware is actually lower than expected (24.5% in Block C-4).

When the individual Shiawassee ware types were plotted by area, they all conformed fairly well to the Shiawassee ware composit. It was noted, however, that while 92 (83.6%) of the 110 Shiawassee Plain and Shiawassee Incised sherds came from Block C-4, only 105 (52.2%) of the 199 Shiawassee Cordmarked sherds came from this block. Of the remaining Shiawassee Cordmarked sherds, 43 (2.16%) are from Block B-3 and 24 (12.0%) are from Block B-4. This reflects not so much a true deviation from the normal Shiawassee ware distribution as the difficulty we encountered in distinguishing some of the Shiawassee Cord-

TABLE 43
UNIT 510E570 STRATIGRAPHIC DISTRIBUTION
(modified)

Ceramics	Levels									
	0-1	1-2	2-3	3-4	4-5	5-6	6-7	7-8	8-9	9-10
Schultz Thick	...	...	...	...	...	...	1	1	...	...
Shiawassee - All Types	...	...	...	4	1	...	52	57	2	10
Shiawassee - Cordmarked	...	...	...	2	1	...	23	39	2	8
Shiawassee Plain	...	...	...	2	...	...	18	13	...	2
Shiawassee Incised	...	...	...	...	...	...	11	5	...	...
Tittabawassee - All Types	3	2	5	1	7	10	16	1	...	...
Tittabawassee Dentate Stick	3	...	4	1	2	4	12	...	...	1
Tittabawassee Cordwr. St. Sta.	...	2	...	...	4	5	2	...	...	...
Tittabawassee Plain Noded	...	...	1	...	1	1	2	1	...	...
Green Point - All Types	1	9	36	20	106	334	7	...	...	...
Green Point Roc. St., Plain	...	2	5	1	13	37	1	...	...	...
Roc. St., Plain, body	...	4	17	8	48	222	5	...	...	...
Green Point Roc. St., Dentate	...	...	...	...	3	1	...	...	...	...
Roc. St., Dentate body	...	...	3	...	10	11	...	...	...	...
Green Point Incised, Crosshatched	1	1	...	1	4	1	1	...	...	...
Incised, Crosshatched, body	...	...	1	...	3	2	...	...	...	...
Green Point Incised, Misc.	...	...	2	...	...	...	...	...	...	...
Green Point Plain	...	...	1	1	1	3	...	...	...	...
Green Point Brushed	...	...	...	...	...	2	...	...	...	...
Brushed (zoned), body	...	...	...	1	...	...	...	...	...	...
Green Point undif. incised, body	...	2	5	7	20	36	...	...	...	...
Green Point undif. punct., body	...	...	2	1	4	19	...	...	...	...
Ruben Lin. Co. Imp., Plain Int.	1	1	5	...	7	14	...	1	...	...
Ruben Lin. Co. Imp., Stria. Int.	...	...	...	2	2	2	...	...	...	...
Plain straight rim	...	...	1	...	2	7	1	...	...	...
Plain excurved rim	...	...	1	2	...	4	...	...	...	...
Cordmarked undecorated rim	1	1	5	1	2	5	...	...	...	...
Cordmarked noded	...	...	...	1	1	...	1	...	...	...
Cordmarked cordwr. st. imp. lip	...	...	3	...	...	...	...	...	...	...
Saginaw Thin Cordmarked	11	77	85	4	2	...	...	...	...	...
Textile Impressed	...	...	2	...	...	...	...	1	...	...
Simple Stamped	...	...	1	...	...	...	...	...	...	...
Cordmarked undecorated, body	4	20	138	7	11	13	13	2	...	...
Cordmarked incised, body	1	1	4	...	...	1	...	...	...	...
Cordmarked punctated, body	...	1	...	...	...	...	...	...	...	...

TABLE 43 Continued

Ceramics	Levels									
	0-1	1-2	2-3	3-4	4-5	5-6	6-7	7-8	8-9	9-10
Plain undecorated, body	2	21	146	84	296	823	76	7	...	...
Scraped body	...	...	11	12	26	20	...	...	...	...
Cordmarked and smoothed, body	...	8	19	11	25	32	13	1	...	...
Plain shell tempered	...	...	...	...	...	...	...	...	...	...
Indeterminate	7	29	101	45	90	316	89	33	3	4

marked from Schultz Thick, particularly when the latter was damaged on the interior or left plain on the interior. A re-sorting of the material, with more attention given to paste characteristics, would probably eliminate this discrepancy.

Shiawassee Ware, Distribution Discussion

Stratigraphically, Shiawassee ware stands between Schultz Thick and Tittabawassee ware. The Shiawassee material is clearly later than the former material and demonstrable earlier than the latter ceramic. The areal distribution analysis confirms the clear-cut separation of these wares.

Sometime during or after the Schultz Thick phase of occupation, the Tittabawassee River channel shifted to the south, perhaps slowly, perhaps in one catastrophic cut-off. Slowly, the old channel filled with earth, and finally, the area of the old channel was occupied by a later group of Early Woodland people—the Shiawassee people. The eventual abandonment of the Schultz site by the Shiawassee ware phase inhabitants appears to have taken place sometime before the arrival of the Tittabawassee ware people with their Havana ceramic tradition. There would appear to be little, if any technological, stylistic, or locational relationship between the Shiawassee ware phase ceramics and the Tittabawassee ware phase ceramics.

Shiawassee Ware, Relationships

Aside from the two sites mentioned above, no Shiawassee ware was observed in the University of Michigan Museum collections. Were it not for the high silt content of the clays utilized for this ware at the Schultz and Bussinger sites, small samples of the plain and cordmarked types would be difficult to distinguish from several later undecorated types from southern Michigan.

Shiawassee Incised is similar in several characteristics to Black Sand Incised, an Early Woodland cordmarked ceramic of west-central Illinois (Griffin, 1952:98-100). In 1930, W. C. McKern described and illustrated several sherds similar to Shiawassee Incised from a site in southern Wisconsin (1945; Plate LXX, 3-10). At the time, these sherds were included with several Late Woodland types. Later, David Baerreis described the type Dane Incised of Wisconsin, a type very similar to Shiawassee Incised (1952). Richard Keslin presented the first formal published description of Dane Incised in 1958 (203-05) using material from the Hahn and Horicon sites in Dodge County, Wisconsin. Keslin's Dodge County material is quite similar to Shiawassee Incised in paste and decorative form and technique, however, it is described as "modeled from a single piece of clay." Several of the Shiawassee Incised sherds from the Bussinger site exhibit definite coil fractures. Keslin also describes Dane Incised as having a conoidal base. Dane Incised is in the earliest stratigraphic context at the Hahn and Horicon sites, and Keslin assigns the type to the Early Woodland period, but states that it may have continued in use into Middle Woodland times. Dane Incised is further described by Ronald Mason in his discussion of the North Bay II Complex material from the Mero site on the Door Peninsula of eastern Wisconsin (1966:94-99; Pl. XVII, Figures 1 and 2 (d)). The rim areas of Mason's material are frequently smoothed before incising.

Mason points out the similarity of Dane Incised of Wisconsin to Black Sand Incised of Illinois (Mason, 1966:97), but suggests that the former ceramic may have enjoyed a considerably longer span (1966:28-31). I would agree with Mason that there are dangers in equating the two types simply on the basis of such generalized attributes as incised decoration over a cordmarked surface. Mason points out that this surface finish—decorative technique combination is frequent in Late Woodland ceramics over much of the Great Lakes region. There is little difficulty, however, in distinguishing the Shiawassee Incised from such later Woodland types if some attention is given to paste and decorative form and motif. In southern Michigan, at least, the similarities to the later materials are superficial.

It is probable that we should look to the south and west for the inspiration of Shiawassee Incised. This is the first in a relatively long series of southern Michigan ceramics that are heavily influenced from the Illinois Valley.

MIDDLE WOODLAND

General

The Middle Woodland period at the Schultz site is represented by three ware groups. Tittabawassee ware is the most abundant ceramic in the lower levels of the Middle Woodland occupation, and it is possible that this ware continued in use throughout the period. The dominant ceramic of the period is Green Point ware. Although these two decorated ware groups share certain general characteristics, they can be easily sorted at the Schultz site. A plain undecorated ware is also present in the Middle Woodland ceramic assemblage at Schultz. This last group is represented by only a few sherds and remains unnamed.

The Middle Woodland period at this site is marked by a high proportion of decorated ceramics. A number of decorative techniques are employed, but there are a limited number of combinations and motifs. Placement and motif seem to conform to prescribed custom. Carelessness is common, but this is not through any spontaneity of execution. The general impression of decorative formality is strong. With the single exception of a zone-painted miniature in Green Point ware, decoration is a plastic art.

The major decorative technique throughout the period is that of texturing certain areas of the vessel to set the design apart from an untextured background. The textured zones are further delineated by bounding incisions or bounding punctations. Texturing is effected by a number of methods, and often this variation serves to distinguish one type from another. Eighty-eight percent of the rim sherds assignable to the Middle Woodland period have a band of this zoned decoration on the upper rim. Bounding punctations usually set this decoration off from a plain neck zone. Bounding incisions delineate body decoration zones.

Tittabawassee Ware, General

Tittabawassee ware is composed of three types: Tittabawassee Dentate Stamped (Fig. 37), Tittabawassee Cordwrapped Stick Impressed (Fig. 38 A-E), and Tittabawassee Plain Noded (Fig. 38 F, G). Tittabawassee Dentate Stamped is the most abundant type in the ware (56.3%). Included in this type sample are twenty-one sherds with incised decoration only. The distinctive bold incising of this latter group is found only on positively identified Tittabawassee Dentate Stamped sherds.

Tittabawassee Cordwrapped Stick Impressed exhibits considerable variation, and some of these sherds probably do not belong in this category. This type accounts for 26.8 percent of the Tittabawassee ware material. Forty-nine Tittabawassee Plain Noded sherds (16.8%) complete the Tittabawassee ware inventory.

Several traits serve to distinguish the Tittabawassee ware from the Green Point ware. The sandier paste of Tittabawassee ware is generally better consolidated. Converse fracture is less common. Tittabawassee ware is generally more massive. It tends to be rather thick, and the decoration, whether incising, punctation, or dentate stamping, is bold and better executed than that of Green Point ware. A simpler vessel form with less neck constriction is indicated. Although some few Tittabawassee sherds exhibit a cambered rim, this trait is much more common with the Green Point ware. Lip decoration is much more frequent in the Tittabawassee series.

Specifically, Tittabawassee vessels appear to be moderately large jars with a scant neck constriction and, consequently, a large orifice. Vessel walls contract toward a rounded or subconoidal base. Rims are usually straight or slightly excurved. Lips are normally flattened or flattened and beveled to the interior on Tittabawassee Dentate Stamped and Tittabawassee Cordwrapped Stick Impressed vessels. Rounded lips are frequent on Tittabawassee Plain Noded vessels.

Exterior and interior surfaces are plain or smoothed, at least on the rim and neck area. Some few rim sherds appear to have been cordmarked and smoothed before decoration. The rims of all three Tittabawassee types have received some form of decoration. The punched exterior rim nodes of Tittabawassee Plain Noded require no further comment here.

Tittabawassee Dentate Stamped has vertical rows of dentate impressions on the upper rim. Each row of impressions is vertical or only slightly inclined to the right. The individual impressions are frequently sharply executed, and they are either square or rectangular in form. The rim stamping usually terminates in a plain neck zone. The termination may be marked by a bold incision or a row of punctations, or the stamping may be unbounded. Punched exterior rim nodes are common.

Tittabawassee Dentate Stamped vessel shoulders and bodies are often decorated with zones of the same bold dentate stamping bounded by broad, shallow incised lines. Where discernible, the motif consists of curvilinear zones forming serpentine bands. Unfortunately, nothing can be said regarding body decoration, if any, of the Tittabawassee Cordwrapped Stick Impressed or Tittabawassee Plain Noded.

As the name indicates, Tittabawassee Cordwrapped Stick Impressed upper rims are stamped with a cordwrapped stick. The impressions are most frequently arranged in vertical rows. Occasionally the impressions are at a slightly oblique angle; and, in one case, crossed oblique impressions present a crosshatched effect. Horizontal impressions are rare. Plain neck zones are most frequent. The rim impression termination is either un-

Fig. 37. Tittabawassee Dentate Stamped. (UMMA Neg. No. 94-2-5).

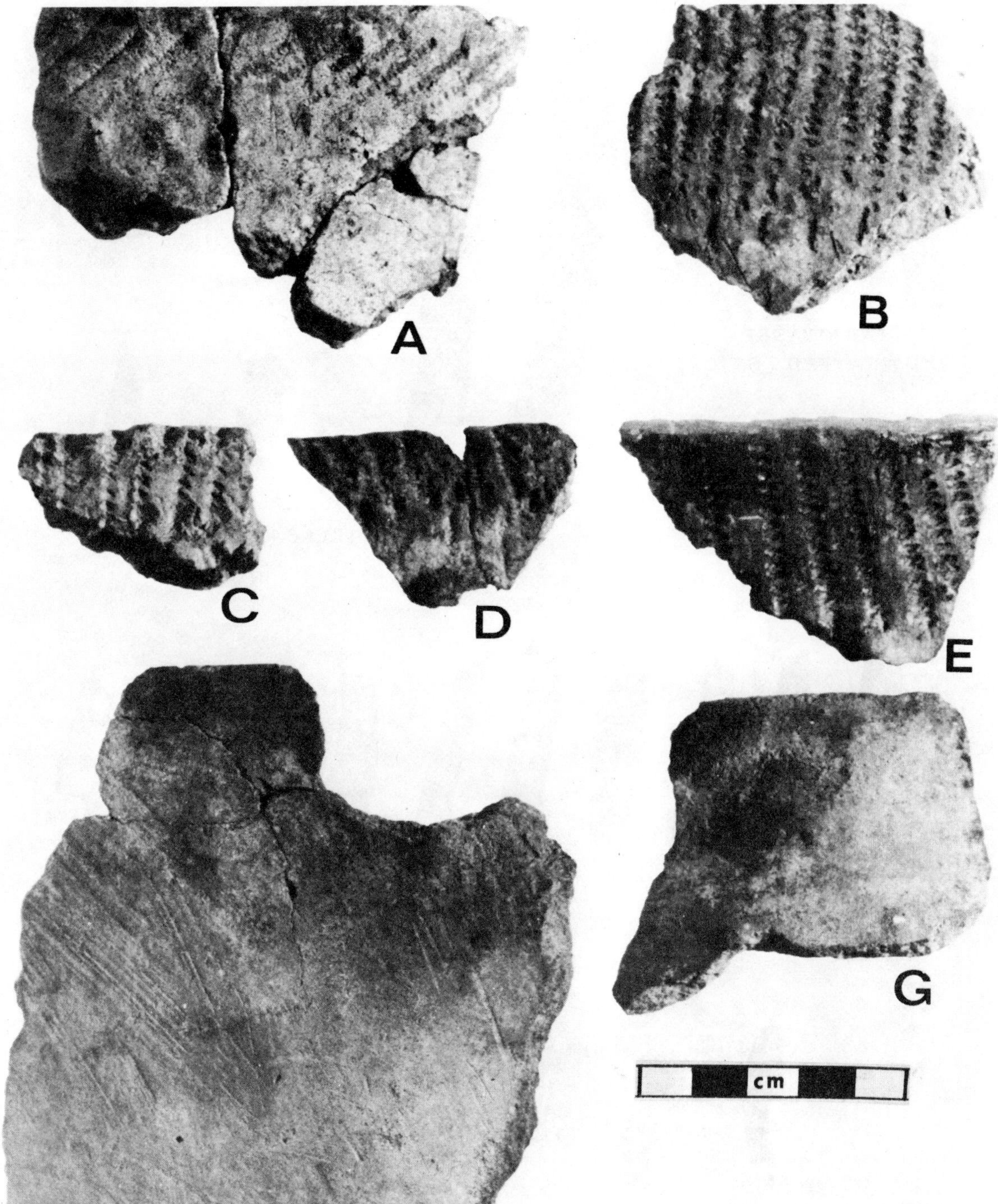

Fig. 38. *A-E,* Tittabawassee Cordwrapped Stick Impressed; *F-G,* Tittabawassee Plain Noded. (UMMA Neg. No. 94-2-3).

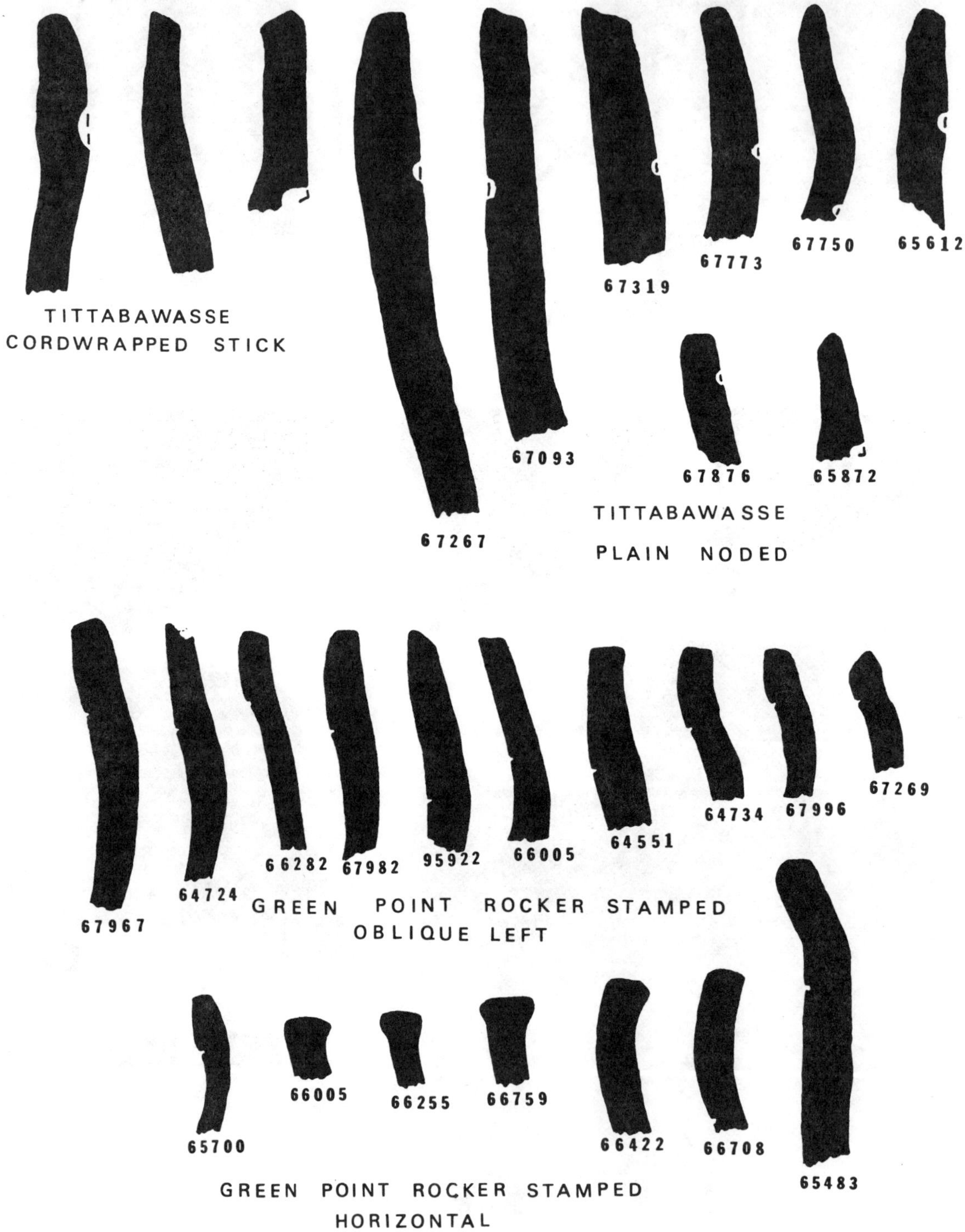

Fig. 39. Schultz site rim profiles. The interior is to the right.

bounded or marked by a horizontal row of punctations or punched exterior nodes.

Some forty-seven percent of the Tittabawassee ware rims have notched lips. Lip notching may occur on the interior edge, exterior edge, the top of the lip, or in combinations of two or all of these placements. Tittabawassee Dentate Stamped and Tittabawassee Plain Noded bear simple lip notches, while the lips of Tittabawassee Cordwrapped Stick Impressed are notched with a cordwrapped stick.

Tittabawassee Ware, Stratigraphic Distribution

The stratigraphic position of Tittabawassee ware at the Schultz site indicates that Tittabawassee succeeded Shiawassee ware and preceded Green Point ware. The composit stratigraphic correlation (Table 42) shows that 43.1 percent (69) of the 160 plotted Tittabawassee ware sherds occur in stratigraphic Unit III*a*. This compares with 30.5 percent (441) of the 1444 Green Point ware sherds in this level. Stratigraphic Unit III*b*, the level directly above III*a*, contained only 6.9 percent (11) of the Tittabawassee ware sherds, while yielding 30.2 percent (435) of the Green Point ware sherds. Tittabawassee ware is strongly represented in stratigraphic Unit IV (*c, b,* and *a*) by 68 sherds (42.5%) as compared to 554 sherds (38.4%) of the Green Point ware. This bimodal distribution of Tittabawassee ware is discussed below.

Both Tittabawassee ware and Green Point ware are well represented in excavation unit 510E570 (Table 43). The major occurrence of Tittabawassee ware is in the square sheet level 6-7, where 36.4 percent (16) of the total 44 Tittabawassee ware sherds are found. Only 1.8 percent (9) of the total 501 Green Point ware sherds are found in this level. The square sheet level immediately above, level 5-6, produced only 9 (20.4%) Tittabawassee ware sherds. This level represents the major occurrence of Green Point ware with 326 sherds (65.0%). Excavation unit 510E570 also serves to demonstrate the chronological relationship of Tittabawassee ware to Shiawassee ware. Although 41.3 percent (52) of the total 126 Shiawassee ware sherds of this excavation unit are from level 6-7, the level with the greatest number of Tittabawassee ware sherds, 54.8 percent (69) of the Shiawassee material is found below this level. Only one Tittabawassee sherd (2.3%) is found below level 6-7.

Stratigraphic distribution comparisons between Tittabawassee ware and Green Point ware were carried through for three other excavation units where both types were sufficiently represented: Trench 6, East Extension; Trench 6, Area B; and 500E585. In each case the observed occurrence of Tittabawassee ware was greater than expected (variation from a random distribution) in the stratigraphic levels below the levels in which sherds of Green Point types occurred in greater than expected numbers. In excavation units Trench 6, Area B and 500E585 a bimodal distribution for Tittabawassee ware similar to that of 510E570 is observed.

Tittabawassee Ware, Areal Distribution

Reference to the areal distribution chart (Appendix AB) for Tittabawassee ware indicates that 30.5 percent of the plotted sherds are on the northernmost (A) blocks. Only 2.0 percent of the Green Point Rocker Stamped sherds are found in these blocks. The high proportion of Tittabawassee ware sherds from these northern blocks takes on added significance when viewed with reference to the composit areal distribution for all sherd groups. This composit plot shows that only 4.5 percent of the total plotted sherds are found in "A" blocks.

The concentrations of Tittabawassee ware in blocks B-1 and C-4 conform to a similar distribution for the marker types of Green Point ware. It should be noted, however, that the proportions of Green Point Rocker Stamped in these blocks are considerably higher than those of Tittabawassee ware. Not only do the relative proportions vary, but the relative proportions for each block are reversed so that block B-1 produced 19.9 percent (25) of the Tittabawassee sherds and 40.2 percent (916) of the Green Point Rocker Stamped, while block C-4 produced 24.5 percent (32) of the Tittabawassee sherds and 35.4 percent (805) of the Green Point Rocker Stamped sherds. Actually, Tittabawassee ware percentages are markedly low for both of these blocks when compared with the composit plot percentages (B-1: 27.7%, C-4: 36.5%). Although the total sherd count of Tittabawassee ware is rather small for blocks B-2, B-3, and B-4, it should be noted that the Tittabawassee percentages for these blocks are dissimilar to the Green Point Rocker Stamped percentages.

Tittabawassee Ware, Distribution Discussion

It was noted earlier that the Tittabawassee ware of excavation units 510E570; Trench 6, Area B; and 500E585 exhibits a bimodal vertical distribution. This would seem to indicate that Tittabawassee ware obtained maximum popularity during the early portion of the Middle Woodland period, was replaced by Green Point ware, and finally enjoyed a resurgence in popularity in the closing phases of the Middle Woodland period.

This interpretation seems incorrect for several reasons. First, one might expect distinguishable physical differences between a pre-Green Point Tittabawassee ware and a late Green Point Tittabawassee ware. Although the sample is admittedly small, no such changes were observed. Second, if Tittabawassee ware was coexistent with Green Point ware for any extended period at the Schultz site, we might expect the two wares to share some very significant attributes, even if the two wares were functionally distinct. Indeed this is the case in a number of western Michigan finds (and represented by at least one vessel at the near-by Bussinger site). At the Schultz site, however, Tittabawassee ware sherds and Green Point ware sherds can be sorted on the basis of decoration, vessel morphology, and paste differences. Finally, if Tittabawassee ware and Green Point ware were manufactured and used by a single group, even if there were a functional difference between the two wares (e.g., ceremonial versus utilitarian, food storage versus food preparation), we would expect that the areal distribution over the site would not be too dissimilar. This is not the case.

I suggest that the occurrence of Tittabawassee material in the upper levels of the southerly excavation units might be the result of mechanical displacement and mixing due to erosion down slope from the northeast. John Speth, in personal communication, has suggested that a period of flooding and cutting occurred at the Schultz site between the end of the Shiawassee occupation and the appearance of Green Point ware. I am not attempting to rule out the possibility that Tittabawassee ware and Green Point ware are at least partly contemporaneous in the Saginaw Valley. With the mixing of several rather specific attributes that we find in western Michigan, it would be surprising to find the two wares completely unrelated, either chronologically or culturally, over such a short distance. I do think, however, that there is little evidence of blending or contemporaneity at the Schultz site.

The plot for the areal distribution of Tittabawassee ware indicates that the major area of occupation during the early portion of the Middle Woodland period was toward the northern portion of the site. This may indicate that the old channel in the southern portion of the site ("C" blocks) had not yet completely stabilized. It is unfortunate that the burial mound or mounds in the northern portion of the site had been almost completely destroyed prior to the University of Michigan excavations. Material associated with some badly disturbed burials, probably representing the truncated remainder of a burial mound, would suggest a Green Point date. Again, this does not rule out the possibility that some of the mound activity may have been of Tittabawassee origin.

Tittabawassee Ware, Relationships

The obvious affiliations of Tittabawassee ware lie to the west and south with the Havana ware of Illinois (summarized by Griffin, 1952:101-14; and Fowler, 1955:213-25). It is a simple matter to trace the dispersion of this rather complex ceramic from its apparent center in west-central Illinois, northeast up the Illinois and Kankakee river valleys into northern Indiana (Quimby, 1941*a*:67-147; Brown, 1964:109-22). From here, the tradition spread up the eastern coast of Lake Michigan, at least as far north as Muskegon, and east up the St. Joseph, Kalamazoo, Grand, and Muskegon river valleys (Quimby, 1941*a*). The headwaters of the Shiawassee, Bad, and Tittabawassee rivers, principal tributaries of the Saginaw River, are only a few miles east of the upper reaches of these western Michigan rivers. Havana material from Illinois appears to be quite variable from site to site. The Tittabawassee ware from the Schultz site is rather homogeneous in technique and motif. Thus, we can make more specific comparisons with the Havana material. This homogeneity is particularly true of Tittabawassee Dentate Stamped which is most similar to Hummel Dentate Stamped (Griffin, 1952:110-12) in form, placement, and motif. Hummel Dentate Stamped is a variety of Naples Dentate Stamped (Griffin, 1941:191-92; 1952:107-12) or a subvariety of Havana Stamped.

It is not surprising that the Illinois sites that produce Hummel Dentate Stamped pottery are more numerous in the upper, or northern, Illinois River Valley. In the south, the Thompson site in Brown County and the Crable Farm in Fulton County have yielded some Hummel Dentate Stamped sherds (sherds in the Ceramic Repository, University of Michigan). Further north, Hummel Dentate Stamped is found at the Rench site in Peoria County (Walker, 1952:37, Pl. XII) and at the Steuben site in Marshall County (Morse, 1963:22-25, Fig. 2). Several complete vessels bearing Hummel Dentate Stamped rim decoration have come from burial mounds still further north. Three vessels from the Utica Mounds Group I, in LaSalle County (Baker, et al., 1941:44-46; Pl. 54, Fig. 1; Pl. 52, Fig. 2; Pl. 57, Fig. 1) are very similar to Tittabawassee Dentate Stamped materials at the Schultz site. At the Adler Mounds in Will County, near Joliet, Illinois, Wilton Krogman excavated two vessels with Hummel (or Naples) Dentate Stamped rims (pictured in Winters, 1961: Fig. 38).

In 1941, George Quimby proposed that certain "Hopewellian" archaeological components in northern Indiana and southwestern Michigan be subsummed under the name Goodall Focus. He describes here (Quimby, 1941*b*:489-94) and in later papers (Quimby, 1941*a*:63-161; 1942:543-48) the ceramics and distribution of the Goodall Focus. Much of the material in Quimby's ceramic type II*b* or Goodall Dentate Stamped (Quimby, 1941*a*: 124-26; 1946:492-93) is the northern Indiana-southwestern Michigan areal equivalent of Hummel Dentate Stamped. We now have samples of this Goodall Dentate Stamped material from a number of sites in northern Indiana and southwestern Michigan.

As noted earlier, my examination of the Bussinger site (20SA194) material was cursory, but mention should be made of the Havana-like material from that site. Although much of the material was similar to the Tittabawassee ware of the Schultz site, the Bussinger sample can generally be characterized as more heterogeneous. Fragments of several diminutive vessels were noted. Rectilinear dentate-filled zones in the form of triangles appeared on the shoulder area of several vessels. At least one deep bowl form was observed. One large rim sherd exhibited characteristics not shared by Tittabawassee ware and Green Point ware at the Schultz site. This rim was cambered but had the large widely space punctations of Tittabawassee ware. The paste was typically Tittabawassee, but the rim zone was filled with fine dentate stamping similar to that described for Green Point ware.

Tittabawassee Dentate Stamped is the eastern Michigan manifestation of the Havana dentate stamping tradition. The justification for adding yet another ware name to an already confusing list of Havana tradition wares is not so much typological as taxonomical. More specifically, it is a matter of variability in ceramic attribute association. As already stated, the Tittabawassee (Havana tradition) material at the Schultz site is easily sorted from the Green Point (Hopewell tradition) material. The distinctions are not so clear-cut in the northern Illinois—northern Indiana—southwestern Michigan area. In that area, vessels of both traditions are often found in the same mound. Indeed, the decorative techniques of both traditions (as described for Tittabawassee ware and Green Point ware) are frequently used on the same vessel. The significance of these counter situations is not clear, at least in the mind of the present writer (for further discussion of this matter see below: Green Point ware, Relationships). Therefore, I feel that the taxonomy should be adequate to delineate the two situations in future discussions.

Tittabawassee Cordwrapped Stick Impressed and Tittabawassee Plain Noded also have their Illinois and Indiana correlates. Pottery similar to both types has been described as Havana Plain by James B. Griffin (1952:101-04). It is difficult to obtain specific information on either the cordwrapped stick or plain noded materials in the literature. Griffin notes that Havana Plain increases in frequency at the expense of Havana Cordmarked as one moves up the Illinois River Valley (Griffin, 1952:104). James Brown, in a reexamination of the ceramics from the Goodall site, notes the occurrence of several Naples Stamped cordwrapped stick impressed sherds (Brown, 1964:111, 113). The University of Michigan collections from the Moccasin Bluff site (20BE26) in Berrien County, Michigan, and the Spoonville site (20OT1) in Ottawa County, Michigan, contain several sherds similar to Tittabawassee Cordwrapped Stick Impressed. Mound I at the Parsons Mound group (20NE100), a Middle Woodland burial mound in Newaygo County, Michigan, produced a plain surfaced cordwrapped stick decorated jar.

Present evidence seems to indicate that Tittabawassee Dentate Stamped came into the Saginaw Valley from southwestern Michigan. Although the ultimate source of this general Havana decorative style may lie in central Illinois, I concur with James Brown (1964:110) in his contention that "the regionally based Havana tradition is made up of locally based traditions" in the northern Illinois-northern Indiana-southwestern Michigan area. Although evidence is admittedly scant, I believe that Tittabawassee Cordwrapped Stick Impressed and Tittabawassee Plain Noded came into the Saginaw Valley as companion types of Tittabawassee Dentate Stamped.

Green Point Ware, General

The Green Point ware group is composed of four types: Green Point Rocker Stamped (Figs. 40, 44, 45A-I), Green Point Incised (Figs. 45J-W, 46), Green Point Brushed (Fig. 47A-H), and Green Point Plain (Fig. 47I-P). Green Point Rocker Stamped and Green Point Incised are each divided into four subtypes (see Table 37). In addition, 450 miscellaneous sherds exhibit sufficient Green Point ware characteristics to permit ware identification.

Green Point ware is notable for its variety of Hopewell derived decorative treatments and a rather poor technological finish. As already noted, the major decorative technique is that of texturing areas or zones to set them apart from a plain background. The following techniques serve as texturing devices: rocker stamping (91.9%), incising (7.0%), brushing (0.7%), and punctating (0.4%). Almost ninety percent of the rim material assignable to this ware class has a band of one of these decorations on the upper rim. Small bounding punctations set this rim decoration off from a plain neck zone. Zones of decoration occur on the shoulder and body of many vessels. These zones are bounded by incised lines.

Zoned motifs, where recognizable, most often consist of a rectilinear band encircling the lower neck with curvilinear festoons or, more often, inverted festoons extending down over the shoulder. On quadrilobate vessels the inverted festoons conform to the interlobe area. Semilunate form body zones sometimes accompany the inverted festoon motif. Unbounded decoration, usually a plain or dentate rocker stamped, is apparently common, but the character of the sample prohibits even an estimate of its frequency. Unbounded decoration is carelessly executed and is probably an overall body decoration. Occasional independent rectilinear and curvilinear incised lines occur.

Other Green Point ware decorative techniques include simple lip notching (7.0% of all Green Point ware rim sherds) and punched exterior rim noding (1.8%). A single fragmented zoned red miniature jar was found near a disturbed burial in the base of one of the plowed-down mounds of the site. The little quadrilobate vessel has inverted festoon-form zones of rocker stamping on a red background. It should be mentioned that Green Point ware incising is done with a rather fine stylus. Line width averages only about 0.8 millimeter as compared with a 3.1 millimeter average line width for Tittabawassee ware incising. Similarly, punctations are considerably smaller and more closely spaced on Green Point ware.

Technologically, the Green Point ware is poor. Heavy inclusive sand and abundant temper result in a friable, irregular transverse fracture. Firing technology was apparently simple. Open fires and poor temperature controls are suggested by the marked color variation in individual vessels of all varieties. The tendency for lamellar converse fracture might also suggest differential interior-exterior firing temperatures.

Over seven thousand plain body sherds were recovered in our excavations at Schultz site. Approximately seventy-five percent of these are from Middle Woodland levels. The same is true of the 369 scraped body sherds. Less than one-quarter of the 1601 cordmarked body sherds are from the Middle Woodland levels. If we use a rough correction factor to eliminate the Tittabawassee ware body sherds, and if we disregard the

Fig. 40. Green Point Plain Rocker Stamped: *A,* vertical variety; *B-I,* oblique left variety; *J-M,* horizontal variety. (UMMA Neg. No. 94-4-4).

probable tendency for differential treatment of the shoulder and base, we obtain the following estimates of nonrim surface finish proportions for Green Point ware: 83 percent plain, 7.5 percent cordmarked and smoothed, 6.5 percent cordmarked, and 3 percent scraped. Thus, the majority of the vessels in this ware group have a plain surface finish. No excessive care was taken in the final smoothing of either the interior or exterior surface. The neck and rim areas of Green Point ware vessels are plain and generally more carefully smoothed.

Green Point ware is represented almost entirely by jar forms. Possibly 2.4 percent of the rim sherds are from vertical rim or inverted rim bowls, but a number of these profiles are questionable. Jars have a globular body with a moderately well-developed shoulder or neck constriction. Rims are short and are of two types. The more common rim is slightly everted and usually has an exterior camber. In addition, this rim form often has an interior upper rim channel resulting in a more pronounced exterior camber. Rim decoration is executed on the cambered area. Less frequently, the rim is markedly everted; in which case the camber and channel are absent or only slightly developed.

The bases of the larger utilitarian ware vessels (Fig. 44A) are sub-conoidal. Several miniature vessels (Fig. 44B), some definitely associated with disturbed burials, have rounded bases. Four small conical feet were excavated, each in a different unit. Paste characteristics indicate that these are from Green Point ware vessels.

While utilitarian ware vessels range from about 19 to 23 centimeters in diameter and 22 to 32 centimeters in height, the miniature vessels range down to 6 centimeters in diameter and 6 centimeters in height. These miniature vessels usually have a quadrilobate body. The paste, technology, decorative treatment, and quality of finish of the miniature vessels does not differ from that of the utilitarian pottery.

Green Point Rocker Stamped is the most prevalent type of the Middle Woodland period at the Schultz site. It is represented by 333 rim sherds and 2,200 body sherds, or about 75 percent of the Green Point ware. The rim material is assigned to four subtypes as follows: 47 percent Plain Oblique Left (Fig. 40C-I), 30.0 percent Plain Vertical (Figs. 40 A, B; 43, 44A), 15 percent Plain Horizontal (Fig. 40J-M), and 7.4 percent Dentate rocker (Fig. 45A-I). Nine percent of the rocker stamped body sherds have been decorated with a dentate tool.

The 193 Green Point Incised sherds make up about 6 percent of the Green Point ware at Schultz site. The 110 rim sherds are distributed into four subtypes as follows: 71.8 percent crosshatched, (Fig. 45J-W), 11.8 percent Vertical (Fig. 46G-M), 9.1 percent Horizontal (Fig. 46A-F), and 7.3 percent Dentate Tool (Fig. 46N-P). Green Point Crosshatched Incised, although morphologically and technologically similar to Green Point Rocker Stamped, is a somewhat finer pottery. The vessels are smaller, vessel walls are thinner, and the decoration is finer and better executed.

Green Point Brushed is the least important Green Point type at the Schultz site. Fourteen rim sherds have a brushed upper rim zone, and seven body sherds exhibit brushed filled zones. The cambered and/or channeled rim is not so common in Green Point Brushed as in the other Green Point ware types.

The name Green Point Plain may be somewhat misleading, for the single partially restorable vessel of this type has a free rocker dentate stamped shoulder and upper body decoration. The name actually refers to the rim type which is typically cambered and, as in other Green Point

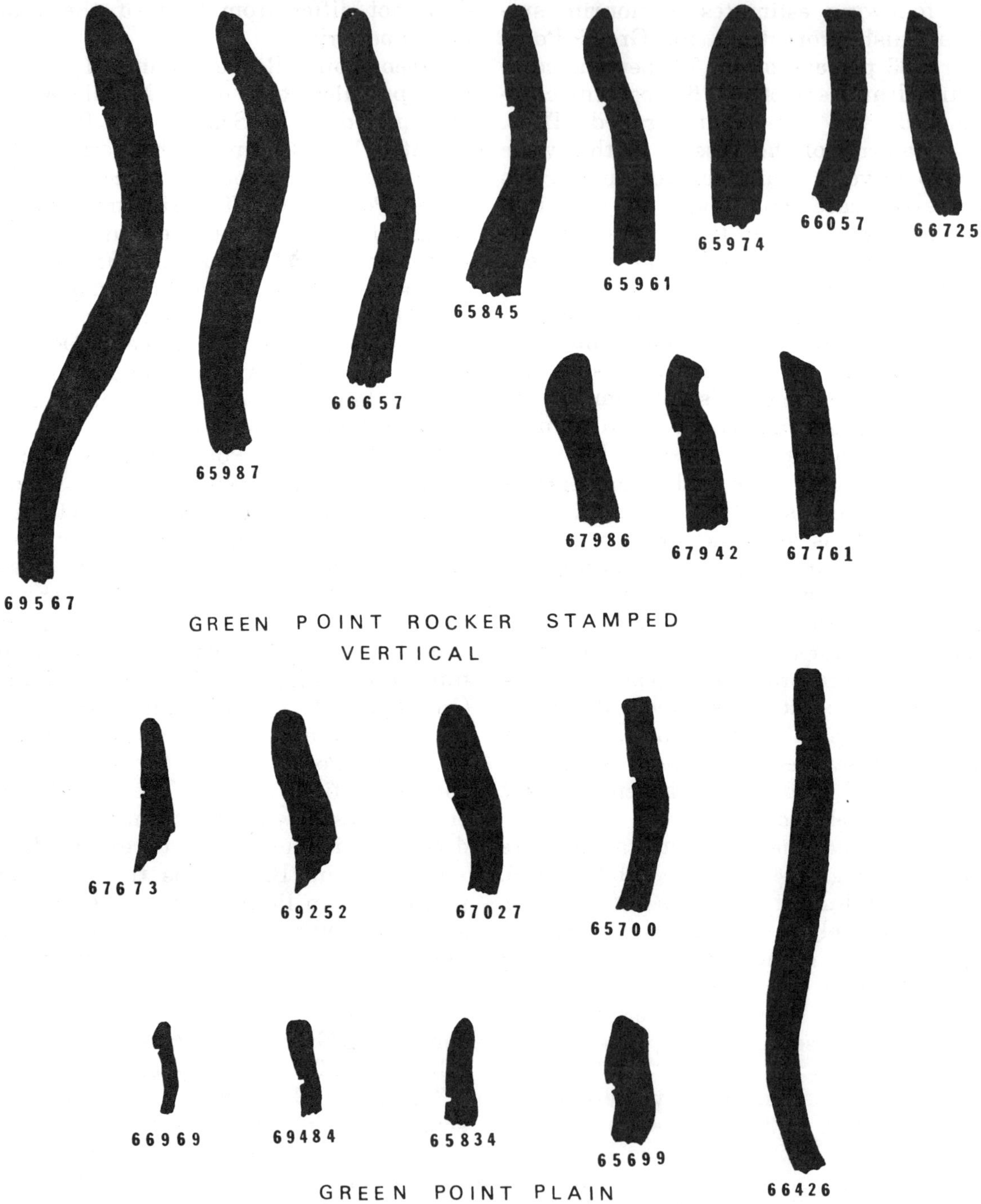

Fig. 41. Schultz site rim profiles. The interior is to the right.

ware types, has a single row of punctations encircling the rim at the base of the camber. The upper rim zone camber, however, is left plain. The 40 Green Point Plain rims at the Schultz site make up 9.8 percent of the Green Point ware rim material.

On the basis of paste and technological characteristics, 2740 decorated body sherds are assigned to the Green Point ware, but cannot be definitely assigned to specific types. The frequency of decorative technique is as follows:

Plain rocker stamped		2002 (73.1%)
zoned	407	
zoning indeterminate	1595	
Dentate rocker stamped		198 (7.2%)
zoned	50	
zoning indeterminate	148	
Plain incised		351 (12.8%)
crosshatched	22	
rectilinear vertical parallel lines	24	
rectilinear	108	
curvilinear	52	
indeterminate form	145	
Dentate tool incised		61 (2.2%)
zoned	21	
zoning indeterminate	40	
Punctated		121 (4.4%)
linear	73	
zoned	12	
zoning indeterminate	36	
Zone brushed		7 (0.3%)

Green Point Ware, Stratigraphic Distribution

It is thought that Green Point ware reached a maximum popularity during the middle portion of the Middle Woodland period. The stratigraphic relationship of Green Point ware with Tittabawassee ware is discussed above. Green Point ware succeeded Tittabawassee ware and was in turn succeeded by other Middle Woodland types. Of the total 2724 Green Point ware rim sherds and decorated body sherds plotted in the composit correlation (Table 42), 1646 (60.5%) are from stratigraphic Units III*a* and III*b*. Reuben Linear Cord Impressed and the unnamed plain excurved rim and plain straight rim types are typologically similar to Middle Woodland ceramics, and their stratigraphic position indicates that they followed the maximum occurrence of Green Point ware at the Schultz site.

There is some evidence that Green Point Plain Rocker Stamped reached a maximum popularity before its companion types, Green Point Dentate Rocker Stamped, Green Point Crosshatched Incised, and Green Point Plain. The composit correlation (Table 42, indicates that sherds of all of these latter types occur in greater than expected numbers (when compared with Green Point Plain Rocker Stamped the marker type for the ware group) in stratigraphic Units III*b* and IV*a*. In excavation Unit 510E570 it appears that Green Point Dentate Rocker Stamped and Green Point Crosshatched Incised achieve maximum popularity slightly later than Green Point Plain Rocker Stamped. A similar situation is indicated for Green Point Plain Rocker Stamped in Trench 6, Area B. In Trench 6, East Extension, Green Point Dentate Rocker Stamped exhibits a bimodal distribution, however. One peak is below the maximum occurrence of Green Point Plain Rocker Stamped and the other is above. There may also be some significant chronological differences between the subtypes of Green Point Plain Rocker Stamped. Using the composit correlation, we find that Green Point Plain Rocker Stamped has its maximum occurrence in stratigraphic Unit III*b*. When the subtypes of Green Point Plain Rocker Stamped were used with the composit stratigraphic units, it was found that Green Point Plain Horizontal Rocker Stamped was most abundant in level III*a*, or below Green Point Plain Oblique Left Rocker Stamped and Green Point Plain Vertical Rocker Stamped. Green Point Brushed, Green Point Vertical Incised, and Green Point

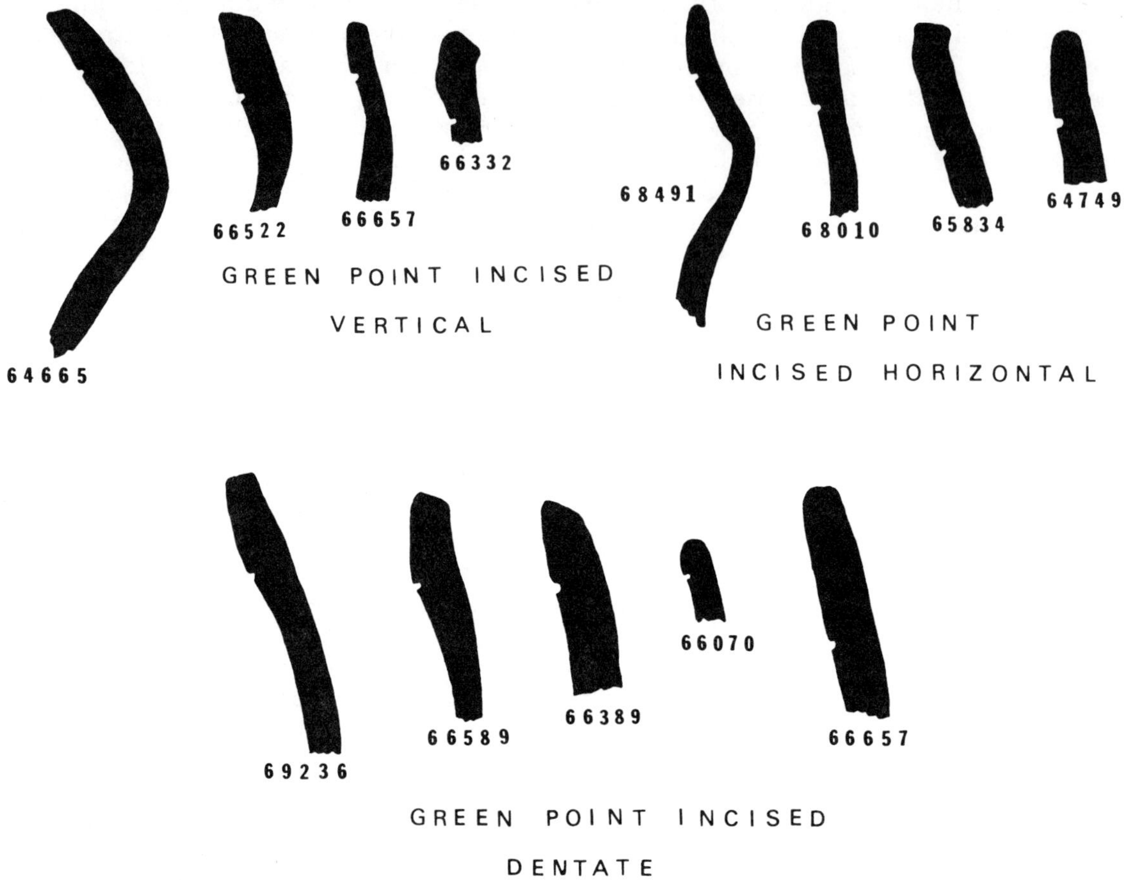

Fig. 42. Schultz site rim profiles. The interior is to the right.

Horizontal Incised occur in such small numbers at the Schultz site that individual stratigraphic analysis would be meaningless.

Green Point Ware,
Areal Distribution

An areal composit of all of the sherd groups attributable to Green Point ware (Appendix AB) was compiled and compared with the areal composit for all of the Schultz site sherd groups. Several interesting deviations are noted in the Green Point ware composit. The proportion of Green Point ware sherds is low in all blocks except B-1. This western block contained 39.5 percent (1011) of the Green Point ware sherds compared with 27.7 percent (3727) of the total areally plotted Schultz site sherds. When the Green Point ware composit distribution is compared with a composit plot for all Schultz site sherds, excluding the Green Point ware, a similar situation is observed.

All of the sherd groups attributable to Green Point ware were plotted individually by area, and the distribution of each was compared with a Green Point ware areal composit chart, in order to discover any significant horizontal distribution differences. Several interesting anomalies were observed.

Green Point Crosshatched Incised has a greater than expected frequency in Block C-4 and a lower than expected frequency in Block B-1.

Block	Crosshatched	Green Point Composit
B-1	33.3%	39.5%
C-4	41.4%	35.0%

The samples of each of the other Green Point incised types are so small that individual consideration would be meaningless. Green Point Incised Horizontal (9 sherds), Green Point Incised Vertical (12 sherds), and Green Point Dentate Tool Incised (44 sherds) were compared as a single group. A similarity is seen in the distribution of this miscellaneous incised material and the Green Point Crosshatched Incised. The frequencies of the former group were low in Block B-1 and high in C-4. This variation from the expected is even more marked than that of Green Point Crosshatched Incised.

Block	Incised Mis.	Green Point Composit
B-1	27.7%	39.5%
C-4	44.7%	35.0%

Only 33 sherds of Green Point Plain were plotted, but there was a higher than expected occurrence in Block B-3. The plotted samples of Green Point Brushed (19 sherds) and Green Point Zone Punctated (10 sherds) were considered too small to be meaningful.

Within the Green Point Rocker Stamped type, the subtype Dentate Rocker Stamped exhibits a lower than expected frequency in Block C-4 and a higher than expected frequency in Blocks B-2 and B-3.

Block	Dentate Rocker Stamped	Green Point Composit
B-1	39.3%	39.5%
B-2	8.4%	4.1%
B-3	16.2%	11.3%
C-4	26.7%	35.0%

The sub-subtype Green Point Rocker Stamped Plain Oblique Left has a greater than expected frequency in Block C-4; the frequency is low in Block B-1. Thus, the Oblique Left has a horizontal distribution most similar to Green Point Crosshatched Incised and Green Point Miscellaneous Incised.

Block	Oblique Left	Green Point Composit
B-1	39.1%	39.5%
C-4	42.4%	35.0%

This situation is reversed for the sub-subtype Green Point Rocker Stamped Plain Horizontal in that the frequency in Block B-1 is higher than expected and Block C-4 is lower than expected.

Block	Horizontal	Green Point Composit
B-1	47.8%	39.5%
C-4	26.1%	35.0%

The observed distribution of Green Point Rocker Stamped Plain Vertical closely conforms to the expected.

The horizontal distributions of the Green Point ware decorated body sherds show some interesting variations from those expected. Green Point Rocker Stamped Plain body sherds compose the largest group of Green Point ware material. Four hundred fifty-seven of these 2200 sherds show that the rocker stamping was confined to zones. The remaining 1743 sherds are either unzoned or indeterminate. It is this latter group that significantly determines the expected distribution of the Green Point ware composit. The zoned rocker stamped body sherds show a tendency to have a greater than expected frequency toward the west.

Fig. 43. Green Point Plain Rocker Stamped, vertical variety. (UMMA Neg. No. 94-8-1).

Block	Zone Rocker Stamped Body	Green Point Composit
B-1	44.7%	39.5%
C-4	28.8%	35.0%

It is interesting to note that Green Point Incised body sherds, particularly those with rectilinear elements, increase in frequency toward the east.

Block	Rect. Incised Body	Curv. Incised Body	Green Point Composit
B-1	22.7%	22.5%	39.5%
C-4	54.7%	45.5%	35.0%

Most of the major sherd groups were plotted in such a way as to determine their spatial relationship with the large circular stockade. This relationship is stated in terms of the relative percentages of sherds of each sherd group occurring in excavation units within the stockade. The other studies of the distribution of cultural and non-artifacial material indicate an avoidance of the stockade area during the Middle Woodland period. The ceramic study also indicates an avoidance of the enclosed area during the Middle Woodland period. More specifically, this avoidance was during the Green Point occupation, or the latter portion of the Middle Woodland period. If all of the Schultz site sherds were in random distribution over the 150,000 square feet of the site considered here, we would expect to find approximately 11.8 percent of the sherds of each group within the roughly 17,700 square feet of the site enclosed by the stockade. The actual percentages of sherds found within the stockaded area are as follows: 10.5 percent Shiawassee ware, 19.9 percent Tittabawassee ware, 3.3 percent Green Point ware, and 16.0 percent Saginaw Thin ware. This distribution would seem to indicate that the stockade area was taboo for certain utilitarian items during the latter portion of the Middle Woodland period.

Green Point Ware, Distribution Discussion

As noted, there is some indication of ceramic change within the Green Point ware period at the Schultz site. Although not conclusive, the vertical distribution information suggests that certain decorative techniques achieve maximum popularity earlier than others. Green Point Rocker Stamped, including the typologically undifferentiated Green Point rocker stamped body sherds, are most frequent in the III*a* and III*b* levels. Green Point Incised types, excluding Green Point Crosshatched Incised, and the typologically undifferentiated Green Point incised body sherds occur most frequently in the III*b* level, and continue into the IV*a* and even IV*b* levels where the frequency of rocker stamped material has declined markedly. Almost 50 percent of the Green Point Crosshatched Incised sherds are found in the III*a* level. This type declines to 16.2 percent in the III*b* level, and then increases to almost 25 percent in the IV*a* level. It would certainly appear that the incised types continued in use after the rocker stamped varieties had begun to disappear.

If the assessment of the changes in ceramic decorative technique through time are correct, then we might expect these changes to be reflected in the horizontal distribution as well. This is indeed the case. With the exception of Green Point Plain Oblique Left Rocker Stamped and Green Point Dentate Rocker Stamped, the rocker stamped sherds occur in greater than expected numbers toward the western part of the site (Block B-1). All of the incised material and the Green Point Plain Oblique Left Rocker Stamped occur with greater than expected frequency toward the east (Block C-4). Green Point Dentate Rocker Stamped would seem to occupy an intermediate areal position. Sherds of this last type are found in greater than expected numbers toward

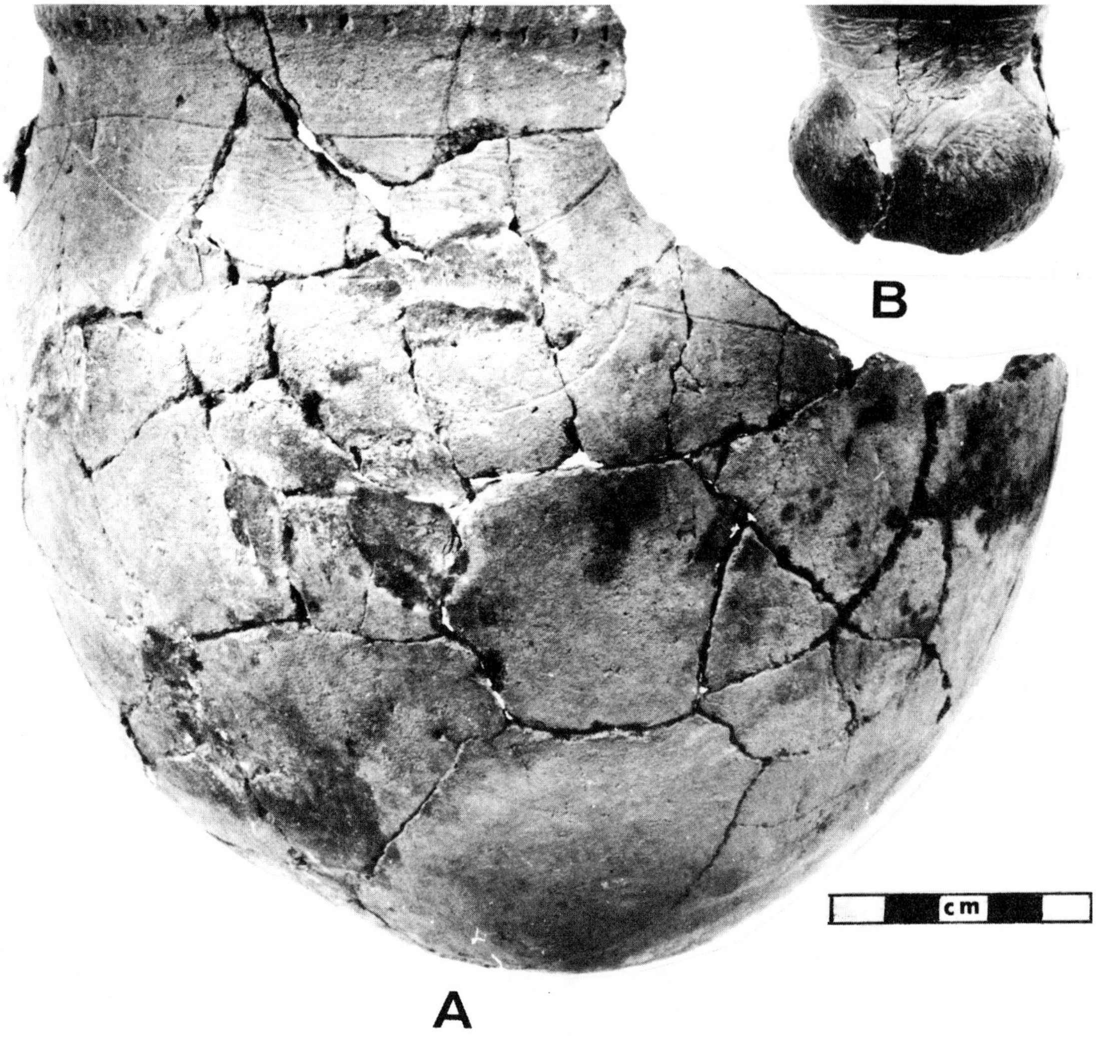

Fig. 44. Green Point ware, restorable vessels: *A,* Green Point Rocker Stamped, vertical variety; *B,* Green Point ware, miniature vessel. (UMMA Neg. No. 94-6-1 and 94-7-1).

the central portion of the excavated area (Blocks B-2 and B-3). Like most of the other rocker stamped types, it is of notably lower than expected frequency toward the east (Block C-4).

Thus, an analysis of both the vertical and horizontal Green Point ware distribution would seem to justify the following conclusions: The basic decorative techniques of the Green Point Ceramic period, rocker stamping and incising, may have been introduced at about the same time, but rocker stamping declined in popularity earlier than incising. During the Green Point period there was a shift, probably gradual, in the area of habitation from the west-northwest portion of the site toward the east-southeast. During the Green Point phase of the Middle Woodland occupation, a large circular palisaded area occupied the northeastern portion of the site. The function of this structure seems to have excluded the use of pottery within.

Green Point Ware, Relationships

As in the case of the Tittabawassee ware, the obvious affiliations of Green Point ware lie to the west and south. Griffin describes such traits as rocker stamping, crosshatching, zoned decoration, and rim cambering and channeling in his discussion of Hopewell ceramics in Illinois (1952:114-21). Griffin, and later Prufer and McKenzie, discuss similar characteristics for the Ohio Hopewell ceramics (Griffin, 1945:240-43; Prufer and McKenzie, 1965:26-32). Like much of the decorated Hopewell material in Ohio (Prufer and McKenzie, 1965:42-43), the Green Point ware is generally characterized by rather careless construction, coarse decoration, and poor finish. In this regard, it is most comparable to the Baehr group, or series, of relatively late Hopewell ceramics (Griffin, 1952:119-21).

Griffin describes the Hopewell rim and the Baehr material as occasionally having a rocker stamped decoration (Griffin, 1952:116, 120). George Quimby's type II*c* (1941*a*:71-72), also called Sumnerville Incised (Quimby, 1941*b*:492), of southwestern Michigan is quite similar to Green Point Rocker Stamped. Quimby notes the occurence of this material at four of the Goodall Focus sites. An illustrated vessel from the Converse site in Kent County, Michigan is strikingly like the Green Point Rocker Stamped vessels at the Schultz site (Quimby, 1941*a*:101-02, Pl. 17, No. 4). More recently, Richard Flanders has described similar material from the Spoonville site. His Crockery Cambered Rim sherds are 18.9 percent plain rocker stamped and 4.8 percent dentate rocker stamped (Flanders, 1965:349). Horizontal rocker stamping appears to be the most common form at the Spoonville site. To the south, in central and southern Ohio, Chillicothe Rocker Stamped pottery exhibits a number of characteristics reminiscent of Green Point Rocker Stamped (Prufer and McKenzie, 1965:29-31). Apparently, no other Hopewell period component has produced such a large proportion of rocker stamped ceramics. In Illinois, this rim treatment is much more infrequent than crosshatching in any series of Hopewell pottery. The same is true of the Ohio material where Hopewell decorative treatment is, in general, rare (Prufer and McKenzie, 1965:32-38). Although much of the Hopewell material from western Michigan is from burial mounds, and perhaps not comparable to the utilitarian ware from the Schultz site, crosshatched rims are much more frequent.

Green Point Crosshatched Incised is the Schultz site correlate of the Hopewell Rim of Illinois (Griffin, 1952:116). Again, it should be pointed out that the Green Point material, including Green Point Crosshatched Incised, would be easily distinguishable from most of the Illinois Hopewell pottery on the basis of quality of construction and finish. Green Point Crosshatched Incised is, therefore, better compared to the Baehr material (Griffin, 1957:119-21). Quimby's type II*a* (1941*a*:70-71) or Norton Crosshatched (Quimby, 1941*b*:491) is the western Michigan correlate to Green Point Crosshatched Incised. Quimby commented that type II*a* was a local "copy" of Hopewell vessels actually imported into southwestern Michigan. He describes these imports under type I (1941*a*:67-70) or Hopewell Zone-stamped (1941*b*:490-91). Flanders reported that 3.5 percent of his Crock-

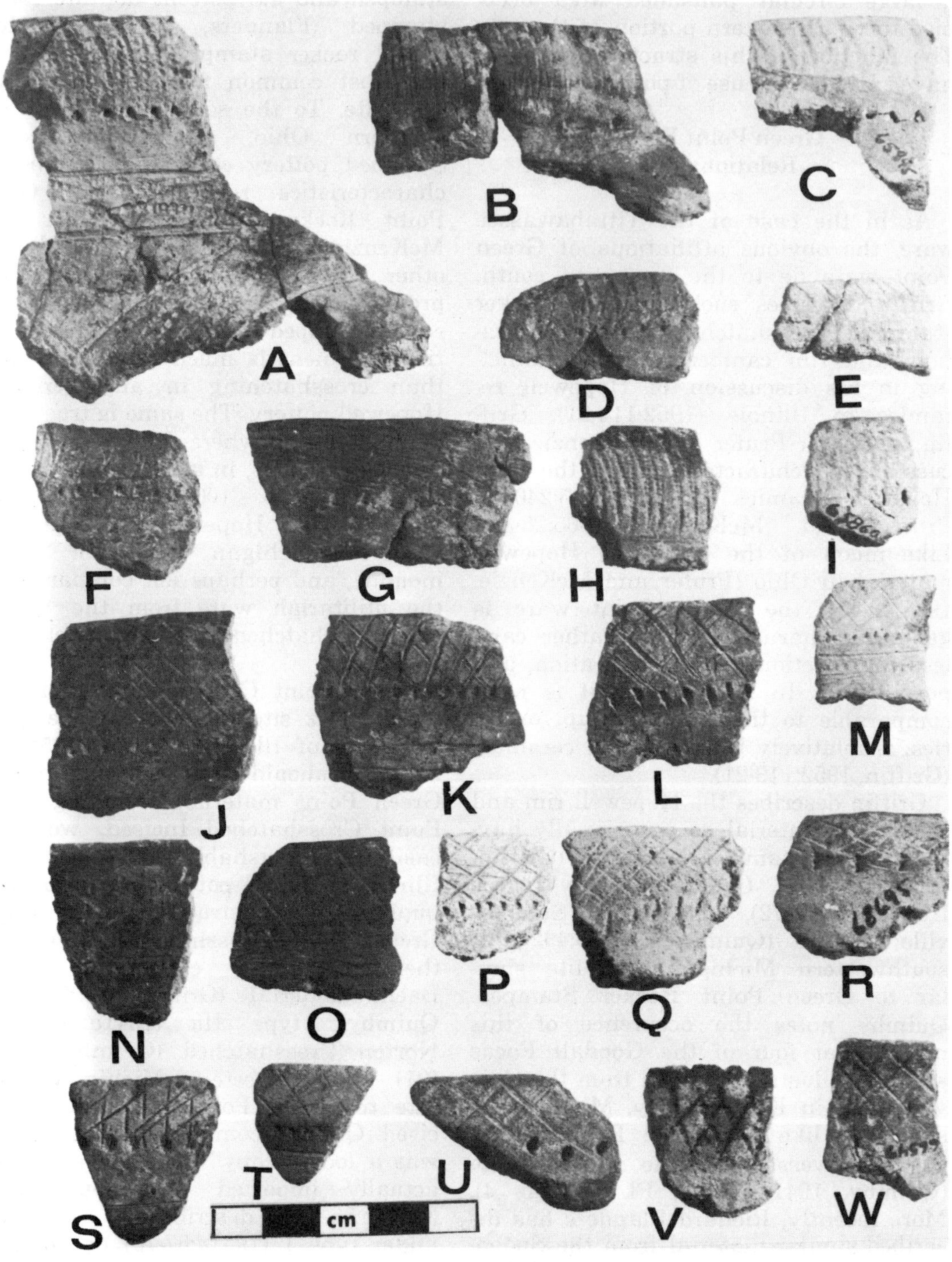

Fig. 45. *A-I,* Green Point Dentate Rocker Stamped; *J-W,* Green Point Incised, crosshatched variety. (UMMA Neg. No. 94-3-5).

ery Cambered Rim material from the Spoonville site had crosshatched rim decoration (1965:349). Many of the Norton Crosshatched vessel bodies bear the bold incising and zoned dentate stamping of the Havana tradition. This is not the case at Schultz site, where the body decoration of Green Point Crosshatched Incised consists of the rocker stamped or crosshatched filled zones, described for Green Point ware, bounded by narrow incised lines. Crosshatching is a common rim decorative treatment to the south in the Ohio Hopewell material. Prufer and McKenzie describe several crosshatched rims in the types Chillicothe Incised and Chillicothe Rocker Stamped (1965:26-27 and 29-31). They also describe a series of 19 crosshatched rims from the McGraw site that could not be specifically assigned to their defined Hopewell types. Prufer and McKenzie feel that the Ohio Hopewell material (Chillicothe) is most comparable to the Baehr series of Illinois. While crosshatching is the most important rim decorative technique of Illinois Valley Hopewell, Ohio Hopewell, and probably southwestern Michigan Hopewell, it is only a minor form at the Schultz site.

Small samples of material similar to Green Point Horizontal Incised have been recovered in Illinois Hopewell sites (Griffin, 1952:120). A portion of Quimby's Sumnerville Incised (1941*b*:492) is very much like the Green Point Vertical Incised. Green Point Brushed may well be related to Baehr Zoned Brushed of the lower Illinois River Valley (Griffin, 1952:120; McGregor, 1958:216-17), however, no intermediary is known from the northern Indiana—southwestern Michigan area. Pottery similar to Green Point Plain may be more common to the west. Approximately 19 percent of the Crockery Cambered Rim pottery at the Spoonville site has a plain rim zone (Flanders, 1965:349). Rims of some of the Baehr material of Illinois were sometimes plain (Griffin, 1952:120). Green Point Plain should not be equated with Brooks Plain of southwestern Michigan (Quimby, 1941*b*:492) or Hopewell Plain of Illinois (Griffin, 1952:119).

Mention should be made of the four small conical feet, presumably from two or more vessels with footed bases, and tentatively assigned to the Green Point phase of the Middle Woodland period. Prufer and McKenzie describe several such feet found at the McGraw site in south-central Ohio (1965:25). They associate the feet, and several other "Southeastern Series" ceramic traits, with the Hopewell component.

The Green Point ware assemblage at the Schultz site represents a local ceramic development of the Hopewell ceramic tradition. This tradition can be traced west into southwestern Michigan, and ultimately southwest into Illinois. Certain similarities are seen in the Hopewell material of Ohio, but, like the ceramics of southeastern Michigan, this Ohio material is seen as a relatively late, attenuated development that has its inspiration to the west. The Schultz site assemblage is notable for the overwhelming proportion of decorated pottery, almost all of which is undoubtedly utilitarian. The literature revealed no other Hopewell component with such a high proportion of decorated material.

The Green Point component at Schultz site is seen as rather late within the Hopewell period. This conclusion is based on a qualitative comparison with other Hopewell ceramics. It appears that the Green Point development at the Schultz site represents the retention of a number of classic Hopewell techniques and elements, modified through time and space. The loss of quality toward the close of the Hopewell period has been noted for several areas. Most of the Green Point ware technological elements

Fig. 46. Green Point Incised: *A-F,* Horizontal Variety; *G-M,* Vertical Variety; *N-P,* Dentate Tool Variety. (UMMA Neg. No. 94-4-1).

Fig. 47. *A-H,* Green Point Brushed; *I-P,* Green Point Plain. (UMMA Neg. No. 94-4-2).

and decorative devices probably came into the Saginaw Valley as a unit. Some new techniques were probably added, and, as we have seen, others were going out of use.

It has already been remarked that certain of the earlier Tittabawassee ware types (Havana-like) seem to continue independently through much of the Green Point ware period. Certain Green Point ware stylistic elements are seen to carry over into the post-Green Point ware period. It seems quite likely that there is little or no hiatus or replacement in occupation and that the disappearance of readily recognizable Hopewell elements was a gradual and continuous process.

Ruben Linear Cord Impressed, General

In the earlier phases of our analysis, it was thought that Ruben Linear Cord Impressed was a Green Point ware ceramic. Some rim form features and certain decorative techniques are quite similar. During the stratigraphic and areal distribution analysis, however, it became apparent that the linear cord impressed material is later than the Middle Woodland types described above. Linear cord impressed sherds also exhibit a horizontal distribution different from that of the Green Point ware material. It was decided that these distributional differences outweighed the typological similarities, so that the type is not included in the Green Point ware group.

Ruben Linear Cord Impressed (Fig. 48) is divided into two subtypes, Plain Interior and Striated Interior (Fig. 48N-W) on the basis of interior surface finish. Of the 47 Ruben Linear Cord Impressed rim sherds analyzed in the descriptive study, 25 sherds (53.2%) have been intentionally roughened on the interior rim. That this roughening was largely confined to the rim area is attested to by the fact that of the 166 body sherds probably attributable to the type, only 32 sherds (19.2%) have striated interiors. The interior striation begins just below the interior edge of the lip and are horizontal to the lip. They are generally deep and sharply defined. The striations might have functioned to prevent slippage while handling or carrying the vessel.

Aside from the interior striations, the two subtypes of Ruben Linear Cord Impressed are similar. Local sandy clay was utilized, and to this, a moderately large amount of crushed stone grit was added. The paste was well mixed and the vessel walls were carefully compacted and smoothed. Although the color variation suggests that the finished vessels were fired in open hearths, some care must have been taken in bringing the ceramics to the proper temperature, for there is scant tendency for lamellar converse fracture. In general, the Ruben Linear Cord Impressed vessels are more carefully manufactured than the Green Point ware ceramics.

The overall sample and the individual sherds are so small that it is difficult to say much regarding the morphology and size of Ruben Linear Cord Impressed vessels. Almost all of the rim sherds appear to represent small jars with a very slight constriction at the neck. In this regard they would be similar to Green Point ware vessels. No Ruben Linear Cord Impressed basal sherds were identified. Three small rim sherds, all of the Striated Interior subtype, may represent vertical rim bowls, but this is highly questionable. Some of the rim and lip features of Ruben Linear Cord Impressed are reminiscent of the earlier Green Point ware material. Of the Ruben Linear Cord Impressed lips, 20.9 percent are flattened and beveled to the interior, and almost 35 percent of the rims are modified by either an exterior camber or an exterior camber and interior channel.

The similarities between Ruben Linear Cord Impressed and Green Point ware do

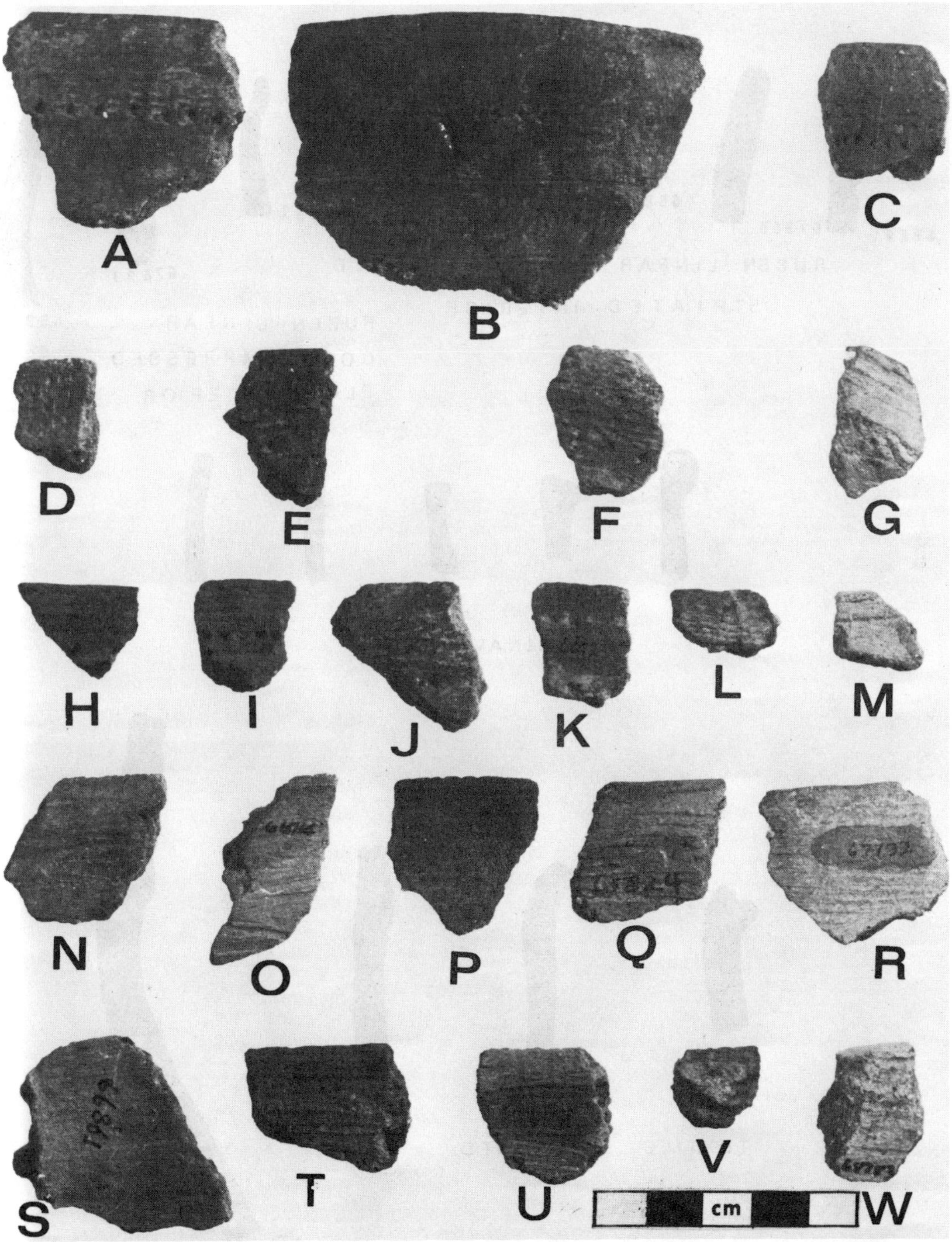

Fig. 48. *A-M,* Ruben Linear Cordimpressed; *N-W,* Interior Striations of Ruben Linear Cordimpressed, Striated Interior Variety. (UMMA Neg. No. 94-5-3).

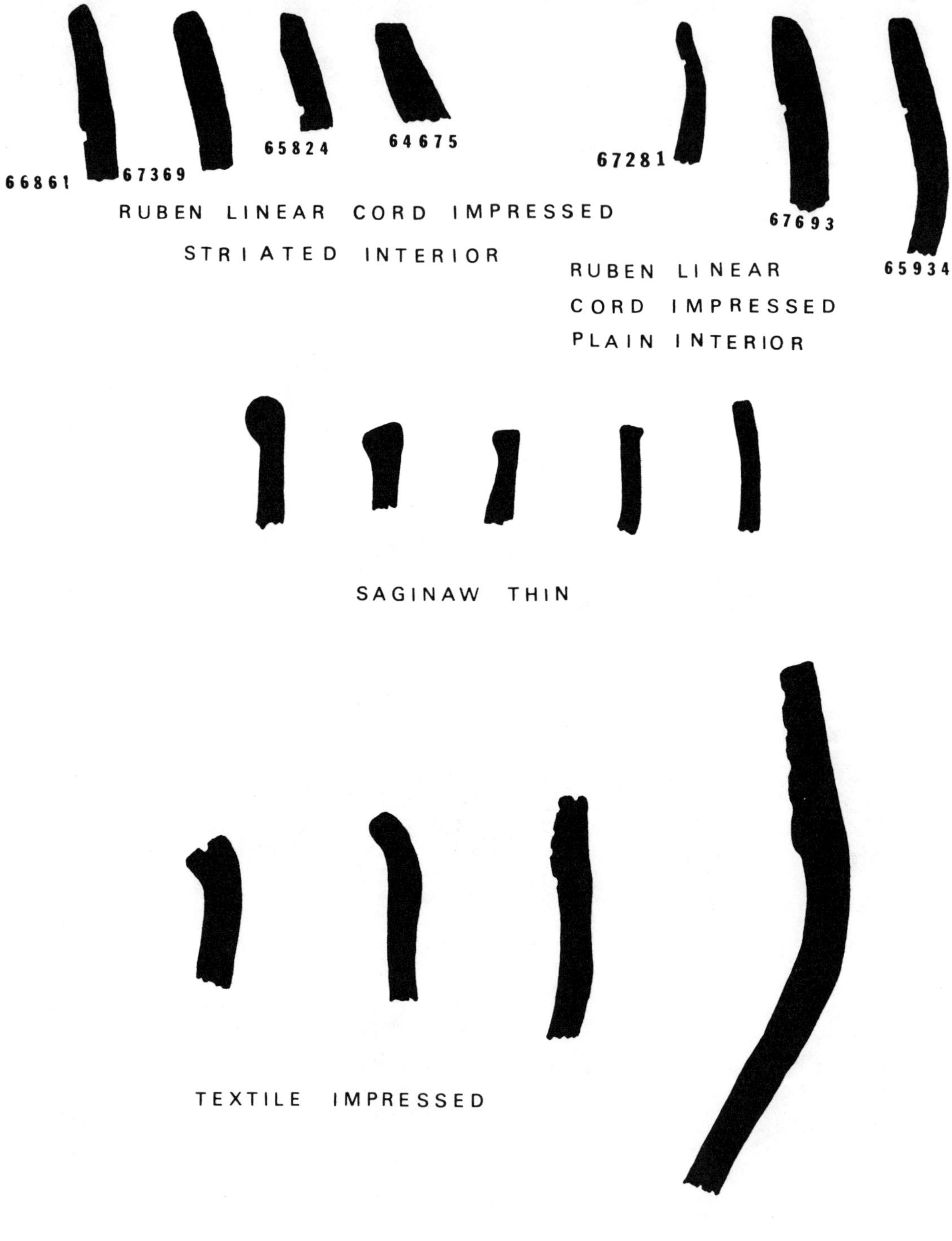

Fig. 49. Schultz site rim profiles. The interior is to the right.

not end with morphology. Certain decorative techniques and styles also continue into the closing phases of the Middle Woodland period. Zoned stamping continues to be the dominant decorative treatment. The upper rim zone is impressed with cord or, in some few cases, with a cordwrapped stick. As in the earlier Middle Woodland periods, this rim zone is bounded by a row of neck punctations. Zoned shoulder and body decoration is also indicated.

Ruben Linear Cord Impressed, Stratigraphic Distribution

As observed above, Ruben Linear Cord Impressed reached its maximum popularity after the decline of the Green Point ware types. While stratigraphic units III*a* and III*b* yielded 60.5 percent of the Green Point ware sherds, only 29.8 percent of the Ruben Linear Cord Impressed sherds came from these levels (Table 42). Stratigraphic units above III*b* yielded 67.5 percent of the Ruben Linear Cord Impressed sherds, but only 39.4 percent of the Green Point ware material.

Ruben Linear Cord Impressed, Areal Distribution

A comparison of the areal distribution of Ruben Linear Cord Impressed (Appendix AB) with the areal composit for all of the Schultz site sherd groups shows that the Ruben material is most frequent toward the south and east. Block C-4 contained 47.3 percent of the Ruben Linear Cord Impressed sherds, while only 36.5 percent of all of the Schultz site sherds come from this unit. The B-1 block yielded only 18.8 percent of the Ruben Linear Cord Impressed sherds, but 27.7 percent of all Schultz site sherds. When the areal distribution of Ruben Linear Cord Impressed is compared with that of Green Point ware, even greater differences are observed.

Block	Ruben Lin. Co. Imp.	Green Point Ware
B-1	18.8%	39.5%
B-3	15.4%	11.3%
B-4	8.8%	3.9%
C-4	43.7%	35.0%

Ruben Linear Cord Impressed, Distribution Discussion

The stratigraphic position of Ruben Linear Cord Impressed is above that of the Middle Woodland Green Point ware and below the Late Woodland cordmarked ceramics. Technologically, morphologically, and stylistically, Ruben Linear Cord Impressed is most similar to Green Point ware and is seen as representing the final phase of the Middle Woodland tradition (Havana: Tittabawassee-Hopewell: Green Point) at the Schultz site.

Unnamed Plain Ware, General

The material described here as Middle Woodland Plain ware bears little typological resemblance to the ceramics described above. The pottery is different technologically and stylistically from both Tittabawassee ware and Green Point ware. The stratigraphic position of this plain ceramic leaves little doubt, however, that it is of Middle Woodland manufacture. The material is placed into a so-called ware solely for descriptive purposes; the two types described are quite dissimilar.

The 108 plain rim sherds are sorted into two unnamed types on the basis of rim form. Sixty-five rims (60.0%) are straight (Fig. 50 L-S) and 43 rims (40.0%) are excurved (Fig. 50 A-K). The excurved rim type is fairly homogeneous internally, while the straight rim type is extremely variable. Indeed, this latter form might best be defined as a residual plain. Certain basic attributes are common to both types. The paste is sandy and contains considerable crushed crystalline stone temper. A moderately large jar with a globular body appears to be the only vessel form represented. A fairly well-developed shoulder and neck constriction is indicated, particularly in the excurved rim sample. Paste consolidation and compaction is generally poor. The interior and exterior surfaces of both types are only carelessly smoothed. Except for occasional lip notching, the straight rim type is without decoration. Some 35.0 percent of the excurved rims have notched lips or rim punctations or both.

As already mentioned, the straight rim type exhibits considerable internal variation. Although the craftsmanship is generally poor, some few vessels were carefully manufactured. A few rims appear to have been intentionally thickened, while other rims are definitely thinned. Lip form ranges from carefully flattened to pointed. It seems doubtful that this material forms a single valid type, if we require a type to have some temporal, areal, or functional significance.

The plain excurved rim type is less varied. The excurvature of the rim is similar in degree and form for most of the sample. None of the rims appear to have been either intentionally thickened or thinned. Of the lips, 84.0 percent are rounded and 15.0 percent are carelessly flattened.

Unnamed Plain Ware, Stratigraphic Distribution

The stratigraphic distribution of the plain material seems to confirm the contention that the two types of this ware are not closely related. Reference to the composit correlation (Table 42) indicates that the straight rim form tends to cocur further down in the cultural deposits. While 58.0 percent of the straight rims were found in stratigraphic unit III*b* or below, only 31.5 percent of the excurved rim type come from these lower levels. The level of maximum occurrence of the straight rim type is in stratigraphic unit III*b*. This is also the level of maximum occurrence for the Green Point ware types. The excurved rim form is most frequent in stratigraphic unit IV*a*. It would seem, then, that the excurved rim, while definitely manufactured during the Middle Woodland period, should be considered as slightly later than the straight rim form. The excurved rim probably attained its greatest popularity at the Schultz site when Green Point ware types were on the decline.

Unnamed Plain Ware, Areal Distribution

Appendix AB shows that the distribution of the straight rim material is not too unlike that of Green Point ware. Comparison of the distribution of the excurved rim form with composit distribution for all sherds (Appendix AB) shows that the plain excurved rim sherds occur with greater than expected frequency in Block B-1 (46.7%) and that the type is deficient in Block C-4 (13.4%). This distribution is unlike that of any other type. It should be noted, however, that the plotted sample of plain excurved rim forms is quite small.

Unnamed Plain Ware, Relationships

Rim sherds similar to the plain excurved rim type of the Schultz site are reported by Flanders from the Spoonville site where 5.5 percent of his Crocker Flared Rim sherds have a plain surface (1965:345-47). Quimby's Brooks Plain (1941*b*:492) includes some similar material. Quimby assigns the material to a late phase of the Middle Woodland Goodall Focus (1941*b*:546-47). The plain excurved rim type of the Schultz site is also similar in form to some of the Weaver Plain of Illinois (Griffin, 1952: 121-22; Wray and MacNeish, 1961:56-

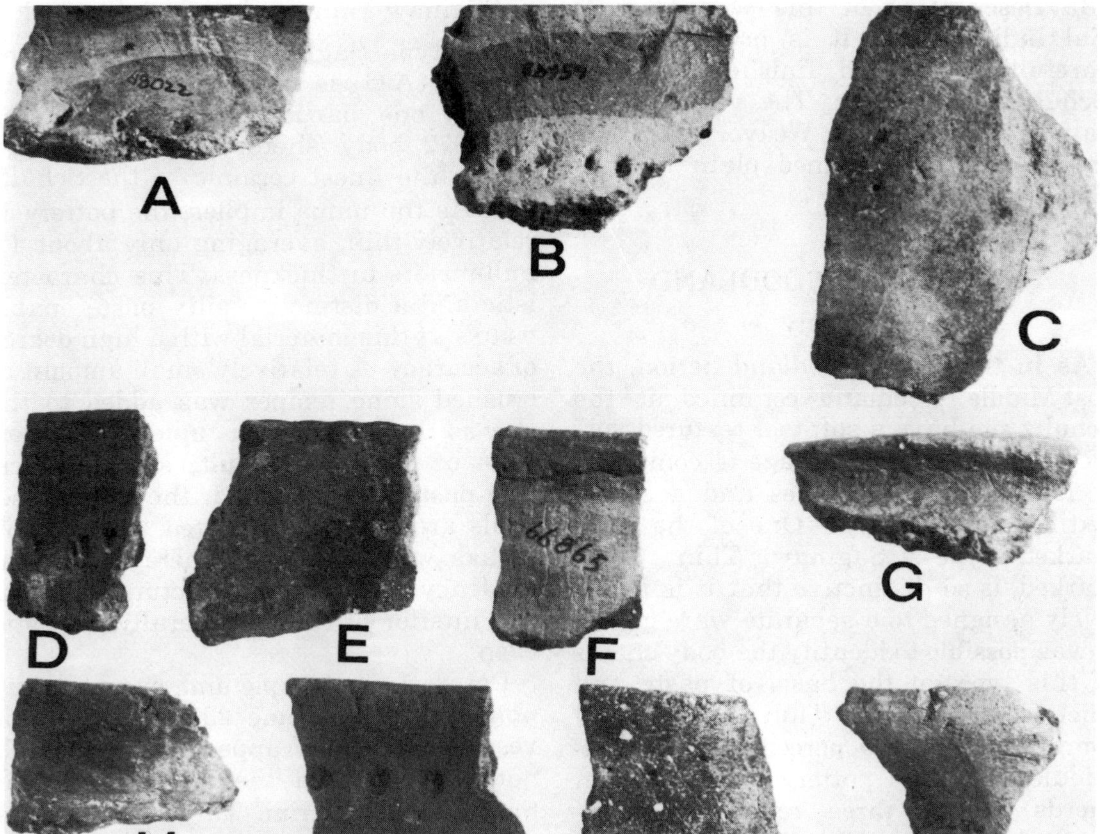

Fig. 50. *A-K,* Unnamed plain excurved rim; *L-S,* unnamed plain straight rim. (UMMA Neg. No. 94-5-4).

58). Descriptions of this Weaver material indicate that it is probably more carefully made and finished than the Schultz site ceramic. The various decorative treatments of Weaver Plain are lacking in the unnamed plain types of Schultz site.

POST-MIDDLE WOODLAND

General

As in the Early Woodland period, the post-Middle Woodland ceramics at the Schultz site have a soft-tool textured surface finish. The assemblage is composed of four cordmarked types and a single textile impressed type. One of the cordmarked types, Saginaw Thin Cordmarked, is so distinctive that it is tentatively assigned to a separate ware group. It was possible to identify the body sherds of this type on the basis of paste and thickness. Saginaw Thin Cordmarked comprises about 29 percent of the post-Middle Woodland pottery. Only the rim sherds of the three remaining cordmarked types could be sorted. The paste characteristics of undecorated rim cordmarked, noded cordmarked, and cordwrapped-stick impressed cordmarked are so indistinctive that no attempt was made to sort the non-Saginaw Thin Cordmarked body sherds into groups. Although most of the 1601 cordmarked body sherds probably belong to one of the three cordmarked types described here, some few were apparently incorrectly sorted from the earlier Woodland ceramics (see Table 42).

Both the body sherds and the rim sherds of the unnamed type, textile impressed, are, of course, identifiable. The type represents no more than 1.4 percent of the post-Middle Woodland material. Six shell-tempered plain sherds, only one of which is from an excavation unit, represent one of the latest aboriginal occupations of the Schultz site.

Saginaw Thin Cordmarked, General

The type Saginaw Thin Cordmarked (Fig. 51 A-O) is represented by 34 rim sherds, one partially restorable vessel, and 672 body sherds. Technologically, this is the finest ceramic at the Schultz site. As the name implies, the pottery is relatively thin, averaging only about 4.2 millimeters in thickness. This characteristic and a distinctive silty paste enable us to sort this material with a high degree of accuracy. A relatively small amount of crushed stone temper was added to the clay so that the paste is much finer than most of the other Schultz site ceramics. The paste is well mixed; the thin vessel walls are highly compacted, and no coil breaks were observed. There is a great tendency for converse fracture. Exterior and interior colors are generally light and even.

Decoration is simple and, except for lip notching, rare. Some 23 percent of the vessels had cordwrapped stick or simple notched lips, and the restorable vessel has a scalloped rim. Three rims had a single row of punctations encircling the neck. Fairly fine clear cordmarking apparently covered the entire exterior. This cordmarking extends to the lip.

All but three of the 35 rims appear to represent jar forms. Rim profiles suggest a poorly developed shoulder with a very slight neck constriction. The partially restorable vessel has a globular body. No basal sherds were identifiable. Three rim sherds may be from small bowl or cup forms. Rims tend to be either slightly everted (80.0%) or vertical (20.0%). Although most of the upper rims show a slight thickening due to finishing compression of the lip, six sherds actually have rim folds. The fold was thin and to the exterior. Finishing and subsequent cordmarking has almost obliterated exterior indications of the fold. Most of the lips are flattened, but some few are rounded and even pointed.

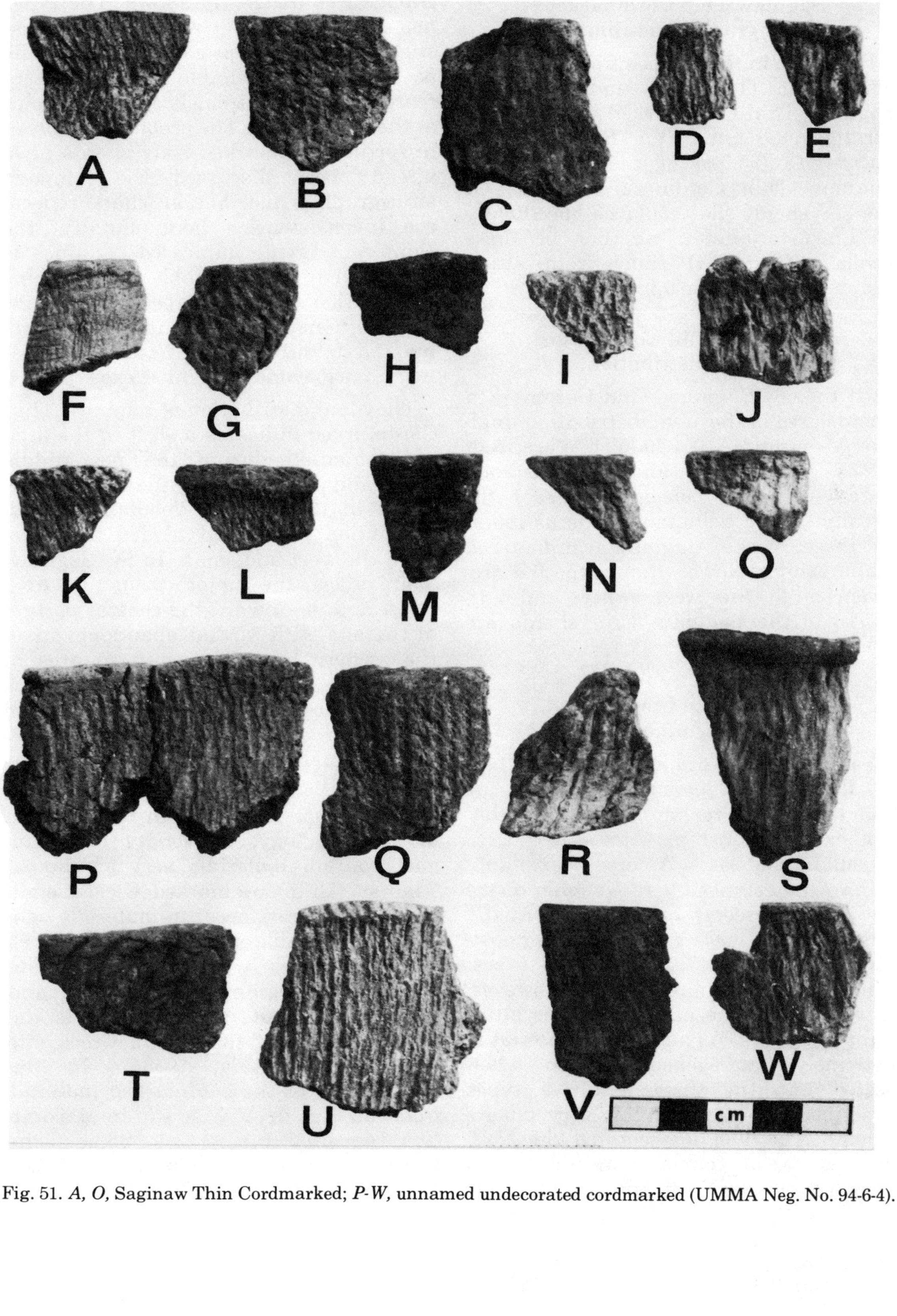

Fig. 51. *A, O,* Saginaw Thin Cordmarked; *P-W,* unnamed undecorated cordmarked (UMMA Neg. No. 94-6-4).

Saginaw Thin Cordmarked, Stratigraphic Distribution

Reference to the composit stratigraphic distribution (Table 42) indicates that Saginaw Thin Cordmarked is quite late. Stratigraphic units IV*a*, *b*, and *c* produced 513 (95.5%) of the 534 plotted Saginaw Thin Cordmarked sherds. Of the 369 sherds that could be specifically assigned to one or another of these levels, 297 (80.7%) came from stratigraphic unit IV*c*, the uppermost unit.

Saginaw Thin Cordmarked, Areal Distribution

Of the 664 Saginaw Thin Cordmarked sherds used in the areal distribution analysis (Appendix AB), 350 (52.6%) are from Blocks A-3, B-3, B-4, and C-3. This compares with 26.8 percent of all of the areally plotted Schultz site sherds found in these blocks. Saginaw Cordmarked Thin exhibits lower than expected frequencies to the west, where only 18 (2.7%) of the Saginaw Thin sherds are found in Block B-1.

Saginaw Thin Cordmarked, Discussion

Saginaw Thin Cordmarked is quite late in the general ceramic sequence at Schultz site. The real problem is its chronological relationship with other Late Woodland materials. A cursory examination of the composit stratigraphic distribution chart seems to indicate that the Saginaw ware is later than the other post-Middle Woodland cordmarked types. This conclusion is unwarranted, however, if we consider the nature of these latter unnamed types. As a unit the material is extremely heterogeneous. Even when sorted into the three tentative types described below, we are on very unsure ground. The type, undecorated rim cordmarked, is, of course, a residual category as the composit stratigraphic distribution chart clearly shows. The types noded cordmarked and cordwrapped stick impressed lip cordmarked, while possibly distinguishable style types, are represented by extremely small samples at the Schultz site. The problems involved in sorting cordmarked body sherds have already been discussed; the composit stratigraphic distribution chart reflects the inconsistencies here. Finally, the sample of textile impressed ceramics is too small to yield reliable stratigraphic information to the degree needed here. The relationships of Saginaw Thin Cordmarked to other Late Woodland types will have to come from other excavations.

The areal distribution of Saginaw Thin Cordmarked indicates a shift in the area of occupation during the post-Middle Woodland period. During the Green Point phase of the Middle Woodland period, occupation areas had tended to be toward the west and south. In the Saginaw Thin phase, the major occupation area appears to be toward the central portion of the site with virtual abandonment of the western area. This shift in area of occupation may have begun during the closing phases of the Middle Woodland period, for the Ruben Linear Cord Impressed material is also poorly represented in Block B-1.

Several site collections in the Museum of Anthropology, University of Michigan, contain materials very similar to Saginaw Thin Cordmarked. Closest similarities, of course, occur in materials definitely assignable to Saginaw ware at nearby sites such as the Hodges site (20SA130), Voeglair site (20SA133), and the Bussinger site (20SA194). It is the major element of the Spring Creek site assemblage (Fitting, 1968*b*). To the south, some of the cordmarked material from the Riviere au Vase site in Macomb County is on a thin ceramic. Some of the Riviere au Vase site material described as Wayne ware by Fitting (1965:158-59) is apparently similar to the Saginaw Thin Cordmarked. Decoration is relatively unimportant on the Wayne Cordmarked pottery. Saginaw Thin Cordmarked may well be a northern variant of Wayne ware equivalent to the Spring Creek Wayne wares.

There is some evidence that there was a trend toward thinner ceramics over a fairly extensive area during part of the Late Woodland period. In northern lower Michigan, some of the Late Woodland material from the Cross Village site in Emmet County and the Juntunen site on Bois Blanc Island in Cheboygan County is thin. In western Michigan, thin cordmarked pottery is found at the Moccasin Bluff site (20BE26) in Berrien County and in a surface collection from Oceana County.

Unnamed Cordmarked Ware, General

Unnamed Cordmarked ware represents a ware group in the loosest sense of the term; in addition to a cordmarked surface finish, the three sorted types share a relatively late chronological position (Table 42). Their relationship beyond this remains to be demonstrated. The 98 cordmarked rim sherds are sorted into three unnamed tentative types. Undecorated rim cordmarked (Fig. 51 P-W) is the largest class with 62 (63.2%) sherds. The type exhibits considerable internal variation, and it should be regarded as a residual class. The 19 (19.4%) noded cordmarked rims (Fig. 52 A-E) and the 17 (17.4%) cordwrapped-stick impressed lip cordmarked rims (Fig. 52 F-N) may represent valid style types. No attempt was made to sort the 1601 cordmarked body sherds into corresponding groups.

Most of the material in this ware is carelessly fabricated and poorly finished. The paste is usually composed of sandy clay with a moderate to large amount of crushed stone added as a tempering material. The paste is poorly mixed and poorly consolidated, resulting in a contorted irregular cross section. There is considerable variation in color, and firing clouds are common. By definition, the exterior surfaces have been finished by stamping with a wide cordwrapped instrument. Overstamping is common, and the cordmarking is frequently partially obliterated.

Rim morphology suggests that jars are the only vessel forms represented. The jars appear to have globular or cylindrical bodies with a slight neck constriction. Rims may be either straight or excurved and are most often vertical. Although the lip is occasionally flattened, carelessly rounded lips are most common.

The defining characteristic of the residual type undecorated cordmarked is its lack of any decoration. Noded cordmarked is simply decorated with a series of exterior nodes encircling the rim or neck. The nodes are punched from the interior. Both the node interval and the distance below the lip show great variation. The notching of cordwrapped stick impressed lip cordmarked is usually across the top of the lip, but may be to the exterior edge, to the interior edge, or to both edges. The long axis of the cordwrapped stick impression is occasionally straight across the lip, but more often the impression is at a slight angle.

Unnamed Cordmarked Ware, Stratigraphic Distribution

Undecorated rim cordmarked rim is represented in almost every stratigraphic level at the Schultz site. This reflects the fact that the type is not only a residual class, but that some of the material actually belongs to Early Woodland types described above. This last point is indicated by the occurrence of 14 undecorated rim cordmarked sherds in stratigraphic composit levels III*a* and III*b* (Table 42). Most of the material in this class is late, however, for 24 (61.6%) of the plotted

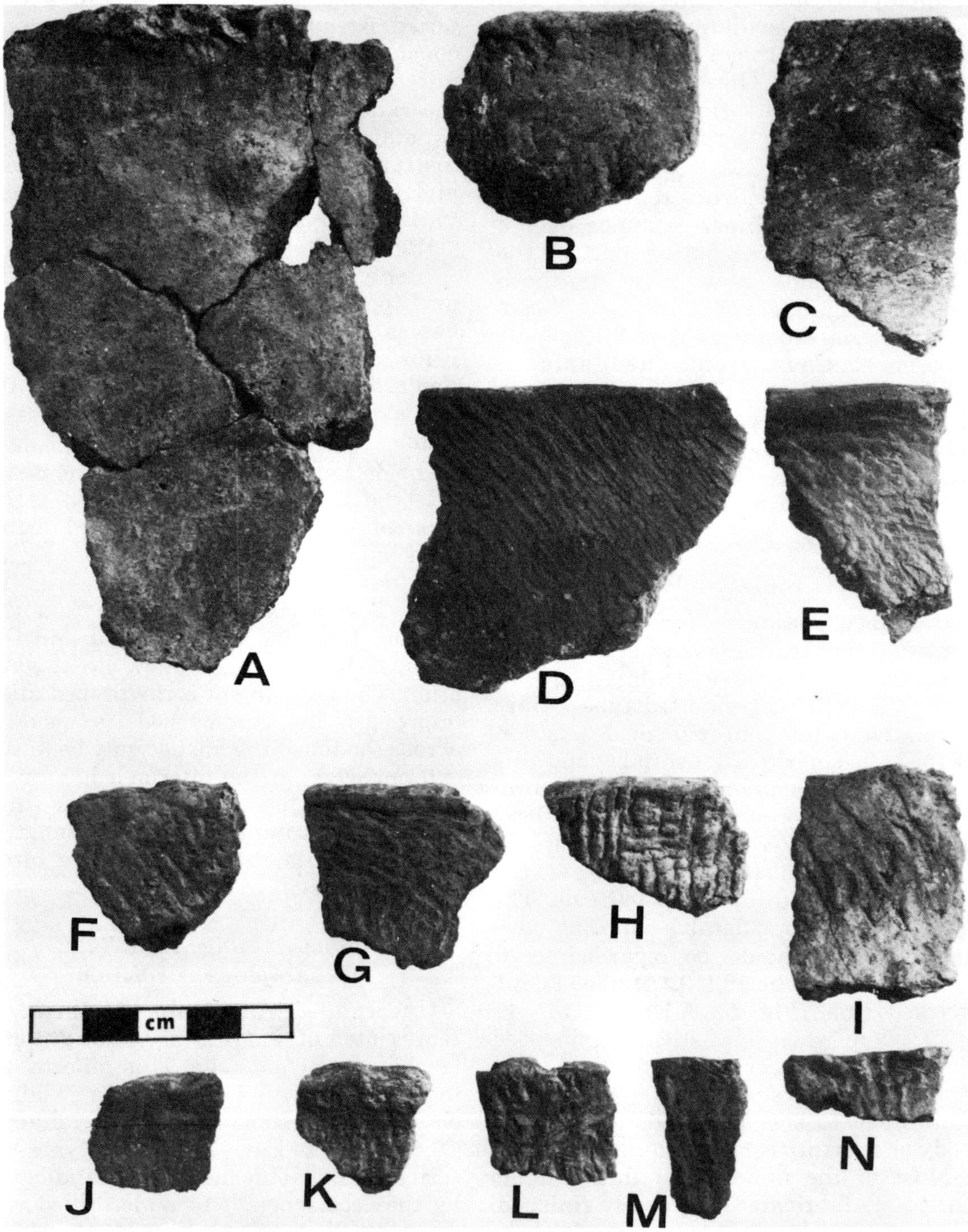

Fig. 52. *A-E,* Unnamed cordmarked and noded; *F-N,* unnamed cordwrapped-stick impressed lip, cordmarked. (UMMA Neg. No. 94-5-1).

undecorated rim cordmarked sherds occurred in the IV*a*, IV*b*, and IV*c* levels.

So few sherds of noded cordmarked and cordwrapped stick impressed lip cordmarked were plotted in the composit that their assignment here to the post-Middle Woodland occupation might seem questionable. This is particularly true of the noded cordmarked, none of which were found above the IV*b* level.

Unnamed Cordmarked Ware, Areal Distribution

Like Saginaw Thin Cordmarked, undecorated rim cordmarked occurs with higher than expected frequency in the eastern portion of the site, particularly in the column 5 blocks (Appendix AB). So little of the noded cordmarked (16 sherds) and cordwrapped stick impressed lip cordmarked (6 sherds) material was areally plotted that discussion would amount to unwarranted speculation.

Unnamed Cordmarked Ware, Relationship

As noted, the precise chronological placement of much of this ceramics is in question. The occurrence of large numbers of cordmarked (non-Saginaw Thin Cordmarked) body sherds in the upper levels of the Schultz site leaves little doubt that most of the Late Woodland ceramics have a cordmarked surface finish. Little can be said of the undecorated rim cordmarked or the noded cordmarked on typological grounds. Pressing a cordwrapped stick into the still-plastic clay, characteristic of cordwrapped stick impressed lip cordmarked, is a common decorative technique during the Late Woodland period throughout eastern Michigan. Fitting (1965:155-59) describes a cordwrapped stick impressed lip element for Vase Tool-impressed and Vase Corded of Riviere ware and for Wayne Cordmarked of Wayne ware. Rim castellation and/or collaring, so characteristic of all of the Riviere ware types, is not found in the Schultz site cordwrapped stick impressed lip sample. This would suggest that the type is more closely related to Wayne ware types.

Miscellaneous Post-Middle Woodland Sherds

The unnamed textile impressed type (Fig. 53 A-C) is represented by 33 sherds, only three of which are rims. All of the material is in a relatively sandy paste with crushed stone temper. Rims are excurved and the textile impressions extend to the exterior edge of the lip. The exterior of one rim is decorated with incisions which form vertical chevrons with the point down. The interior of one of the rim sherds bears textile impressions which extend to 9 millimeters below the lip. Another has either textile impressions or cordwrapped stick impressions on the interior rim; these impressions extend to 28 millimeters below the lip. One lip is flattened and fabric impressed and has a deeply incised line along the top. The other two lips are rounded and textile impressed. Nineteen of the 24 plotted textile impressed sherds are from stratigraphic composit level IV (Table 42). Textile impressed surfaces are noted for both Riviere ware and Wayne ware (Fitting, 1965:154-59).

Five Late Woodland rim sherds have a linear cord impressed decoration (Fig. 53 D-F). This decoration consists of four to five horizontal lines encircling a plain or cordmarked-and-smoothed rim zone. All of the rims are from sandy paste, crushed stone tempered vessels. The rims are straight to slightly excurved. Lips are flattened on four of the sherds and one example has a rounded lip. Two of the sherds have linear cord impressions along the top of the lip, while two others have oblique cord impressions across the lip.

Fig. 53. *A-C,* Unnamed textile impressed; *D-F,* unnamed linear cord impressed; *G-I,* unnamed simple stamped. (UMMA Neg. No. 94-6-2).

One of the sherds has a row of interior-punched nodes 29 millimeters below the lip. The material appears to be related to Wayne Cordmarked, Cordimpressed variant.

Four very small sherds have a linear knotted-cord impressed decoration. The paste is quite similar to the linear cord impressed material described above. Surface finish is plain or smoothed on three sherds while the fourth is impressed with cord or textile. Horizontal knotted-cord impressions encircle the exterior rims. The interior rim of one sherd bears vertical knotted-cord impressions, and another has vertical cordwrapped stick impressions on the interior rim. The lip of one sherd is notched with a cord-wrapped stick and another is simply gashed. Interior-punched nodes occur 15 millimeters below the lip of one sherd. Fitting (1965:155-57) notes that a knotted-cord is occasionally used to decorate Vase Corded and Macomb Linear Corded of Riviere ware.

Two rim sherds and eleven body sherds have a simple stamped surface finish (Fig. 53 G-I). The finish is apparently achieved by carelessly stamping a plain surface with a carved paddle. The lines are parallel and average about 2.0 millimeters in width; the grooves are slightly wider. All of the sherds are tempered with crushed stone. The rims and lips are undecorated. One large body sherd indicates that the vessel had a definite rim or neck constriction. Although carved paddle stamping is usually thought to be a Middle Woodland decorative technique, the occurrence of eleven of the simple stamped sherds in stratigraphic composit level IV (Table 42) suggests that the material described here is of Late Woodland origin. Fitting (1965:37) notes several simple stamped sherds from the Late Woodland site of Riviere au Vase in Macomb County, Michigan.

MISCELLANEOUS CERAMIC OBJECTS

Miniature Vessels

Thirteen Schultz site rim sherds represent miniature vessels. Although there are no complete or restorable examples, all of the vessels appear to have been quite small. Most of the cuplike miniatures are obviously constructed by modeling from a single lump of clay. They are generally thick and, although seven of the rims exhibit some form of crude decoration, the finish is in most cases very poor. The paste is often poorly mixed and consolidated. Four of the vessels lack tempering material, and two appear to be unfired. Thickness ranges from 2.5 to 10.0 millimeters and averages 5.9 millimeters. Lips are usually rounded and three examples have simple notched lips. Four vessels had a single horizontal row of punctations 5.5, 6.0, 7.0, and 13.3 millimeters below the lip. One sherd has irregular rectilinear incised lines below the punctations, and one sherd has a small flat applique node at the lip with narrow incised lines radiating out and down from the node.

It is suspected on typological grounds that these miniature vessels are of Late Woodland origin. Of the eight examples plotted by composit stratigraphic level, one is from Level II*c*, one from III*a*, one from III*b*, two from IV*a*, two from IV*c*, and one is from General Level IV. Fitting describes similar miniature vessels in the late phase at the Riviere au Vase site (1965:46 and Pl. XIX-XXI). The small size, crude fabrication, and poor quality of decoration and finish suggests that all of these miniature vessels were made for, or perhaps by, children; they probably served as toys.

Clay Pipe Fragments

Three fragments of pipe bowl and a large pipe stem fragment were recovered at the Schultz site. Two of the bowl fragments are from the same pipe and came from the 5*a*-6 level of Unit 510E570 (stratigraphic composit level III*b*). The pipe was made from a sandy clay tempered with feldspar. The buff paste is well consolidated and the surfaces are well smoothed. The cylindrical bowl stood about 29 millimeters above the stem. The exterior bowl diameter was approximately 26 millimeters. The bowl expands very slightly toward the base. It is 6.0 millimeters thick near the rounded lip and 7.2 millimeters thick near the base.

The third bowl fragment is from near the base of a cylindrical pipe bowl. It was less carefully made than the pipe described above. It is made from untempered sandy clay and has a plain orange-buff exterior. It was found in the same unit and level as the above fragments.

A flattened pipe stem fragment was found in the eastern extension of Trench 6 at the base of the plow zone (stratigraphic composit level IV). The stem is oval in cross section and expands toward the bowl. The hole appears to have been punched into the plastic clay. The pipe was made from a sandy, untempered, well-mixed clay. The plain gray exterior was carefully burnished, but the bite has worn to a chalky orange. The maximum thickness is 16.0 millimeters, while it is only 8.0 millimeters thick at the bite. Width at the bite is 9.0 millimeters, and the maximum width is 22.0 millimeters. The hole diameter is 3.4 millimeters.

Miscellaneous

Five small objects appear to be fired coil fragments. The sandy feldspar tempered paste is well consolidated. All have a plain buff colored surface. Three of the objects are straight and have a circular cross section, one is curved and circular in cross section, and one is straight and slightly flattened. Three are broken at both ends, one is broken at one end and pointed at the other, and one is broken at one end and flattened at the other, perhaps for applique attachment. The objects range from 17.0 to 42.0 millimeters in length. The diameter ranges from 4.1 to 8.3 millimeters and averages 6.45 millimeters. All of these objects are from Trench 6. Three are from Level 2-3 and two are from Level 3-4. The objects probably represent vessel fabrication coil fragments that were accidentally fired when brushed into an open hearth.

X

LITHIC INDUSTRIES OF THE SCHULTZ SITE

James E. Fitting

A fairly large sample of lithic material was recovered from the Schultz site, and to date it has been only superficially analyzed. This report covers 1,870 chipped stone tools, 46 other stone tools and a brief appraisal of 191,053 flint chips (462 pounds of chippage) recovered between 1962 and 1965.

The sections of this study are, in turn, descriptive and interpretive but not comparative. The analysis will be of the artifacts themselves, their vertical and horizontal distribution within the site, but not their relationships with other sites.

Fred Dustin noted long ago that the majority of flint artifacts found in the eastern portion of the Michigan lower peninsula were made of Bayport chert (Dustin, 1968). The Schultz site is no exception. In only one artifact class, that of blades, is the occurrence of exotic chert high enough to be significant. The rare occurrence of unusual forms on the site can be explained by a similar rare occurrence of these forms in the Saginaw area (Dustin, 1968).

LITHIC MATERIAL

The numbers of artifacts and cores from various levels at the Schultz site are given in Table 58 and the counts and percentages for the main occupational levels in Table 59.

Cores

The University of Michigan collections from the Schultz site contained 213 cores; 72 from pure stratigraphic units and the remainder from surface collections, areas of machine stripping and stratigraphically mixed units.

Three types of cores were recognized, including block cores, plano-convex cores and bipolar cores. Block cores (Fig. 54) were described in the report of the Eastport site (Binford and Papworth, 1963:83). Identical cores were found with some of the earlier burials at the Riviere au Vase site (Fitting, 1965:53-55), where I referred to them as "amorphous cores" and noted that the area where a flake had been removed served as the striking platform for the removal of the next flake. After comparing these cores, I would defer to the earlier descriptive term used at the Eastport site.

The most common core type is the plano-convex core (Fig. 55). This includes both flake and blade cores, although the latter are very rare. The flat side serves as the striking platform and a series of flakes are taken off around the edges. Occasionally the striking platform is worked, giving an impression of bifacial working. When this has been done, it is the removal of an additional series of flakes which distinguishes them from bifacial tools.

The final core type is the bipolar core

Fig. 54. Block cores.

which may have served as a tool rather than an actual core (Fig. 56). This core type has been discussed at length by Binford and Quimby (1963), McPherron (1967), and Fitting (1968*a*, and 1968*b*), all of whom considered its function as a tool type. Wright (1965) and Harrison (1966:61-63) have considered these objects to be "wedges."

Bifaces

We have 825 bifacially worked artifacts from the site including 386 from units of fairly pure provenience and 439 from surface collections, machine stripping and areas of mixed provenience. These were subdivided into 17 artifact categories.

Fig. 55. Plano-convex cores.

Fig. 56. Bipolar cores.

One of the most distinctive projectile point forms was a group of straight to contracting ground stemmed points, to be referred to hereafter as stemmed points, represented by 66 specimens (Fig. 57, 58C). All of these exhibit heavy grinding on the stems and bases and six broken examples have been reworked with perforator tips; an additional example has been reworked as a scraper (Fig. 58B). Examination under a binocular microscope revealed wear along the sides of

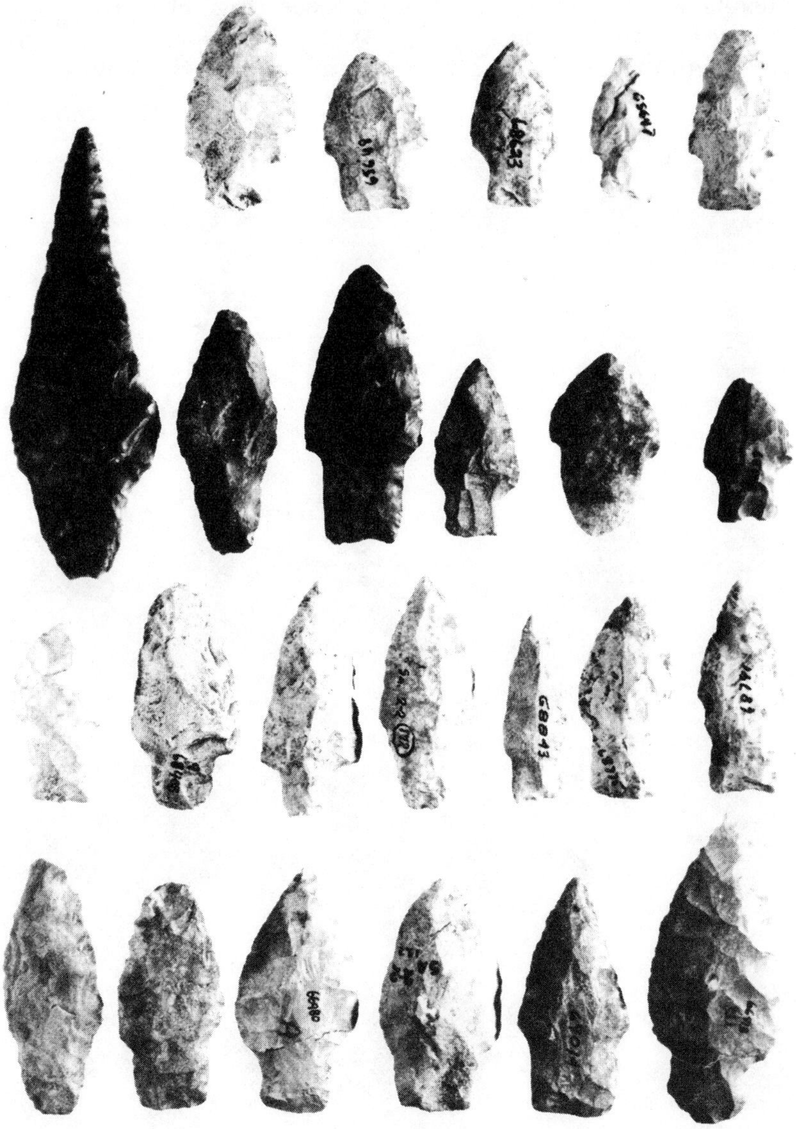

Fig. 57. Stemmed points.

many of these objects. Normally, this would indicate use as a knife but in this instance it may be the by-product of basal and stem grinding. The metric attributes for this series are summarized in the table below.

The bifacial tools found in greatest numbers in levels with stemmed points were plano-convex ovate bifaces (Fig. 59). We have a sample of 44 of these. Traces of wear are found on both the bases and the sides which would seem to indicate use as a scraper of some sort. A summary of the metric attributes of this group of artifacts is given in Table 45.

Twenty-eight large triangular pointed bifaces (Fig. 60) also served as a knife-type at the site. Wear is consistently found along the edges of these objects.

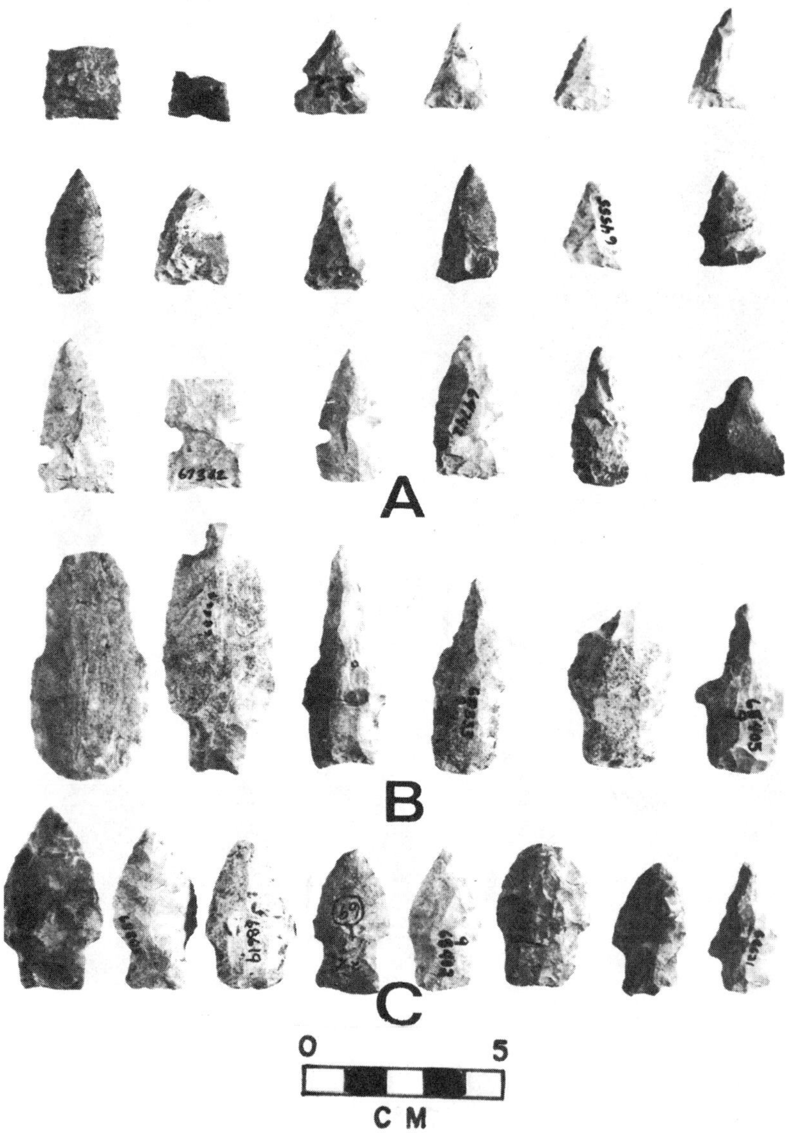

Fig. 58. *A*, triangular; *B*, stemmed points reworked as drills; *C*, stemmed points.

Fig. 59. Plano-convex ovate bifaces.

Fig. 60. Triangular pointed bifaces.

The metric attributes are summarized in Table 46.

TABLE 44
STEMMED POINTS
(In Centimeters)

	Length	Width	Hafting Width	Hafting Length	Thickness
N	45	62	64	57	66
Sx	233.7	152.8	113.2	99.6	59.8
Sx^2	305.11	389.68	208.57	192.22	55.64
$\bar{x}$	5.19	2.47	1.77	1.75	.91
s	1.44	.46	.36	.57	.15

TABLE 45
PLANO-CONVEX OVATE BIFACES
(In Centimeters)

	Length	Width	Thickness
N	29	44	44
Sx	158.0	122.0	57.3
Sx^2	882.35	349.72	78.43
$\bar{x}$	5.45	2.77	1.30
s	.88	.52	.30

TABLE 46
LARGE TRIANGULAR POINTED BIFACES
(In Centimeters)

	Length	Width	Thickness
N	15	28	28
Sx	90.2	85.3	24.6
Sx^2	559.26	262.19	22.99
$\bar{x}$	6.01	3.05	.89
s	1.10	.29	.23

The most common type of projectile point on the site was an expanding stemmed form. Initially, I divided these into a group of 76 large points, over 4.0 centimeters long (Fig. 61), and a group of 93 short points, under 4.0 centimeters (Fig. 62). When these measurements were pooled it was found that there was no evidence of a bi-modal distribution, so on typological grounds this distinction was not warranted. I did find, however, that this division had a temporal significance, so I have continued to use it. Tables 47 and 48 contain a summary of the metric attributes of these two groups of expanding stemmed points.

TABLE 47
SMALL EXPANDING STEMMED POINTS
(In Centimeters)

	Length	Maximum Width	Hafting Width	Thickness
N	77	91	90	93
Sx	250.2	185.1	126.0	72.3
Sx^2	821.20	382.02	178.57	57.77
$\bar{x}$	3.25	2.03	1.40	.78
s	.33	.25	.16	.13

TABLE 48
LARGE EXPANDING STEMMED POINTS
(In Centimeters)

	Length	Maximum Width	Hafting Width	Thickness
N	39	76	76	76
Sx	195.4	185.9	118.6	66.8
Sx^2	999.14	467.22	188.25	60.18
$\bar{x}$	5.01	2.45	1.56	.91
s	.73	.42	.21	.14

There is a small group of 12 narrow expanding stemmed points (Fig. 63A) which is of special significance. It was a search for a "Dustin Lamoka" site which originally led University of Michigan field parties to the Schultz site. The

Fig. 61. Large expanding stemmed points.

Fig. 62. Small expanding stemmed points.

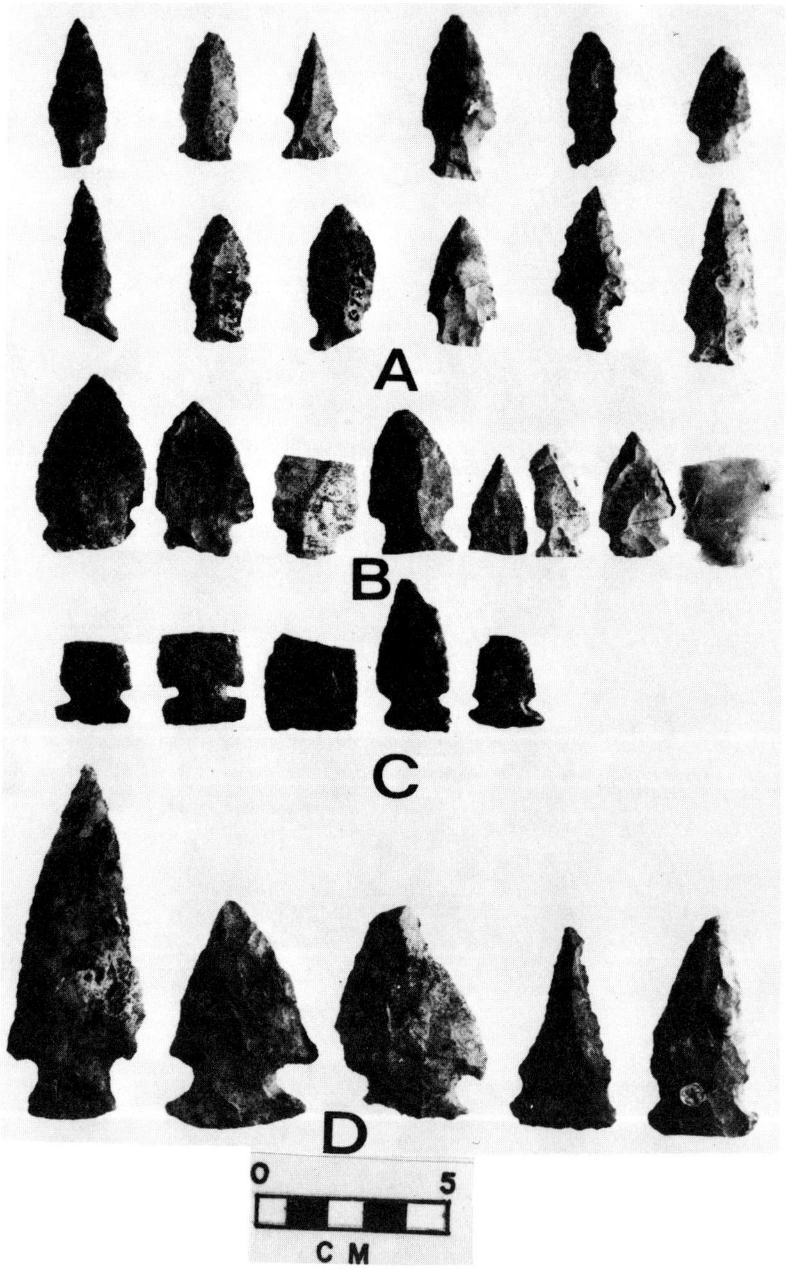

Fig. 63. *A,* Narrow expanding stemmed points; *B,* unifacial points; *C,* Pomranky cache blades; *D,* hafted knives.

Dustin point was first mentioned by Ritchie (1961:29-30) in relation to New York Lamoka points and Binford and Papworth (1963:105) reported a single specimen of presumably Archaic age from the Eastport site. More recently, University of Michigan field parties have excavated a site with a "Dustin" component (Harrison, 1966). The narrow expanding stemmed points from Schultz were separated from the other expanding stemmed points because of their similarity to Dustin and Lamoka points. At the Schultz site these are exclusively late Middle Woodland and Late Woodland forms. The metric attributes are summarized in Table 49.

TABLE 49
NARROW EXPANDING STEMMED POINTS
(In Centimeters)

	Length	Width	Hafting Width	Thickness
N	12	12	12	12
Sx	45.2	19.5	12.9	9.5
Sx^2	172.56	32.11	14.03	7.75
$\bar{x}$	3.76	1.63	1.08	.79
s	.46	.20	.12	.14

A group of ten expanding stemmed pointed bifaces has an extremely wide haft element and heavy wear on the blade edges (Fig. 63D). I believe that these served as hafted knives. Several exhibit extensive resharpening and there is a great deal of size variation (Table 50).

Eighteen small triangular points were found on the site (Fig. 58A). Four of these are notched but this notching appears almost as an afterthought. One expands slightly above the base but agrees with the series in all other respects. The metric attributes are summarized in Table 51.

TABLE 50
HAFTED KNIVES
(In Centimeters)

	Length	Maximum Width	Hafting Width	Thickness
N	5	10	10	10
Sx	31.9	33.5	23.0	9.3
Sx^2	213.65	114.07	53.67	9.01
$\bar{x}$	6.38	3.35	2.30	.93
s	(range 5.4-9.2)	.45	.29	.20

TABLE 51
SMALL TRIANGULAR POINTS
(In Centimeters)

	Length	Width	Thickness
N	14	18	18
Sx	41.0	32.5	9.5
Sx^2	125.22	59.95	5.23
$\bar{x}$	2.93	1.81	.53
s	.64	.27	.11

Ten corner notched points were found at the Schultz site (Fig. 64D). Most of these are fragmentary but what metric information is available is summarized in Table 52.

TABLE 52
CORNER NOTCHED POINTS
(In Centimeters)

	Length	Width	Hafting Width	Thickness
N	2	7	10	10
$\bar{x}$	3.70	3.00	1.70	.74
Range	3.3-4.0	1.5-4.0	1.2-2.2	.4-1.0

Five Pomranky cache blades were found on the site (Fig. 63C), four notched and one unnotched. This will be the only named point type I will use in this section, and I am doing this only after trying and rejecting other terms. I use it with the restriction that it is a type limited to one river drainage of the Saginaw Valley. These objects are all made of Pomranky chert and are almost identical to the one found at 20SA1 (Wright, 1964:Pl. I) in an Early Woodland context. It is unfortunate that none were found in stratigraphic context at 20SA2. Measurements are summarized below.

TABLE 53
POMRANKY CACHE BLADES
(In Centimeters)

	Length	Width	Thickness
N	0	5	5
$\bar{x}$	0	2.13	.44
Range	0	1.9-2.4	.4-.5

Four hafted scrapers (Fig. 64B) were found on the site. These may have been manufactured on broken expanding stemmed points. Their metric attributes are summarized in the table below.

TABLE 54
HAFTED SCRAPERS
(In Centimeters)

	Length	Width	Hafting Width	Thickness
N	4	4	4	4
$\bar{x}$	2.9	2.5	1.7	.9
Range	2.7-3.1	2.3-2.7	1.2-1.9	.7-1.0

Thirty-eight expanding stemmed point bases and 145 point tips were recovered from the Schultz site. Other bifaces include two gravers and 20 drills or perforators or fragments of these tools. Most of these were very small. The exception was a long expanding base drill found in the lower levels of the site (Fig. 64C). It is 10 centimeters wide along the blade and 1.6 centimeters wide at the base. It is made of an exotic brown and white banded chert.

Our collection also contained 34 complete bifaces of several forms ranging from ovate to nearly triangular (Fig. 65). This miscellaneous group of bifaces probably contains both preforms and knives. There were 220 other fragmentary objects with some evidence of bifacial workmanship.

Unifaces

A sample of 832 unifacial artifacial artifacts, manufactured on both flakes and blades, were recovered from 20SA2. This included 339 from areas of certain stratigraphic placement and 493 from the surface, areas of machine stripping and culturally mixed excavation units.

Eight unifacial points were found at this site (Fig. 63B). These are similar in form to the small expanding stemmed forms and, since they are found in the same cultural levels, they are probably a variant of this form (see Table 55).

TABLE 55
UNIFACIAL POINTS
(In Centimeters)

	Length	Width	Hafting Width	Thickness
N	4	8	8	8
$\bar{x}$	3.85	2.23	1.48	.56
Range	3.2-4.6	1.6-2.8	.9-2.1	.3-.8

Endscrapers formed a significant part of the assemblage. Two variants were recognized: a form with a sloping end (Fig. 66); and a form with a steep retouch

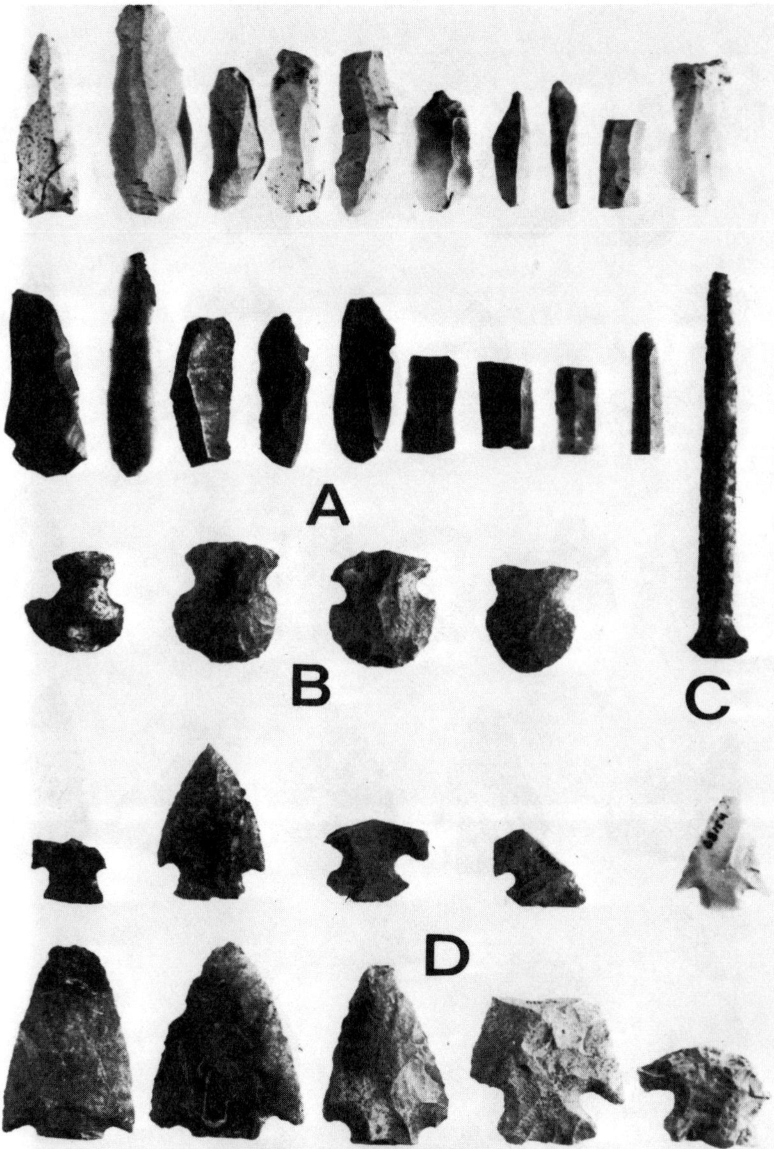

Fig. 64. *A,* Exotic blades; *B,* hafted scrapers; *C,* drill; *D,* corner notched points.

Fig. 65. Miscellaneous bifaces.

Fig. 66. Sloping retouch endscrapers.

on the end (Fig. 67). Our collections contained 51 sloping endscrapers and 82 steep endscrapers.

The largest category of unifacial artifacts were retouched flakes, predominantly side scrapers. This category contained 511 specimens, and I am certain that it will eventually be broken down into a number of tool categories as significant as those of projectile points. So far, only a series of distinctive flakes with retouch on the bulbar surface have been separated from the rest. There were 26 of these in our collections.

Our collections contain 154 blades, 55 of exotic chert (Fig. 64A) and 99 of Bayport chert (Fig. 68). The metric attributes of the exotic blades are summarized in Table 56 and the Bayport blades in Table 57.

TABLE 56
EXOTIC BLADES
(In Centimeters)

	Length	Width	Thickness
N	17	55	55
Sx	70.7	82.6	18.0
Sx^2	303.01		
$\bar{x}$	4.16	1.50	.33
s	.75		

TABLE 57
BAYPORT BLADES
(In Centimeters)

	Length	Width	Thickness
N	51	99	99
Sx	223.7	165.9	47.1
Sx^2	1028.18		
$\bar{x}$	4.39	1.68	.48
s	.97		

Among the exotic blades, 15 (26%) are a white chert which grades into a pinkish chert found on 16 blades (28%). Twenty-one blades (29%) are made on a fine-grained grey chert. Among the remaining three exotic blades one is black, one tan and one a banded grey and red flint (each representing 2%).

Retouch on one or both sides or the end is found on 28 of the exotic blades (52%) and 78 of the Bayport blades (79%).

We might also point out that while several Bayport chert blade cores were found on the site, we did not recover a single exotic blade core. There was no other fragment of exotic chert large enough to represent the remnant of such a core. I would suspect that exotic blades were brought to the site in a finished form.

CHRONOLOGICAL DIFFERENCES

Differences between the industries of the several occupations of the site are marked in a number of tool and core types. The numbers of tool and core types found in clear stratigraphic context is given in Table 58. In Table 59, this information has been grouped to contrast the Early Woodland, early and late Middle Woodland and Late Woodland industries at the site.

There is a clear succession of core types from Early Woodland through late Middle Woodland (Fig. 69). Plano-convex cores are replaced through time by block cores. The Late Woodland occupation was not included in this comparison since only four cores were recovered and three of these were bipolar cores (which may be a form of tool). On the cumulative graph in Figure 69, the Late Woodland curve would crosscut all other distribution lines, but demonstrate nothing of significance.

The dearth of cores in the Late Woodland levels is significant when we view it as a part of a trend. Cores account for more than ten percent of the items in Early and early Middle Woodland levels

Fig. 67. Steep retouch endscrapers.

Fig. 68. Bayport chert blades

TABLE 58
STRATIGRAPHIC DISTRIBUTION

Chipped Stone Artifacts	Stratigraphic Levels										
	II*a*	II*b*	II*c*	II*d*	III*a*	III*b*	IV*a*	IV*b*	IV*c*	Other	Total
I. Cores											
Block Cores	...	...	1	...	7	7	1	...	...	21	37
Plano-convex	...	1	13	1	16	4	6	1	...	53	95
Bipolar	1	1	2	...	4	1	2	2	1	67	81
II. Bifaces											
Stemmed Points	...	2	25	1	8	1	...	...	1	28	66
Ovate Bifaces	...	1	13	...	5	6	3	...	1	15	44
Large Triangular	...	...	3	...	4	6	1	2	...	13	29
Large Expanding Stem	...	...	...	...	12	8	4	4	2	45	75
Small Expanding Stem	...	...	3	...	11	8	10	6	3	52	93
Narrow Expanding Stem	...	...	...	...	...	3	1	1	1	6	12
Notched Knives	...	...	1	...	...	2	1	...	...	6	10
Small Triangular	...	...	...	...	1	...	1	...	2	14	18
Expanding Stem Bases	...	...	1	6	4	7	1	1	...	18	38
Point Tips	1	7	17	1	15	19	7	3	8	67	145
Corner Notched	...	...	...	...	4	2	2	...	...	2	10
Pomranky	...	...	...	...	...	...	...	...	...	5	5
Hafted Scrapers	...	...	...	...	1	1	...	...	...	2	4
Gravers	...	...	1	...	...	...	...	...	...	1	2
Drills	1	...	3	...	...	2	1	...	1	12	20
Miscellaneous Bifaces	...	...	2	...	3	3	1	...	3	22	34
Biface Fragments	...	4	21	3	24	16	9	3	9	131	220
III. Unifaces											
Unifacial Points	...	...	...	...	...	2	1	1	...	4	8
Steep Endscrapers	...	...	...	...	13	9	4	2	3	51	82
Sloping Endscrapers	...	...	9	...	7	3	2	2	1	27	51
Retouch Flakes	1	5	37	2	66	50	21	15	9	305	511
Bulbar Retouch Flakes	...	...	2	...	7	4	2	2	...	9	26
Blades	...	1	6	3	19	14	12	1	1	97	154
Total	4	22	160	17	231	178	93	46	46	1073	1870

in Table 59. From Late Middle Woodland to late Woodland, there is a decline in both relative and absolute numbers of cores. If we include bipolor cores as a tool type, we have a single Late Woodland core.

Seven bifacial tools furnish us with good evidence of artifact style change through time. The counts and percentages of stemmed points, Plano-convex ovate bifaces, large triangular pointed bifaces, large expanding stemmed points, small stemmed points, small triangular points and narrow expanding stemmed points are given in Table 60 and compared on a cumulative graph in Figure 70. Stemmed points and plano-convex ovate bifaces account for 87 percent of the Early Woodland artifacts in this series. Some continuity might be suggested by the 37 percent occurrence of these two groups in the early Middle Woodland industry and

19 percent in the late Middle Woodland industry. It also might be a reflection of the fact that all earlier artifact types were available to later occupants who could not avoid finding them while digging pits or walking eroded areas of the site.

Large triangular pointed bifaces are found in all levels but are most frequent during the Middle Woodland occupations. While several small expanding stemmed points were found in the Early Woodland levels, they are most common in later occupations. In the early Middle

TABLE 59
STRATIGRAPHIC DISTRIBUTION
(By Component)

Chipped Stone Artifact	Early Woodland		Early Middle Woodland		Late Middle Woodland		Late Woodland		Total
	N	%	N	%	N	%	N	%	N
I. Cores									
Block Cores	1	.5	7	2.8	8	3.0	...	...	16
Plano-convex	14	7.5	17	6.9	10	3.7	1	1.1	42
Bipolar Cores	4	2.2	4	1.6	3	1.1	3	3.2	14
Total	19	10.2	28	11.3	21	7.8	4	4.3	72
II. Bifaces									
Stemmed Points	27	14.5	9	3.3	1	.4	1	1.1	38
Ovate Bifaces	14	7.5	5	2.0	9	3.3	1	1.1	29
Large Triangular	3	1.6	4	1.6	7	2.6	2	2.2	16
Large Expanding Stem	...	...	12	4.8	12	4.4	6	6.5	30
Small Expanding Stem	3	1.6	11	4.4	18	6.6	9	9.8	41
Narrow Expanding Stem	...	...	...	...	4	1.5	2	2.2	6
Notched Knives	1	.5	...	...	3	1.1	...	...	4
Small Triangular	...	...	1	.4	1	.4	2	2.2	4
Expanding Stem Bases	1	.5	10	4.0	8	3.0	1	1.1	20
Point Tips	25	13.4	16	6.5	26	9.6	11	12.0	78
Corner Notched	...	...	4	1.6	4	1.5	...	...	8
Pomranky	...	...	...	...	...	...	...	...	...
Hafted Scrapers	...	...	1	.4	1	.4	...	...	2
Gravers	1	.5	...	...	...	...	...	...	1
Drills/Perforators	4	2.2	...	...	3	1.1	1	1.1	8
Miscellaneous Bifaces	2	1.1	3	1.2	4	1.5	3	3.3	12
Biface Fragments	25	13.4	27	10.9	25	9.2	12	13.0	89
Total	106	57.0	103	41.5	126	46.5	51	55.4	386
III. Unifaces									
Unifacial Points	...	...	...	...	3	1.1	1	1.1	4
Steep Endscrapers	...	...	13	5.2	13	4.8	5	5.4	31
Sloping Endscrapers	9	4.8	7	2.8	5	1.8	3	3.3	24
Retouch Flakes	43	23.1	68	27.4	71	26.2	24	26.1	206
Bulbar Retouch Flakes	2	1.1	7	2.8	6	2.2	2	2.2	17
Blades	7	3.8	22	8.9	26	9.6	2	2.2	57
Total	61	32.8	117	47.2	124	45.8	37	38.1	339
TOTAL	186		248		271		92		797

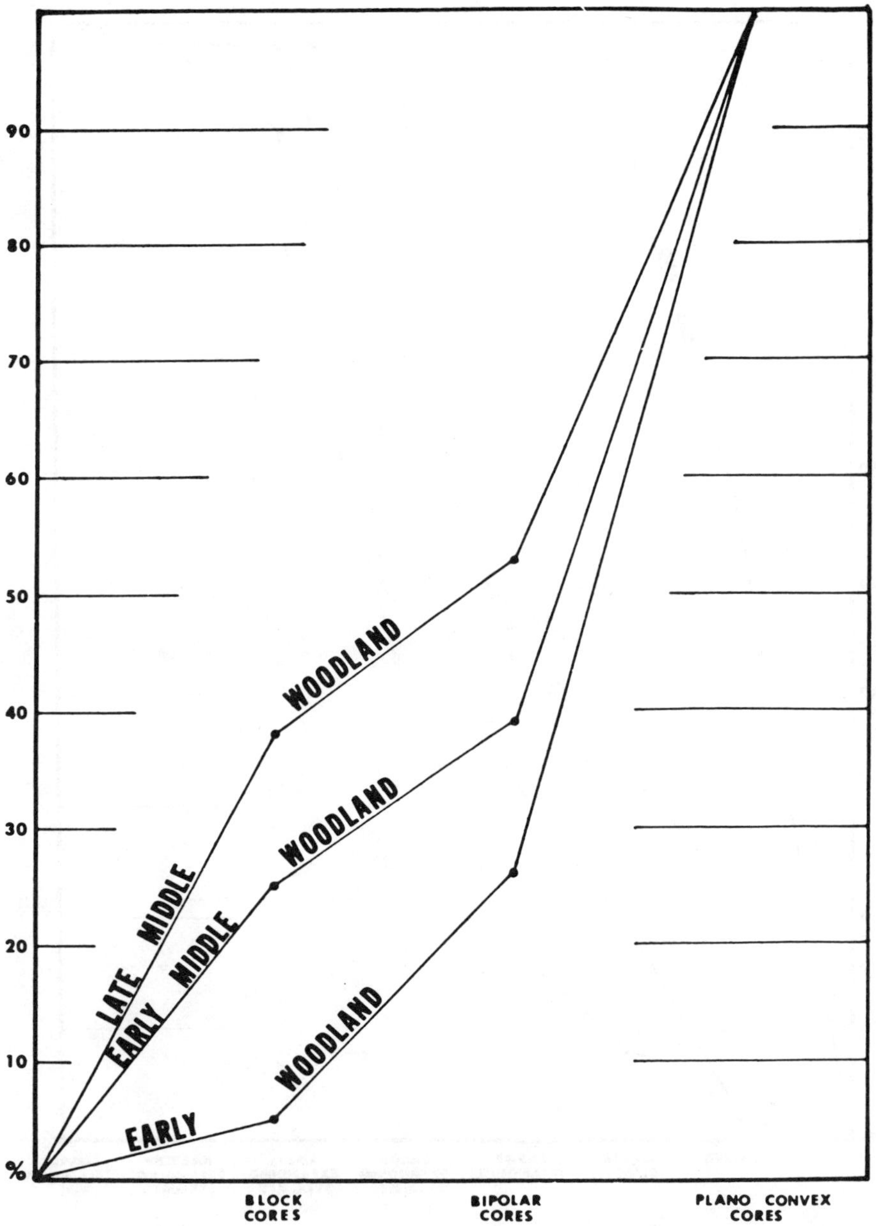

Fig. 69. Cumulative comparison of core frequency.

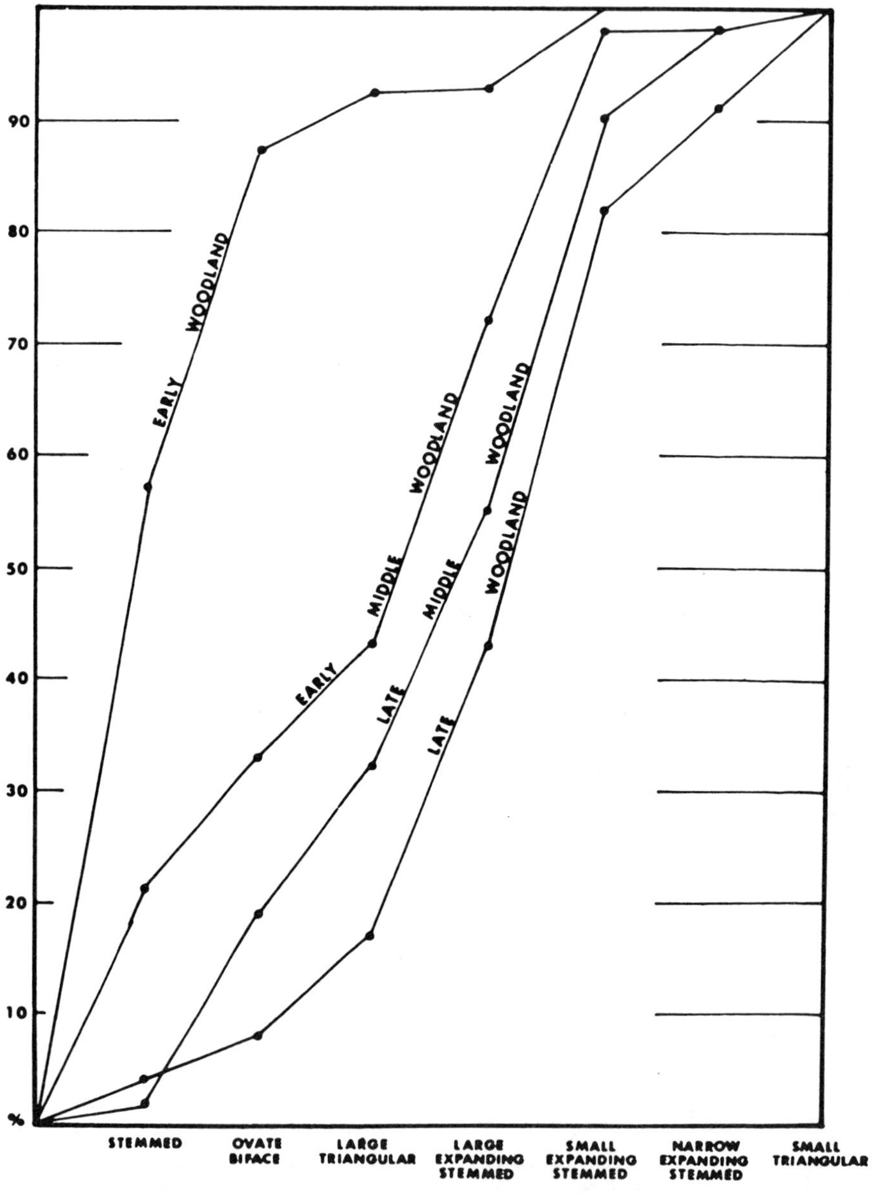

Fig. 70. Cumulative comparison of projectile point styles.

TABLE 60
STRATIGRAPHIC DISTRIBUTION
(By Component)

Key Chipped Stone Artifacts	Early Woodland		Early Middle Woodland		Late Middle Woodland		Late Woodland	
	N	%	N	%	N	%	N	%
Stemmed Points	27	57	9	21	1	2	1	...
Ovate Bifaces	14	30	5	12	9	17	1	4
Large Triangular	3	6	4	10	7	13	2	9
Large Expanding Stem	...	...	12	29	12	23	6	26
Small Expanding Stem	3	6	11	26	18	35	9	39
Small Triangular	...	...	1	2	1	2	2	9
Narrow Expanding Stem	...	...	...	...	4	8	2	9
Total	47		42		52		23	

Woodland levels the expanding stemmed forms outnumber the small expanding stemmed forms. In the later occupations, the small forms outnumber the larger ones three to two. Within the Middle Woodland occupations, the drop in large expanding stemmed points, many of which show evidence of use as knives, is partially compensated for by an increase in large triangular pointed bifaces, another knife form. There is a general drop in percentage of knife forms in the entire Late Woodland occupation which may have functional as well as chronological significance.

The narrow expanding stemmed points and small triangular points are clearly associated with the later occupations. The forms which resemble Lamoka points are found in late Middle Woodland and Late Woodland levels. One of the small triangular points was found in an unquestionable early Middle Woodland feature. While reaching their greatest frequency in later time periods, similar small triangular points have been found stratified below the Archaic occupations at the Schmidt site (Harrison, 1966:60) and one was found in the single component Middle Woodland midden at the McGraw site (Pi-Sunyer, 1965:84).

Several other biface groups have chronological significance. Hafted scrapers and corner notched points are exclusively Middle Woodland types. Our category of miscellaneous bifaces reaches its highest percentage in the Late Woodland levels.

While no Pomranky cache blades were found in clear stratigraphic context at 20SA2, one was found in the Early Woodland level at 20SA1 (Wright, 1964), suggesting an Early Woodland association for these objects. The single graver found in context from the site came from the Early Woodland levels. Drills and perforators, are twice as common in the Early Woodland levels as in later occupations. If we add the six broken stemmed points that have been reworked as perforators, the drill/perforator ratio of Early Woodland to any other level is at least five to one.

There are several chronologically significant categories of unifacial tools. Steep endscrapers are absent from the Early Woodland industry. There are only half as many flakes with retouch on the bulbar surface in the Early Woodland industry as in any other industry.

Blades are found in all levels. The Early Woodland blades, however, are all made of Bayport chert and are larger than the Middle Woodland blades. Blades are still predominantly a Middle Woodland artifact and exotic blades are exclusively Middle Woodland.

The blade assemblage from the Schultz site was not large in comparison to Middle Woodland sites further to the south. At the Schultz site they accounted for approximately eight percent of the total tool and core assemblage from the entire site and seven percent of the assemblage from the areas of certain provenience. This is in strong contrast to such sites as McGraw in Ohio where 58 percent of the approximately 300 chipped stone artifacts were blades (Pi-Sunyer, 1965) or Snyders in Illinois where 55 percent of both surface and excavated materials were blades (White, 1963:66).

These blades, however, offer a basis for comparison with other areas and with some rather interesting results. Pi-Sunyer, in his study of McGraw blades, noted a significant difference in width to length ratios between Illinois and Ohio Hopewell sites. The Ohio blades were much thinner in relation to their length. The sample from the Schultz site conforms more closely to those two samples readily available from Illinois than it does to the Ohio samples studied by Pi-Sunyer (see below).

Flanders (1965:186), in his analysis of the Knight Mounds materials from Illinois, observed that blades from mounds which he considered to be "early" averaged 5.7 centimeters in length while those from "late" mounds averaged only 4.3 centimeters in length. The average length of blades from the Renchville Mound in Illinois (Bluhm and Beeson, 1960), which dates to the first century B.C., is 5.3 centimeters. The Snyders site represents a long occupation but White's (1963:68) study indicates that many chipped stone artifacts suggest "... association with late Hopewell or Late Woodland occupations." The average blade length at this site is 4.9 centimeters, slightly less than the Renchville average.

Pi-Sunyer observed differences in blade length between the earlier Russell

TABLE 61
BLADE RATIOS

Sites	Width: Length	Sample Size
OHIO		
Brown's Bottoms	1: 3.23	13
Russell Brown Mound No. 3	1: 3.68	4
McGraw	1: 3.70	60
Turner Mound No. 2	1: 3.85	64
Turner Mound No. 1	1: 4.00	43
Russell Brown Mounds No. 1 & No. 2	1: 4.04	7
ILLINOIS		
Renchville Mound	1: 2.57	14
Snyders	1: 2.66	194
SCHULTZ SITE, MICHIGAN		
Early Woodland	1: 2.9	3
Early Middle Woodland	1:2.9	10
Late Middle Woodland	1: 2.6	15
Exotic Blades (entire site)	1: 2.8	17
Bayport Blades (entire site)	1: 2.6	51

TABLE 62
BLADE MEASUREMENT
(In Centimeters)

Sites	Average Length	Average Width	Sample Size
OHIO			
Russell Brown Mound No. 1 & No. 2	4.63	1.14	7
Turner Mound No. 2	4.0	1.03	64
McGraw	3.97	1.07	60
Brown's Bottoms	3.52	1.09	13
Russell Brown Mound No. 3	3.50	.95	4
ILLINOIS			
Renchville Mound	5.27	2.05	14
Snyders	4.87	1.83	194
SCHULTZ SITE, MICHIGAN			
Early Woodland	4.97	1.74	3
Early Middle Woodland	4.56	1.59	10
Late Middle Woodland	4.08	1.60	15

Brown Mound assemblages (Mounds No. 1 and No. 2) and the later assemblage from Mound No. 3 at that site with a decrease in blade length over time. The McGraw site, with radiocarbon dates clustering between the two groups of dates for the Russell Brown Mounds, also produced blades with measurements intermediate between the two groups. The only blade assemblage examined by Pi-Sunyer, where length does not decrease in later assemblages is that from Turner Mound No. 1. Pi-Sunyer indicated that this rather long blade assemblage for Ohio (average length of 4.6 centimeters) was probably late but the blades were of uncertain provenience within the mound.

The significance of the admittedly small sample from the Schultz site is that the trend of blade size reduction through time is demonstrated at a single site.

A vast quantity of chippage was recovered from the site which has not yet been fully analyzed. The counts and weights of flakes from the 1963 and 1964 excavations are given in Table 63. In 1963, a half-inch screen was used for most of the excavation while a fine screen was used for large parts of the Early Woodland level. In 1964, a quarter-inch screen was used uniformly over the entire site. As a result, the average weight of the early Middle Woodland chippage is nearly twice as great for the 1963 season as for the 1964 season. On the other hand, the average weight of lots of chippage from the 1963 Early Woodland excavation average less than those from the 1964 excavations, but there is a great deal more variation from lot to lot depending on the recovery technique used.

The chippage pattern gives us additional information on changing patterns of industrial activity at the site. There appears to be a nice correlation between the percentage of cores in any level and the average weight of flakes from that level: Early Woodland, 10.2 percent cores, .0308 ounces average weight for flakes; early Middle Woodland, 11.3 percent cores, .0391 ounces average weight for flakes; late Middle Woodland, 7.8 percent cores, .0284 ounces average

TABLE 63
STRATIGRAPHIC DISTRIBUTION OF CHIPPAGE
(Weights in Ounces)

Occupational Levels	Lots of Chippage	Count	Weight	x̄ Weight	Flake to Artifact Ratio
Early Woodland					
1963	70	11,134	302	.0271	
1964	92	15,900	532	.0334	
Total	162	27,034	834	.0308	145/1
Early Middle Woodland					
1963	54	5,790	373	.0644	
1964	200	28,504	971	.0340	
Total	254	34,294	1,344	.0391	138/1
Late Middle Woodland					
1964	135	57,579	1,638	.0284	212/1
Late Woodland					
1964	38	8,623	230	.0266	93/1
Total from Provenience Excavations		127,530	4,046	.0317	
Total from Site		191,053	7,391	.0386	

weight for flakes; Late Woodland, 4.3 percent cores, .0266 ounces average weight for flakes. I believe that flake size increases with increased dependence on cores for tool blanks at the site. When cores are not present for manufacture of new tool blanks, old tools or preforms are utilized and the average flake weight is less since more secondary and fewer primary flakes are present in the sample.

Several other correlations also support this position. The miscellaneous biface category (Table 59) varies inversely with the number of cores recovered from any particular level of the site. If these include preforms, then the pattern of variation is between dependence on cores and dependence on preforms. It also seems clear that later occupants of the site were reusing tools left by earlier occupations. At the first two levels of the site there are 38 artifact groups with 434 artifacts while in the upper two levels there are 44 artifact groups with 363 artifacts. All of the "diagnostic" early artifact classes are found in later levels. It appears, therefore, that dependence on cores decreases while reuse of older artifacts increases over time.

The degree of industrial activity is perhaps reflected in the ratio of flakes to artifacts: 145 to 1 in the Early Woodland level; 138 to 1 in the early Middle Woodland level; 212 to 1 in the late Middle Woodland level; and only 94 to 1 in the Late Woodland level.

FUNCTIONAL INFERENCES

Chipped stone tools were made for specific economic purposes. At the

Schultz site we are fortunate in having nonartifactual material which gives an indication of both season of occupation and the intensity with which a variety of resources were exploited. One of the things which I first noticed was the close correlation between changes in the frequency of mammal bone (more specifically, the percentage of the total meat represented by animal bone for any particular level) and the frequency of bifacial artifacts. In those Middle Woodland horizons where fishing, clamming and, indirectly, gathering of plant food species became more important, there was an increase in the percentage of unifacial tools. The use of this biface to uniface ratio as a rough index of the relative importance of hunting to other activities has been extended to a number of other sites in Michigan with fairly consistent results. The trend follows for the Spring Creek site (Fitting, 1968*b*) and the Goodwin-Gresham site (Fitting, Brose, Wright and Dinerstein, 1969) where they can be checked against the actual bone refuse recovered from the sites. It also seems to hold true for Summer Island (Brose, 1969) and several sites where fishing was inferentially important. Bone preservation was poor or sampling slight at the following sites, but all are located in areas more satisfactory for fishing than for hunting; Naomikong Point (Janzen, 1968*a*), Berquist, Riverview Cemetery and Bear Creek (Fitting, 1968*a*).

The ratios of fragmentary point tips to point bases also varies inversely from level to level. In the Early and Late Woodland levels point tips outnumber point bases by larger margins than in the two Middle Woodland levels. This could be interpreted as indicating more kills near the site in those two horizons with more distant hunting taking place in the two middle levels. During Middle Woodland times more projectiles were refurbished with new points and the old ones removed directly at the site. Actual breakage took place elsewhere and, perhaps, at a different season of the year.

The Early and Late Woodland horizons, with their greater dependence on mammals, also contain relatively more broken biface fragments, representing both knives and preforms. They also have greater frequencies of sloping retouch endscrapers.

I am unable to offer any technological reason for the parallel distribution of tool types and certain food types over time. I would be most reluctant to apply it to areas outside of the Great Lakes without extensive testing. It does, however, seem to hold together rather well in this restricted area and is useful for site interpretation.

The absolute densities for both artifacts and chippage in the major cultural horizons on the site are given in Table 64. These were determined by dividing the sample from each horizon by the number of cubic feet of earth excavated for each horizon. In spite of the differences in raw count, the ratios for Early, early Middle and Late Woodland are surprisingly similar. The density of chipped stone in the late Middle Woodland horizon is three to six times as great as that of any other horizon depending on what ratio you use for comparing density.

There are indications, from the features and nonartifactual materials, that some of the differences between occupations are seasonal with exploitation of different resources at different times.

The infrequency of certain animal species suggests that the Early Woodland occupation was primarily a winter occupation. The living floors and the relatively high core to flake ratio might indicate a fairly stable occupation. The relatively high frequency of drills in this level may be a reflection of some type of winter activity.

TABLE 64
TOOL AND FLAKE DENSITIES
(In Cubic Feet)

Horizon	Volume	Artifacts	Chippage
Late Woodland	980	.09	9
Late Middle Woodland	950	.28	61
Early Middle Woodland	3849	.06	9
Transitional (II*d*)	965	.02	(Not calculated)
Early Woodland	3100	.06	9

It has been suggested that the early Middle Woodland occupation is a fall to winter occupation. The change of tool ratios and the nonartifactual material indicated more emphasis on fishing and clamming and less storage of nuts. It is a very low density occupation but, again, seems to be fairly stable with a relatively high flake to artifact ratio.

The late Middle Woodland horizon seems to be a spring to summer occupation. There is a significant increase in occupational density as well as an absolute increase in sample size. The flake to artifact ratio of over 200 to 1 is suggestive of a great deal of industrial activity but there is a decrease in the number of cores and the average weight of flakes. The highest percentage of cores is found in earlier occupational levels. I would suggest that cores are obtained from the Bayport chert quarries, located approximately 40 miles from the site, during the late summer and early fall. Prior to July and August, the occupants of the site would be engaged in spring industrial activity. During this time of year tools appear to have been more commonly resharpened and tools of older occupations reused than new tools manufactured. Cores could have been obtained just before that fall round of economic activities began. The fall and winter occupants had a supply of cores to use for making new tools.

The Late Woodland occupation seems to have been a winter hunting occupation. I would suspect that this is really a series of many small occupations covering a very long time period; at least from A.D. 600 until A.D. 1300. Although the absolute density of artifacts and chippage does not differ greatly from that of the Early and early Middle Woodland levels, the lower chippage to artifact ratio suggests that much less industrial activity is taking place right on the site. There are also fewer cores in this level than in any other level so whatever industrial activity did take place was probably secondary, the reworking of old tools and preforms, rather than primary knapping from cores.

An examination of internal distributional patterns for each level was not as productive as I hoped it would be. This may have been because of the gross methods I used. I am certain that a more detailed examination of individual artifact placement would yield much better results.

The rough areal distribution of cores, bifaces and unifaces in the Early Woodland level is given in Table 65. All of the Early Woodland tools were found on the old levee, either inside or outside of the stockade. None were found in the mound area. The relative percentage of tools outside and inside of the stockade, as measured by the ratio of percentage of Early Woodland tools to Early Woodland site in each area, suggests a great deal of similarity with a slightly lower frequency of tools inside the stockade. This may be a result of extensive sampling inside of the stockade in 1964 as opposed to the intensive sampling of a particularly rich Early Woodland area outside the stockade in 1963.

TABLE 65
EARLY WOODLAND TOOL DISTRIBUTION*

Tool	Outside Stockade	Inside Stockade
Cores		
Number	5	14
Percent	8	9
Bifaces		
Number	29	77
Percent	48	62
Unifaces		
Number	26	35
Percent	44	28
Total Tools	60	126
Percent of Total Tools	31	69
Ratio: Percent Total Tools / Percent of Site	1.19	.93
Ratio: Biface / Uniface	1.13	2.20

*Taken from Table 3.

The biface to uniface ratio also changes between these two areas. I would not interpret this as being related to the stockade since it is fairly clear from other evidence that the stockade was not there during the Early Woodland period. I would suggest a relationship to artifact density. The intensive concentration outside of the stockade may represent an actual habitation area where women were carrying out maintenance activities. Such areas are also present inside of the stockade, but in 1964 we also sampled intervening areas of lesser artifact density which might represent butchering and men's work area between habitations. A slightly higher percentage of cores is found in this area too.

In the early Middle Woodland level (Table 66) materials were found in the channel area and along the levee both inside and outside of the stockade. The greatest concentrations of material, in relation to the percentage of the excavated amount of site in each area, was found in the old river channel fill. The biface to uniface ratio in the old river channel area is very low and may indicate that fishing or gathering activities took place in this part of the site.

The concentrations of chipped stone tools are greater on the levee outside of the stockade than they are inside; a position in agreement with the other indications that the stockade was built during this time period. However, this is not a very strong difference and is actually less than for the Late Woodland period. The biface to uniface ratio between various areas of the site varies in the same way as in the Early Woodland level. Larger percentages of bifaces are found in areas of lower artifact density. The same explanation, butchering and primary flint working activities being carried out between household areas where maintenance activities were more important and unifaces were more frequent. Again, the percentage of cores is higher in just those areas where bifaces are most common and artifact densities lowest.

Almost all of the late Middle Woodland chipped stone tools are found in the channel area (Table 67), as are all of the cores from this occupation. No chipped stone material definitely ascribable to this occupation were found outside of the stockade along the levee. Five bifacial implements from this occupation were found inside of the stockade. Not only is this an extremely low artifact density in relation to the percentage of the site excavated in this area, but the occurrence of all bifaces is very unusual since almost one-half of the late Middle Woodland sample consists of unifacial im-

TABLE 66
EARLY MIDDLE WOODLAND TOOL DISTRIBUTION*

Tool	Channel	Outside Stockade	Inside Stockade
Cores			
Number	8	7	13
Percent	8	12	16
Bifaces			
Number	37	24	42
Percent	35	40	51
Unifaces			
Number	61	29	27
Percent	57	47	33
Total Tools	106	60	82
Percent of Total Tools	43	24	33
Ratio: Percent Total Tools / Percent of Site	2.39	.80	.63
Ratio: Bifaces / Uniface	.61	.83	1.56

*Taken from Table 3.

plements. This seems to again indicate a special function for the stockade.

There are late Middle Woodland implements in the mound area of the site so all areas of the site would have been available to these people. The avoidance of the entire levee, as far as stone tools are concerned, is at slight variance with the distributional patterns for other materials where only the stockade is avoided.

Materials from the Late Woodland horizon were found in all areas of the site except the mounds (Table 68). The greatest density of Late Woodland chipped stone is within the area of the old river channel; there it is almost two and one-half times as great as on the levee. On the levee there is a tendency for more material to be found outside of the stockade area than inside of the stockade area, but I find it difficult to relate this to the stockade which must have been long gone by the time of the latest occupation.

There is a correlation between artifact density and biface to uniface ratio at this time, but it is the exact opposite of the pattern present in the Early and early Middle Woodland levels. In the Late Woodland occupation, the biface to uniface ratio decreases with a decrease in artifact density. I believe that this reflects a major change in the pattern of site use between the earliest and latest occupations although both were based on hunting. I would suggest that during the earlier periods, the site was primarily a habitation site with evidences of hunting activity in areas around habitations. The sparse Late Woodland occupation, which already has been demonstrated to cover a rather long time period, is represented by many small hunting camps which were possibly even established on actual kill sites. Hunting and butchering activities are the primary activities at the site and

TABLE 67
LATE MIDDLE WOODLAND
TOOL DISTRIBUTION*

Tool	Channel	Inside Stockade	Mound
Cores			
Number	21	...	...
Percent	8	...	...
Bifaces			
Number	120	5	1
Percent	46	100	25
Unifaces			
Number	121	...	3
Percent	46	...	75
Total Tools	262	5	4
Percent of Total Tools	97	2	1
Ratio: Percent of Total Tools / Percent of Site	4.40	.03	.06
Ratio: Bifaces / Unifaces	.99	...	.33

*Taken from Table 3.

TABLE 68
LATE WOODLAND TOOL DISTRIBUTION*

Tool	Channel	Outside Stockade	Inside Stockade
Cores			
Number	1	2	1
Percent	2	9	4
Bifaces			
Number	30	10	11
Percent	68	45	41
Unifaces			
Number	13	10	14
Percent	29	45	54
Total Tools	44	22	26
Percent of Total Tools	48	24	28
Ratio: Percent of Total Tools / Percent of Site	2.66	.80	.54
Ratio: Bifaces / Unifaces	2.40	1.00	.79

*Taken from Table 3.

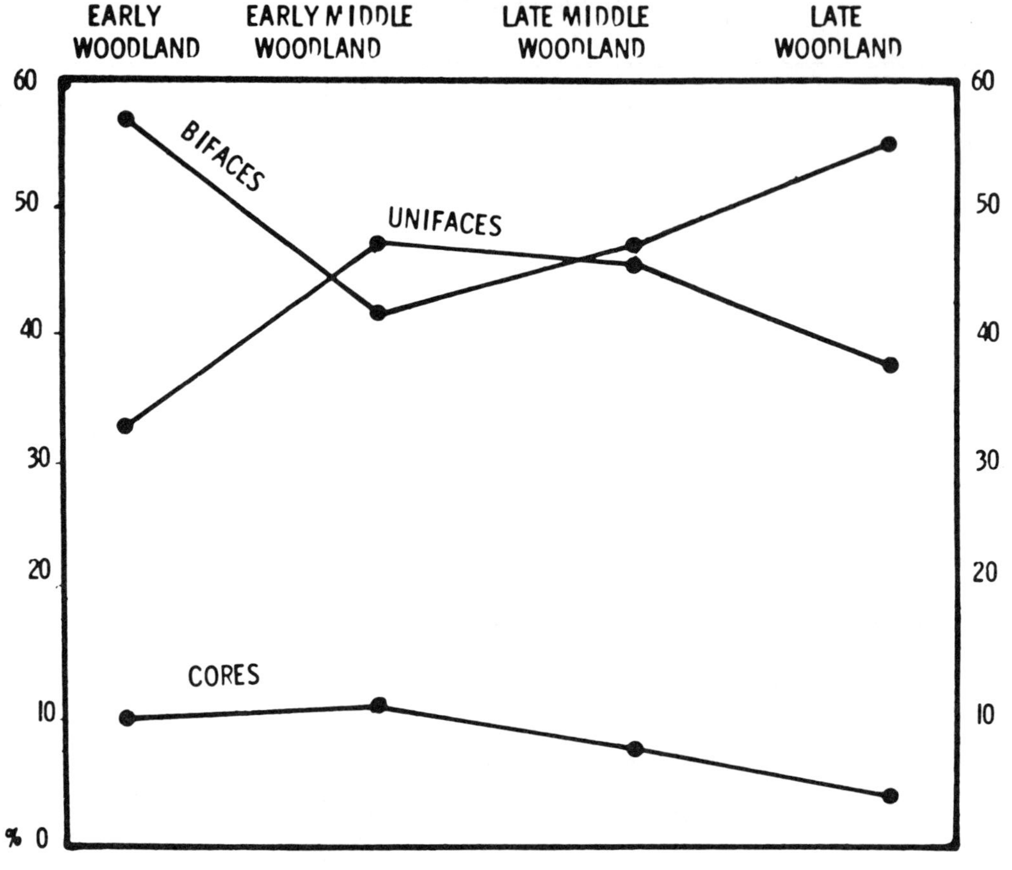

Fig. 71. Percentages of bifaces, unifaces and cores.

group maintenance activities, if preformed at all, were carried out in the marginal low occupational density areas between the major activity areas.

XI

BONE, ANTLER AND SHELL ARTIFACTS

Peter F. Murray

The Schultz site yielded over nine hundred pieces of modified bone antler and shell. This substantial number and variety of implements were fashioned from the skeletal remains of several species of Michigan vertebrates and a few exotic Molluscan species from the Gulf of Mexico or the Southeastern Atlantic coast. Nearly half of this total number of artifacts are the remains of freshwater turtles of the family Emydidae which were modified by the Schultz inhabitants into containers. The percentages of the various faunal representatives by class or phylum is as follows: Reptilia, 41.0 percent; Mammalia, 23.0 percent; Aves, 2.0 percent; Mollusca, 1.0 percent; and Pisces, 0.5 percent.

A selective use of certain mammalian species for the production of artifacts is evident. Deer, for instance, provided the most substantial amount, about 45 percent. This factor is probably the result of the importance of deer as a food source. For the same reason, black bear remains total 13 percent, ranking next to deer. Other species only periodically or rarely utilized include: beaver *(Castor canadensis)*, 5.0 percent; elk (*Cervus canadensis*), 3.0 percent; porcupine (*Erithizon dorsatum*), 3.0 percent; dog (*Canis familiaris*), 3.0 percent; *lynx* sp., 1.0 percent; and raccoon (*Procyon lotor*), 0.5 percent. The remaining 25.0 percent consists of unassignable remains or forms which could not be identified with confidence.

Certain mammalian bones were selected with great frequency due to their naturally convenient shape and durability. Deer and elk antler comprise 46.0 percent; maxillae, mandibles and teeth, 38.0 percent; metapodials, 7.0 percent; ulnae, 6.5 percent; ribs, 1.0 percent; scapulae, 1.0 percent, plus a small percentage of unassignable bone flakes and chips, 5.0 percent.

The high incidence of turtle remains is due to the ease with which the components of the carapace separate along the natural sutures combined with the characteristic brittleness yet durability of the bone.

In general, the condition of the bone artifacts is excellent, indicating that the sample is representative of the occupation and unskewed by differential preservation, with the possible exception of the Early Woodland levels.

About seven hundred artifacts were functionally recognizable or lent themselves to classification and could thus be described. These have been categorized first by material, then functionally, and finally grouped by types. The typology constructed here is somewhat arbitrary, due to the limited sample, though some cultural and chronological validity is apparent.

DESCRIPTION OF ARTIFACTS

Artifacts of Antler

Socketed Conical Projectile Points: Socketed conical points (Fig. 72*b*) were fashioned by cutting away the distal portion of an antler tine, then gouging out the cancellous bone, producing a concavity of a depth sufficient to secure the point to a tapered shaft. Hollow portions of cut antler discards suggest that a larger piece of antler was previously removed, then cut to the desired length in the process of fitting the point more closely to the shaft. The metric attributes in millimeters follow:

	Length	Diameter of Base	Diameter of Socket	Depth of Socket
N	7	14	5	3
x̄	61.0	12.0	10.0	29.0
Range	43.0-90.0	10.0-16.0	8.0-10.0	25.0-34.0

Toggled Harpoon Points: (Fig. 72*a*) Two toggle head harpoons were present in the assemblage (see Mason, 1965:156-63). These were fashioned in the same manner as the socketed points with the exception of the circular and squarish perforations for line attachment. The line holes are gouged rather than drilled conoidal or square, and are positioned in the central portion of the body of the point. In addition, there is some indication of a barb produced by cutting away about half of the circumference of the base leaving the rest to project at an angle over the shaft. The metric attributes appear at the bottom of this page.

Solid Conical Points: (Fig. 72*c, d, e*) A third type of conical point was manufactured by removing a portion of antler point and occasionally polishing or grinding the proximal and distal ends. These were probably hafted with mastic.

	Length	Diameter of Base
N	4	4
x̄	22.0	7.5
Range	14.0-30.0	6.0-8.0

Awl Handles: (Fig. 74*d, b, c*) Five small socketed handles were manufactured from short pieces of antler cut and ground flat at each end. The end with the largest diameter has been drilled to receive a narrow, pointed implement such as an awl. One handle from Level III*a* contains a cylindrical piece of copper which is probably an awl fragment

	Length	Diameter of Base	Diameter Socket	Depth of Socket	Diameter Perforation	Perforation to Tip Distance	Perforation to Base Distance
N	2	2	2	2	2	2	2
x̄	54.0	11.5	9.2	30.0	7.7	35.5	32.0
Range	51-57	10-12	8-10.5	25-35	7.5-8	35-36	30-35

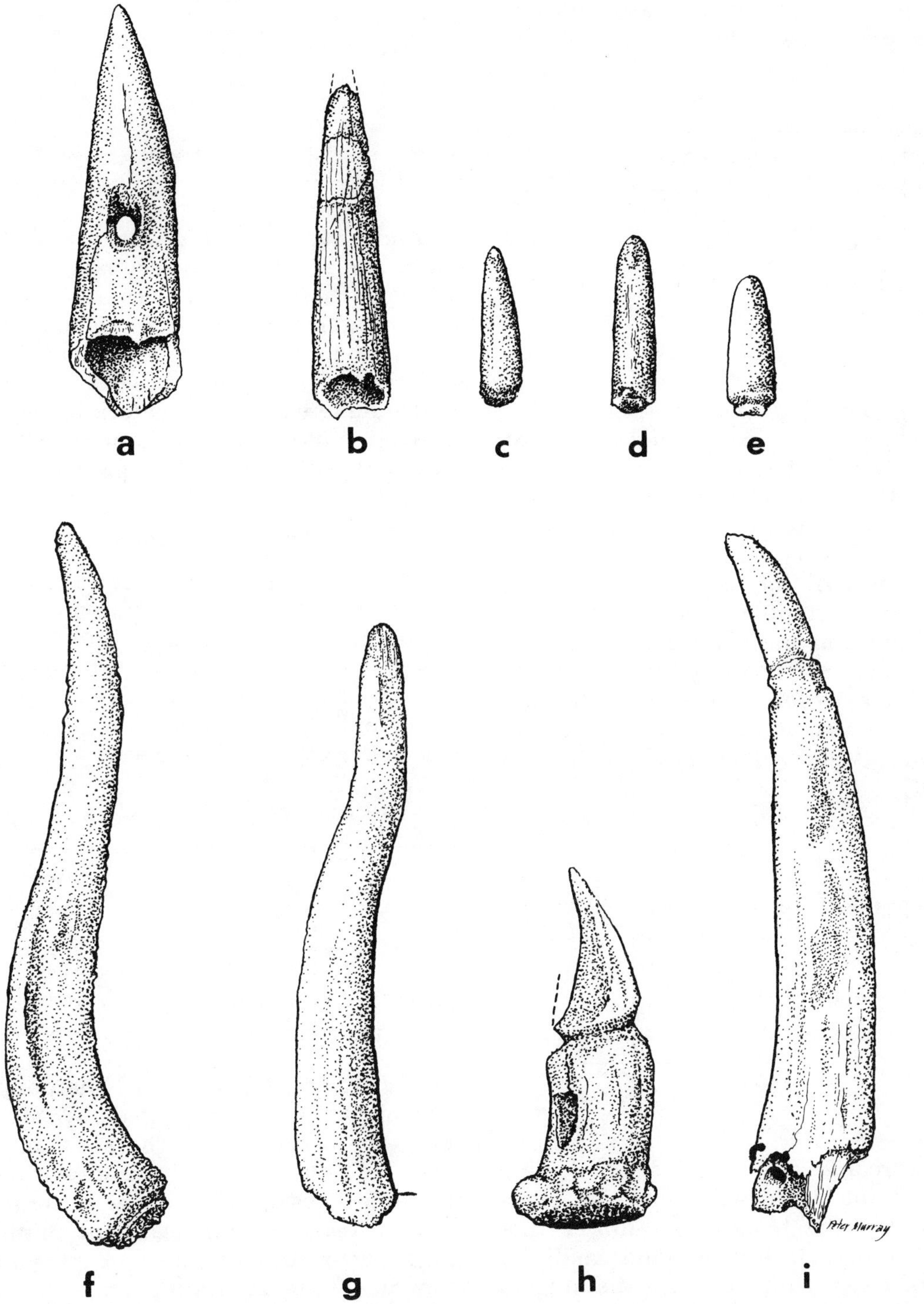

Fig. 72. Antler artifacts: *a,* toggle head harpoon; *b,* socketed conical point; *c, d, e,* solid conical projectile points; *f, g, i,* antler tine flakers; *h,* sawed antler spur.

(see Fig. 74*b*). The metric attributes in millimeters are listed below:

	Length	Diameter Base	Diameter Socket
N	5	5	5
$\bar{x}$	46.0	12.0	3.2
Range	32.0-50.0	10.0-15.0	3.0-3.5

Large Socket Handles: (Fig. 73*i, j*) One hollow antler section and three very curved but hollowed pieces of antler suggest their use as handles for lithic and bone implements. The short, hollow antler section is similar to the antler sleeves utilized as handles for ground and chipped stone in certain European mesolithic and neolithic industries. The remaining three pieces of hollowed tine are not shaped for the greatest efficiency as projectile points, and are thus placed in this category. The metric attributes follow:

	Length	Diameter Base	Diameter Socket
N	3	3	3
$\bar{x}$	61.0	17.0	10.5
Range	48.0-85.0	14.0-20.0	10.0-11.0

Pressure Flakers: (Fig. 72*f, g, i*) Tine flaking implements were made by incising around the base of an antler tine with a stone tool until it could easily be knocked free with a blow. The distal ends are dulled, striated and scarred from working flint. The metric attribute follow:

	Length	Diameter
N	4	7
$\bar{x}$	55.0	17.0
Range	30.0-17.0	15.0-20.0

Other Cut Antler: (Fig. 73*e, f, g, h*) Cut antler is a residual category having arisen due to the variety of sizes and shapes, and the general condition and state of preservation of these artifacts. The majority of them are broken and discarded flakers or waste material from the production of points and handles. Others represent antler artifacts in process.

Artifacts of Bone

Cylindrical Awls: (Fig. 75*g*) These are bone awls which exhibit a circular cross section and show deliberate and unusual care in manufacture. With few exceptions, these implements have received a glossy polish and taper to a fine, elongated point. The metric attributes follow:

	Length	Average Width
N	4	4
$\bar{x}$	52.5	7.40
Range	38.0-59.0	5.0-10.0

Ulna Awls: (Fig. 74 *d, e*) Nine pointed implements were fashioned by sharpening the distal end of the shaft of the ulna. These awls could be used with considerable pressure since the olecranon process becomes an excellent handle. Eight out of nine of the ulna awls were from deer, the remaining one was prepared from a bobcat. Several of these awls have a sharpened anterior border which implies their use as a cutting tool

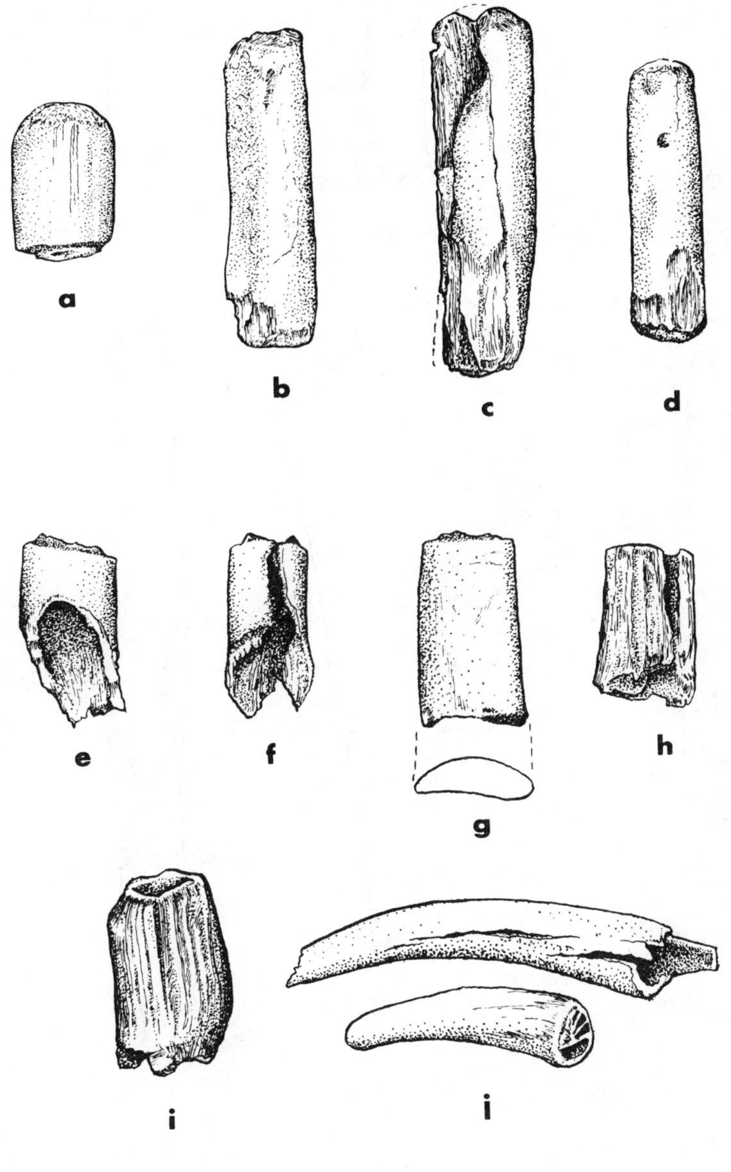

Fig. 73. Antler artifacts: *a, b, c, d,* antler percussion flakers; *e, f, g, h,* discarded proximal ends of tines; cut and abraded antler section; *i, j,* antler handles.

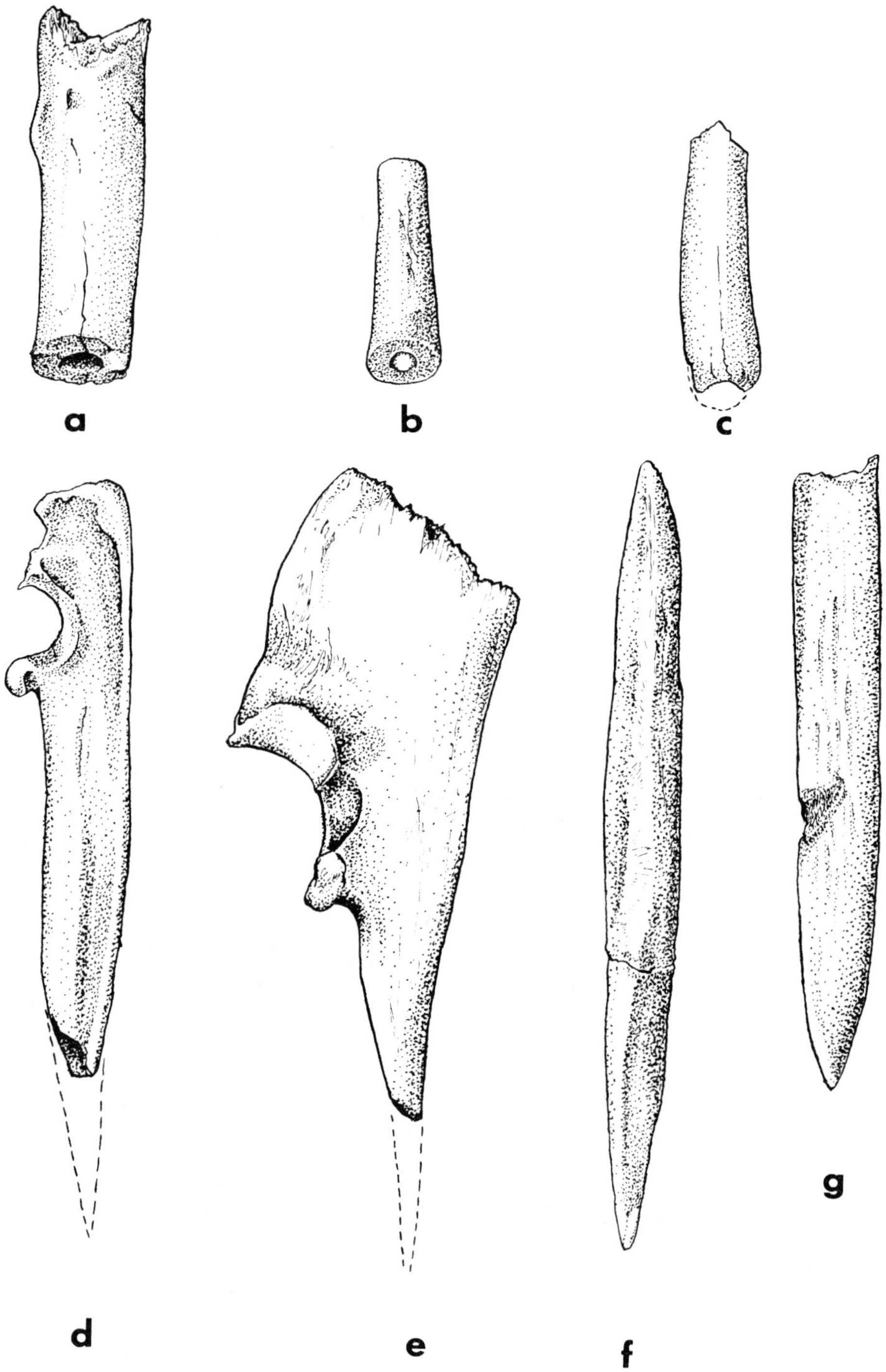

Fig. 74. Bone and antler artifacts: *a, b, c,* antler handles (*b* contains a copper fragment); *d, Lynx* sp. ulna awl; *e,* deer ulna awl; *f,* bipointed bone implement; *g,* flat bone awl or projectile point.

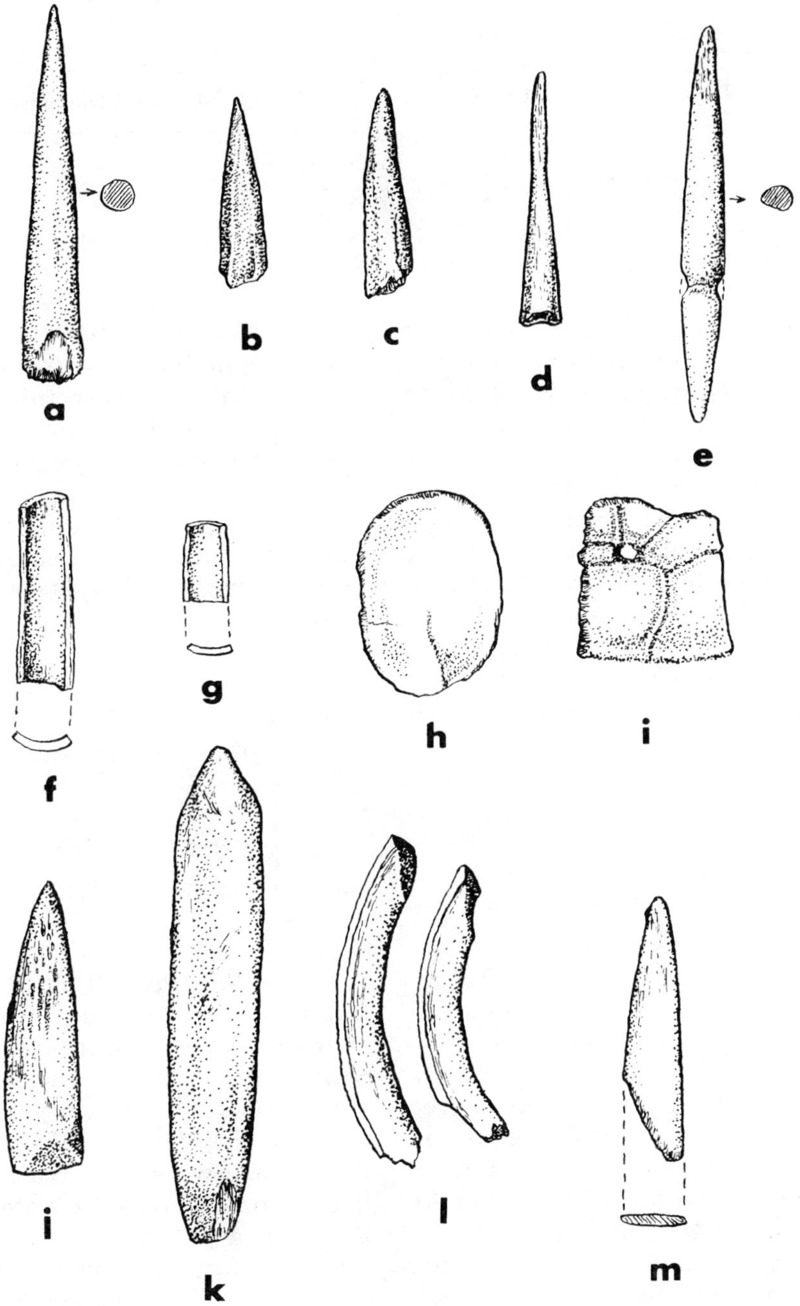

Fig. 75. Bone artifacts: *a,* cylindrical awl; *b, c,* splinter awls; *d,* drum spine awl; *e,* pin; *f, g,* longitudinally split and polished bird bone sections; *h,* cut and polished disk of turtle carapace; *i,* ground and perforated turtle carapace; *j, k,* possible flat bone projectile points; *l,* beaver incisor chisels; thin, flat ground bone object, possibly a fragment of a weaving tool.

as well. The metric attributes are listed below:

	Length	Average Width of Shaft
N	9	9
x̄	83.0	11.0
Range	67.0-101.0	10.0-12.0

Splinter Awls: (Fig. 75*b, c*) Splinters and chips of bone which have received additional sharpening or show evidence of utilization on the pointed ends are considered awls or punches. A total of 15 such artifacts were recovered from the Schultz site. These rather crude implements are highly variable in size, shape and source but all are commonly manufactured from the splinters which result from forcibly striking a longbone with a heavy stone or similar object. The metric attributes in millimeters are listed below:

	Width	Length
N	13	13
x̄	7.0	58.0
Range	5.0-9.0	35.0-95.0

Fish Spine Awls: (Fig. 75*d*) Three drum spines (*Aplodinotus grunniens*) and one sturgeon dermal bone scale (*Acipenser fulvescens*) have been included here in the probability that at least some of these were used as awls. Only one drum spine has obviously recognizable modification, this being the result of usage.

Pins: (Fig. 75*e*) Pins are circular or semicircular in cross section with evenly tapered points at both ends. The points show no evidence of heavy usage and do not appear to be awls. The metric attributes in millimeters follow:

	Greatest Diameter	Length
N	2	1
x̄	65	66.0
Range	6.0-7.0	66.0

Flat Bone Projectile Points: (Fig. 75*j, k*) Four bone implements which are semi-rectangular in cross section and abruptly pointed rather than tapered may have been employed as projectile points. There is little evidence of wear or utilization on the pointed ends, and two specimens have a thinned base, possibly for hafting. The metric attributes in millimeters follow:

	Length	Thickness	Width of Base
N	4	4	4
x̄	69.0	7.0	10.0
Range	48.0-84.0	5.0-8.0	9.0-11.0

Large Shuttles: (Fig. 76*a, b*) Eight fragmentary weaving implements or shuttles were identified among the Schultz artifacts. These implements display unusual uniformity in shape and size and deliberate skill in manufacture. All of them were prepared from a strip of bone removed from the anterior border of the metacarpal of deer. The flattened surfaces were ground smooth until the vascular groove running down the center of the bone is faintly visible. A perforation or eye has been positioned in the center of the vascular groove 15 to 18 millimeters from the notched proximal end. It is suggested that these implements

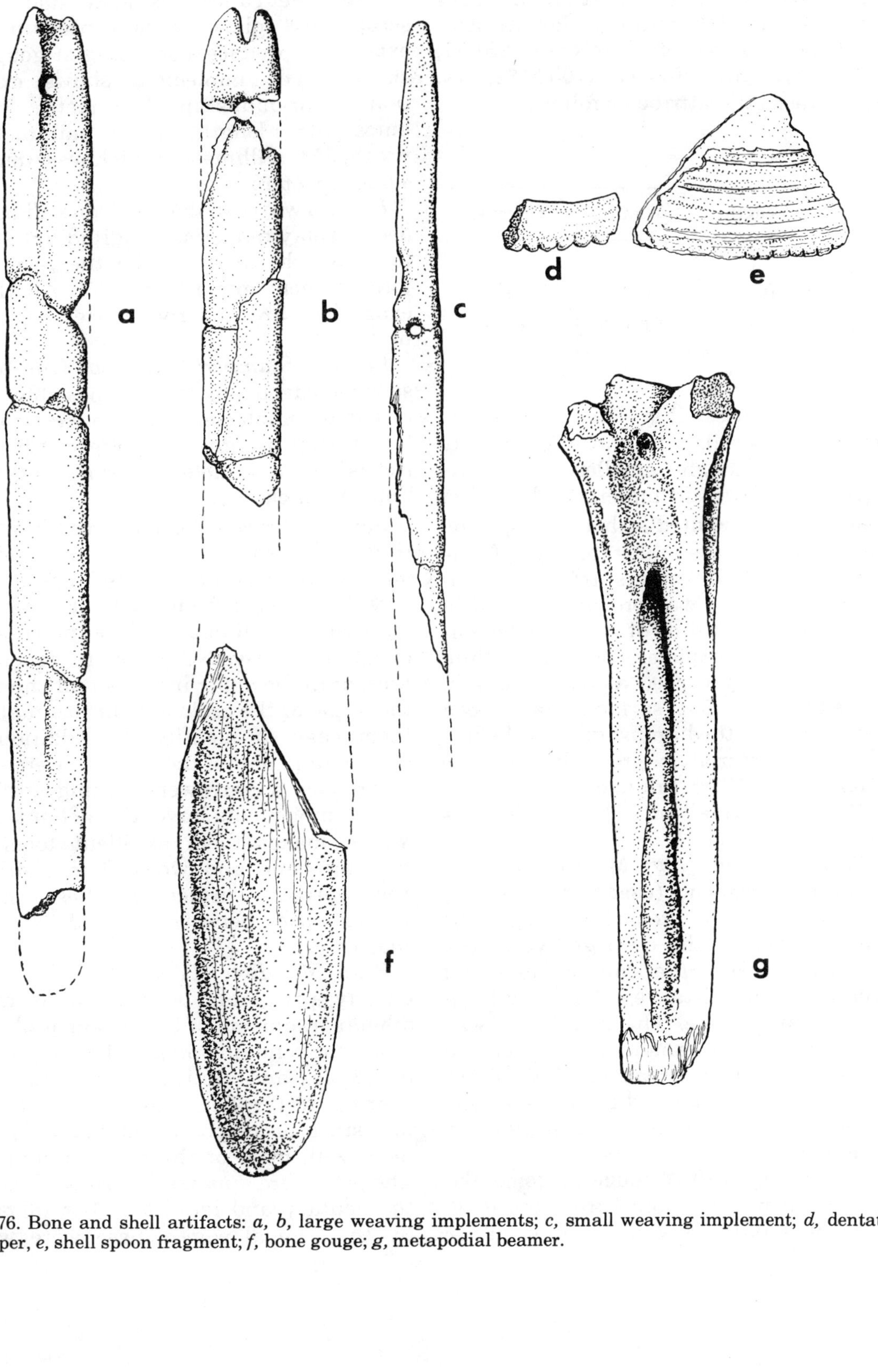

Fig. 76. Bone and shell artifacts: *a, b,* large weaving implements; *c,* small weaving implement; *d,* dentate stamper, *e,* shell spoon fragment; *f,* bone gouge; *g,* metapodial beamer.

were used in the preparation of grass matting and fish netting. Similar artifacts are figured in Winters (1961:77; Fig. 43*ff*) and Fowler (1952:162; Pl. L, i). The metric attributes follow:

	Length	Width	Thickness
N	1	8	8
$\bar{x}$	182.0	14.0	4.0
Range	182.0	12.0-14.0	3.0-4.0

Small Shuttles: (Fig. 76*c*) This is an implement similar to those previously described, though smaller and prepared from different material. The object is apparently pointed at both ends, judging from the gradual tapering of the shaft in both directions from the perforation. The eye was probably placed in the distal one-third of the implement when it was complete. The tool is thin, flat and lightly curved along its length; the edges and flat surfaces have been carefully smoothed and slightly polished. The raw material is probably rib. The fragment is 123.0 millimeters long, 8.0 millimeters wide and 2.0 millimeters thick.

Beamers: (Fig. 76*g*) Metapodial hide scraping implements (used to remove hair from hides) were prepared by splintering the bone in the deep groove of the posterior border of a cannon-bone and removing the distal epiphysis with a blow from a stone. The distal end was then flaked and ground until a chisel-like working surface was acquired. Three functionally similar artifacts were prepared from spirally fractured sections of long bone.

Gouge: (Fig. 76*f*) A gouge or gougelike implement was fashioned from the long-bone of a large cervid, possibly elk or moose. The cancellous bone had been scraped out following the contour of the exterior to produce a scooping or gouging surface. The implement shows exceptional workmanship. The metric attributes are: length, 102.0 millimeters; width, 35.0 millimeters; thickness, (mean) 4.0 millimeters.

Hoes: Two scapulae and one ilium of deer display numerous longitudinal striations which appear to be the result of forcing them into the ground. All three examples are poorly preserved and broken.

Dentate Stamper: (Fig. 75*d*) One bone serrated-edged object may possibly represent an implement for producing dentate stamp designs on pottery. The object is 25.0 millimeters long and 4.0 millimeters thick.

Beaver Incisor Carving Implements: (Fig. 75*l*) Ten beaver incisors received additional grinding on the lingual surface due to wear from usage or to sharpen them intentionally. The process of grinding removes the notch generally present in the upper incisors and changes the angle of the occlusial surface making them easy to identify. In addition to sharpening, half of the incisors were split to produce a narrower working surface. These implements have a trenchant edge which makes them excellent tools for carving bone and wood. The width of the working surface of these implements varies between 3.0 and 8.0 millimeters.

Bear Mandible Pendants: (Fig. 77*c*) Over twenty ground teeth and a few mandibular fragments of black bear probably represent pendants prepared from ground mandibles and sections of cut maxillae bearing teeth. The mandibular portion has since decomposed leaving only the teeth with most of the roots ground off. The jaws were apparently drilled through the dentary and laced together in pairs by the ventral edge. These were worn

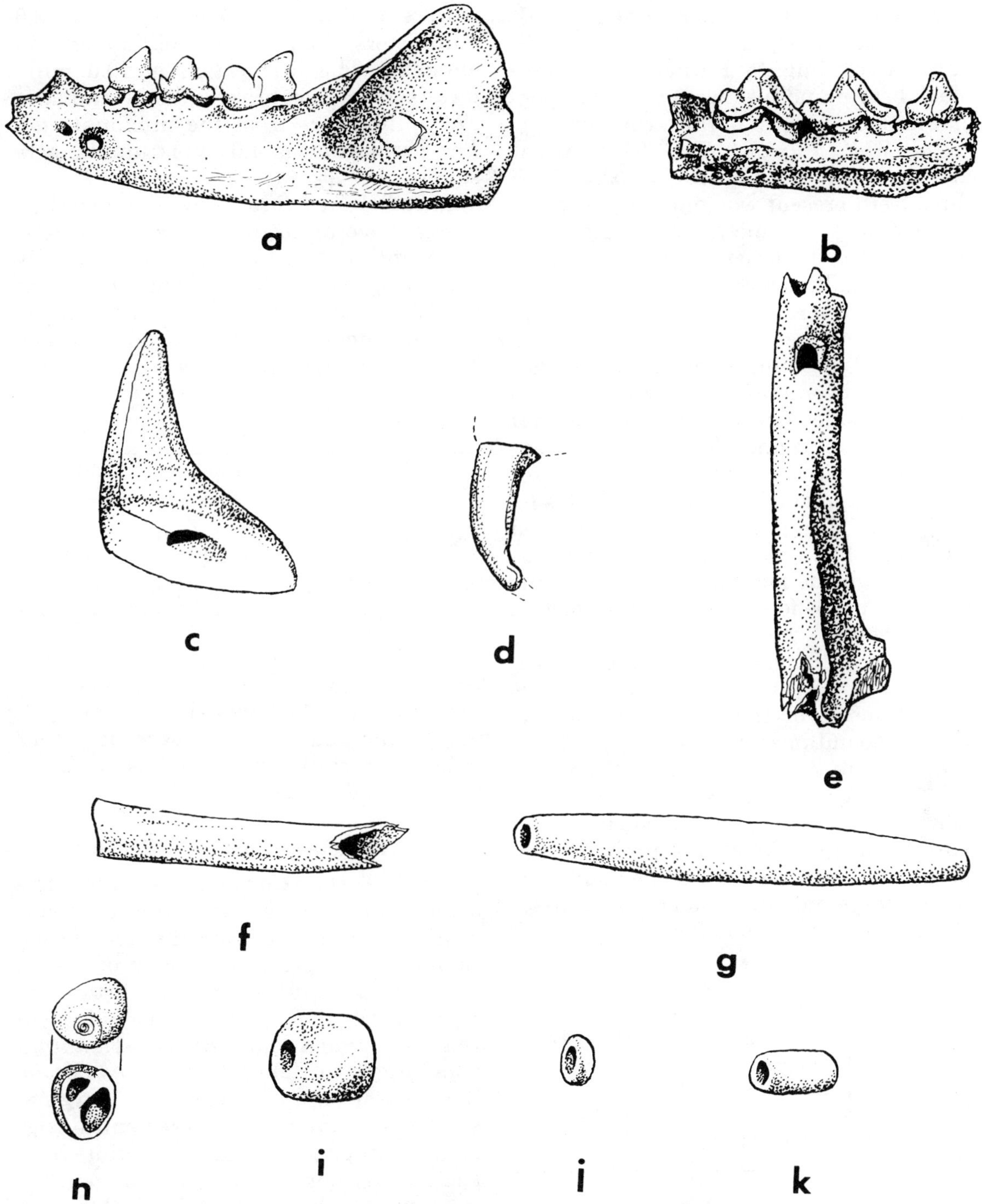

Fig. 77. Bone and shell artifacts: *a,* cut and polished bobcat mandible pendant; *b,* cut wolf maxilla; *c,* ground bear tooth; *d,* shell claw effigy; *e,* whistle from loon humerus; *f,* cut and polished bird bone bead; *g,* elongate columella bead; *h,* Anculosa sp. bead; cylindrical columella bead; *j, k,* other shell beads.

around the neck in combination with beads and other decorative paraphernalia. According to Parmalee (1959:86) black bear mandibles were the most popular and prized form of this ornament.

Cut Wolf Maxilla: (Fig. 77*b*) A cut and ground portion of wolf maxilla with three teeth present was probably worn as a pendant. The metric attributes are: length, 48.5 millimeters; width to top of P_1, 21.0 millimeters.

Ground Bobcat Mandible: (Fig. 77*a*) A complete bobcat mandible with grinding around the ventral edge and posterior border of the ramus is yet another pendant. Parmalee (1959:93) points out that *Lynx rufus* mandible pendants are rare in Illinois aboriginal sites. No count of them was made from Michigan sites by this writer. The entire bone has received a slight polish and perforations are present through the mental foramen and the ramus. The pendant is 69.0 millimeters long; dentary width through P_1 is 13.0 millimeters; diameter of the conoidal perforation in the dentary, 4.0 millimeters; and diameter of the perforation in the ramus, 7.0 millimeters.

Bird Bone Tubes: (Fig. 77*f*) Tubes are polished sections of avian long bone which have been cut into segments of variable length. They were probably employed as beads, though some could represent fragments of whistles or "flutes." The metric attributes follow:

	Length	Diameter
N	5	5
$\bar{x}$	54.0	9.0
Range	16.0-111.0	4.5-14.0

Bird Bone Whistle: (Fig. 77*e*) A section of Loon (*Gavia immer*) humerus with a square perforation near the head may represent a whistle. The object is 73.0 millimeters long; 10.0 millimeters in diameter. The perforation is 10.0 millimeters from the broken distal end and 57.0 millimeters from the proximal end. The perforation is 4.0 by 4.0 millimeters square.

Split Polished Bird Bone Sections: (Fig. 75*f, g*) Several sections of polished bird bone appear to have been intentionally split lengthwise. These may represent gaming pieces or counters, though no known function could be found for them. The metric attributes follow:

	Length	Width	Thickness
N	3	4	4
$\bar{x}$	34.0	6.9	3.4
Range	12.0-54.0	6.0-9.0	3.0-5.0

Polished Mammal Bone Fragments: One rectangular piece of cut bone resembling an inlay plus eleven other polished and cut bone fragments defy orderly description and are thus placed in this residual category.

Artifacts of Turtle Carapace

Plain Turtle Carapace Dishes: The astounding number of turtle carapace fragments collected from the Schultz excavations are primarily pieces of dishes or bowls. Several species of turtles are represented, the most common of them were assigned to *Emys blandingi* (Blanding's turtle) and *Chrysemys picta,* the eastern painted turtle. The marginal shields were ground from the ventral edge of the carapace and all projecting bone such as vertebrae were scraped from the interior of the vertebral shields producing a container suitable for holding liquids. The dorsal side of the carapace is often polished.

Engraved Turtle Carapace Dishes: (Fig. 78*a, b*) A few dishes had been further embellished with geometric and curvilinear designs shallowly engraved into the dorsal surface of the carapace.

Carapace Bangles: (Fig. 75*i*) Two perforated carapace fragments of an Emydidae turtle and one *Trionyx* sp. are probably bangles.

Carapace Disk: (Fig. 75*h*) One fragment of polished carapace was cut into an oval. Its function is unknown.

Artifacts of Shell*

Effigy Claw: (Fig. 76*d*) A fragment of an effigy sillouette cut from the nacreous layer of a fresh water mussel is one of the few pieces of an artistic nature from the Schultz site. The example resembles the claw core of a large raptorial bird such as a hawk or eagle. The fragment is 23.0 millimeters long and 10.0 millimeters wide, tapering to a point.

Spherical Beads: These beads were prepared from the thickened umbo portion of fresh water clams. A total of 28 of these small beads were counted ranging from 4.0-8.0 millimeters in length.

Short, Cylindrical Collumella Beads: (Fig. 77*i, j, k,*) Eight of these larger oval or cylindrical forms were encountered. It appears that the majority of them were prepared by grinding and drilling sections of marine gastropod collumellae. The size ranges are: length, 9.0-12.0 millimeters.

Elongate Cylindrical Columella Beads: (Fig. 77*g*) A particularly superb example of a cylindrical columella bead measures 74.0 millimeters long by 10.0 millimeters in diameter through the central portion. Both ends are evenly tapered to a diameter of 5.0 millimeters.

Anculosa Beads: (Fig. 77*h*) One *anculosa* sp. bead was prepared for stringing by grinding down the aperture and part of the body whorl exposing the columella as a loop.

Shell Dipper: (Fig. 78*c*) One vessel or dipper was prepared from the shell of the gulf coast marine gastropod *Busycon contrarium.* The spire had been cut and ground evenly with the aperture producing a pleasing container with considerable capacity for holding and transferring liquids. The anterior portion of the shell has been broken. The measurements are: length, 140 millimeters; width 108.0 millimeters.

Spoons: (Fig. 76*e*) One serrated marginal fragment of mussel (see Griffin and Morse, 1961:562, Fig. 3) and one notched unidentified species were probably employed as spoons.

DISCUSSION OF ARTIFACTS

The stratigraphic, spatial and temporal relationships of bone and shell artifacts can not, due to several reasons, be as instructive as the study of other materials. Some information can, however, be derived from a few distinctive categories of bone implements where they are found to relate to specific known assemblages of limited distribution in time and space.

The quantitative distribution of bone and shell artifacts from the Schultz site is well demarcated when compared throughout the successive occupations (see Table 69).

The dearth of bone artifacts from the Early Woodland levels is due to several factors: (1) the lower artifact count correlates roughly with that of the lithic material (see Fitting, this volume), indicating a population differential; and (2) the considerably greater age and different conditions of the Zone II soils (see Speth, this volume) show little in favor of bone preservation. Less than one-fourth of a percent of all bone artifacts were derived from these levels, with II*c* containing the largest quantity.

*Editor's Note: Brose (pp. 125-26) found a number of additional shell artifacts with the molluscan remains from the site which were discussed earlier.

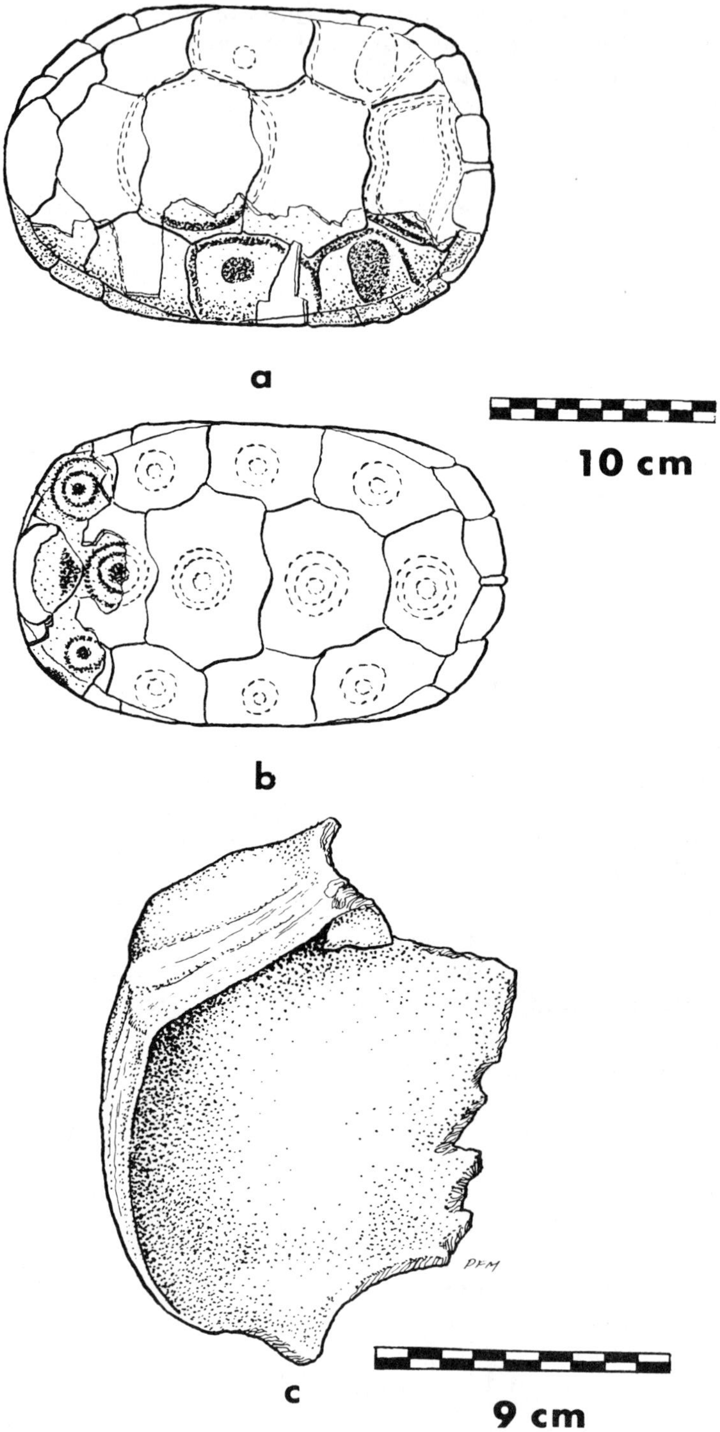

Fig. 78. *a,* Engraved carapace dishes; *b, Busycon contrarium* shell dipper.

Early Middle Woodland

Slightly less than ten percent of the total number of nonlithic artifacts were derived from Levels II*d* and III*a*, constituting an unproportional increase in the number and variety of bone implements. While there is an abrupt decrease in quantity from Level II*c* to II*d*, Level III*a* contains the most varied assemblage of all occupations though not the largest total number. Nearly all of the artifact types are represented during this period, suggesting the rapid and complete establishment of a more varied bone and shell technology, though differential preservation and sampling error are not to be disregarded entirely.

Late Middle Woodland

The previously established technology reaches its peak in Level III*b* and culminates with an obvious quantitative decline in Level IV*a*, again in agreement with the lithic material. A gradual decline in the variety of artifacts can be observed along with a slight increase in specific tool types. Approximately one fourth of the total number of nonlithic artifacts were derived from these levels.

Late Woodland

An obvious decline in the quantity and variety of bone implements is evident by Late Woodland times. Only 4.6 percent of the total nonlithic assemblage was derived from Levels IV*b* and IV*c*, as is proportionally true of the lithic assemblage.

STRATIGRAPHIC, SPATIAL AND TEMPORAL DISTRIBUTION

The first appearance of conical socketed projectile points is in Level II*c* of the Early Woodland occupation. By the Middle Woodland period, all four projectile point categories had been established. Flat, ground bone projectile points appear only in Levels III*a* and III*b*; the toggle head harpoons are similarly restricted. Plain socketed conical points are the least restricted stratigraphically, ranging into all units of the Schultz occupation. Solid conical points range from Level II*a* to IV*a*, spanning a slightly greater period than flat bone and harpoon points. Antler projectile points occur in Late Archaic through Historic times in the Eastern United States.

Perhaps the most unusual antler artifacts in the Schultz assemblage are the toggle head harpoons. Mason's (1965) discussion of the spatial and temporal affinities of harpoons suggests a wide distribution of similar artifacts, with occurrences in the Tchefuncte middens at Lake Ponchartrain, Louisiana; Late Woodland sites in Kansas and Nebraska; and elsewhere as far west as Oregon (Mason, 1965:156-60). Several Michigan and Wisconsin occurrences have been reported variously from the Porte de Mortes, Mero and Spider cave sites, relating to the Middle Woodland components; and one similar artifact—also assignable to Middle or Late Woodland—was reported from the Heins Creek site, Door County, Wisconsin (Wells, 1964:99-101). It is assumed that these detachable harpoon heads were employed in taking large fish such as northern pike or sturgeon.

Virtually all of the cylindrical awls of a known stratigraphic context were derived from the Middle Woodland strata. Ulna and splinter awls reveal a somewhat broader distribution and do not, therefore, seem to relate to any specific assemblage. All of the previously described categories of awls are generally distributed in the Archaic through Woodland periods in the Eastern United States.

Weaving implements, on the other hand, relate specifically to the Middle Woodland assemblage of the Schultz site with no previous or subsequent appearances in the archaeological record.

TABLE 69
STRATIGRAPHIC DISTRIBUTION OF BONE, ANTLER AND SHELL ARTIFACTS FROM THE SCHUTLZ SITE

Artifact	II*a* N/%	II*b* N/%	II*c* N/%	II*d* N/%	III*a* N/%	III*b* N/%	IV*a* N/%	IV*b* N/%	IV*c* N/%	OTHER N/%	TOTAL N/%
Projectile points	...	...	...	...	...	...	...	...	...	...	...
Flat bone projectile points	...	...	...	...	2/50.0	2/50.0	...	...	...	...	4
Socketed conical projectile points	...	...	1/7.0	...	5/360	2/14.0	1/7.0	1/7.0	...	4/29.0	14
Toggle head harpoons	...	...	...	...	1/50.0	1/50.0	...	...	...	...	2
Solid conical projectile points	...	...	...	...	2/25.0	3/37.5	1/12.5	...	...	2/25.0	8
Cylindrical awls	...	...	...	...	2/40.0	1/20.0	1/20.0	...	...	1/20.0	5
Ulna awls	...	...	...	...	2/22.0	2/22.0	...	...	1/11.0	4/44.0	9
Splinter awls	...	...	2/15.3	...	2/15.3	1/7.6	1/7.6	...	...	7/53.0	13
Fish spine awls	...	...	...	...	...	3/75.0	...	...	...	1/25.0	4
Pins	...	...	...	...	...	...	...	...	...	2/100.0	2
Large shuttle	...	...	...	...	2/25.0	4/50.0	2/25.0	...	...	...	8
Small shuttle	...	...	...	...	1/100.0	...	...	...	...	...	1
Small socket handles	...	...	...	...	1/20.0	...	...	...	...	4/80.0	5
Large socket handles	...	...	...	...	1/33.3	...	...	...	...	2/66.6	3
Tine flakers	...	1/14.0	...	...	2/28.0	2/28.0	...	...	...	2/28.0	7
Percussion flakers	...	...	...	...	...	...	2/29.0	...	1/14.0	4/58.0	7
Cut antler	...	...	1/7.7	...	1/7.7	1/7.7	1/7.7	...	1/7.7	8/62.0	13
Hoes	...	...	...	...	1/33.3	1/33.3	...	...	...	1/33.3	3
Beaver chisels	...	...	...	...	...	1/.10	3/33.3	3/33.3	...	3/33.3	10
Ground teeth	...	1/2.5	...	1/2.5	6/15.0	5/13.0	5/03.0	4/12.0	...	17/44.0	39
Beamers	...	1/25.0	...	...	...	1/25.0	...	...	...	2/50.0	4
Gouges	...	...	...	...	...	...	...	...	...	1/100.0	1
Dentate stamper	...	...	...	...	1/100.0	...	...	...	...	...	1
Birdbone tubes	...	...	...	...	2/29.0	2/29.0	2/29.0	...	...	1/13.0	7
Birdbone "tallies"	...	...	...	...	1/25.0	2/50.0	...	...	...	1/25.0	4
Dishes, turtle carapace	...	...	...	...	24/5.2	123/26.0	55/12.0	7/1.5	8/1.6	240/52.5	457
Dishes, engraved carapace	...	...	...	...	1/16.0	3/50.0	1/16.0	...	...	1/16.0	16
Carapace bangles	...	...	...	...	...	...	...	...	1/50.0	1/50.0	2
Ground carapace	...	...	...	...	...	...	...	...	...	1/100.0	1
Tabular polished bone	...	...	...	...	...	1/100.0	...	...	...	...	1
Other polished bone	...	...	...	...	5/38.0	8/62.0	...	...	...	...	13
Effigy claw	...	...	...	...	...	...	1/100.0	...	...	...	1
Beads, spherical	...	...	...	...	1/3.1	1/3.1	23/82.0	...	1/3.1	2/6.2	28
Beads, cylindrical, columella	...	...	...	...	2/25.0	...	1/12.5	1/12.5	1/12.5	3/37.5	8
Beads, snail (*anculosa*)	...	...	...	...	...	...	...	...	...	1/100.0	1

TABLE 69 (Continued)
STRATIGRAPHIC DISTRIBUTION OF BONE, ANTLER AND SHELL ARTIFACTS FROM THE SCHULTZ SITE

Artifact	II*a*	II*b*	II*c*	II*d*	III*a*	III*b*	IV*a*	IV*b*	IV*c*	OTHER	TOTAL
	N/%	N/%	N/%	N/%	N/%	N/%	N/%	N/%	N/%	N/%	N/%
Breads, elongate	...	...	...	...	...	...	...	...	...	...	...
Columella	...	...	...	...	1/100.0	...	...	...	...	...	1
Dipper	...	...	...	...	...	...	...	...	...	1/100.0	1
Spoons	...	...	...	...	...	...	1/20.0	2/40.0	1/20.0	1/20.0	5
Notched Shell	...	...	...	...	...	...	...	...	...	1/100.0	1
Grand Total	0/0.0	3/.43	4/.57	1/.13	69/9.8	162/23.1	109/16	18/2.6	15/2.0	319/43	700 100.0

"Shuttles" (variously termed spatulae, spatulate needles, net menders and mat needles) are discussed by Ritchie (1965) as occurring throughout the Middle and Late Woodland occupations of New York State. Other occurrences of shuttles from the Northeastern United States include specimens from the Adler Mound Group (Winters, 1961:57-88) and the Clear Lake Hopewellian (Fowler, 1952:133-48). In the Plains, similar implements have been noted historically as large needles utilized in the preparation of grass and reed mats. The shuttles in the Schultz assemblage however, are somewhat distinctive in that most of them have been prepared from the metapodial rather than ribs and a notched proximal end is characteristic. It is also feasible that these implements were employed in the preparation of fish-netting.

Antler handles were contained only within Level III*a*, perhaps in correlation with the use of the slender cylindrical bone and copper awls. Tools of this sort imply sophisticated leather work or the production of specialized and ornamental goods typical of some Middle Woodland occupations. Large socket handles may have held scrapers or other flint and ground stone implements.

Flint knapping implements show a weak but perhaps significant correlation with the nature of the lithic material. Tine flakers are restricted to the Early and Middle Woodland periods of the Schultz site, possibly relating to a more sophisticated pressure flaking flint industry. Antler percussion flaking implements however, range from Levels IV*a* to IV*c*, perhaps in conjunction with the diminished use of cores and the increased production of large bifaces discussed by Fitting.

Fragments of cut antler representing implements in process or discarded material are distributed in consistent numbers throughout the occupation.

Scapula grubbing or digging implements make their appearance in Levels III*a* and III*b*, and consistent with this specific assemblage, there is no subsequent appearance of the implements in clear stratigraphic context. Scapula hoes have a general distribution in the Eastern United States from Middle Woodland through historic times.

Beaver tooth carving implements appear during the Late Middle Woodland strata and persist through the Late Woodland period. Beaver incisor chisels are widely distributed spatially and temporally throughout the Northeastern states and are not distinctive chronologically in relation to the Schultz site.

Ground mandibles and teeth of several species of carnivores however, are impressively Hopewellian. In the Schultz assemblage there is an abrupt increase in the number of such artifacts in Levels III*a* through IV*b* with a subsequent disappearance of them in Level IV*c*. Mandible pendants occur in the Archaic through Late Woodland periods, but are most prevalent in the Hopewell phase of Middle Woodland occupations (Parmalee, 1959:85).

A tool suggested to represent a dentate stamper was yielded by Level III*a*, but due to a lack of confidence as to its genuine function, little can be said here.

Cut and polished bird bones are similarly restricted to the Middle Woodland units, with a slightly wider distribution of tubes. "Tallies" were identified only in Levels III*a* and III*b*.

A more statistically valid distribution, owing to its size, is that of the turtle carapace dishes. Scraped and polished carapace dishes make their first stratigraphically well-defined appearance during the Middle Woodland unit in Level III*a*. In Level III*b*, there is a five-fold increase in the number of uniform-sized fragments until a subsequent and gradual decline in number culminates with the

Late Woodland Level IV*c*. Engraved carapace dishes have an expectedly narrower distribution at the Schultz site, being restricted entirely to the Middle Woodland period. The curvilinear and geometric designs on these dishes strongly resemble those from the Norton mounds, another Michigan Middle Woodland site.

Shell artifacts were derived only from the Middle and Late Woodland units: a likely feature of poor preservation. Spherical beads of fresh water mussel shell range from Early Middle Woodland through Late Woodland with the vast majority of them, about 82 percent, yielded by Level IV*a*. Oval or cylindrical columella beads are more uniformly distributed through Levels III*a* to IV*c*, though one-quarter of them were from Level III*a* alone. Both the effigy claw and the elongate columella bead were from the Middle Woodland period; the former from Level IV*a* and the latter was removed from Level III*a*. The *Busycon contrarium* dipper unfortunately was collected from the surface.

The bone tool assemblage of the Schultz site, viewed in conjunction with the faunal analysis by Cleland and Luxenberg, provided some additional data on the subsistance activities of these people during the various occupations.

Early Woodland

The few bone artifacts derived from these levels can at best only provide us with negative evidence. By virtue of a complete lack of fishing and related utilitarian implements, it is safe to assume that the primary economic activity was hunting, as Cleland points out.

Middle Woodland

The presence of a well-developed and varied nonlithic technology would indicate that the Middle Woodland occupants exploited several food resources with considerable intensity. A variety of conical and flat bone projectile points suggests the use of large game, while the presence of shuttles and toggle head harpoons might point to a well-developed fishing economy (see Wedel, 1961:95, 173-74).

The occurrence of scapula hoes or digging implements indicates the practice of some agricultural techniques or at least the maintenance of wild plants. As a general observation, the more elaborate and carefully made implements, in conjunction with the artistic and exotic goods, certainly implies a more sophisticated, intensive and selective exploitation of the environment than the previous occupations.

Late Woodland

Again, with the decline in production of nearly all categories of bone implements known to the preceding occupation, the evidence points to a hunting and plant gathering economy. The total lack of elaborate and specialized equipment during the late Woodland period implies a less intensive and directional exploitation of the environment.

XII

OTHER CULTURAL MATERIAL

James E. Fitting

In addition to ceramics, chipped stone, and bone tools, items belonging to several other classes of cultural material were recovered from the Schultz site. These included some ground stone tools and ornaments, hammer stones, worked and unworked fragments of copper, small fragments of mica, red ocher and limonite and a quantity of firecracked rock. A brief discussion of each of these types of materials and some information on vertical and horizontal distribution of each class is given below.

OTHER STONE TOOLS

The remaining stone tools from the Schultz site have been classified as gorgets, abraders, polishing stones (?), celts and adzes, hammer stones and a pitted stone similar to objects which have been called "nutting stones" (Fig. 79).

The seven gorgets and gorget fragments from the site were all made of slate (Fig. 80*B*). Only two were complete. One is irregular with signs of drilling on both sides in addition to the two complete perforations. The small complete gorget was found in the late Middle Woodland burials excavated in 1964 and was clearly associated with them. Only one other gorget fragment was found in an unmixed provenience unit and this was from an Early Woodland level.

Four sandstone objects with grooves worn into them have been classified as abraders (Fig. 80*A*). One was found on the surface, two in Late Woodland levels, and one in the Early Woodland level. This might be another reflection of the hunting activities of these two occupations.

Three stone objects (Fig. 80*C*) have one or more smoothed, polished faces. For want of a better term, I have called them "polishing stones." Since all came from surface areas, we cannot use their location as an indicator of function.

Six adzes, two celts and five fragments which could be either adzes or celts were recovered from the site (Fig. 81). Again, we had the problem that only three were from areas of certain cultural association. Two were Early Woodland and one was Late Woodland. This follows the same pattern as abraders and some of the chipped stone tools.

The remaining seventeen stone tools are cobbles with battering on one or both ends. We weighed the fourteen complete examples and found a cluster of eight weighing between 4 and 10 ounces, a single 15 ounce specimen, a group of four between 22 and 32 ounces, and one weighing 40 ounces. I am assuming that the different sizes were used for different types of chipping activity. One hammer stone was found in the Early Woodland

Fig. 79. "Nutting stone."

level while the remaining three from unmixed units were Middle Woodland.

The ground stone tools, ornaments and hammer stones from the site are numerically insignificant in comparison to the chipped stone industry. Abraders and adzes seem to be associated with Early and Late Woodland occupations. We cannot, however, rule out sampling error as the cause of this distribution. Still, the fact that only one gorget and three hammer stones can be related to the intensive Middle Woodland occupations is remarkable. The occurrence of only 17 positive hammer stones on a site with over 191,000 flint chips is also remarkable.

COPPER

Only 32 pieces of copper, with a total weight of 26.5 grams, were recovered from the Schultz site during the several years of excavation. Small, amorphous pieces accounted for 23 of these 32 items, with a total weight of 15.5 grams.

Three small copper beads (Fig. 82 H-I) weighing one gram each, one rolled tubular copper bead weighing one gram (Fig. 82 A) and a small copper ring, also weighing one gram, (Fig. 81*C, D*) accounted for the items of personal adornment from the site. The tubular bead was found on the surface, but the other items were from Middle Woodland levels. Two of the beads were from Feature No. 43, while the ring was from the late Middle Woodland level in the channel.

Items which may have had more economic significance consisted of two tightly rolled fragments of sheet copper which at first glance seemed to be awls (Fig. 82 B). It is suggested that these were awls in the making; small fragments of copper may have been beaten into sheets

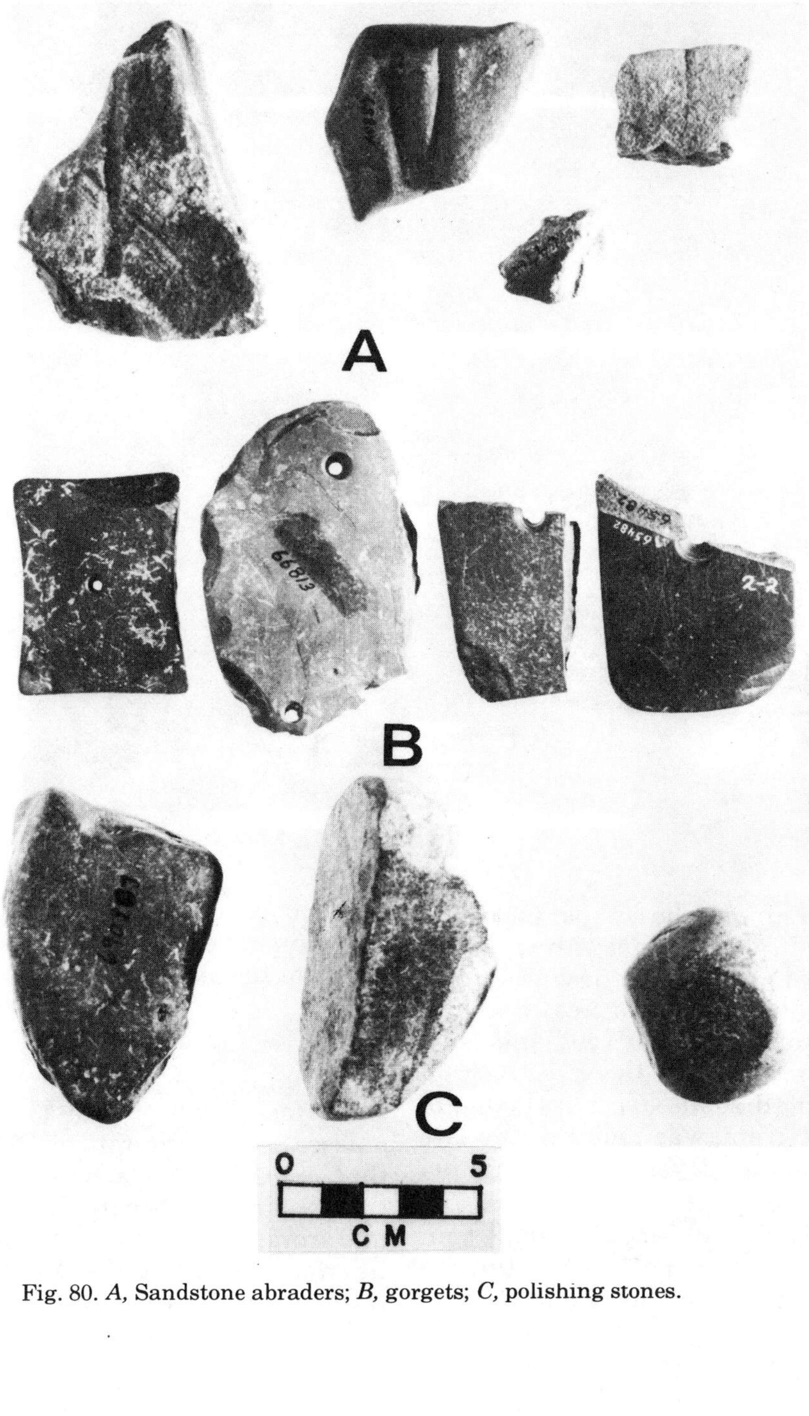

Fig. 80. *A,* Sandstone abraders; *B,* gorgets; *C,* polishing stones.

Fig. 81. Adzes and celts.

(as are found among the scraps) and these sheets rolled and pounded until they formed a solid awl. One of these was from an area of mixed provenience, and the other was from the Late Woodland level in the channel area of the site. A fragment of a small solid copper awl, weighing only one gram, was found in the late Middle Woodland level in the channel area (Fig. 82 E).

The last copper object is a small pin about an inch and a half long with one chisel-like end and the other end blunted from pounding (Fig. 82 F). It was recovered from an early Middle Woodland level inside of the stockade.

LIMONITE

A number of fragments of limonite were found on the site. These small masses often contained fragments of flint, and they have been interpreted as the remains of fire-making kits of flint and iron pyrite. Five fragments of limonite were found in the Early Woodland level, three in the early Middle Wood-

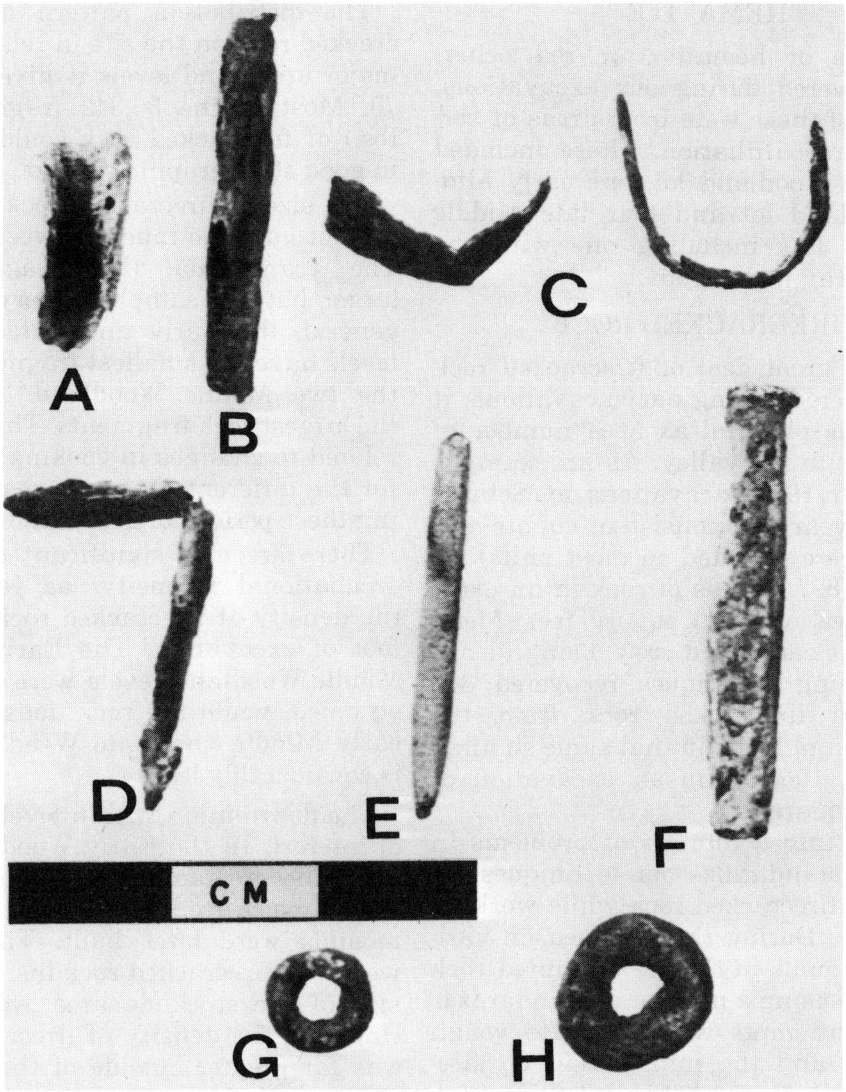

Fig. 82. Copper artifacts: *A*, tubular bead; *B*, rolled copper fragment; *C*, copper ring fragments; *D*, barbed awl; *E*, awl; *F*, drift; *G*, *H*, beads.

land level and two in the Late Woodland level with two other fragments from the areas of mixed provenience. However, only four areas of excavation are involved in all twelve finds. I would more readily account for one early Woodland kit in Unit D and one in 670E570, a late Middle Woodland kit in Unit A and a Late Woodland kit in the channel area.

MICA

Flecks of mica were noted several times in the course of excavation but only 12 were large enough to recover with the sampling technique which we were using. Nine of these were from the east extension of Trench No. 6 from the 1963 season. Two of the other fragments were from the early Middle Woodland level, one inside and one outside the stockade, and one was from the late Middle Woodland level in the channel.

HEMATITE

Ten lots of hematite, or red ocher, were recovered during our excavations. Only six of these were from areas of certain cultural affiliation. These included one Early Woodland lot, one early Middle Woodland lot and four late Middle Woodland lots including one with the burials excavated in 1964.

FIRECRACKED ROCK

While a great deal of firecracked rock was recovered during our excavations, it was not as plentiful as at a number of other sites in the valley. As an example, during our 1964 excavations at Schultz (the only year that consistent counts and weights were recorded on most units) we recovered 897 pounds of rock in an excavation area of 3,620 square feet. Members of this same field crew, using identical sampling techniques recovered 343 pounds of firecracked rock from the nearby Schmidt site in that same summer (Harrison, 1966:54) in an excavation of only 350 square feet.

We ran into a number of problems in trying to standardize our techniques for recording firecracked rock while working at Schultz. During the 1962 season various individuals in the crew counted rock fragments using a number of standards of size. No attempts were made to weigh this rock, and the information on firecracked rock from 1962 is not too useful. Some individual field workers were quite conscientious about recording firecracked rock in 1963, but the consistency and the completeness of the data is similar to that from 1962. In 1964, we attempted to count and weigh all rock which did not pass through the sampling screen. This was done for all units with the exception of one five-by-ten and two ten-by-tens excavated during the closing week of the field season which, for the most part, were peripheral to our major sampling area.

The distribution pattern of the firecracked rock on the site in relation to the major areas and levels is given in Table 70. Most of the 36,342 fragments (897 lbs.) of firecracked rock could be placed in good stratigraphic context.

The size of firecracked rock fragments did not vary too much between horizons. The Transitional (II*d*) fragments are larger but the sample is very small. In general, the Early and Late Woodland levels have the smallest fragments, while the two Middle Woodland levels have the largest rock fragments. This might be related to changes in cooking techniques for the different resources exploited during these periods of occupation.

There are also significant changes in occupational intensity, as reflected by the density of firecracked rock per cubic foot of excavation. The Early and late Middle Woodland levels were intensively occupied, while the rock density for the early Middle and Late Woodland levels is considerably less.

The distribution within levels was also of interest. In the Early Woodland level, all of the firecracked rock came from the levee area in front of the area where the mounds were later built. The average weight of firecracked rock inside and outside of the stockade area was similar. However, the density of firecracked rock was far greater outside of the stockade. This is probably a result of the proximity of this part of the site to the channel.

The distribution pattern of firecracked rock in the early Middle Woodland level is the most complex on the site. The average weight of firecracked rock from the channel area and the living floors below the mounds in back of the stockade is very similar, suggesting that the same type of cooking activities may have been pursued in both areas. The intensity with which this activity took place was much greater in the channel area. The average size of firecracked rock on the levee is

TABLE 70
FIRECRACKED ROCK
(weight in ounces)

Horizon	Channel (750 ft²)	Outside Stockade (380 ft²)	Inside Stockade (1745 ft²)	Mound (745 ft²)	Total (3620 ft²)	Volume 1964
Late Woodland						(615 ft³)
N	1940	22	*X*	*X*	1962	3.19
Wt.	757	29			786	1.27
x̄	.39	1.32			.40	
	2.57	.06				
Late Middle Woodland						(840 ft³)
N	5193	0	0	1218	6411	7.63
Wt.	2729			463	3192	3.80
x̄	.53			.38	.48	
	6.92			1.63		
Early Middle Woodland						(2585 ft³)
N	2281	2104	3758	217	8360	3.23
Wt.	1505	376	1443	152	3476	1.34
x̄	.66	.18	.70	.42		
	3.04	5.54	2.15	.29		
Transitional (II*d*)						(830 ft³)
N	87	*X*	*X*	*X*	87	.10
Wt.	99				99	.12
x̄	1.14				1.14	
	.11					
Early Woodland						(2170 ft³)
N	*X*	6618	8967	0	15585	7.18
Wt.		2586	3203		5789	2.67
x̄		.39	.36		.37	
		17.42	5.14			

Total Units of Certain Provenience	N 32,405 Wt. 13,142
Mixed and Uncertain Provenience	N 3937 Wt. 1013
Total Site	N 36342 Wt. 14355

Note: The symbol *X* signifies that a particular part of the site was not occupied by groups at a particular horizon. The symbol 0 indicates that a group occupied that area of the site at that horizon but that no fire-cracked rock was recovered.

much smaller both inside and outside of the stockade. It is particularly small outside of the stockade which gives a distorted view of the density based on number of fragments per square foot of excavated area. While the count indicates a density nearly two and one half times as great outside of the stockade as inside of the stockade, the average weight per square foot is only 30 percent larger. It does suggest differences in the type and possibly intensity of activities carried out inside and outside of the stockade.

In the late Middle Woodland level firecracked rock was found only in the channel area and in the mound fill or prepared floors below the mounds. No firecracked rock was recovered from the levee either inside or outside of the stockade.

Almost all of the late Woodland firecracked rock from the 1964 season was recovered from the channel area, with only a few fragments from the levee and none from the area of the mounds.

XIII
OCCUPATIONAL HISTORY

James E. Fitting

THE EARLY WOODLAND OCCUPATION

In the latter part of the sixth century B.C., man was able to occupy the Schultz site at Green Point for the first time in 1500 years. This occupation seems to have taken place on a natural levee between the then active river channel and an extensive area of marsh. The entire eastern part of Green Point was a marsh, with the 20SA1 occupation taking place on a small knoll in this marsh during the drier months.

The earliest occupation seems to have taken place after initial formation of the levee when Green Point was decidedly swampy. During the occupation, the site itself became less swampy but the surrounding area remained a marsh. The rate of flow of the Tittabawassee may have increased during this occupation with the channel gradually shifting away from the site.

Some forest cover seems to have developed directly on the site as soon as it was dry enough. Brunett has reported charcoal of maple, shagbark hickory, white ash, black ash, eastern hophornbeam, quaking aspen, northern red oak and eastern hemlock.

The occurrence of a number of forest animal species suggested that mature forest existed in the surrounding higher areas; possibly further up the main stream of the Tittabawassee. This level produced one of the rare occurrences of coniferous charcoal. Cleland noted several northern animal species, particularly marten and fisher, and suggested more coniferous cover than at present in the valley with the possibility of a cooler climate than today. The molluscs also indicated a cooler climate.

The human occupation of the site seems to have been extensive but of short duration. Most of the cultural material is found on a single horizon. The occupation seems to have been heaviest in the areas closest to the river channel and to have decreased in intensity with distance from the channel. The close clustering of radiocarbon dates also indicates a very short occupation. The placement of materials on the living floors suggest that the site was finally abandoned after a particularly disasterous flood. It appears that the Early Woodland occupants did not return after this abandonment.

The cultural inventory of these people was more limited than in later occupations. The principal, if not sole, ceramic type was Schultz Thick, represented by 30 rim sherds, 328 body sherds and several base and other fragments. These were moderately large jars with flat bases and lug handles. They were coarse tempered and generally marked by both exterior and interior cordmarking although both the exterior and interior surface might be smoothed near the lip. Lips were usually square but some were rounded.

Large stemmed projectile points and plano-convex ovate bifaces, probably a type of knife, were the most common bifacial implements. There are relatively high frequencies of projectile point tips, drills and fragments of bifaces. Unifacial tools are relatively rare and amorphorus retouched flakes are the most common type of uniface. The only endscrapers have a sloping edge, and the few large blade tools which were recovered were made of local Bayport cherts. Plano-convex cores were the most common core type with this occupation.

Bone artifacts were rare. They included several splinter awls and ground teeth, a bone point, a flaker and a beamer. All bone implements had an economic rather than ceremonial function.

One sandstone abrader, two celts, a gorget fragment and several hammerstones belonged to this occupation. No mica was found in this level but several fragments of copper and small quantities of limonite and red ocher were recovered.

Cleland felt that the absence of water fowl and turtles in his small sample may have been indicative of a winter occupation of the site. Luxenberg also was dealing with a small sample but found some turtles suggesting some summer occupation. She also identified several species of fish which spawn in the early spring.

Allison's plant data is not particularly helpful in interpreting the season of occupation since only a single fragment of acorn was identified among the materials recovered from the Early Woodland features of the 1964 season. Her biggest sample was from an excavation unit in the channel area which lacked any trace of this earliest occupation.

While the site may have been lightly occupied throughout most of the year, I would still regard the late fall, winter and early spring as the period of most intensive occupation.

All seventeen Early Woodland features were Type C pits, oval features averaging approximately two feet wide, three feet long with a depth of slightly over one foot. They were straight sided and the bottoms were marked by traces of fire suggesting sunken hearths. The density of Early Woodland features was greatest along the edge of the channel on the levee and seemed to drop with distance from the river.

The density of features per total volume of occupation in this level was lower than any other occupation at the site. This is in line with the interpretation of the occupation as a short one. The density of both artifacts and chipping per cubic foot of excavation was low but still very similar to that of all occupations except that of the late Middle Woodland period.

The density of firecracked rock, in relation to both the area and volume of the occupation, is extremely high. The distribution of artifacts, chippage and firecracked rocks is heaviest along the edge of the channel and decreases toward the north of the site.

The low density and distribution of the features, the extremely low density and poor quality of ceramics and the high density of firecracked rock may indicate a different cooking technique for this early occupation. Stone boiling in skin lined pits might be one possibility although the area of fire reddened soil is at the bottom of the pits which would argue against this.

A detailed examination of the location of pits and firecracked rock at several areas of intensive Early Woodland occupation on the site indicated that firecracked rock was not found *in* these pits. It tended to be piled around the edges of these pits. The pits also tended to cluster around a large single post mold. It is possible that these pits were located within structures of some sort. This would be expected if this were a winter occupation. The fires in the pits may have been used to heat rocks which were moved elsewhere for stone boiling or, possibly, even for warmth. It is also possible that the pits were earth ovens where food was steamed or roasted with a cover of stones which had been warmed in the pit earlier.

Both Cleland and Luxenberg found an abundance of small animal species in the faunal remains from this occupation. Cleland, in particular, noted that hunting was more generalized than for later occupations. I would suspect that this generalized diet was extended to plant foods but that they may have been collected at other places in the valley, like 20SA1. If they were brought back to the site, it would have been in a partially processed form and, as Allison has suggested, they might have been totally consumed.

The numbers of small aquatically oriented animals like muskrat, raccoon, beaver, and otter would be expected if the site were located in a marsh. Larger species such as deer and bear were of major importance in the diets of these people but birds and turtles were almost ignored.

Luxenberg found a difference in the pattern of internal distribution of faunal remains at this period. Deer were the most important single food source, but their bones were found well back on the levee. Small mammals, particularly muskrat, and fish were found in greater numbers nearer the channel. This foreshadows the site utilization pattern which occurs in several later occupations.

The fish that were represented in the bone refuse are generally of a large size and belonged to species that could either have been caught on a year-round basis or species that would have been more likely to have been caught in the early spring. The size of the fish suggests that they were speared. This might have been done from the shore, from canoes or through holes in the river ice. Fish play a smaller part in the diet than in any subsequent occupation.

Brose's data indicates that molluscs were used as food but the relative density of their remains is not as great as in the later Middle Woodland period. He has, however, pointed to the difficulty of gathering them in winter, and if the Early Woodland occupation was primarily a winter occupation their scant occurrence is not surprising. The type of pits characteristic of this occupation could easily have been used for steaming molluscs in the manner described by Brose.

Molluscs, for this occupation as for all levels, would probably have played a small part in the diet of the site occupants and would not even have been as useful in supplying amino acids as in later levels where animal protein played less a part in the diet.

The general pattern of artifact distribution, several small but dense clusters with two to three Type C pits each, along the edge of the river channel suggests that the site, located on a newly formed levee surrounded by marsh, was occupied by a number of distinct family units. The site seems to have been occupied primarily in the fall, winter and early spring, although a few people may have stayed on through the summer while the others went elsewhere searching for food.

Fish, turtles and molluscs seem to have been summer, fall and spring foods but are found in small numbers. Small mammals were an important food source but larger mammals were the mainstay in the diet. They were probably hunted in the surrounding upland forests which may have had a larger coniferous element than today.

This would have been a precarious existence subject to flood during much of the year. It is quite possible that this area was occupied for only a short time and the site inhabitants were finally driven off by a particularly severe flood.

THE TRANSITIONAL (II*d*) OCCUPATION

The transitional (II*d*) occupation at the site is the most elusive of all the occupations. It is difficult to date, and it is not even possible to call it Early or Middle Woodland with any certainty.

After the abandonment of the site by the Early Woodland peoples, the flooding activity continued to decrease. This could have been in response to the final draining of the Algoma stage in the Lake Huron Basin after the final downcutting of the St. Clair or Detroit River channels. The backswamp area of the site dried up as did the marsh at 20SA1. The channel on the south edge of the site, possibly one of many channels of the Tittabawassee through the marsh in the Early Woodland period, decreased in size and shifted further to the south. There seems to have been a general filling in of the old channel with some slump from the old river bank and some redeposition of Early Woodland cultural material.

As the channel filled, a thin humic zone was formed on the still moist channel fill in an area which almost certainly would have been subject to seasonal flooding with ponded water standing in places for several months of the year. The transitional occupation of the site took place on this soil zone and was restricted to the old channel area.

There may have been an increase in the forest cover on the site itself. Brose has suggested more hickory and elm with the climate similar to that of today. Allison's data on plant remains suggests that walnut, butternut and hickory were available in the area and that nuts from these trees were a more important food source than in any other occupation.

Cultural material is very sparse. The ceramic sample is represented by Shiawassee ware. The sherd count for this ware, 309, is almost as large as that from the Early Woodland level, but the rim sherd count suggests that only nine vessels are represented. However, since the total bulk of the excavated portion of the Early Woodland occupation is approximately three times as great as the transitional occupation, the ceramic densities are similar. Ceramics do not seem to have been an important cultural item in either the Early Woodland or transitional occupation.

Shiawassee ware is marked by a sandy paste with a high silt content which gives this ware its distinctive feel and appearance. It has large tempering fragments. The vessels seem to have been wide jars with generally excurved walls and, possibly, flat bases. The most common variant is Shiawassee Cordmarked with its careless application of loose twisted cord to the exterior surface. Even this decoration is often obliterated. Almost a quarter of the sample consisted of smoothed or smoothed-over cordmarked sherds. The remaining ten percent were incised with broad lines, usually at right angles to each other, over a plain surface. Shiawassee ware sherds from other sites in the valley show some variation on this pattern of incising but the small Schultz site sample was fairly uniform.

The density of chipped stone artifacts to volume of site excavated is much less than for the Early Woodland level. The one straight stemmed point may be redeposited or salvaged from the earlier occupation. The typical projectile point type was probably an expanded stem form represented by six point bases. No standardized scrapers were found, but more Bayport chert blades were found in proportion to other unifaces than in any other level. The bone assemblage from this level was limited to a single ground tooth. No copper, mica, hematite, or limonite were found with this occupation.

The season of occupation is not clear, but both Cleland and Luxenberg note a great deal of similarity in fauna to that of the Early Woodland occupation. The apparently greater concentration on fish might indicate more warm weather occupation, but the sample of bone material from this level is very small.

There are seven features in this horizon, all hearths. The volume of the features in this level, in relation to the volume of excavation, is almost identical to that of the Early Woodland period although there is no overlap in feature type. Many of the early III*a* features, all hearths again, probably belong with this occupation rather than with the early Middle Woodland occupation where they were placed for the feature analysis. No post molds were noted and there is no evidence of structures.

The volume of chipped stone artifacts to volume of site excavated is only one-third that of the Early Woodland occupation. This would mean that ceramics were relatively more important in the total cultural assemblage. Firecracked rock was extremely rare with a density far less than for any other occupation. The few fragments which were present were over twice as heavy as for any other level.

Allison's floral analysis indicates a particularly heavy emphasis on nuts for this horizon. However, the rodent burrows, the presence of nutmeats in the shell and the unreliable radiocarbon date discussed by Speth cast some doubt on the reliability of the small sample from this level.

Cleland found one deer and two muskrats in this level; Luxenberg found one deer and one muskrat. They both found remains of several large fish. The combined samples indicated that while fish remains accounted for over 100 pounds of meat, mammals still accounted for three-quarters of the meat diet. Birds and turtles seem to have been unimportant.

The transitional occupation seems to represent a series of small camps occupied for extremely short periods of time by passing groups of hunters or fishermen. These occupations must have started several centuries after the Early Woodland abandonment since there was some evidence for the incomplete development of a soil horizon. It was still before the beginning of our era; possibly some time between 400 B.C. and 10 B.C.

The cultural inventory was simple with ceramics playing a larger part in the total assemblage. I would suggest that this was an occupation of small family groups. Food may have been consumed on the spot. The base camp for such a group would have been located elsewhere.

THE EARLY MIDDLE WOODLAND OCCUPATION

Around 2,000 years ago there appears to have been a considerable increase in flooding at Green Point. Speth has suggested that the deposits of this period were formed under conditions associated with a long term rise in river level. He has suggested that the entire cycle was as long as 300 years with as much as 100 years of constant inundation. This seems to have been associated with a general rise in lake level in the Michigan and Huron basins. During the peak of this postulated lake stage, even the highest areas of the site may have been under water.

Brose's information on molluscs confirms, in part, Speth's conclusions. Brose has suggested a damper climate with a decrease of forest cover on the site itself, which we would expect with the higher water level. While the molluscs suggest a possibly warmer temperature, Speth has suggested a colder temperature with a decreased evaporation rate as one possible cause for the increased water level. As Speth indicates, however, a number of factors may be involved in this water level increase and Brose's data, largely from features, may be selected from intervals on either side of the high lake stage.

During the early part of this period, there seems to have been some occupation along the levee and on the edge of the filled-in channel. As flooding activity increased, cultural materials from this occupation were washed into the channel area providing additional fill. The active channel of the Tittabawassee, after the high water stage, was probably somewhere near its present location to the south of the site.

Brunett has recorded a number of tree species from the area in his examination of charcoal from features. These include maple, yellow birch, shagbark hickory, chestnut, hackberry, white ash, black walnut, red mulberry, white oak, swamp white oak, burr oak, northern red oak and American elm. Allison recognized shells of walnuts, butternuts and hickory nuts from both features and the general site level. Several of these species have a distinctly southern orientation and were not represented in the charcoal from the Early Woodland levels. This might indicate a slightly warmer temperature. On the other hand, a variety of habitats are represented. It seems likely that some of these trees originated at some distance from the site and were brought to the site by flooding.

Cleland suggested that the fauna from the early portion of the Middle Woodland period indicated a trend toward more open forest conditions. Luxenberg has some question about the significance of this change and suggested that if it did occur, it may have been a local development. Both are impressed by the increased percentages of aquatically oriented forms in the faunal assemblage although both point out that species from other habitats are represented in the assemblage.

The cultural material from this occupation has been recovered from all major areas of the site. While some features were found, there is evidence of extensive postoccupational disturbance and redeposition. The assemblage which we have is mixed and some of the material is clearly waterworn. Our reconstruction of the assemblage of this horizon needs to be in part typological.

The ceramics from this early Middle Woodland occupation were Tittabawassee wares. These seem to have been moderately large jars with wide mouths, which contracted toward rounded or subconoidal bases. Rims were slightly curved with flattened to beveled lips. Bodies were most commonly smoothed and decoration was primarily on the neck and lip although some zoned body decoration was present. These vessels were grouped into three types on the basis of decoration: Tittabawassee Dentate Stamped, Tittabawassee Cordwrapped Stick Impressed and Tittabawassee Plain Noded.

There is some evidence of a bimodal distribution of Tittabawassee wares but I would concur with Speth and Fisher that this is probably caused by redeposition. While some of the generally later Green Point ware may have been manufactured at this time, I feel that the principle early Middle Woodland ceramics were Tittabawassee wares.

Only about 160 rim and neck sherds were assigned to this ware although many of the untypeable plain bodysherds would probably belong to these vessels. Only 30 to 40 vessels are represented in this sample, so ceramics are not too frequent. If only Tittabawassee wares were manufactured at this time, then the density of ceramics is less than that for either of the first two occupations of the site.

The lithic assemblage in the early Middle Woodland levels is marked by moderate percentages of older tool types as well as early Middle Woodland forms. This could again be caused either by a reworking of early deposits or by salvage and reuse of tools found after floods or while digging pits. The most typical projectile point form for this level is the expanding stemmed variant which marks most of the Middle and Late Woodland occupation of the site. The length of these expanding stemmed forms is, on the average, greater than for any subsequent level. A small triangular point of the type usually associated with Late Woodland occupations was recovered from one of the features. A hafted scraper and some biface fragments round out the biface assemblage. Gravers and drills were absent. Steep retouched endscrapers appear for the first time and there is a new emphasis on blade tools with blades of exotic materials appearing for the first time.

The bone assemblage for this period is the most varied, but not the most plentiful, of all the occupations. There are 69 items; 25 of these are turtle shell dishes including one engraved dish. Ground teeth, bone projectile points and polished bone (beads?) were very common. The variety of the bone industry is perhaps a reflection of the variety of activities carried out at the site.

One copper implement and some fragments of copper, two pieces of mica and one lot of red ocher have been attributed to this occupation.

The season of occupation seems to have varied but both Cleland and Luxenberg note a considerable increase in animal and fish species which would have been more available during the warmer months. At the same time, Allison noted a slight shift in nut resource utilization. If the Early Woodland occupation can be described as primarily a fall, winter and spring occupation, then the early Middle Woodland occupation took place primarily in the summer and fall.

All areas of the site would probably have been available to the early Middle Woodland inhabitants when not flooded. Features for some part of this occupation have been found in all parts of the site. There is a wide variety of features including Type A and Type B pits, empty pits and hearths. The hearths were found primarily in the old river channel area (on top of, and mixed with, II*d* hearths) of the site as well as in the northernmost areas of our excavations at some distance from the river channel. We also noted that the average weight of firecracked rock in these two areas was higher than in any other part of the site or in any other occupation except the transitional (II*d*) occupation. The type of features and firecracked rock in the lower elevation areas of the site suggest a site use similar to that of the transitional (II*d*) period.

One of the principal site features, the ceremonial stockade, was apparently built during the very last part of this occupation. This seems to have been late in the early Middle Woodland occupation of the levee since some Type A and Type B pits and hearths are found within the stockade area. The empty pits are clearly early Middle Woodland features associated with the stockade.

I would suspect the following occupational pattern based on the feature distribution. A preflood pattern of site utilization with shallow hearths, using few large firecracked rocks, is characteristic of the low-lying areas of the site. After the peak of the high water stage, the site was occupied as it again emerged from the waters as a knoll in a swamp. As the water level dropped further and the intensity of seasonal flooding decreased, the stockade, a ceremonial structure, was built. The zone of occupational intensity shifted to the old river channel since the levee area, which was first dry, became a restricted area.

The distribution of cultural material on the site, even allowing for the construction of the stockade some time during this period, is perplexing. Ceramics are found in greatest numbers along the channel side of the levee between the channel and the stockade. They are not particularly frequent in the channel area. Stone tools are most frequent in the channel area. Relatively large fragments of firecracked rock are found in the channel area but even larger quantities of very small fragments of firecracked rock are found on the levee just outside of the stockade; moderate amounts of intermediate-sized fragments were found within the stockade.

If we intuitively factor out the initial preflood occupation, we could suggest that men concentrated on fishing in the lower southern portion of the site near the river while women carried on more generalized activities and some men processed the results of their hunting on the drier higher areas of the site. No clear-cut pattern can be observed because of the shifting pattern of artifact concentration and the variable nature of the site itself during this time period.

Cleland, Luxenberg and Brose all note a new emphasis on aquatic food sources. Fish, in particular, became a most important item in the diet of the people. Luxenberg has suggested, however, that mammals still accounted for two-thirds of their diet and there seems to have been a greater concentration on a few large mammals. Both Cleland and Luxenberg suggest that nets were used to catch a wide variety of sizes of fish. Molluscs begin to take on more significance as a food source.

Allison noted a decrease in dependence on nuts but suggested that it might be related to an increase in the consumption of other plant foods which either were totally consumed or were not recovered by screening with a quarter-inch mesh screen. This position has been partially supported by some other lines of evidence. The pattern of site utilization which characterized that late Middle Woodland occupation certainly began to develop by the end of the early Middle Woodland period and coprolites from this later occupation suggest a strong emphasis on plant foods.

As we mentioned earlier, living floors are not clearly present and the nature of the site utilization is variable and changing. However, it is possible to suggest some changes in social organization. The occupational intensity, measured by the economic scale of density of artifacts per cubic foot of deposit excavated, is equal to that of the Early Woodland period. This, however, is an average of an early low-density occupation and a later, post-flood, occupation which must have been of a higher density.

Where the concentration of cultural material in the Early Woodland occupation could be related to family living areas, the distribution pattern for the early Middle Woodland occupation suggests large site areas were used for specialized activities. This might suggest work groups, divided on a sexual basis, which could have formed along extended family or lineage lines. Certainly the stockade was the product of group effort and the focus of group attention. The carrying potential of the site would have been greater during the warmer periods of the year, and more people may have gathered at the site during this time than during the early period when winter population concentration took place. Green Point was well on the way to becoming the focal occupation of the Saginaw Valley during the early Middle Woodland period.

THE LATE MIDDLE WOODLAND OCCUPATION

The trend toward less flooding of the site and a further decrease in swampy conditions in the surrounding area continued on into the later of the two Middle

Woodland occupations at the site. This shift probably took place near the end of the third century A.D., and there is a distinct change in the nature and intensity of the occupation as well as in the cultural material.

The site was again a stabilized levee with only seasonal backswamp formation by at least A.D. 350. By A.D. 450 the site was high enough above the water level for erosion from higher to lower levels to have taken place. Speth feels that both the lower and upper portions of this occupational level are reworked with only the middle part representing true midden formation.

Brose's environmental data, derived from the molluscs, complements the pattern suggested by Speth. The early part of the late Middle Woodland occupation sees a decrease in the flooding which marked the earlier Middle Woodland occupation. Conditions were still wetter than present. By the end of the late Middle Woodland occupation he has suggested a climate which was drier, and possibly cooler, than at present.

Brose feels that the molluscs indicate a considerable decrease in forest cover on Green Point itself although well-forested areas may surround the site. Cleland and Luxenberg have also considered the possibility of more open country in the local area at this time. Allison noted a further decrease in the consumption of nuts and found the only seed refuse from the 1964 excavations associated with this occupation. It may be that the site itself was cleared by man.

Brunett has noted woods among the charcoal from the site which are generally similar to those present in the early Middle Woodland level with the addition of shell bark hickory, black ash and slippery elm, and the deletion of red mulberry, swamp white oak and burr oak. This might also argue for slightly cooler and drier conditions at the site. Allison noted the food use of hazelnut, hackberry and goosefoot at this level. These are all plants which would colonize newly drained areas and would continue to grow there if a climax plant cover was not allowed to develop.

The pattern of site occupation seems to have been very complex and there is a great quantity of cultural material. More material was recovered from this very limited volume of excavation than from any other occupation.

The characteristic ceramics for this level were Green Point wares. They may have appeared in the early Middle Woodland levels but they are certainly paramount in this level. Green Point ware vessels are almost all medium to small jars with constricted necks, moderately developed shoulders and subconoidal to rounded bases. Miniature vessels of this type have quadrilobate bodies. Vessel walls tend to be considerably thinner than the walls of earlier ceramic types.

Over 80 percent of these vessels seem to have had plain bodies. The remainder were almost evenly divided between cordmarked and smoothed-over cordmarked bodies with a small occurrence of scraping. Over 90 percent of the decorated bodysherds were impressed with rocker stamping and an additional seven percent were decorated with incising.

Four types were recognized on the basis of rim decoration or lack of it: Green Point Rocker Stamped, Green Point Incised, Green Point Brushed and Green Point Plain. Green Point Rocker Stamped accounted for 75 percent of this ware category, 333 rimsherds and 2,200 bodysherds. Green Point Incised was the next largest type with 110 rimsherds. There were 14 brushed rims and 40 Green Point Plain rims.

We estimated that slightly over 400 vessels were represented for this occupation. This is more than 12 times as many vessels as were represented in any earlier occupation. This is even more significant when we note that the total volume of the late Middle Woodland deposits which we excavated was less than one-third that of either the Early Woodland or the early Middle Woodland excavations.

Again, some stone tools seem to be redeposited or salvaged from earlier occupations. The principle projectile point types are still expanding stemmed forms although there is a decrease in the average length. A triangular point was recovered as was a notched scraper. Narrow expanding stemmed points, somewhat similar to the forms often called Dustin Points, make their appearance for the first time in this occupation.

A wide range of unifacial tools, including unifacial points, were found with this occupation. Blades reached their greatest percentage (excluding the transitional level) and exotic blades are most prevalent at this level.

There is a decreasing emphasis on cores in general and on plano-convex cores in particular. Block cores are almost as common as plano-convex cores.

There are nearly three and one-half times as many bone artifacts in the late Middle Woodland level as there are in the early Middle Woodland level and nearly ten times as many as in the Early and Late Woodland occupations. The density of bone artifacts is almost ten times as great as for any other level. The variety of bone artifacts, however, is less than for the early Middle Woodland occupation.

Turtle carapace dishes are even more important than in the early Middle Woodland period and make up approximately 60 percent of the assemblage, about twice what they did in early Middle Woodland times. A higher percentage of these are also engraved. At the same time, there is a distinct increase in bone and shell beads and decorative items. There is an actual decrease in the numbers of bone points, awls and flaking implements. The "florescence" of the bone industry does not appear to have been associated with the economic activities of these people.

Almost all of the copper, mica and red ocher found at the site are clearly of late Middle Woodland origin. Considering, however, the increase in density of all artifact categories and the tendency for these exotic materials to be found in the mound area, copper and red ocher decrease in proportion to other artifact categories in the living areas of the site. Shell beads and ornaments and cut animal teeth also are concentrated in the mound area.

The information on the season in which the site was occupied is generally the same as for the early Middle Woodland occupation. The further decrease in dependency on nuts and the increase in dependency on fish might indicate a warmer weather occupation. This might be a result of a decrease in river level with less spring flooding and a longer potential period for summer occupation.

No empty pits, even within the stockade, have been associated with the late Middle Woodland level. Type A and Type B pits and hearths are all found with this occupation but Type B pits are most common. These are pits with quantities of debris and some evidence of burning. They are found in about three times the number that would be expected by chance alone. Late Middle Woodland pits and hearths are found almost exclusively in the channel area. The occurrence of these clearly defined features in this part of the site argues against both a total redeposition of the late Middle Woodland material or a "sweeping out" of a stockaded village and subsequent dumping in the channel.

The density of features per cubic foot of excavation is generally high for both Middle Woodland occupations but reaches its peak for the entire site, with features accounting for over two percent of the bulk of the excavation, during this time.

The stockade area seems to have been avoided by late Middle Woodland peoples. Even the empty pits are no longer found within its walls. However, the occurrence of one Type B pit within its confines and another located directly over a post mold, might indicate that the stockade itself had vanished by A.D. 450. All that then remained may have been a restricted or "sacred" area which was suffering from encroachment by the dense population concentration in the channel area.

The mounds were built during the late Middle Woodland period and there is some debris from this occupation in the fill. No burials have been found that we know of in the two largest mounds (the only ones that could be recognized as mounds from surface indications). The few burials that we did find were on the edge of a basket loaded area which was on a level with the surrounding site. The burials were probably secondarily deposited in the mound. Even the grave goods could have been redeposited.

Feature density is high and both the density and average size of firecracked rock are very high. The density of chippage and artifacts is five to six times as great as for any other occupational level. Over 80 percent of the firecracked rock, most of the chipped stone and virtually all of the artifacts were found in the channel area.

Earlier variants of Green Point ware, which may be contemporary with Tittabawassee ware, are found in the northwestern areas of the site (under Mound A?) while the later variants are found in the southern (channel) parts of the site. The channel area seems quite clearly to have been where the action was during this occupation.

There are some significant changes in the extractive activities carried out at the site. Cleland's analysis of the 1962 and 1963 bone refuse indicated an increase in fishing with fish accounting for a third of the meat eaten by the people. Luxenberg's data from the 1964 season is even more striking with fish accounting for two-thirds of the meat. This difference may be, in part, distributional. Cleland's sample overrepresents the levee with very little material from the channel area while Luxenberg's sample contains material from several large units in the channel. This type of differential bone refuse distribution is not unique for this occupation.

Deer is the most important meat source. There is a decline in the variety of mammals hunted but small, aquatically oriented mammals are still much in evidence. The deer appear to have been hunted in the fall.

Molluscs play a greater part in the diet of the late Middle Woodland people than for any other group. There are not only more molluscs, but there are higher percentages of food species in this level.

Allison was able to duplicate the work of others in demonstrating the avoidance of the stockade area during this occupation. She also could demonstrate a decreasing dependence on nuts and she suggested, largely on the basis of negative evidence, that other plant foods played an important role in the diet of these people. No plant material was recovered which might suggest in any way that agriculture was known to these people.

McClary's very provocative paper largely supports the work of other specialists in addition to making a contribution of its own. Fish were found to be important in the diet of these people and quantities of still unidentified plant material were found. The parasites indicate that some of the fish were eaten before being completely cooked. McClary's comments on the hygenic conditions at the site add another dimension to our picture of the late Middle Woodland occupation.

The late Middle Woodland occupation of the Schultz site was probably a summer occupation in a relatively stable area, an area which may have been intentionally kept clear of large trees to favor the growth of certain types of plants. During the summer more people came to the site than ever before but used a smaller area of the site for living purposes. The economic focus of the people seems to have been on fishing, but fishing may have been only one of the reasons for the occupation. The avoidance of the stockade area, the construction of mounds and the burial activity indicate another function for the site. The presence of public works (mounds) and the density of population suggest that the type of social organization was at least as well developed as that of the early Middle Woodland period.

THE LATE WOODLAND OCCUPATION

The drop in level of the lake and the river at the site, which started in the early Middle Woodland period, continued on into the early part of the Late Woodland period at the Schultz site. There was a period of erosion in the sixth century and some of the deposits were completely reworked. Taggart considered the possibility of an "occupational hiatus" during this time, but there is some evidence for a continued occupation of lesser intensity in the channel area.

There is a suggestion in Brose's data of an increase in forest cover. Coupled with the decrease in cultural material, this suggests a drastic change in site function and a new pattern of site use.

The information on flooding indicates that a high water level was again present in the later part of the first millennium A.D. Some time between A.D. 700 and A.D. 900 the site again became marshy although it does not appear to have been inundated as during the early Middle Woodland period. It appears to have been dry again around A.D. 1100 although it has been continually subjected to seasonal floods right up to recent times when an artificial levee was built.

It is perhaps deceptive to even talk of the Late Woodland occupations; sporadic occupations, for different reasons, seem to have taken place many times between A.D. 600 and A.D. 1300.

Brose has suggested that the climate was warmer and damper during this period. Brunett reported more tree species in the charcoal from the Late Woodland midden and features than for any other occupation. All tree species found in earlier levels, with the exception of the red mulberry and burr oak of the early Middle Woodland period, are found in this level. In addition, pignut hickory, American beech and black gum were found only in this level. I would interpret Brunett's data as generally indicative of considerable diversity over this time.

Both Cleland and Luxenberg have interpreted the faunal evidence as indicative of deciduous woodland in the area of the site. Cleland also felt that this would have been open woodland with occasional prairies, a condition similar to that of the early historic period.

The cultural inventory from this level is small and does not show the variation which would be expected over this amount of time. On typological grounds, fragments of 86 vessels have been assigned to this occupation. The only clearly defined type is Saginaw Thin, a thin, hard paste jar form with cordmarking right up to the rim. These vessels seem to have been small- to medium-sized with slightly constricted necks and straight to slightly outflaring rims.

Some sherds of Saginaw Thin may have had rim or lip decoration but those vessels with rim or lip decoration seem generally to be thicker and to have a softer paste. There is a minority type which is textile impressed, but these seem to be large elongated vessels which can be relegated to the last part of the Late Woodland occupation.

The density of ceramics is less than one-fourth that of the late Middle Woodland occupation, although it is still considerably greater than that of earlier occupations. The density of Late Woodland chippage and chipped stone artifacts is also less than one-fourth that of the late Middle Woodland occupation. The ratio of vessels to artifacts is, however, still the same.

The Late Woodland projectile points are still primarily expanding stemmed forms. There is an increase in the percentage of the small expanding stemmed forms. Narrow expanding stemmed forms and triangular points also become more popular through time. There seems to be little standardization of knife forms, and the category of "miscellaneous bifaces" is larger than in any other occupation.

There is little change in the unifacial assemblage from the late Middle Woodland level except that blades are less important than during any earlier occupation. Cores almost completely disappear, and the ratio of chippage to artifacts is the lowest for any level. There is a decline in both quantity and quality of tools from the Middle Woodland levels although there are still more than in the Early Woodland occupation. Turtle carapace dishes still account for nearly half of the assemblage, and decorative items are still common.

A sandstone abrader and an adze were found with this level as were several copper fragments. One possible fire-making kit was found.

The season of site occupation varied through the long Late Woodland time span at the site. Cleland noted a drastic decline in fish as a source of food and suggested a return to a primarily hunting occupation. Luxenberg, on the other hand, has information which seems to contradict Cleland's. She has levels within the Late Woodland sequence where fishing is still decidedly important. This difference is, however, probably a function of the areas of the site represented in each sample. The plant refuse could either indicate more summer occupation or a more transient occupation.

Late Woodland features were few in number and consisted almost entirely of Type A pits; refuse pits with no evidence of fire. Only two features with evidence of firing could be attributed to this level.

These features were found in greater than expected numbers on the levee but the stockade seems to have little influence on their distribution. Almost all of the cultural material from this period seems to be equally distributed inside and outside of the stockade which would indicate that it not only was gone but that the area was no longer differentiated from the rest of the site. The return of a high river level would also have made the higher part of the site, the levee, a more secure area from the renewed flooding.

The distribution of cultural material is interesting. While most of the features were found on the levee, more of the cultural material was found in the channel area. Almost all of the firecracked rock and chippage were found in the channel, as were the greatest densities of sherds and stone. There is a complete avoidance of the mound area, but this might be caused by the concentration of economic activities in the southern part of the site.

Two explanations could be offered for this distribution. In the late Middle Woodland occupation, I rejected the hypothesis that the stockade was the living area and that the channel fill was village refuse cleaned out of the stockade. I did this because features occurred in the channel area and were absent in the stockade. In the Late Woodland occupation the features are found on the levee indicating that occupation took place there, but the living debris appears to have been cleaned away and deposited in the channel.

An alternative explanation is that the Late Woodland midden accumulation was actually washed down into the lower areas of the site leaving only the subsurface features in the higher areas. The actual explanation is probably a combination of these factors as well as others which we have not yet even considered.

There was certainly an increase in hunting activity over that done in the late Middle Woodland occupation, and there was also a decrease in the number of species hunted. A few large species, primarily deer and bear, accounted for most of the meat. There is a drop both in the frequency of molluscs and in the frequency of food species among those molluscs which were recovered. Nuts were also less important in the diet.

Cleland found a drastic decrease in fish utilization in Level IV*c* while Luxenberg found fish to be "the most important single source of meat" in that level. Cleland's sample was primarily from the levee while Luxenberg had a very large sample from the channel area where fish bone always seems to be more common. Mammal bone is usually most common on the levee. This trend, noted in earlier occupations, is carried to a point of near exclusion in this Late Woodland level.

Either the social situation, seasonality, redeposition, or the long time span considered as a single unit or a combination of these factors could be involved in this distributional pattern. It could be that fishing was a warm weather activity carried out in the channel area by women. Men could have processed and possibly cached meat in the pits at the higher parts of the site.

It also could be that the channel was occupied in the spring and fall while the levee served as the site of a winter occupation. It could be that fish bone eroded into the channel with other cultural material while the larger mammal bone is characteristic of the sporadic post A.D. 1000 occupation when flooding would have been less likely.

In general, the Late Woodland occupations seem to have been brief, to have occurred for varied reasons and seem to have occurred over a long period of time. It is possible that the site served more as a spring and fall fishing site in the earlier portions of the Late Woodland period, as in the late Middle Woodland times, and later became more the focus for a series of winter hunting camps. There is again no evidence for agricultural activity at the site. This would not be expected with the transient nature of any single occupation. A base camp must have existed somewhere else for these people, and this may have been agricultural.

XIV

THE SCHULTZ SITE IN THE VALLEY AND BEYOND

James E. Fitting

So far, we have viewed the Schultz site as an isolated area of occupation in the Saginaw Valley. From some of the earlier chapters, however, it is clear that the site can only present a portion of the regional adaptation of prehistoric peoples in the Saginaw Valley and the upper Great Lakes. The Schultz site has been considered as one site in the larger regional context in another volume now in press (Fitting, n.d.*a*). There is no need to duplicate that work here; the following pages represent only a brief summary of interpretations derived from Schultz and, quite literally, hundreds of other sites.

The Late Archaic occupation of the Saginaw Valley, recently studied by Papworth (1967), Taggart (1967) and others, furnishes us with the necessary base for understanding the early occupation at the Schultz site. Prior to the late high water stage in the Lake Huron Basin, the Nipissing stage, there appears to have been scant settlement in the Saginaw Valley. The reasons for this are to be found in the environmental potential of the area (Fitting, 1968*a*); the closed boreal forest and newly flooded lake shores could not support a dense population. Even the greater rate of stream flow which must have occurred with the low stages of the Great Lakes would have been detrimental to most of the food species of fish utilized by the Late Archaic populations of later times.

With the high water lake stage, reached just prior to 2000 B.C., the center of the valley was a shallow lake, the Shiawassee Embayment. Extensive Late Archaic settlements are found around the shores and on islands in this westward extension of the Saginaw Bay. Cleland (1966) and Taggart (1967) have suggested that the Late Archaic seasonal pattern involved winter population concentrations based on deer hunting and summer population dispersal, with larger groups breaking up into smaller family units during the summer months. This is the same pattern suggested by Morse (1967) for the inhabitants of the Robinson site in Tennessee. I would interpret the entire pattern as that of a southern group moving into the area when the valley could again support a higher population level.

For years, archaeologists have been impressed by the uniformity of Late Archaic-Early Woodland burial practices throughout northeastern North America. The Glacial Kame, Red Ocher, Old Copper and Meadow Wood complexes of the northeast all share certain similarities. There appears to have been more communication along this newly opened ecological frontier and with the better established areas to the south.

The principle characteristics of the

burial cult have been discussed in a number of places (Ritchie, 1955; 1965; Ritzenthaler and Quimby, 1962). The most elaborate developments seem to have taken place within several centuries of 1000 B.C. The burials from the Andrews (Papworth, 1967), Hodges (Binford, 1963*a*) and Pomranky (1963*b*) sites are examples of this burial tradition in the Saginaw Valley.

After 2000 B.C. the Shiawassee Embayment began to drop with a general drop in lake level. Although there were subsequent rises in lake level, the valley was never again as rich for hunting and gathering populations as it had been at the Nipissing high stage. The greater attention to burial activity mentioned above, seems to have taken place as the potential carrying capacity of the environment was once again decreasing.

By the sixth century B.C., it was possible to occupy a small rise in the swamp in the very center of the valley. The lakeshore winter camps of a thousand years earlier were, by this time, dry sand ridges; perhaps already colonized by the pines which marked these former beaches in the early historic period.

The inhabitants of the Schultz site in the sixth century B.C. have been classed as Early Woodland people because of their pottery. However, the occurrence of notched cache blades with this occupation at the Schultz site, furnishes us with a link with the Late Archaic burials located elsewhere in the valley. It seems fairly clear that we are dealing with cultural continuity between the preceramic and early ceramic-using peoples here.

There is certainly a continuity in the settlement system. The Early Woodland Schultz site presents an extensive camp which was occupied primarily during the winter. It is the equivalent of the Schmidt site (Harrison, 1966) of an earlier period. The Early Woodland occupations at the Kantzler site downriver in Bay City (Crumley, 1967) and 20SA1 (Wright, 1964) are to the Early Woodland Schultz camp what the Feeheley (Taggart, n.d.*a*) and Hart (Wright and Morlan, 1964) sites are to the Schmidt site in the Late Archaic. At Kantzler, fish are more important in the Early Woodland occupation than in any subsequent occupation. The scanty Early Woodland materials from the Bussinger, Andrews, Mahoney, Fraizer and Fletcher sites probably represent the same type of small summer camp.

The degree of similarity between the Early Woodland occupations of the Saginaw Valley and surrounding areas is striking. This is particularly true of the "Marion" culture of the Sheets and Larsen sites in Illinois (Munson, 1966; Munson and Hall, 1966) and the Leimbach site in northern Ohio (Shane, 1967*a*; 1967*b*). Details of features, artifact styles and even settlement system (Shane, personal communication) seem to be similar. The radiocarbon dates for these complexes center within a century of each other as well.

We have virtually no information on the transitional period between the Early Woodland and Middle Woodland occupations in the valley; that is, between 500 B.C. and 100 B.C. The Shiawassee ware level at Schultz with its shallow hearths, fish and muskrat bone, is the only living area so far excavated in the valley. At least one Shiawassee ware sherd was recovered from Kantzler, and I have seen additional Shiawassee ware in the Michigan State University collections from the Fletcher site. As Fischer mentioned, the largest extant collection is from the Bussinger site and has yet to be analyzed. Until more information is available, I would not want to speculate on even the Saginaw Valley adaptive pattern for this horizon, let alone any form of external relationship.

The Middle Woodland occupation seems to have started in the first century

B.C. The ceramics suggest a relationship with the Havana and Hopewell-Baehr materials from the Illinois River Valley (Griffin, 1952; Struever, 1965). This relationship is probably not based on an actual movement of people, but rather on the adoption of specific traits, often out of context, by a local group. The population during the entire Middle Woodland period does not seem to have been too high. Out of the nearly 200 sites from the valley listed in the University of Michigan Museum of Anthropology, only 10 have Middle Woodland components. The evidence from Schultz suggested that the earlier phase of the Middle Woodland occupation may have been flooded out by rising lake levels. So far, no early (Tittabawassee) Middle Woodland living areas have been excavated elsewhere in the valley, although scattered Tittabawassee ware sherds have been found in several excavations. There is at least one late Middle Woodland component which can be compared with the Schultz material at the Kantzler site.

During the early Middle Woodland period, Schultz tended more toward a summer occupation with population concentration and possibly ritual activity. This pattern was even stronger during the late Middle Woodland occupation. Fishing at Schultz became more important and hunting became less important at the site as a summer activity. Again, Kantzler is the foil for Schultz. Hunting takes on increased importance in the Middle Woodland occupation at that site.

Such a settlement system which appears to be based on summer population concentrations and the dispersal of population in the winter is similar to that suggested for northern sites of this same time period (Brose, 1968; Fitting, Brose, Wright and Dinerstein, 1969; Janzen, 1968*a*) and the Chippewa sites of the Historic period (Fitting and Cleland, 1969). It is certainly unlike the settlement pattern suggested for Ohio Hopewell by Prufer (1965) and seems to be unlike the pattern implied for the Illinois area (Struever, 1965).

A review of the Middle Woodland occupation in the Saginaw Valley (Fitting, n.d.*b*) suggests that most of the Hopewell and Havana traits (methods of decorating pottery, bone ornaments) are superficial or occupy a different role in the lives of people (percentages of pottery variants, mounds without burials, low frequencies of blades, etc.) than in areas further to the south. The toggle head harpoons and most of the projectile points could easily be found in northern Lake Forest Middle Woodland assemblages.

The earliest of the Late Woodland occupations at the Schultz site seems to be a continuation of the late Middle Woodland occupation on a much reduced level but later occupations are quite variable. This variety in Late Woodland occupations is characteristic of the entire valley. Both hunting and fishing occupations are represented at Schultz as well as at Stadelmeyer, while the Mahoney and Fosters sites both seem to be winter hunting sites (Bigony, n.d.). The Hodges site (Fitting and Sasse, n.d.) may have been a fishing station along the Flint River. Bernard Spencer (personal communication) feels that the Malone site which he is currently excavating is a high density village of agricultural peoples of the 13th century A.D. or later.

Spencer (1968) has shell tempered pottery, which he feels is related to certain Illinois complexes, recovered from Malone and other sites. Bigony (n.d.) is impressed with the northern influences in the ceramics from the Stadelmeyer site, a situation also true of the Butterfield site (Wobst, 1968) which is located in neighboring Bay County, although not in the Saginaw Valley proper. Fischer, at Schultz, and Fitting and Sasse, at Hodges, have distinctive ceramic complexes which, if anything, find similarities in the western Michigan Spring Creek (Fitting, 1968*c*) and Spoonville (Flanders, 1965) sites. Halsy (1967) sees similarities in the Bussinger site burial complex ceramics to Wayne wares from southeastern Michigan as well as the Ohio Intrusive mound culture and the Kipp Island Phase in New York.

Actually, this much variation in occupation pattern is not surprising. It could almost be predicted from the early historic sources. The Nouvel account (Guta, 1957) gives the impression that you could expect to find almost anyone wandering about the valley.

Fitting and Cleland (1969) have suggested three types of settlement systems in the Late Woodland period in the upper Great Lakes; the Chippewa, Ottawa and Potawatomi systems. The Chippewa system involved summer population concentrations based on fishing with winter population dispersal into small hunting groups, essentially the same pattern that was characteristic of the Middle Woodland period in the Saginaw Valley.

The Potawatomi system involved stable summer camps, usually surrounded by a stockade, where women practiced agriculture and men hunted or fished close to the village. During the winter, the entire group would move, as a unit, to a winter hunting ground where a large, temporary camp was established.

The Ottawa pattern was the most complex with large, semipermanent agricultural villages occupied primarily by women, with men gone for much of the year. The men hunted, fished and traded along the lakes in the summer and hunted in the interior of the state in the winter.

As Fitting and Cleland (1969) pointed out, the Chippewa, Potawatomi and Ottawa patterns are found to roughly correspond with the Canadian and Carolinian biotic provinces and the transition zone between these provinces. The settlement systems are geared to the maximum exploitative efficiency of each of these areas. The Saginaw Valley, as we indicated earlier, is environmentally diverse and, in effect, contains elements characteristic of all of these areas. In the Late Woodland period it seems to be a part of the buffer or transition zone between the major adaptive patterns and could easily have been incorporated into all three types of settlement systems.

It is quite likely that groups with a Chippewa type of settlement system could spend one winter, or a part of a winter, hunting in the valley while a group with a Potawatomi pattern could move north from Illinois, southwestern Michigan or northern Ohio to hunt there the next winter.

The Saginaw Valley could have supported any part of an Ottawa adaption as well, but I would suspect that only transient camps occupied primarily by men will be found for this pattern. One of the requisites for the very early historic Ottawa villages was a degree of isolation than could not be found along the busy streams and rivers of the Saginaw Valley. In fact, with the possible exception of the Malone site, which may be a small agricultural village with southern and western influence, all prehistoric Late Woodland occupations in the valley seem to be transient ones. It might even be better to talk of the Late Woodland utilization of the valley rather than occupation. We might speculate that it was possible to support a larger *total* population throughout the Great Lakes region by moving different groups in and out of the valley on a seasonal basis, each occupying a slightly different ecological niche.

The nature and impact of the Late Woodland agricultural adaptation is an important factor in understanding the Late Woodland land use pattern in the Saginaw Valley. Cleland (1966) and Fitting and Cleland (1969) have emphasized the importance of agriculture in the Late Woodland period with an increase in population as the first visible result. An increase in population density also occurred in nonagricultural areas to the north of the effective limits of agriculture. It has been suggested (Fitting, n.d.*a*) that this was a result of the establishment of a Late Woodland regional symbiosis. This symbiotic relationship was based on trade between ecologically diverse subareas. It has been documented for the seventeenth century by G. A. Wright (1967, 1968).

It might be that in many cases, as with the historic Chippewa, it was better to be a specialized hunter than a marginal agriculturalist. Southern settled groups might have also benefited by a buffer zone, a hunting area open to all comers, between themselves and their more mobile northern neighbors.

The seventeenth century Nouvel account of the Saginaw Valley records almost no settlement. His party traveled up the river to a point near Midland, noting only one occupation, a recently abandoned hunting camp. If there had been settled agricultural villages along the river bank, they would have been mentioned. For the prehistoric period such villages were almost, if not completely, absent.

With the diverse types of settlement and archaeological materials recovered from the valley, it would seem that attributing the prehistoric occupation of the valley to any specific ethnic group, such as the Sauk, Chippewa or Ottawa, would be difficult. It is only after 1701, with the establishment of the French Fort at Detroit, that the Chippewa came into the area in any numbers. Throughout the eighteenth century the Chippewa became more strongly identified with the valley, and the highly acculturated groups represented at the Valley Sweet site (Brose, 1966) and the Fletcher site (excavated by Dr. Moreau Maxwell in 1967 and 1968) are historic Chippewa. Several non-Indian traders were operating in the area from established posts in the late eighteenth century, and it is very possible that even the acculturated Chippewa were agricultural by this late date.

I think that maize agriculture in the valley itself, as opposed to agriculture practiced elsewhere by people who seasonally utilized the valley, is probably a very late historic development. Accounts mention Indian cornfields in the valley only in the nineteenth century. In Chapter I of this volume, we noted that Albert Miller attempted to establish a farm on Green Point in the early 1830's which he soon abandoned. Several years later, McCormick described the Indian cornfields at Green Point. This was probably a frequent happening because of the almost complete population replacement in the valley between 1820 and 1840.

The Schultz site was not an isolated site. Its occupants were, for more than 2000 years, participants in larger, regional settlement systems, systems which can, in turn, be related to the overall patterns of cultural developments in northeastern North America. It has proven to be a key site, perhaps *the* key site in our interpretations of Saginaw Valley prehistory. The types of analysis presented in this volume, as well as others which we have not used, need to be applied to many other sites before the above interpretive statements can be fully tested and rise above the level of speculation on which all too many are still based.

APPENDIX A
SCHULTZ SITE CERAMICS

Fred W. Fischer

APPENDIX AA. Ceramic Description

Schultz Thick

Sample: 30 identifiable rim sherds, 2 partially restorable vessels, 328 body sherds including 3 lugs, 3 lug fragments and basal fragments

Technology:

Method of manufacture—coiled

Paste—sandy clay with large amount of tempering material

Temper—crushed crystalline stone, usually feldspar. Tempering particles 12 mm and average about 2.3 mm

Texture—fairly well consolidated and compacted, irregular transverse fracture, coil breaks common

Color—exterior colors range from buff to dark gray, interior and core colors range from yellowish-buff to black: 70.5% of exteriors are buff, 16% are light gray, 9% are dark gray, and 4.5% are medium brown; 68% of interiors are buff, 13% are light gray, 6% are yellowish buff, and 13% are dark gray to black; 47% of cores are buff, 20% are light gray, 18% are dark gray, 9% are black, and 6% are yellow buff

Surface finish—exteriors smoothed before cordmarking. Cordmarked over entire vessel. Frequent bidirectional overstamping. Cordmarks occasionally obliterated in small areas. Surface fairly regular. Interiors poorly smoothed with random direction smoothing marks and frequent finger impressions. Vessels were apparently cordmarked over entire interior surface. Cordmarks obliterated on 38% of rims. Irregular undulating surface. Lip: 77% cord impressed, 23% smoothed. Cordmarking is coarse, loosely twisted cord, twisted to right. Individual impressions contiguous and parallel. Undulating surface indicates that cord was wrapped around hand for interior impressions: 47% of exterior impressions are left oblique from lip, 23% are vertical or at right angle to lip, 7% are indeterminant; 67% of interior impressions are horizontal and 33% are vertical

Metrics—cord impression width: 1.2 mm to 3.1 mm. Average is 1.9 mm.

Decoration:

Technique and motif—incising

Incising: one sherd has 2 pairs of narrow rectilinear incised lines that converge at *ca.* 45° angles. Apex is toward base of vessel

Metrics—line width: 0.3 mm

Vessel form:

Lip—61% flattened and 39% rounded

Rim—

Attitude (11 sherds): 55% vertical, 36% inverted, and 9% everted

Form: all straight

Modification: 89% are thinned toward upper rim

Body—

Form: moderately large jar. Elongate cylindrical body contracts toward small flat base. Large orifice with scant rim constriction and no shoulder

Appendages: lugs (6). Four are riveted, two may be applique, three are elongate strips, two are ovoid knobs, and one is of indeterminate form. All are cordmarked

Metrics—(one complete ovoid lug): 4.9 cm long, 2.5 cm wide, and 1.9 cm protrusion. Protrusion of three incomplete strip lugs is 1.0, 1.1, and 1.2 cm

Size—body measurements below on two partially restorable vessels and on large rim section

Metrics—height: approximately 31.0 cm, orifice diameter: approximately 25.0, 23.0 and 22.0 cm

Maximum body diameter: 28.0 and 23.0 cm, thickness, rim (taken 1.0 cm below lip): 6.1 mm to 11.7 mm. Average is 9.0 mm. Thickness, body: 8.2 mm to 18.9 mm. Average is 12.7 mm.

Base—Small, flat, cordmarked on interior and exterior. Body-base juncture approximately 45°

Metrics—diameter: approximately 6.0 and 8.0 cm, thickness: average is 12.2 mm

Tittabawassee Dentate Stamped

Sample: 34 identifiable rim sherds. One extends to vessel body, 13 extend to vessel neck. No complete or restorable vessels

Technology:

Method of manufacture—probably coiled and paddled

Paste—sandy clay with large amount of tempering material

Temper—crushed stone, *ca.* 47% granitic material, 29.5% quartzite, 20.5% feldspar, and one sherd with no apparent temper. Tempering particles reach 6.9 mm and average about 2.0 mm

Texture—moderately well consolidated and compacted. No coil breaks observed. Irregular transverse fracture and scant tendancy for lamellar converse fracture

Color—core, exterior, and interior colors range from black to buff: 50% of cores are black, dark gray, dark brown, and dark gray-brown, 14.5% are medium gray, 35.5% are light gray, light brown, or buff; 35.5% of the interiors are black, dark gray, dark gray-brown, or dark brown, 20.5% are medium gray or medium brown, 41% are light brown or buff. 50% of the exteriors are black, dark gray, or dark brown, 23.5% are medium gray or medium brown, 26.5% are light gray or buff

Surface finish—94% of exteriors are plain and moderately well smoothed. Two sherds appear to have been cordmarked and smoothed. Tool marks are rare on exterior and interior surfaces. Interiors are smoothed but often irregular. Tempering particles are apparent on the interior surface

Decoration:

Technique—dentate stamping (100%), incising (54%), noding (23.5%), punctation (6%), and lip notching (38.3%)

Dentate Stamping: upper portion of rim is stamped with dentate tool to form parallel vertical rows of square or rectangular impressions with narrow lands between. Stamping lines are usually concave to the left. Stamping is generally deep, bold, and clear. Rim zone stamping begins at lip and extends down rim 12.0 mm to 44.0 mm. Dentate stamping terminates plain zone on 5 vessels, with bounding incision on 5 vessels, and with bounding punctations on 2 vessels. Interior rims of 2 vessels have dentate stamping similar to exterior rim. Dentate stamping occurs as zone filler on the shoulder of one vessel and on the shoulder and body of one vessel.

Metrics—lip to rim zone stamping termination: 12.0 mm to 44.0 mm, average is 27.9 mm.

Individual impressions (squares): 0.5 mm to 4.0 mm, average is 2.0 mm

Incising: zone-bounding incisions on neck or shoulder of 13 of sherds that extend below the stamped rim zone. Incising is shallow to moderately deep and is done with broad blunted or broad rounded end tool

Metrics—incision width: 1.8 mm to 6.0 mm, average is 3.1 mm

Noding: eight sherds have exterior punched nodes on rim (4) or neck (4)

Metrics—node interval: 14.0 mm to 21.0 mm, average is 17.2 mm

Lip to node: 18.0 mm to 40.0 mm, average is 26.4 mm

Punctation: lower limit of rim zone dentate stamping is bounded by a single row of punctations on 2 vessels. Bold punctations are impressed at an acute angle from the left on one sherd and at an acute angle from the right on one sherd. Punctations made with blunted tool

Metrics—punctation diameter: 3.9 mm to 4.1 mm; punctation interval: 7.2 mm to 12.5 mm

Lip notching: 13 rim sherds have notched lips, 7 sherds have simple notched lips. Of these, 4 are notched to lip interior, 2 are notched to lip exterior, and 1 on top of the lip; 5 sherds have lips notched with a denticulate tool. Of these, 4 are notched to lip interior and one on top of the lip. One sherd is notched on top of the lip with a cordwrapped stick or cordwrapped paddle edge.

Motif—upper rim zone dentate stamping described above. Dentate-stamped filled zones bounded by incised lines occur on shoulder and body of vessel. Two sherds extending to vessel shoulder exhibit portion of rectilinear zoned band encircling neck 34.0 mm and 60.0 mm below the lip. One sherd extending to the body exhibits narrow (11.5 mm to 16.5 mm) curvilinear bands in form of large circular spirals extending from upper shoulder to lower body.

Vessel form:

Lip—59% flattened, 35% flattened and beveled to interior, and 6% rounded.

Rim—

Attitude (16 sherds): 56.3% everted, 37.4% vertical, and 6.3% inverted.

Form (27 sherds): 67% straight, 22% excurved, and 11% incurved

Modification: 9% cambered only, 6% cambered and channeled, and 85% unmodified

Body—

Form: rim morphology and attitude suggest that jar form is exclusively represented. Jars appear to have cylindrical form with undeveloped shoulder and only slight constriction at neck.

Size—

Metrics—orifice diameter: 1 sherd approximately 19.0 cm. Maximum body diameter: 1 sherd approximately 24.0 cm.

Thickness (taken at neck): 5.8 mm to 13.5 mm, average is 8.8 mm

Base—none identifiable

Green Point Rocker Stamped, Plain Oblique Left

Sample: 117 identifiable rim sherds of which 8 extend to vessel shoulder and 30 extend to vessel neck. One restorable vessel approximately 75% complete

Technology:

Method of manufacture—probably coiled

Paste—sandy clay with moderate amount of tempering material

Temper—crushed stone, 80.5% white and pink feldspar and possibly quartzite, 15.2% granitic material. One sherd limestone tempered and four small sherds have no apparent temper. Tempering particles reach 7.0 mm and average about 2.0 mm

Texture—moderately well consolidated and compacted. No coil breaks observed. Irregular transverse fracture and some tendency for lamellar converse fracture

Color—core, exterior and interior colors range from black to yellow-buff; 77% of cores fall into black, dark grays, and dark browns; 8% into medium browns; and 15% into orange and yellow-buffs; 43% of exteriors fall into black and dark browns; 17% into medium browns and 40% into light browns and buffs; 59% of interiors fall into black and dark gray-browns; 8.5% into medium grays; and 32.5% into buffs

Surface finish—exteriors and interiors are plain and well smoothed. Some few sherds have horizontal smoothing marks on interior, and one sherd has horizontally brushed interior. Neck area is relatively better finished. One sherd is burnished over exterior rim, neck, and shoulder, partially obliterating decoration.

Decoration:

Technique—rocker stamping, punctation, incising, noding, and lip notching

Rocker stamping: plain rocker stamped upper rim zone. Rockers at oblique angle from left to right from lip. Impressions are concave to left. Plain rocker stamp as zone filler on neck, shoulder and body. One sherd with free horizontal plain rocker stamp on shoulder. Rim stamping is generally clear and well executed.

Metrics—rim rocker length (56 sherds): 8.0 mm to 35.0 mm; average is 19.1 mm; trimodal peaks at 13.0 mm, 16.0 mm, and 20.0 mm

Punctation: lower limit of rocker stamped rim zone is bounded by single row of punctations. One sherd has double row of punctations. Punctations shallow to moderately deep and made with a blunted tool in most cases: 83% are angular in form, 15% are hemiconical, and 2% are elongate; 38% are impressed from right, 10% from left, 17% from below, 30% at 90° angle, and 4% from above

Metrics—punctation diameter: 1.0 mm to 5.0 mm; average is 2.09 mm, mode at 1.5 mm

Punctation interval: 2.0 mm to 12.0 mm; average is 4.4 mm; mode is 3.0 mm

Lip to punctation: 8.0 mm to 35.0 shoulder, and body. Incisions are shallow and are made with a blunted tool

Incising: zone-bounding incision on neck, shoulder, and body. Incisions are shallow and are made with a blunted tool

Metrics—Incision width: 0.7 mm to 1.9 mm; average is 1.1 mm

Noding: one sherd with exterior punched node 27.0 mm below lip

Lip notching: six sherds (5.1% of sample) with simple notched lips, two notched to lip exterior and four notched on top of lip

Motif—upper rim zone rocker stamping described above. Rocker-stamped filled zones bounded by incised lines occur on neck and shoulder of 13 sherds and on body of restorable vessel (11.9% of total sample). Twelve examples are in form of narrow rectilinear band encircling neck with narrow curvilinear bands forming inverted festoons extending to shoulder or upper body.

Metrics—zone band width: 6.5 mm to 13.0 mm; average is 9.6 mm

Lip to decoration zone: 15.0 mm to 48.5 mm; average is 29.8 mm

Vessel form:

Lip—56% flattened, 27% flattened and beveled to interior, and 17% rounded

Rim—

Attitude (21 sherds): 76% everted 20% vertical and 4% inverted.

Form (85 sherds): 54% straight, 39% slightly incurved (most due to channel and camber treatment), and 7% excurved

Modification: 49% cambered only, 29% cambered and channeled, and 22% modified

Body—

Form: rim morphology and attitude suggest jar form exclusively represented. Neck and shoulder decoration of several small vessels further suggest presence of body lobes. Large restorable vessel has unlobed globular body with relatively short rim and neck. Neck constriction is pronounced.

Size—Metrics—

Height (1 vessel): approximately 32.0 cm

Orifice diameter: restorable vessel approximately 20.0 cm; four sherds approximately 10.0 cm, 14.0 cm, 20.0 cm, and 24.0 cm

Maximum body diameter: restorable vessel approximately 23.0 cm

Thickness (taken at neck): 3.3 mm to 9.1 mm; average is 7.4 mm

Base—one identifiable as subconoidal, thickness 8.5 mm

Green Point Rocker Stamped, Plain Vertical

Sample: 77 identifiable rim sherds of which 5 extend to vessel shoulder and 23 extend to vessel neck. Two restorable vessels, one approximately 80% complete and one approximately 15% complete

Technology:

Method of manufacture—probably coiled

Paste—very sandy clay with moderate amount of tempering material

Temper—crushed stone: 47% white and pink feldspar and possible quartzite, 38% granitic material, 15% have no apparent tempering material. Tempering particles reach 5.0 mm and average about 1.5 mm

Texture—moderately well consolidated, but friable due to sandy nature of clay. Irregular transverse fracture. Only slight tendancy for lamellar converse fracture. No coil breaks observed. One sherd has probable firing "pop out" scar on lower shoulder

Color—core, exterior, and interior colors range from black to orange-buff: 63% of cores fall into black, dark grays, and dark browns, 10% into medium grays, and 27% into light browns and buffs; 55% of exteriors fall into black, dark grays, and dark browns, 17% into medium browns, and 28% into light browns and buffs; 61% of interiors fall into black, dark grays, and dark browns; 12% into medium grays and browns; and 27% into light grays and buffs.

Surface finish—exteriors are moderately well smoothed. One restorable vessel is well smoothed over cordmarking. All others in sample appear to have plain surfaces. Neck areas are especially well smoothed. Interiors are even and well smoothed. Two sherds have horizontally brushed interiors. Tool marks rare on exterior and interior.

Decoration:

Technique—rocker stamping, punctation, incising, noding, lip notching

Rocker stamping: plain rocker stamped rim zone. Rockers at 90° angle to lip. Impressions are concave to left. Plain rocker stamp as zone filler on neck, shoulder. One vessel with free vertical rocker stamp on shoulder. Rim stamping is generally distinct and well executed but is light and poorly done on several sherds.

Metrics—rim rocker length (45 sherds): 8.0 mm to 32 mm; average is 18.1 mm trimodal peaks at 12.0 mm, 17.5 mm, and 22.0 mm

Punctation: lower limit of rocker stamped rim zone usually bounded by single row of punctations. Three sherds lack punctations and punctations are 21.0 mm below lower limit of rocker stamping on another example. Punctations shallow to moderately deep and made with blunted implement in most cases. One example shows use of hollow tool 2.6 mm in diameter: 72% are angular in form, 24% hemiconical, and 4% are elongate; 30% are impressed from right, 30% at 90° angle, 27% from left, and 13% from below

Metrics—punctation diameter: 1.0 mm to 6.0 mm; average and mode are 2.5 mm

Punctation interval: 1.0 mm to 9.0 mm; average is 5.4 mm; bimodal peaks at 3.0 mm and 8.0 mm

Lip to punctation: 9.0 mm to 40.0 mm; average is 19.2 mm; bimodal peaks at 15.0 mm and 25.0 mm

Incising: zone-bounding incision on neck, shoulder, and body. Incisions are moderately deep to shallow and made with blunted tool

Metrics—incision width: 0.3 mm to 1.0 mm

Noding: three sherds with exterior punched nodes

Metrics—node interval (1 sherd): 31.0 mm. Lip to node: 19.0 mm, 32.0 mm, and 33.0 mm

Lip notching: four sherds (5.2% of sample) exhibit simple notched lips. One notched to lip exterior and three notched on top of lip

Motif—upper rim zone rocker stamping described above. Rocker-stamped filled zones bounded by incised lines occur on neck and shoulder of three sherds and two restorable vessels (6.5% of total sample). One example is in form of narrow rectilinear band encircling neck with double curvilinear bands forming inverted festoons extending over shoulder to upper body. One restorable vessel has six contiguous semilunar festoons on shoulder; the other exhibits a narrow shoulder band forming inverted festoons. In addition, this vessel has semilunar-shaped body zones of rocker stamping complimenting each festoon segment.

Metrics—zone band width (1 sherd): 6.5 mm to 17.0 mm. Lip to decoration zone: 27.0 mm, 29.0 mm, 32.0 mm, 37.0 mm, and 53.0 mm.

Vessel form:

Lip—38% flattened and beveled to interior, 35% flattened, 18% rounded, and 9% pointed

Rim—

Attitude (16 sherds): 81% everted and 19% vertical

Form (52 sherds): 71% straight, 27% incurved (most due to channel and camber treatment), and 2% excurved

Modification: 43% cambered only, 38% cambered and channeled, 19% unmodified

Body—

Form: rim morphology and attitude suggest jar form exclusively represented. Restorable vessels are jars with unlobed globular or subconoidal bodies. Maximum body diameter is at lower shoulder; relatively short rims and necks

Size—Metrics—height (1 vessel): 22.9 cm

Orifice diameter: restorable vessels, 17.2 cm and 17.0 cm; sherds, approximately 15.0 cm, 22.0 cm, 26.0 cm, and 28.0 cm

Maximum body diameter: restorable vessels approximately 20.6 cm and 19.0 cm

Thickness (taken at neck): 4.7 mm to 8.4 mm; average is 6.5 mm

Base—one identifiable as subconoidal; thickness is 8.2 mm

Green Point Rocker Stamped, Plain Horizontal

Sample: 55 identifiable rim sherds of which 7 extend to vessel shoulder and 12 extend to vessel neck. One restorable miniature vessel approximately 70% complete

Technology:

Method of manufacture—probably coiled

Paste—sandy to very sandy clay with moderate amount of tempering material

Temper—crushed stone (where identifiable): 54% white and pink feldspar and possibly quartzite, 25% granitic material, and 21% with no apparent temper. Tempering particles reach 7.2 mm and average about 2.0 mm

Texture—well consolidated and compacted. No coil breaks observed. Irregular transverse fracture and some tendancy for lamellar converse fracture

Color—core, exterior, and interior colors range from black to yellow-buff: 79% of cores fall into black and dark gray-browns, 7% into medium browns, and 14% into light grays, light browns and orange and yellow buffs; 73% of exteriors fall into black and dark gray-browns, 2% into medium browns, and 25% into buff and orange-buff; 12% of interiors fall into black, 36% into medium grays and 52% into light grays, light browns, and buffs

Surface finish—exteriors and interiors are plain. Quality of finish on exterior and interior ranges from well smoothed with even surface to poorly smoothed with uneven surface. Smoothing and tool marks are common on interiors. Neck area seldom receives special care.

Decoration:

Technique—rocker stamping, punctation, incising, noding, and lip notching

Rocker stamping: plain rocker stamped upper rim zone. Rockers parallel to lip. Impressions are convex toward lip. Plain rocker stamp as zone filler on neck, shoulder and body. One sherd has free vertical plain rocker stamping on exterior shoulder and interior rim. Stamping is poorly executed and often partially obliterated on larger vessels. Smaller vessels were stamped with more care.

Metrics—rim rocker length (13 sherds): 12.0 mm to 29.0 mm; average is 20.2 mm

Punctation: lower limit of rocker stamped rim zone is usually bounded by a single row of punctations. Three sherds extending to lower neck area lack punctation. One sherd has double row of punctation. Punctations shallow to deep and usually made with blunted implement: 71% are angular in form, 25% are hemiconical, and 4% are elongate; 42% are impressed from right, 17% from left, 17% from below, 16% at 90° angle, and 8% from above

Metrics—punctation diameter: 1.0 mm to 5.0 mm; average is 2.7 mm; bimodal peaks at 2.0 mm and 4.0 mm

Punctation interval: 2.0 mm to 11.0 mm; average is 4.9 mm; bimodal peaks at 3.0 mm and 9.0 mm

Lip to punctation: 5.0 mm to 32.0 mm; average is 14.0 mm; bimodal peaks at 11.0 mm and 22.0 mm

Incising: zone-bounding incision on neck, shoulder, and body of three small vessels. Incised line below and parallel to rim zone punctations on rim of two small vessels, independent curvilinear incision on shoulder of one small vessel. Incisions are generally shallow and made with blunted tool.

Metrics—incision width: 0.5 mm to 1.6 mm; average is 0.9 mm

Noding: two sherds with exterior punched nodes

Metrics—node interval: 26.5 mm and 32.0 mm. Lip to node: 25.5 mm and 34.5 mm

Lip notching: two sherds (3.5% of sample) with lips notched to exterior. One simple notched and one cord notched.

Motif—upper rim zone rocker stamping described above. Rocker-stamped filled zones bounded by incised lines occur on neck and shoulder of two small vessels and on neck, shoulder, and body of restorable miniature vessel. Neck and shoulder zones of restorable vessel form four inverted festoons complimenting a circular zone of rocker stamping on each of four body lobes. Free incision on shoulder of small vessel is in form of horizontal curvilinear meander bounded below by rectilinear row of punctation

Metrics—lip to decoration: 8.0 mm, 10.0 mm, and 14.0 mm

Vessel form:

Lip—61% flattened, 28% rounded, and 11% flattened and beveled to interior

Rim—

Attitude (14 sherds): 79% everted and 21% vertical

Form (43 sherds): 58% straight, 37% incruved (most due to channel and camber treatment), and 5% excurved

Modification: 41% cambered only, 22% cambered and channeled, 27% unmodified, and 10% with interior thickened lip and profile suggesting incurved rim bowl sherds rather than channeled and cambered rim jar sherds

Body—

Form: rim morphology and attitude suggest 90% jar forms and 10% bowl forms. Larger jars have relatively low rim necks. Restorable miniature jar has high neck rim and quadrolobate body. Six sherds appear to be from incurved rim bowls.

Size—in addition to restorable miniature vessel described above, five sherds are from similar miniature vessels; all are jar forms (10% of total sample)

Metrics—height (1 miniature vessel): 6.3 cm

Orifice diameter: restorable miniature jar, 5.4 cm; jar rim sherds approximately 16.0 cm, and 20.0 cm; bowl rim sherd approximately 22.0 cm

Maximum body diameter: restorable miniature jar, 5.7 cm

Thickness (taken at neck): 2.2 mm to 9.2 mm; average is 5.85 mm; bimodal peaks at 4.5 mm and 6.0 mm

Base—one miniature vessel base identifiable is rounded. Thickness is 2.8 mm

Green Point Rocker Stamped, Dentate

Sample: 17 identifiable rim sherds of which 2 extend to vessel shoulder and 8 extend to vessel neck. No complete or restorable vessels.

Technology:

Method of manufacture—probably coiled

Paste—sandy clay with small amount of tempering material

Temper—crushed stone (where identifiable): 71% white and pink feldspar and possibly quartzite; 29% with no apparent temper. Tempering particles reach 6.2 mm and average about 1.5 mm

Texture—well consolidated and compacted. No coil breaks observed. Irregular transverse fracture and some tendancy for lamellar converse fracture.

Color—core colors range from black to medium grays and browns with 76.5% falling into blacks and dark brown and 23.5% into medium grays and medium browns. Exterior colors range from black to buff with 65% falling into black and dark browns, 17.5% into medium browns and 17.5% into buff. Interiors range from black to buff with 76.5% falling into black and dark browns and 23.5% into buff.

Surface finish—exteriors plain and well smoothed. Horizontal smoothing marks visible on about 53% of exterior surfaces. Interiors are even and well smoothed and horizontal smoothing marks are rare. Neck area is relatively better finished.

Decoration:

Technique—rocker stamping, punctation, and incising

Rocker stamping: dentate rocker stamped upper rim zone: 47% vertically stamped, 41% oblique from upper left stamped, and 12% horizontally stamped. Impressions are concave to left on vertical and oblique stamped rims and convex toward lip on horizontally stamped rims. Dentate rocker stamp occurs as zone filler on neck and shoulder of one vessel.

Metrics—rim rocker length (14 sherds): 9.0 mm to 23.0 mm; average is 16.4 mm; bimodal peaks at 13.0 mm and 18.0 mm

Punctation: lower limit of rocker stamped rim zone is bounded by single row of punctations. Punctation shallow to moderately deep and made with blunted implement: 73% are angular in form, 18% are hemiconical, and 9% are elongate; 37% are impressed from right, 27% at 90° angle, 18% from below, 9% from right, 9% from above.

Metrics—punctation diameter: 1.0 mm to 3.0 mm; average is 1.9 mm; mode is 2.0 mm

Punctation interval: 2.0 mm to 9.0 mm; average is 4.4 mm; mode is 4.5 mm

Lip to punctation: 1.0 mm to 27.0 mm; average is 17.4 mm; mode is 20.0 mm

Incising: zone-bounding incision on neck and shoulder (1 vessel). Incisions made with blunted tool.

Metrics—incision width: 1.0 mm to 1.9 mm

Motif—upper rim zone stamping described above. Rocker-stamped filled zones bounded by incised lines occur on neck and shoulder of one vessel. In form of narrow rectilinear band encircling neck with curvilinear bands forming inverted festoons extending to shoulder or upper body.

Metrics—zone width; 11.0 mm to 16.5 mm

Lip decoration zone 29.0 mm

Vessel form:

Lip—76% flattened and 24% flattened and beveled

Rim—

Attitude (6 sherds): 5 everted and one vertical

Form (16 sherds): 81% straight and 19% incurved due to camber and channel modification

Modification: 53% cambered only, 12% cambered and channeled, and 35% unmodified

Body—

Form: rim morphology and attitude suggest jar form exclusively represented. Relatively short neck indicated.

Size—one sherd large enough to permit gross approximation of orifice diameter of 20.0 cm

Metrics—thickness (taken at neck): 4.1 mm to 8.4 mm; average is 6.2 mm; trimodal peaks at 4.0 mm, 6.0 mm and 7.5 mm.

Base: none identifiable.

Green Point Incised, Cross Hatched

Sample: 55 identifiable rim sherds of which 5 extend to vessel shoulder and 31 extend to vessel neck. No complete or restorable vessels.

Technology:

Method of manufacture—probably coiled

Paste—sandy clay with small amount of tempering material

Temper—crushed stone. White feldspar and possibly quartzite predominate. Pink feldspar is common and granitic material is rare. Tempering particles range from about .3 mm to 4.0 mm, and average about 1.5 mm

Texture—moderately well consolidated and compacted. No coil breaks observed. Irregular transverse fracture and some tendancy for lamellar converse fracture.

Color—core, interior, and exterior colors range from black to buff: 84% of core colors fall into black, dark grays, and dark browns, and 16% fall into orange-buffs; 61% of exteriors fall into black, dark grays, dark brown, and dark gray-brown, and 39% fall into buff and orange-buff; 53% of interiors fall into black and dark grays and 47% into light grays, buff, and orange-buffs.

Surface finish—exteriors and interiors are plain and well smoothed and tool marks are rare. Neck area is relatively better finished, but burnishing occurs on only one miniature vessel.

Decoration:

Technique—incising, punctation, rocker stamping, dentate stamping, noding, and lip notching

Incising: crosshatched upper rim zone. Zone-bounding incision on neck, shoulder, and body. Incisions are shallow to deep and are made with pointed or blunted tool. Rim crosshatching is generally poorly executed and resulting lands form parallelograms.

Metrics—incision width: 0.1 mm to 1.3 mm; average is about 0.6 mm

Crosshatch incision interval: 1.5 mm to 8.1 mm; average is 4.0 mm

Punctation: lower limit of crosshatched rim zone is bounded by a single row of punctations in 95.4% of the sample. Punctations are moderately deep, and made with a blunted tool in most cases. One example shows use of hollow implement: 78% are angular in form, 19% are hemiconical, and 3% are elongate; 37% are impressed from right, 22% from left, 19% from below, 19% from above, and 3% at 90° angle.

Metrics—punctation diameter; 1.0 mm to 7.0 mm; average is 2.5 mm, mode is 2.0 mm

Punctation interval: 1.0 mm to 16.0 mm; average is 4.1 mm; mode is 3.0 mm

Lip to punctation: 7.0 mm to 28.0 mm; average is 15.4 mm; trimodal peaks at 12.0 mm, 15.0 mm, and 28.0 mm

Rocker stamping: six sherds have rocker stamped decoration on neck and shoulder. Of these, four are zoned elements and two are free. Four are plain rocker elements and two are dentate rocker.

Dentate stamping: one sherd with zoned dentate decoration on neck and shoulder. Small dentations are in straight rows at 1.4 mm intervals.

Noding: one sherd with exterior punched nodes 16.0 mm below lip. Interval between nodes is 14.0 mm

Lip notching: three sherds (5.8% of sample) with simple notched lips. Two notched to lip exterior and one on top of lip.

Motif—upper rim zone crosshatching described above. Rocker-stamped or dentate-stamped filled zones bounded by incised lines occur on neck and shoulder of 7 sherds (12.7% of total sample). All appear to form a narrow rectilinear band encircling neck with narrow curvilinear bands forming inverted festoons, extending to shoulder or upper body. One sherd with nonzoned rocker stamping is stamped over entire neck below punctations and one is stamped on shoulder.

Metrics—zone band width: 3.0 mm to 5.1 mm

Lip to decoration zone: 15.0 mm to 34.0 mm; average is 21.2 mm

Vessel form:

Lip—36% flattened and beveled to interior, 34% flattened, 25% rounded, and 5% pointed

Rim—

Attitude (10 sherds): Seven everted, two vertical, and one inverted.

Form (48 sherds): 46% straight, 44% slightly incurved (due to channel and camber treatment), and 10% excurved

Modification: 38% cambered only, 36% cambered and channeled, and 26% unmodified

Body—

Form: rim morphology and attitude suggest jar form exclusively represented. Neck and shoulder decoration further suggest that some of these vessels have body lobes.

Size— two sherds large enough for approximation of orifice diameter of about 13.5 cm and 20.0 cm. In addition, three sherds appear to be from miniature vessels.

Metrics—thickness (taken at neck): 2.8 mm to 8.7 mm; average is 5.5 mm

Base—none identifiable

Green Point Incised, Vertical

Sample: 12 identifiable rim sherds of which 3 extend to vessel shoulder, and 4 extend to vessel neck. No complete or restorable vessels.

Technology:

Method of manufacture—probably coiled

Paste—sandy clay with large amount of tempering material

Temper—crushed stone. 92% white and pink feldspar and 8% granitic material. Tempering particles reach 11.5 mm and average about 2.0 mm

Texture—well consolidated and compacted. No coil breaks observed. Irregular transverse fracture

Color—core, exterior and interior colors range from black to orange-buff. 75% of cores fall into black and dark browns and 25% into orange-buff; 64% of exteriors fall into black and dark browns and 36% into light brown, buff and orange-buff; 67% of interiors fall into black, dark grays, and dark browns and 33% into light brown, buff, and orange-buff.

Surface finish—exterior surfaces are plain, regular, and well smoothed. Interiors are regular and well smoothed. Exterior and interior tool marks rare.

Decoration:

Technique—incising, punctation, rocker stamping, cord stamping, and lip notching.

Incising: vertical incised lines on upper rim zone. Zone-bounding incision on neck and shoulder. Incisions generally of careless execution, at irregular intervals, shallow, and made with both pointed and blunt tools.

Metrics—line interval: 1.0 mm to 6.8 mm; average is 3.7 mm, mode at 3.0 mm

Incision width: 0.2 mm to 1.3 mm; average is 0.8 mm

Punctation: lower limit of incised rim zone is bounded by a single row of punctations. Punctations generally shallow and made with blunted tool. Five sherds have angular punctation, two hemiconical, and one elongate. Three sherds have punctations impressed from right; two from left; and one each from above, below, and at 90° angles.

Metric—punctation diameter: 1.0 mm to 2.0 mm; average is 1.8 mm

Punctation interval: 4.0 mm to 7.0 mm; average is 5.0 mm; mode at 4.0 mm

Lip to punctation: 9.0 mm to 15.0 mm; average is 12.1 mm; bimodal peaks at 9.0 mm and 14.5 mm

Rocker stamping: plain rocker stamp as zone filler on lower neck of two vessels

Cord stamping: cord impressions as zone filler on neck and shoulder of one vessel. Transverse cord impressions within narrow rectilinear band.

Lip notching: three sherds (25% of sample)

with notched lips. Two notched to lip exterior and one on top of lip.

Motif—upper rim zone incising described above. Rocker-stamped filled zones bounded by incised lines on lower neck of two sherds. Appear to form rectilinear bands encircling neck. Cord-stamped filled zones bounded by incised lines on neck and shoulder of one sherd; in form of narrow rectilinear band encircling neck and narrow curvilinear band on shoulder.

Metrics—zone band width (single cord stamped zone sherd); 7.0 mm and 10.5 mm

Lip to decoration zone: 21.0 mm, 21.0 mm and 31.0 mm

Vessel form:

Lip—58% flattened and beveled, 17% flattened, 17% rounded and 8% pointed

Rim—

Attitude (4 sherds): All everted

Form (3 sherds): 5 straight and 3 curved (due to channel and camber treatment)

Modification: 42% unmodified, 33% cambered only, and 25% cambered and channeled

Body—

Form: rim morphology and attitude suggest jar form exclusively represented. One large sherd indicates pronounced neck constriction with short flared rim

Size—single sherd large enough to permit approximation of orifice diameter of 19.0 cm

Metrics—thickness (taken at neck): 4.0 mm to 8.0 mm; average is 5.5 mm

Base—none identifiable

Green Point Incised, Horizontal

Sample: 11 identifiable rim sherds of which 3 extend to vessel neck. One restorable vessel approximately 15% complete

Technology:

Method of manufacture—probably coiled

Paste—sandy clay with small amount of tempering material.

Temper—crushed stone (where identifiable). 50% white and pink feldspar and 17% granitic material. Four sherds have no apparent temper. Tempering particles reach 3.5 mm and average is about 1.5 mm

Texture—well consolidated and compacted. No coil breaks observed. Irregular transverse fracture and some tendancy for lamellar fracture

Color—core, exterior, and interior colors range from black to buff. 83% of cores fall into black, dark grays, and dark browns; 8.5% into medium gray; and 8.5% into buff; 83% of exteriors fall into black, dark browns, and dark gray-browns, and 17% into buff. 67% of interiors fall into black and dark browns; 8% into medium brown, and 25% into buff.

Surface finish—92% of exteriors are plain and smoothed. One sherd is incised over scraped or brushed surface. Interiors are well smoothed. Tool marks rare on exterior and interior.

Decoration:

Technique—incising, punctation, and rocker stamping

Incising: 3 to 7 (average of 5) horizontal incised lines encircling upper rim zone. Zone-bounding incision on neck and shoulder. Rim incisions are carelessly executed and often interrupted. Made with both blunt and pointed tools.

Metrics—incision width: 0.2 mm to 1.5 mm; average is about 0.5 mm

line interval: 0.8 mm to 5.5 mm; average is 2.8 mm; mode is 2.0 mm

Punctation: lower limit of incised rim zone is bounded by single row of punctations. Punctations moderately deep to shallow and made with blunted tool. Two sherds have hemiconical punctations, one angular, and one elongate. Two sherds have punctations impressed from right, one from left, and one at 90° angle.

Metrics—punctation diameter: 2.0 mm to 4.0 mm; average is 2.8 mm; mode at 2.0 mm

Punctation interval: 3.0 mm to 10.0 mm; average is 5.0 mm; mode at 3.0 mm

Lip to punctation: 12.0 mm to 23.0 mm; average is 16.0 mm

Rocker stamping: plain rocker stamp as zone filler on neck and shoulder of one vessel

Motif—upper rim zone incising described above. Rocker-stamped filled zones bounded by incised lines at neck and shoulder of one restorable vessel. Narrow rectilinear band encircling neck with narrow curvilinear bands in form of inverted festoons extending to shoulder or upper body.

Metrics—zone band width: 5.2 mm to 8.3 mm. Lip to decoration zone: 22.0 mm

Vessel form:

Lip—75% flattened, 17% rounded, and 8% flattened and beveled

Rim—

Attitude (3 sherds): 2 everted and 1 vertical

Form (8 sherds): 5 incurved (due to channel and camber treatment) and 3 straight.

Modification: 50% cambered and channeled, 25% cambered only and 25% unmodified

Body—

Form: rim morphology and attitude suggest jar form exclusively represented. Single restorable vessel has pronounced neck constriction and body is apparently unlobed. Relatively short rim neck.

Size—single restorable vessel large enough to permit gross approximation of orifice diameter of 12.5 cm

Metrics—thickness (taken at neck): 4.0 mm, 5.1 mm, 5.7 mm, and 6.0 mm

Base—none identifiable

Green Point Incised, Dentate Tool

Sample: 7 identifiable rim sherds, of which 3 extend to vessel shoulder and 2 extend to vessel neck. No complete or restorable vessels

Technology:

Method of manufacture—probably coiled

Paste—sandy clay with small to moderate amount of tempering material

Temper—crushed stone: 5 sherds with white and pink feldspar, 1 sherd with granitic material and 1 sherd with gray chert. Tempering particles reach 5.2 mm and average about 2.0 mm

Texture—well consolidated and compacted. No coil breaks observed. Irregular transverse fracture.

Color—core colors range from black to medium browns. Five fall into black and dark grays and 2 into medium browns. Exterior and interior colors range from black to buffs. Five sherds have black or dark brown exteriors, 1 medium brown, and 1 buff. Five sherds have black or dark brown interiors, 1 medium brown, and 1 buff.

Surface finish—exteriors and interiors are plain and well smoothed. Tool and smoothing marks are rare.

Decoration:

Technique—dentate tool incising, punctation, and plain incising

Dentate tool incising: upper rim zone incised by means of denticulate tool resulting in a series of parallel incised lines. Incisions are interrupted (alternate dragging and lifting of tool) on 5 sherds, 3 are applied paralled to lip and 2 are at oblique angle from the left. Incisions are continuous and parallel to lip on 2 sherds. One sherd has vertical continuous dentate tool incision on the neck. Two sherds have interrupted dentate tool incision as zone filler on upper shoulder. Dentate incising is generally well executed. Narrow impressions range from deep to very shallow.

Metrics—incision width (individual line): 0.3 mm to 1.0 mm; average is 0.6 mm

Dentate interval: 0.4 mm to 3.8 mm; average is 1.4 mm

Punctation: lower limit of dentate tool incised rim zone is bounded by a single row of punctations. Punctations are shallow to deep and made with blunted tool. Punctations are rounded in form on 4 sherds and angular on 3 sherds. Punctations are from right on 2 sherds, from below on 2 sherds, and at 90° angle on 2 sherds.

Metrics—punctation diameter: 0.9 mm to 2.4 mm; average is 1.7 mm

punctation interval: 1.6 mm to 4.8 mm; average is 3.2 mm

lip to punctation: 5.0 mm to 28.0 mm; average is 15.3 mm

Incising: zone-bounding incision on upper shoulder of 3 sherds. Incisions shallow and made with blunted tool.

Metrics—incision width: 0.9 mm, 1.0 mm, and 1.0 mm

Motif—Upper rim zone dentate tool incising described above. Dentate tool-incised filled zones occur on upper shoulder of at least two vessels. Fragmentary material suggests rectilinear zones.

Metrics—lip to decoration zone 28.0 mm, 30.0 mm, and 33.0 mm

Vessel form:

Lip—4 flattened, 2 flattened and beveled to interior, and 1 rounded

Rim—

Attitude (6 sherds): 4 everted and 2 vertical

Form (7 sherds): 5 straight and 2 slightly incurved (due to channel and camber treatment)

Modification: 2 cambered only, 2 cambered and channeled, and 3 unmodified.

Body—

Form: rim morphology and attitude suggest jar form exclusively represented

Size— one sherd appears to represent a miniature vessel. Single sherd large enough to permit approximation of orifice diameter of 15.0 cm

Metrics—thickness (taken at neck): 4.0 mm to 8.8 mm; average is 5.7 mm

Base—none identifiable

Green Point Plain

Sample: 39 identifiable rim sherds of which 19 extend to vessel neck and 3 extend to vessel shoulder. One restorable vessel, approximately 35% complete.

Technology:

Method of manufacture—probably coiled

Paste—sandy clay with moderate to large amount of tempering material

Temper—crushed stone: 40.5% quartzite, 21.5% feldspar, 19% granitic material, and 5% limestone; 14% have no apparent temper. Tempering particles reach 6.7 mm and average about 1.8 mm

Texture—well consolidated and compacted. No coil breaks observed. Irregular transverse fracture. Tendancy for lamellar converse fracture.

Color—core, exterior, and interior colors range from black to buffs: 59.5% of core colors fall into black, dark grays, dark browns, and dark gray-browns, 19% into medium grays and medium browns, and 21.5% into light grays, light browns, and buffs; 42% of exteriors fall into black, dark grays and dark browns, 17% into medium grays and medium browns, and 40% into light grays, light browns, and buffs; 57% of interiors fall into blacks, dark grays, and dark browns, 7% into medium browns, and 36% into light grays, light browns, and buffs.

Surface finish—exterior and interior of rims and necks are plain and well smoothed. Tool marks are present, but rare, on rim and neck interiors. Exterior neck area generally better finished. Exterior shoulder and body of restorable vessel is lightly brushed and subsequently partially smoothed.

Decoration:

Technique—punctation, rocker stamping, incising, and lip notching.

Punctation: single row of punctations encircling rim 6.0 mm to 25 mm below lip. This approximates the lower limit of convexity on vessels with upper rim zone camber. Punctations are moderately deep in most cases and are made with a blunted tool. Punctations practically obliterated by smoothing on restorable vessel: 64% are angular in form, 29% are hemiconical, and 7% are elongate; 25% are impressed from above, 21% from the left, 18% from the right, 18% from below, and 18% at 90° angle.

Metrics—punctation interval: 2.0 mm to 15.0 mm; average is 5.7 mm; mode at 4.0 mm. Lip to punctation: 6.0 mm to 25.0 mm; average is 15.1 mm; mode at 14.5 mm

Rocker stamping: plain rocker stamp as zone filler on neck of one miniature vessel. Free plain rocker stamping on upper shoulder of one vessel. Free dentate rocker stamping over brushed surface on shoulder and body of single restorable vessel.

Incising: zone-bounding incision on neck and shoulder of miniature vessel. Incised horizontal line on shoulder of single vessel. Incisions shallow and made with blunted tool.

Metrics—incision width 0.5 mm and 1.0 mm

Lip notching: three sherds (7.5% of sample) have simple lip notching. Two notched on top of lip and one notched to lip exterior.

Motif—rocker-stamped filled zone bound by incised line occurs on neck and shoulder of one miniature vessel. Upper rectilinear bounding incision appears to encircle neck; lower curvilinear bounding incision in form of inverted festoon on shoulder, apparently outlining body lobes. Free horizontal rocker stamping on body of restorable vessel occurs in vertical tiers on shoulder and body of restorable vessel.

Metrics—lip to decoration zone (single miniature vessel): 8.5 mm

Vessel form:

Lip—50% rounded, 40.5% flattened, 7% flattened and beveled to interior, and 2.5% flattened and beveled to exterior

Rim—

Attitude (12 sherds): 67% everted and 33% vertical

Form (29 sherds): 69% straight, 24% incurved (most due to channel and camber treatment), and 7% excurved

Modification: 42.5% cambered only, 25% cambered and channeled, and 32.5% unmodified

Body—

Form: rim morphology and attitude suggest jar form exclusively represented. Restorable vessel is cylindrical jar constricting slightly from body to orifice. It has no actual shoulder or neck development: 18 rim sherds appear to represent vessels with a definite neck development and suggest that this is the more common form.

Size—2, and possibly 3, sherds are from miniature vessels.

Metrics—maximum body diameter (1 vessel): approximately 20.0 cm

Orifice diameter (1 vessel): 13.0 cm

Thickness (taken at neck): 2.1 mm to 7.7 mm; average is 5.2 mm

Base—one identifiable as subconoidal; thickness is 8.0 mm

Green Point Brushed

Sample: 14 identifiable rim sherds, 6 of which extend to vessel neck and 1 to vessel shoulder. No complete or restorable vessels.

Technology:

Method of manufacture—probably coiled

Paste—sandy clay with large amount of tempering material

Temper—crushed stone: 64.3% granitic material, 21.4% feldspar, and 14.3% quartzite. Tempering particles reach 5.3 mm and average about 2.0 mm

Texture—moderately well consolidated and compacted. No coil breaks observed. Irregular transverse fracture.

Color—core colors range from black to buff with 57% falling into black, dark browns, dark grays, and dark gray-brown; 21.5% into medium grays and medium browns; and 21.5% into light brown and buffs. Exterior colors range from dark gray and dark brown to buff with 35.5% into dark grays, dark browns, and gray-brown; 29.0% into medium grays and medium brown; and 35.5% into light browns and buffs. Interior colors range from black to light brown with 42% falling into black, dark grays, and dark brown; 29% into medium grays and medium browns; and 29% into light browns.

Surface finish—where discernable, exteriors are plain and well smoothed and subsequent brushing has obliterated any possible tool marks on upper rim zone: 86% of interiors are moderately smoothed to well smoothed. Interiors of two sherds exhibit horizontal striations similar to brushed exterior. One sherd has burnished lip and burnished interior.

Decoration:

Technique—brushing, punctation, noding, and lip notching

Brushing: brushed upper rim zone: 57% are brushed at oblique angle from left to right from lip, 36% are horizontally brushed and one sherd is vertically brushed. Parallel brushing marks are irregular and often overlapping. A grass or twig bundle may have been used to obtain this effect.

Punctation: lower limit of brushed rim zone is bounded by single row of punctations in 43% of sample. Punctations are shallow to deep. Punctations are angular in form on four sherds, hemiconical on one, and elongate on one. Punctations are impressed from right on two sherds, at 90° angle on two sherds, and from below on one sherd.

Metrics—punctation diameter: 1.0 mm to 4.0 mm; average is 2.8 mm

punctation interval: 3.0 mm to 7.0 mm; average is 4.6 mm

lip to punctation: 14.0 mm to 24.0 mm; average is 18.7 mm

Noding: one sherd with horizontal row of exterior punched nodes on plain neck.

Metrics—node interval: 9.0 mm.

lip to node: 38.0 mm.

Lip notching: two sherds (14.3% of sample) with simple notched lips. One notched to lip exterior and one notched to lip interior.

Motif—upper rim-zone brushing described above. Shoulder and body decoration, if any, not indicated in sample.

Vessel form:

Lip—43% flattened, 28.5% flattened and beveled to interior, and 28.5% rounded.

Rim—

Attitude (4 sherds): all everted

Form (12 sherds): 92% straight and 8% incurved (due to channel and camber treatment)

Modification: 14% cambered only, 7% cambered and channeled, and 79% unmodified

Body—

Form: rim morphology and attitude suggest that at least 86% of sample represent jar forms. Two sherds, one with interior striations and one with burnished interior, are possibly from vertical rim bowls. Rim attitude suggests that jar forms have fairly well defined neck.

Size—Metrics—orifice diameter: 1 sherd approximately 18.0 cm

Thickness (taken at neck): 6.1 mm to 7.8 mm; average is 7.0 mm

Base—none identifiable

Reuben Linear Cord Impressed, Plain Interior

Sample: 18 identifiable rim sherds of which 4 extend to vessel neck and 2 extend to vessel shoulder. No complete or restorable vessels.

Technology:

Method of manufacture—probably coiled

Paste—sandy clay with large amount of tempering material

Temper—crushed stone: 84% white and pink feldspar and possibly quartzite and 16% granitic material. Tempering particles reach 6.6 mm and average about 1.5 mm

Texture—well consolidated and compacted. No coil breaks observed. Irregular transverse fracture

Color—core, exterior, and interior colors range from black to light buffs: 47% of core colors fall into black and dark grays, browns and gray-browns, 31.5% into medium grays, and 21.5% into orange and yellow-buffs; 37% of exterior colors fall into black and dark browns, 47% into medium browns, and 16% into orange-buffs; 42% of interior colors fall into black and dark browns, 21% into medium browns, and 37% into light browns and buffs.

Surface finish—exteriors are plain and smoothed, and interiors are well smoothed. Tool marks rare on exterior and interior.

Decoration:

Technique—linear cord stamping, punctation, incising, and lip notching.

Cord stamping: parallel linear cord impressions on upper rim zone. Three upper rims may be vertically impressed with cord-wrapped stick. Of the 15 sherds with definite linear cord impressions, 80% have horizontal impressions (7 or 8 lines) and 20% have vertical impressions. Transverse cord impressions occur as zone filler on neck of one vessel. Cord impressions are carelessly made and often partially obliterated by smoothing.

Metrics—cord width: 0.5 mm to 1.8 mm; average is 1.2 mm; mode at 1.35 mm

Punctation: lower limit of cord-impressed rim zone bounded by single row of punctations. Punctations are moderately deep and made with blunted tool. Five sherds have angular punctations and one has hemiconical punctations. Three sherds have punctations impressed from the right, two from the left and one at 90° angle.

Metrics—punctation interval: 3.0 mm to 6.0 mm, average is 4.4 mm
punctation diameter: 1.0 mm to 3.0 mm, average is 2.0 mm
lip to punctation: 8.0 mm to 21.0 mm; average is 17.5 mm, mode at 18.5 mm

Incising: zone-bounding incision on neck of one vessel. Lower limit of cord-impressed upper rim zone of one vessel bounded by broad incised line. Shallow incision

Metrics—incision width: 0.7 mm and 2.1 mm

Lip notching: two sherds (11% of sample) with simple notching on top of lip.

Motif—upper rim zone linear cord impressing described above. Transverse cord impressions as incision-bounded zone filler on one sherd. Zone in form of rectilinear band encircling neck of vessel.

Metrics—zone band width: 14.5 mm
lip to decoration zone: 30.0 mm

Vessel form:

Lip—58% flattened, 26% rounded, and 16% flattened and beveled to interior.

Rim—

Attitude (5 sherds): all everted

Form (18 sherds): 72% straight, 22% incurved (due to channel and camber treatment), and 6% excurved

Modification: 39% cambered only, 17% cambered and channeled, and 44% unmodified

Body—

Form: rim morphology and attitude suggest jar form exclusively represented. Relatively short rim neck with only slight neck constriction.

Size—single sherd large enough to permit approximation of orifice diameter of 16.0 cm

Metrics—thickness (taken at neck): 4.1 mm to 7.0 mm, average is 5.3 mm

Base—none identifiable

Reuben Linear Cord Impressed, Striated Interior

Sample: 25 identifiable rim sherds of which 8 extend to vessel neck. No complete or restorable vessels.

Technology:

Method of manufacture—probably coiled

Paste—sandy clay with moderate to large amount of tempering material.

Temper—crushed stone: 48% granitic material, 40% white quartzite, 4% feldspar, and 8% with no apparent temper. Tempering particles reach 7.7 mm and average about 2.2 mm

Texture—well consolidated and compacted. No coil breaks observed. Irregular transverse fracture. Slight tendancy for lamellar converse fracture.

Color—core, exterior, and interior colors range from black to buffs. 88% of cores fall into black, dark grays, and dark browns; 8% fall into medium browns, and 4% into buff; 52% of exteriors fall into black and dark browns, 16% into medium browns, and 32% into light brown and buffs. 52% of interiors fall into black and dark browns, 20% into medium browns and 28% into buffs.

Surface finish—interiors are scraped or scoured with grass, bark, or some other tool. Result is a series of irregular horizontal lands and grooves. These are usually deep and distinct. One sherd appears to have actually been incised. Scoring begins just below lip and covers entire interior of all rims in sample. Exterior rim is usually plain and well smoothed. Cord-wrapped stick decoration as overall surface finish on two sherds. Neck of one vessel is vertically brushed and all others are plain.

Decoration:

Technique—linear cord stamping, cord-wrapped stick or paddle-edge stamping, punctation, incising, rocker stamping, lip notching, and possibly brushing.

Linear cord stamping: 80% of sample has parallel linear cord impressions on upper rim zone: 80% of these are applied horizontally and 20% are applied vertically. Two sherds have linear cord impressions encircling top of lip. Cord impressions are carelessly made. They are often shallow and/or partially obliterated. Interval between impressions is often irregular.

Metrics—cord width: 0.6 mm to 2.1 mm; average is 1.2 mm; mode at 1.05 mm

Cordwrapped Stick or Paddle-edge Stamping: 20% of sample has cordwrapped stick or cord-wrapped paddle-edge impressions on upper rim zone. All are applied vertically. Impressions are shallow and partially obliterated.

Metrics—width of Stick or Paddle-edge Impression: 3.5 mm to 4.9 mm; average is 4.0 mm
Cord Impressions: 0.5 mm to 1.8 mm; average is 1.05 mm

Punctation: lower limit of cord-impressed rim zone bounded by single row of punctations in 82% of sherds with complete upper rim zone (11 sherds). Punctations are moderately deep and made with blunted tool. 6 sherds have angular punctations, 2 sherds have circular punctations, and 1 has elongate punctations. 3 sherds have punctations impressed from the right, 2 from the left, 2 from below, and 2 at 90° angles.

Metrics—punctation diameter: 2.0 mm to 3.0 mm; average is 2.2 mm

punctation interval: 3.0 mm to 11.0 mm; average is 6.4 mm; mode at 5.0 mm

lip to punctation: 10.0 mm to 30.0 mm; average is 21.0 mm; mode at 20.5 mm

Incising: one sherd has a shallow, rectilinear, horizontally incised line 27.0 mm below the lip. It is 1.2 mm wide. One sherd has a series of parallel vertically incised lines extending down 6.0 mm below lip on interior surface. They are 4.0 mm wide.

Rocker stamping: one cordwrapped stick or cordwrapped paddle impressed sherd has free horizontal plain rocker stamping on neck area beginning 22.0 mm below lip.

Lip notching: 6 sherds (24% of sample) exhibit simple notched lips, 4 notched on top of lip and 2 notched to lip exterior.

Brushing: as noted above, one sherd is vertically brushed on neck area below a plain upper rim zone with linear cordimpressed decoration. It is not possible to say whether brushing is decorative treatment or surface finish.

Motif—upper rim zone decoration described above. No sherds in sample extend below vessel neck.

Vessel form:

Lip—68% flattened, 24%* flattened and beveled to interior, and 8% rounded.

Rim—

Attitude (5 sherds): 3 everted and 2 vertical.

Form (17 sherds): 70.5% straight and 29.5% excurved.

Modification: 20% cambered only, none cambered and channeled, 80% unmodified.

Body—

Form: rim morphology and attitude suggest at least 88% of sample represents jar forms. Three sherds are possibly from vertical rimmed bowls.

Size—no sherds large enough for vessel measurements or approximations other than thickness. No miniature vessels in sample.

Metrics—thickness (taken at neck): 5.2 mm to 8.7 mm; average is 6.6 mm

Base—none identifiable.

Plain Excurved Rim

Sample: 58 identifiable rim sherds and one restorable vessel, about 15% complete

Technology:

Method of manufacture—probably coiled

Paste—93% sandy clay with large amount of tempering material: 7% silty clay with moderate amount of tempering material.

Temper—crushed stone (where identifiable). 60% feldspar, 21% granitic material, and 3 sherds with no apparent temper. Tempering particles reach 7.8 mm and average about 2.0 mm

Texture—only moderately well consolidated and compacted, resulting in friable texture. Irregular transverse fracture and scant tendancy for lamellar converse fracture. No coil breaks observed.

Color—core, exterior, and interior colors range from black to buff. 66% of cores are black, dark grays, and dark browns, 24% fall into medium grays and medium browns; and 10% into light gray, light brown and buffs. 59% of exteriors fall into black, dark grays, dark browns, and dark gray-browns, 24% into medium grays and medium browns, and 17% into light browns, buffs and orange-buff. 59% of interiors fall into black, dark grays, dark browns, and dark gray-browns, 17% into medium browns, and 24% into light browns, buffs, and yellow-buff.

Surface finish—exteriors are plain, 73% are well smoothed, while 27% are but poorly smoothed. Tool marks are common on all exteriors. Interiors are plain, well smoothed, and regular and tool marks are common.

Decoration:

Technique—punctation, lip notching, and noding.

Punctation: twelve sherds (20.5% of sample) have a single row of punctations encircling neck. Punctations are shallow to very deep. 58% are angular in form, 33.5% are hemiconical, and one sherd has punctations made with a round hollow tool, 4.2 mm in diameter. 50% are impressed from below, 42% at 90° angle, and 8% from left.

Metrics—punctation diameter: 1.2 mm to 5.1 mm, average is 3.4 mm

punctation interval: 4.5 mm to 12.0 mm; average is 7.9 mm

lip to punctation: 9.5 mm to 30.9 mm; average is 13.7 mm

Lip notching: 13 sherds (22% of sample) have notched lips. Ten sherds have simple notches (apparently fingernail impressions on nine of the ten sherds). Of these, six are notched to

lip exterior, three on top of lip, and one to lip interior. Two sherds are notched with cordwrapped stick or cordwrapped paddle edge. One is notched to lip exterior, the other to lip interior. One sherd appears to have textile impressions to lip interior.
Noding: single restorable vessel has single row of exterior punched nodes encircling neck 27.0 mm below lip. Node interval is 28.0 mm

Vessel form:
Lip—84% rounded, 15% flattened, 0.5% beveled to interior, and 0.5% pointed.
Rim—
Attitude and form: all sherds in class have excurved rim form by definition. Excurvature of neck and rim is continuous and generally constant curve
Modification: none
Body—
Form: rim morphology suggests that jar form is exclusively represented. Globular body is suggested by single restorable vessel. Moderately well defined to very well defined neck.
Size—Metrics—orifice diameter: restorable vessel approximately 27 cm
Maximum body diameter: Restorable vessel approximately 36 cm
Thickness (taken at neck): 3.2 mm to 8.9 mm; average is 6.3 mm
Base—none identifiable

Cordmarked Noded

Sample: 12 identifiable rims. No complete or restorable vessels.

Technology:
Method of manufacture—probably coiled
Paste—sandy clay with large amount of tempering material
Temper—crushed stone: 41.5% quartzite, 33.5% granitic material, and 25% feldspar. Tempering particles reach 5.2 mm and average about 1.7 mm
Texture—poorly consolidated and compacted resulting in friable texture. No coil breaks observed. Transverse fracture plane is irregular and often appears contorted. No tendancy for converse fracture observed.
Color—core, exterior, and interior colors range from black to buff: 75% of cores are black, dark gray, or dark brown, 8.5% are medium brown, and 16.5% are buff and yellow-buff; 66.5% of exteriors are black, dark gray, or dark brown, 8.5% are medium brown, and 25% are light brown or buff: 50% of interiors are black, dark gray, or dark brown, 8.5% are medium brown, and 41.5% are light brown or buff.
Surface finish—exteriors are cord impressed. Individual cord impressions are usually distinct but about 33% of sample exhibit subsequent partial smoothing and impressions are completely obliterated in some areas. Individual cord impressions are contiguous: 25% of impressions are vertical or at right angles to lip, 41.5% are left oblique from lip, and 8.5% are right oblique from lip. Interiors are plain and poorly smoothed. Tempering particles frequently protrude in an undulating interior surface. Horizontal tool marks are common. One sherd has a cord impressed and smoothed lip; all others are plain.
Metrics—cord impression width: 0.8 mm to 3.2 mm. Average is 1.8 mm

Decoration:
Technique—noding (100%) and lip notching (8.5%).
Noding: all sherds of this class have exterior punched node decoration by definition. This usually consists of a single row of nodes encircling rim or neck. One sherd has a double row of nodes encircling neck.
Metrics—node interval: 15.0 mm to 38.0 mm; average is 26.7 mm
lip to node: 18.0 mm to 38.0 mm; average is 26.1 mm
Lip notching: one sherd has a cordwrapped stick or cordwrapped paddle-edge notched lip. Notching is to lip exterior and lip interior.

Vessel form:
Lip—66.5% rounded, 25% flattened, and 8.5% flattened and beveled to interior.
Rim—
Attitude (9 sherds): Seven vertical and two everted
Form (12 sherds): 50% straight and 50% excurved
Modification: none
Body—
Form: rim morphology and attitude suggest jar form exclusively represented. Jars appear to have cylindrical body with scant shoulder development and neck constriction.
Size—
Metrics—orifice diameter: two sherds, both approximately 28.0 cm
Thickness (taken 1.0 cm below lip): 5.5 mm to 8.4 mm. Average is 6.9 mm
Base—none identifiable

Saginaw Thin Cordmarked

Sample: 34 identifiable rim sherds and one restorable vessel about 25% complete

Technology:
Method of manufacture—probably coiled
Paste—silty clay with small to moderate amount of tempering material.

Temper—crushed stone: 44.5% feldspar, 39% granitic material, 11% dark fine-grained material, and 5.5% quartzite. Tempering particles reach 4.2 mm and average about 1.5 mm

Texture—well compacted. No coil breaks observed. Irregular but well rounded transverse fracture. Transverse fracture plane appears contorted and sometimes exhibits a converse lamination. Great tendency for converse fracture.

Color—core colors range from black to buff with 34.5% black, dark gray, dark brown, and dark gray-brown; 37% medium gray and medium brown; and 28.5% light brown and buff. Exterior colors range from dark gray to buff with 20% dark gray and dark brown; 43% medium gray and medium brown; and 37% light brown, buff, and orange-buff. Interior colors range from black to light brown with 20% black, dark gray, and dark gray-brown, 34.5% medium gray and medium brown, and 45.5% light gray and light brown.

Surface finish—exteriors are cord impressed. Impressions are usually deep and individual cords are distinct. About 14% of sample shows subsequent partial smoothing. Individual cord impressions are contiguous. Overstamping is rare on rim area: 86% of impressions are vertical or at right angles to lip, 8.5% are left oblique from lip, and 5.5% are right oblique from lip; 97% of interiors are plain and very undulating, apparently from finger smoothing. Horizontal tool marks are common in interior rim area. One sherd has vertical cord impressions on interior rim; 51% of lips are cord impressed or cord impressed and partially smoothed; 49% of lips are plain.

Metrics—cord impression width: 0.6 mm to 2.3 mm. Average is 1.5 mm

Decoration:

Technique—lip notching, (23%), punctation (8.5%), rim scallop (3%).

Lip notching: Eight sherds have notched lips. Six sherds have cordwrapped stick notched lips. Of these, four are notched obliquely from the right on top of lip and two are notched to lip exterior and interior. Two vessels have plain notches on top of lip.

Punctation: three vessels have single row of punctations encircling neck. Punctations are deep and are executed with angular pointed tool in two cases. Punctations are made with cordwrapped stick on third example. Punctations are impressed from above on two sherds and from below on one sherd.

Metrics—punctation diameter: 2.2 mm, 3.5 mm, and 4.2 mm.
punctation interval: 4.5 mm and 9.5 mm.
lip to punctation: 15.0 mm, 16.5 mm, and 18.9 mm

Rim Scallop: restorable vessel has single large rim scallop (complete vessel probably had two to four such scallops) 68.0 mm wide and extending 9.0 mm above lip.

Vessel form:

Lip—72% flattened, 22% rounded, and 6% pointed: 77% of all lips show slight to pronounced thickening due to compression in finishing lip.

Rim—

Attitude (15 sherds): 80% everted and 20% vertical

Form (35 sherds): 60% straight, 37% excurved, and 3% incurved.

Modification: 6 sherds (17% of sample) have a thin exterior rim fold. Flattening and subsequent cordmarking has almost completely obliterated exterior indications of fold.

Metrics—lip to lower limit of fold: 6.6 mm to 14.2 mm, average is 9.9 mm

Body—

Form: rim morphology and attitude suggests that at least 91.5% of sample represent jar forms. Three sherds are possibly from small bowl or cup forms. Jars appear to have a poorly developed shoulder, only a slight neck constriction, and an everted to slightly flaring rim. Single restorable vessel has an elongate globular body with scant neck constriction and an everted rim.

Size—body measurements below are on single restorable vessel which appears to be larger than average vessel in this class.

Metrics—height: approximately 22.0 cm
Maximum body diameter: approximately 24.0 cm
thickness (taken 1.0 cm below lip): 2.5 mm to 5.3 mm; average is 4.2 mm

Base—none identifiable

APPENDIX AB.
Areal Distribution of Ceramics

B-1 Composit Areal Distribution for 13488 Schultz Site Sherds

	1	2	3	4	5
A	. . .	2 < 0.1%	317 2.3%	256 1.9%	20 0.2%
B	3727 27.7%	582 4.3%	1825 13.4%	1077 7.9%	82 0.6%
C	1 < 0.1%	266 2.0%	436 3.2%	4897 36.5%	. . .

B-2 Schultz Thick Areal Distribution (333 Sherds)

	1	2	3	4	5
A	. . .	2 0.6%	4 1.2%	31 9.3%	2 0.6%
B	5 1.5%	5 1.5%	155 46.6%	96 28.8%	22 6.6%
C	1 0.3%	2 0.6%	1 0.3%	7 2.1%	. . .

B-3 Shiawassee Ware Areal Distribution (309 Sherds)

	1	2	3	4	5
A	. . .	. . .	14 4.5%	4 1.3%	2 0.6%
B	12 3.9%	1 0.3%	45 14.6%	25 8.1%	3 1.0%
C	. . .	6 1.9%	1 0.3%	196 63.5%	. . .

B-4 Tittabawassee Ware Areal Distribution (131 Sherds)

	1	2	3	4	5
A	. . .	. . .	17 13.0%	17 13.0%	6 4.5%
B	25 19.9%	10 7.6%	10 7.6%	9 6.9%	1 0.8%
C	. . .	2 1.5%	2 1.5%	32 24.5%	. . .

B-5 Green Point Ware Composit Areal Distribution (2558 Sherds)

	1	2	3	4	5
A	. . .	. . .	30 1.2%	30 1.2%	2 < 0.2%
B	1011 39.5%	106 4.1%	209 11.3%	99 3.9%	9 0.4%
C	. . .	42 1.6%	45 1.8%	194 35.0%	. . .

B-6 Green Point Rocker Stamped, Plain Oblique Left Areal Distribution (146 Sherds)

	1	2	3	4	5
A	. . .	. . .	3 2.0%	1 0.7%	2 1.4%
B	57 39.1%	5 3.4%	9 6.2%	3 2.0%	1 0.7%
C	. . .	2 1.2%	1 0.7%	62 42.4%	. . .

B-7 Green Point Rocker Stamped, Plain Vertical Areal Distirubiton (90 Sherds)

	1	2	3	4	5
A	. . .	. . .	. . .	1 1.1%	. . .
B	40 44.5%	4 4.4%	10 11.1%	1 1.1%	. . .
C	. . .	. . .	. . .	34 37.8%	. . .

B-8 Green Point Rocker Stamped, Plain Horizontal Areal Distribution (46 Sherds)

	1	2	3	4	5
A	. . .	. . .	2 4.3%	1 2.2%	. . .
B	22 47.8%	3 6.5%	4 8.7%	1 2.2%	. . .
C	. . .	1 2.2%	. . .	12 26.1%	. . .

B-9 Green Point Rocker Stamped, Plain (Non-zoned or Indeterminant), Body Sherd Areal Distribution (1454 Sherds)

	1	2	3	4	5
A	. . .	. . .	9 0.6%	15 1.2%	. . .
B	558 38.3%	50 3.4%	164 11.4%	66 4.5%	5 0.3%
C	. . .	31 2.1%	16 1.1%	540 37.1%	. . .

B-13 Green Point Incised, Miscellaneous Areal Distribution (65 Sherds)

	1	2	3	4	5
A	. . .	. . .	1 1.5%	4 6.1%	. . .
B	18 27.7%	3 4.6%	5 7.7%	3 4.6%	. . .
C	. . .	. . .	2 3.1%	29 44.7%	. . .

B-10 Green Point Rocker Stamped, Plain (Zoned), Body Sherd Areal Distribution (367 Sherds)

	1	2	3	4	5
A	. . .	. . .	5 1.4%	7 1.9%	. . .
B	164 44.7%	12 3.4%	47 12.7%	14 3.8%	. . .
C	. . .	5 1.4%	7 1.9%	106 28.8%	. . .

B-14 Green Point Incised, Body Sherd Areal Distribution (146 Sherds)

	1	2	3	4	5
A	. . .	. . .	3 2.1%	. . .	. . .
B	33 22.6%	8 5.5%	10 6.9%	4 2.7%	1 0.7%
C	. . .	1 0.7%	11 7.5%	75 51.3%	. . .

B-11 Green Point Rocker Stamped, Dentate, Rim and Body Sherd Areal Distribution (191 Sherds)

	1	2	3	4	5
A	. . .	. . .	4 2.1%	1 0.5%	. . .
B	75 39.3%	16 8.4%	31 16.2%	5 2.6%	2 1.0%
C	. . .	3 1.6%	3 1.6%	51 26.7%	. . .

B-15 Green Point Plain Areal Distribution (33 Sherds)

	1	2	3	4	5
A	. . .	. . .	. . .	. . .	. . .
B	8 24.2%	2 6.1%	7 21.2%	2 6.1%	. . .
C	. . .	. . .	1 3.0%	13 39.4%	. . .

B-12 Green Point Incised, Crosshatched Areal Distribution (87 Sherds)

	1	2	3	4	5
A	. . .	. . .	3 3.5%	. . .	. . .
B	29 33.3%	5 5.7%	8 9.2%	2 2.3%	. . .
C	. . .	. . .	4 4.6%	36 41.4%	. . .

B-16 Reuben Linear Cord Impressed, Plain and Striated Interior Areal Distribution (181 Sherds)

	1	2	3	4	5
A	. . .	. . .	1 0.6%	2 1.1%	. . .
B	34 18.8%	10 5.5%	28 15.4%	16 8.8%	1 0.6%
C	. . .	6 3.3%	4 2.2%	79 43.7%	. . .

B-17 Plain Body Sherd Areal Distribution (6461 Sherds)

	1	2	3	4	5
A	. . .	. . .	147 2.3%	94 1.4%	8 0.1%
B	1921 29.7%	257 4.0%	746 11.6%	377 5.8%	29 0.4%
C	. . .	125 1.9%	189 2.9%	2568 39.9%	. . .

B-21 Unnamed Plain Excurved Rim Areal Distribution (30 Sherds)

	1	2	3	4	5
A	. . .	. . .	. . .	1 3.3%	. . .
B	14 46.7%	2 6.7%	5 16.6%	1 3.3%	1 3.3%
C	. . .	2 6.7%	. . .	4 13.4%	. . .

B-18 Scraped Body Sherd Areal Distribution (329 Sherds)

	1	2	3	4	5
A	. . .	. . .	. . .	4 1.2%	. . .
B	64 19.5%	14 4.3%	32 9.7%	21 6.4%	3 0.9%
C	. . .	2 0.6%	22 6.7%	167 50.7%	. . .

B-22 Saginaw Thin Cordmarked Areal Distribution (664 Sherds)

	1	2	3	4	5
A	. . .	. . .	30 4.5%	11 1.7%	. . .
B	18 2.7%	31 4.7%	89 13.4%	112 16.8%	1 0.1%
C	. . .	12 1.8%	119 17.9%	241 36.4%	. . .

B-19 Cordmarked and Smoothed Body Sherd Areal Distribution (853 Sherds)

	1	2	3	4	5
A	. . .	. . .	28 3.3%	19 2.2%	. . .
B	359 42.0%	37 4.3%	108 12.6%	73 8.8%	3 0.4%
C	. . .	13 1.5%	17 2.0%	196 22.9%	. . .

B-23 Unnamed Undecorated Rim Cordmarked Areal Distribution (58 Sherds)

	1	2	3	4	5
A	. . .	. . .	2 3.5%	3 5.2%	. . .
B	13 22.4%	4 6.9%	3 5.2%	7 12.0%	. . .
C	. . .	. . .	1 1.7%	25 43.1%	. . .

B-20 Unnamed Plain Straight Rim Areal Distribution (56 Sherds)

	1	2	3	4	5
A	. . .	. . .	2 3.6%	. . .	. . .
B	17 30.3%	2 3.6%	4 7.1%	6 10.7%	. . .
C	. . .	2 3.6%	1 1.8%	22 39.0%	. . .

B-24 Cordmarked Body Sherd Areal Distribution (1384 Sherds)

	1	2	3	4	5
A	. . .	. . .	41 3.0%	40 2.9%	. . .
B	209 15.1%	92 6.6%	300 21.7%	233 16.8%	9 0.6%
C	. . .	47 3.4%	30 2.2%	383 27.7%	. . .

APPENDIX AC
Distribution of Sherd Groups in Relation to Stockade

Units Outside Palisade	Units Within Palisade	Samples	Ceramic
58.5%		333	Schultz Thick Ware
89.5%		309	Shiawassee Ware
80.1%		132	Tittabawassee Ware
96.5%		87	Green Point Incised, Crosshatched
96.3%		191	Green Point Rocker Stamped, Dentate
96.0%		2115	Green Point Rocker Stamped, Plain
95.0%		240	Green Point Incised, Miscellaneous
100.0%		62	Green Point Ware, Miscellaneous
90.0%		182	Reuben Linear Cord Impressed
92.9%		56	Plain Straight Rim
90.0%		30	Plain Excurved Rim
84.0%		664	Saginaw Thin Ware
88.0%		58	Cordmarked Rims (all other post-Middle Woodland)
94.9%		6499	Plain Body Sherds
94.3%		330	Scraped Body Sherds
93.0%		857	Cordmarked and Smoothed Body Sherds
84.8%		1401	Cordmarked Body Sherds

APPENDIX AD
Ceramics from Features*

Ceramic	1	2	3	4	5	8	12	15	16	18	23	24	29	30	32	33	34	35
Schultz Thick																1		1
Shiawassee—all types						1						2						
Shiawassee Cordmarked												1						
Shiawassee Plain						1						1						
Shiawassee Incised																		
Tittabawassee—all types									1									
Tittabawassee Dentate Stamped									1									
Tittabawassee Cordwr. St. Sta.																		
Tittabawassee Plain Noded																		
Green Point—all types	3			1		12	1	1	6	1						1		
Green Point Roc. St., Plain																		
Roc. St., Plain, body	1					2	1	1	2	1			3					
Green Point Roc. St., Dentate																		
Roc. St., Dentate, body						1			2									
Green Point Incised, Crosshat.				1												1		
Incised, Crosshat., body						1												
Green Point Incised, misc.									1									
Green Point Plain																		
Green Point Brushed																		
Brushed (zoned), body																		
Green Point undif. incised, body	2					7			1				1					
Green Point undif. punct., body						1												
Reuben Lin. Co. Imp., Plain Int.						1			1						1			
Reuben Lin. Co. Imp., Stria. Int.		1																
Plain straight rim					1								1					
Plain excurved rim													1					
Cordmarked undecorated rim																		
Cordmarked noded																		
Cordmarked cordwr. st. imp. lip																		
Saginaw Thin Cordmarked	5		1				1									1		
Textile Impressed																		
Simple stamped																		
Cordmarked undecorated, body						1							2	1		2	2	
Cordmarked incised, body						1												
Cordmarked punctated, body																		
Plain undecorated, body	5		1	2		41	1	3	15	1	1		16	2	1	2	1	2
Scraped body						13			3									
Cordmarked and smoothed, body	3					2			1				3			1	1	
Plain shell tempered																		
Indeterminate	5					2	3	2	5			2	1	1	1		1	

*Pages 293-296 show ceramics (by type) from 1962 and 1963 Schultz site features. Pages 297-300 show data from 1964 features.

Ceramic	36	37	38	39	40	41	42	43	44	45	46	47	48	49	51	52	53
Schultz Thick							4	4		2		4	4		1		
Shiawassee—all types					1										1		
Shiawassee Cordmarked					1										1		
Shiawassee Plain																	
Shiawassee Incised																	
Tittabawassee—all types				1										1			
Tittabawassee Dentate Stamped				1													
Tittabawassee Cordwr. St. Sta.														1			
Tittabawassee Plain Noded																	
Green Point—all types			1				32	70						9	4	4	
Green Point Roc. St., Plain							1	7						1	1		
Roc. St., Plain, body							21	47			1			6	3	3	
Green Point Roc. St., Dentate																	
Roc. St., Dentate, body							9	4			1						
Green Point Incised, Crosshat.								5								1	
Incised, Crosshat., body																	
Green Point Incised, misc.																	
Green Point Plain								2									
Green Point Brushed																	
Brushed (zoned), body																	
Green Point undif. incised, body			1				1	4						1			
Green Point undif. punct., body								1						1			
Reuben Lin. Co. Imp., Plain Int.							2	1									
Reuben Lin. Co. Imp., Stria. Int.																	
Plain straight rim								1									
Plain excurved rim							1	2									
Cordmarked undecorated rim																	
Cordmarked noded								1									
Cordmarked cordwr. st. imp. lip																	
Saginaw Thin Cordmarked	4				1											1	
Textile Impressed																	
Simple stamped																	
Cordmarked undecorated, body	1	1		1	1	1	2	13	1					2		2	
Cordmarked incised, body																	
Cordmarked punctated, body																	
Plain undecorated, body		1	1		3	2	72	149						12		3	2
Scraped body							4	1									
Cordmarked and smoothed, body	1	1			1		8	18						2		2	
Plain shell tempered																	
Indeterminate	8		2	1	2	1	18	44	1		1			6	1	1	

Ceramic	56	57	58	59	62	64	65	68	71	72	73	74	75	76	77	78	79	80
Schultz Thick			1	8														
Shiawassee—all types	1			2												1		
Shiawassee Cordmarked				2			1											
Shiawassee Plain																1		
Shiawassee Incised	1																	
Tittabawassee—all types																		
Tittabawassee Dentate Stamped																		
Tittabawassee Cordwr. St. Sta.																		
Tittabawassee Plain Noded																		
Green Point—all types	5	41			1	2		2	1		23	23	1	2		5	17	
Green Point Roc. St., Plain		3									1	1						
Roc. St., Plain, body	4	38						1	1		18	15		2		1	8	1
Green Point Roc. St., Dentate												1					1	
Roc. St., Dentate, body												2				2		
Green Point Incised, Crosshat.	1												1				2	
Incised, Crosshat., body																		
Green Point Incised, misc.												1				1	4	
Green Point Plain					1	2												
Green Point Brushed																		
Brushed (zoned), body																		
Green Point undif. incised, body								1			4	3				1	1	
Green Point undif. punct., body																	1	
Reuben Lin. Co. Imp., Plain Int.									2			1						
Reuben Lin. Co. Imp., Stria. Int.																		4
Plain straight rim		1								1	1	1						
Plain excurved rim																		
Cordmarked undecorated rim											1		1		1			
Cordmarked noded																		
Cordmarked cordwr. st. imp. lip																		
Saginaw Thin Cordmarked													4	2				
Textile Impressed																		
Simple stamped																		
Cordmarked undecorated, body		3									9	13	2	1		1	1	2
Cordmarked incised, body																		
Cordmarked punctated, body																		
Plain undecorated, body	35	44							8		15	38		2		2	11	9
Scraped body	1	1						1	2		2	5						2
Cordmarked and smoothed, body	3	11						3			4	3	1				1	6
Plain shell tempered																		
Indeterminate	4	19		2							5	14	2	1		4	4	4

Ceramic	81	82	83	84	87	88	89	90	91	92	93	94	95	96	97	98	100
Schultz Thick															1		
Shiawassee—all types												1			1		
Shiawassee Cordmarked												1			1		
Shiawassee Plain																	
Shiawassee Incised																	
Tittabawassee—all types							3			1			1		2		
Tittabawassee Dentate Stamped							1			1							
Tittabawassee Cordwr. St. Sta.																	
Tittabawassee Plain Noded							2						1		2		
Green Point—all types	1	2	4		1	5	39			20	1			3	219		
Green Point Roc. St., Plain	1					2	3			2					20		
Roc. St., Plain, body		1	2			3	34			7	1			3	126		
Green Point Roc. St., Dentate										1					3		
Roc. St., Dentate, body			1				1			7					19		
Green Point Incised, Crosshat.					1					1					2		
Incised, Crosshat., body															2		
Green Point Incised, misc.							1								3		
Green Point Plain															3		
Green Point Brushed										1					2		
Brushed (zoned), body																	
Green Point undif. incised, body			1							1					28		
Green Point undif. punct., body		1													11		
Reuben Lin. Co. Imp., Plain Int.							1			1				1	12		
Reuben Lin. Co. Imp., Stria. Int.															7		
Plain straight rim							1						1		3		
Plain excurved rim							1								2		
Cordmarked undecorated rim															1		
Cordmarked noded															1		
Cordmarked cordwr. st. imp. lip																	
Saginaw Thin Cordmarked						3									6		
Textile Impressed																	
Simple stamped																	
Cordmarked undecorated, body				1		3	4	1					3		24		
Cordmarked incised, body																	
Cordmarked punctated, body																	
Plain undecorated, body		1		5		13	65	1		26	2	1	2	4	440	1	1
Scraped body						1	3			1					30	1	
Cordmarked and smoothed, body		2	1	1	1		6		4	1					46		
Plain shell tempered																	
Indeterminate				3	1	5	24	1		12		1	1	1	163		

Ceramic	2	3	5	6	7	8	9	10	11	12	13	14	17	19	20	21	22
Schultz Thick												1			1	1	
Shiawassee—all types													1				
Shiawassee Cordmarked																	
Shiawassee Plain																	
Shiawassee Incised													1				
Tittabawassee—all types							1										3
Tittabawassee Dentate Stamped							1										1
Tittabawassee Cordwr. St. Sta.																	
Tittabawassee Plain Noded																	2
Green Point—all types			10	11	1								2		6	39	41
Green Point Roc. St., Plain					1											6	2
Roc. St., Plain, body			7	10									2		6	26	32
Green Point Roc. St., Dentate																	
Roc. St., Dentate, body																1	1
Green Point Incised, Crosshat.			1														
Incised, Crosshat., body																	2
Green Point Incised, misc.																1	
Green Point Plain																	1
Green Point Brushed																	
Brushed (zoned), body																	
Green Point undif. incised, body			1	1											1	5	1
Green Point undif. punct., body			1														2
Reuben Lin. Co. Imp., Plain Int.																1	2
Reuben Lin. Co. Imp., Stria. Int.			1													1	2
Plain straight rim		1															1
Plain excurved rim																	1
Cordmarked undecorated rim													1				
Cordmarked noded			1														
Cordmarked cordwr. st. imp. lip		2															
Saginaw Thin Cordmarked		1		1			4	1					1				
Textile Impressed					1		1										
Simple stamped													1				
Cordmarked undecorated, body	2		24		3	2	4	1		1	1		5		3		5
Cordmarked incised, body																	
Cordmarked punctated, body																	
Plain undecorated, body	4		25	27	6	2	1	1	5				9	2	13	60	127
Scraped body								1	1							6	15
Cordmarked and smoothed, body			8	3									2		3	1	5
Plain shell tempered																	
Indeterminate			8	1	4	1	3	2	1				4		8	24	34

Ceramic	23	26	27	29	31	32	33	34	35	36	37	38	39	40	41	42	43	45
Schultz Thick											1							
Shiawassee—all types							1										1	
Shiawassee Cordmarked																	1	
Shiawassee Plain							1											
Shiawassee Incised																		
Tittabawassee—all types													1					
Tittabawassee Dentate Stamped													1					
Tittabawassee Cordwr. St. Sta.																		
Tittabawassee Plain Noded																		
Green Point—all types		4	18	1	1	7	20					1	2	30		1		
Green Point Roc. St., Plain			2				1							3				
Roc. St., Plain, body		2	14	1	1	5	13					1	1	19		1		
Green Point Roc. St., Dentate		1				1												
Roc. St., Dentate, body						1	1							1				
Green Point Incised, Crosshat.			1				1											
Incised, Crosshat., body		1																
Green Point Incised, misc.			1				3							5				
Green Point Plain														1				
Green Point Brushed																		
Brushed (zoned), body													1					
Green Point undif. incised, body							1											
Green Point undif. punct., body														1				
Reuben Lin. Co. Imp., Plain Int.			1			1												
Reuben Lin. Co. Imp., Stria. Int.			1									1						
Plain straight rim														1				
Plain excurved rim																		
Cordmarked undecorated rim																	1	
Cordmarked noded																		
Cordmarked cordwr. st. imp. lip																		
Saginaw Thin Cordmarked																		
Textile Impressed																		
Simple stamped																		
Cordmarked undecorated, body				1			2			1								
Cordmarked incised, body																		
Cordmarked punctated, body																		
Plain undecorated, body		9	28	5	1	21	28						13	54		6	16	8
Scraped body	1	1	2				3											
Cordmarked and smoothed, body					1							1		5	2	1	2	
Plain shell tempered																		
Indeterminate		10	9			2	7	2	1			5	5	16		2	7	

Ceramic	46	47	48	49	51	52	53	55	57	58	59	60	61	65	67	68	73	74
Schultz Thick																		
Shiawassee—all types	3					7			1	1	1					1		1
Shiawassee Cordmarked	2					6			1	1	1					1		1
Shiawassee Plain						1												
Shiawassee Incised	1																	
Tittabawassee—all types																		
Tittabawassee Dentate Stamped																		
Tittabawassee Cordwr. St. Sta.																		
Tittabawassee Plain Noded																		
Green Point—all types		13																
Green Point Roc. St., Plain		1																
Roc. St., Plain, body		6																
Green Point Roc. St., Dentate																		
Roc. St., Dentate, body																		
Green Point Incised, Crosshat.		2																
Incised, Crosshat., body																		
Green Point Incised, misc.																		
Green Point Plain																		
Green Point Brushed																		
Brushed (zoned), body																		
Green Point undif. incised, body		3																
Green Point undif. punct., body		1																
Reuben Lin. Co. Imp., Plain Int.								1					1					
Reuben Lin. Co. Imp., Stria. Int.																		
Plain straight rim		1																
Plain excurved rim																		
Cordmarked undecorated rim												1						
Cordmarked noded							1											
Cordmarked cordwr. st. imp. lip																		
Saginaw Thin Cordmarked																		
Textile Impressed																		
Simple stamped																		
Cordmarked undecorated, body		1												1				
Cordmarked incised, body																		
Cordmarked punctated, body																		
Plain undecorated, body		8	2	1	1	1	1	1					3		1			
Scraped body																		
Cordmarked and smoothed, body				2												1		
Plain shell tempered																		
Indeterminate	2			1												4		1

Ceramic	75	77	78	79	80	81	82	83	84	85	86	88	89	90	91	92	93	94	96
Schultz Thick		1																	
Shiawassee—all types																			
Shiawassee Cordmarked																			
Shiawassee Plain																			
Shiawassee Incised																			
Tittabawassee—all types					3			4		1									
Tittabawassee Dentate Stamped					2			3		1									
Tittabawassee Cordwr. St. Sta.								1											
Tittabawassee Plain Noded					1														
Green Point—all types				2	24		8	2					3	1	3	5	3		
Green Point Roc. St., Plain					5		1	2					2						
Roc. St., Plain, body				1	15		3							1	3	3	2		
Green Point Roc. St., Dentate																			
Roc. St., Dentate, body							2						1				1		
Green Point Incised, Crosshat.					2														
Incised, Crosshat., body																			
Green Point Incised, misc.							1												
Green Point Plain					1														
Green Point Brushed																			
Brushed (zoned), body																			
Green Point undif. incised, body				1	1											2			
Green Point undif. punct., body							1												
Reuben Lin. Co. Imp., Plain Int.					2														
Reuben Lin. Co. Imp., Stria. Int.							2		1				1						
Plain straight rim																			
Plain excurved rim																			
Cordmarked undecorated rim	2				1														1
Cordmarked noded																			
Cordmarked cordwr. st. imp. lip																			
Saginaw Thin Cordmarked	2					3					1								
Textile Impressed	1																		
Simple stamped																			
Cordmarked undecorated, body	2			10	2	11													3
Cordmarked incised, body						1													
Cordmarked punctated, body																			
Plain undecorated, body	1		1	10	30	4	9	4	2			3		2	4	7	4	3	2
Scraped body					1		3								1	2			
Cordmarked and smoothed, body	2		1	2			1		1						1				
Plain shell tempered																			
Indeterminate	1		1	7	15	5	2	3	5						4	2	2		2

APPENDIX B
BONE ARTIFACTS

Peter F. Murray

APPENDIX BA. List of Bone Artifacts

CATEGORY I: PROJECTILE POINTS

Artifact: flat bone projectile points
Species: probably deer
Material: longbone fragments
Use: large and small game
Number: 4
Levels: III*a*, III*b*
Distribution: general distribution in time and area

Artifact: socketed conical projectile points
Species: *Odocoileus virginianus,* white-tailed deer
Material: antler tine
Use: large and small game
Number: 14
Levels: II*c*, III*a*, III*b*, IV*a*, IV*b*
Distribution: Great Lakes states and elsewhere, Late Archaic through Historic periods

Artifact: toggle head harpoon points
Species: *Odocoileus virginianus,* white-tailed deer
Material: antler tine
Use: fishing
Number: 2
Levels: III*a*, III*b*
Distribution: Middle and Late Woodland in Michigan (Spider Cave, Mero and Porte de Mortes sites), Middle and Late Woodland of Wisconsin, Late Woodland of Kansas, Nebraska and elsewhere (Mason, 1965:156-63)

Artifact: solid conical points
Species: *Odocoileus virginianus,* white-tailed deer
Material: antler
Use: large and small game
Number: 8
Levels: III*a*, III*b*, IV*a*
Distribution: Late Archaic through Late Woodland in Eastern United States

CATEGORY II: AWLS

Artifact: cylindrical awls
Species: bird (Anseriformes), beaver, deer and unidentified mammal
Material: ulna, antler, unidentified longbones
Use: piercing leather, etc.
Number: 5
Levels: III*a*, III*b*, IV
Distribution: present in most all bone assemblages of Eastern United States

Artifact: ulna awls
Species: *Odocoileus virginianus, Lynx* sp., unidentified mammals
Material: ulna
Use: piercing implement
Number: 9
Levels: III*a*, III*b*, IV*c*
Distribution: Archaic through Late Woodland in Eastern United States

Artifact: splinter awls
Species: unidentified mammals, mostly deer
Material: splintered longbone
Use: piercing and punching leather, etc.
Number: 15
Levels: II*c*, III*a*, III*b*, IV*a*
Distribution: in most all bone assemblages

Artifact: fish spine awls
Species: *Aplodinotus grunniens,* (drum) *Acipenser fulvescens* (sturgeon)
Material: dorsal spine of drum, dermal bone scale of sturgeon
Use: punches or piercing implements
Number: 4
Levels: III*b*
Distribution: ---

CATEGORY III: BIPOINTED BONE IMPLEMENTS

Artifact: pins or leister points
Species: unidentified mammal
Material: unidentified longbone splinter
Use: either pins or fish-spear points
Number: 2
Levels: 20x20B, 1.9 ft—2.1 ft; 20x20B, 1.3 ft—1.4 ft

CATEGORY IV: WEAVING IMPLEMENTS

Artifact: large shuttles
Species: *Odocoileus virginianus*

Material: metapodial
Use: preparation of grass mats and possibly fish-netting
Number: 8
Levels: III*a*, III*b*, IV*a*
Distribution: Middle and Late Woodland New York state (Ritchie, 1965), Clear Lake Hopewellian (Fowler, 1952: 133-48), Adler mound group (Winters, 1961: 57-88), Late Woodland and historic plains

Artifact: small shuttles
Species: *Odocoileus virginianus*
Material: rib
Use: preparation of grass and reed mats
Number: 1
Levels: III*a*
Distribution: ---

CATEGORY V: HANDLES

Artifact: small socket handles
Species: *Odocoileus virginianus*
Material: antler
Use: awl handles
Number: 5
Levels: III*a*
Distribution: general distribution, occur with greatest frequency in Middle Woodland assemblages

Artifact: large socket handles
Species: *Odocoileus virginianus*
Material: antler
Use: awl and scraper handles
Number: 3
Levels: III*a*
Distribution: ---

CATEGORY VI: FLINT KNAPPING IMPLEMENTS

Artifact: tine flakers
Species: *Odocoileus virginianus*
Material: antler
Use: pressure flaking
Number: 7
Levels: II*b*, III*a*, III*b*
Distribution: general

Artifact: drifters
Species: *Odocoileus virginianus*
Material: antler
Use: percussion flakers
Number: 7
Levels: IV*a*, IV*c*
Distribution: general

Artifact: miscellaneous cut antler
Species: *Odocoileus virginianus, Cervus canadensis*
Material: antler
Use: antler artifacts in process or discards
Number: 13
Levels: II*c*, III*a*, III*b*, IV*c*,
Distribution: general

CATEGORY VII: HOES

Artifact: hoes
Species: *Odocoileus virginianus*
Material: scapulae, ilium
Use: digging and grubbing
Number: 3
Levels: III*a*, III*b*
Distribution: Middle and Late Woodland, Hopewellian occupations, Late Woodland and historic plains, Mississippian, etc.

CATEGORY VIII: MODIFIED TEETH AND MANDIBLES

Artifact: incisor chisels
Species: *Castor canadensis,* beaver
Material: upper and lower incisors
Use: carving and gouging bone, antler and wood
Number: 10
Levels: III*a*, III*b*, IV*a*
Distribution: Late Archaic through Late Woodland of Eastern United States

Artifact: ground teeth
Species: *Ursus americanus,* black bear canines, incisors, molars
Use: ground mandible pendants, personal adornment
Number: 22
Levels: II*c*, II*d*, III*a*, III*b*, IV*a*
Distribution: Middle Woodland occupations of Eastern United States

Artifact: pendant
Species: *Lynx rufus,* bobcat
Material: mandible
Use: perforated through ramus and dentary for suspension
Number: 1
Levels: not in stratigraphic context
Distribution: Hopewellian and Middle Woodland occupations

Artifact: cut maxilla
Species: *Canis lupus,* wolf
Material: portion of maxilla with P_1, M_1 and M_2 present
Use: pendant
Number: 1
Levels: not in stratigraphic context
Distribution: same as above

Artifact: notched tooth
Species: *Urocyon cinereoargenteus,* fox

Material: canine tooth
Use: unknown
Number: 1
Levels: III*b*
Distribution: ---

Artifact: cut and ground maxilla
Species: *Ursus americanus,* black bear maxilla with one molar present
Use: pendant
Number: 1
Levels: IV
Distribution: same as round jaws and teeth

CATEGORY IX: SCRAPING IMPLEMENTS

Artifact: beamers
Species: *Odocoileus virginianus*
Material: metapodial
Use: remove hair from hides
Number: 4
Levels: II*b*, III*b*
Distribution: Late Archaic through Late Woodland, Historic and Late Woodland plains

Artifact: gouge or scraper
Species: large cervid
Material: unidentified longbone
Use: possibly hide preparation or fleshing tool
Number: 1
Levels: not in stratigraphic context
Distribution: ---

CATEGORY X: POTTERY TOOLS

Artifact: notched bone
Species: unidentified mammal
Material: unidentified bone
Use: produce dentate stamp design on pottery
Number: 1
Levels: III*a*
Distribution: ---

CATEGORY XI: CUT AND POLISHED BIRD BONE

Artifact: tubes
Species: unidentified bird
Material: unidentified longbone
Use: beads
Number: 4
Levels: III*a*, III*b*, IV*a*
Distribution: Late Archaic through Middle Woodland

Artifact: tube
Species: Heron ?
Material: humerus, tibiotarsus
Use: beads
Number: 2
Levels: III*a*
Distribution: general

Artifact: whistle
Species: *Gavia immer,* common loon
Material: humerus
Use: whistle
Number: 1
Levels: IV*a*
Distribution: general in Late Archaic, Middle and Late Woodland sites

Artifact: longitudinally split bird bone sections
Species: unidentified bird
Material: unidentified longbone
Use: unknown
Number: 4
Levels: III*a*, III*b*
Distribution: Middle and Late Woodland, Historic Eastern United States

CATEGORY XII: SCRAPED AND POLISHED TURTLE CARAPACE

Artifact: dishes
Species: *Emys blandingi,* wood turtle, *Chrysemys picta,* painted turtle
Material: carapace
Use: holding and transferring liquids
Number: 457 uniform-sized fragments, estimated minimum number of dishes:15
Levels: III*a*, III*b*, IV*a*, IV*b*, IV*c*
Distribution: Middle and Late Woodland Eastern United States

Artifact: dishes, engraved
Species: *Emys blandingi*
Material: carapace
Use: holding and transferring liquids, burial goods
Number: 20 + fragments, minimum number of dishes: 3
Distribution: Michigan occurrence in Norton Mounds

Artifact: bangles
Species: Emydidae
Material: carapace, ground and perforated
Use: suspension for personal adornment
Number: 2
Levels: IV*c*, one not in stratigraphic context
Distribution: ---

Artifact: bangle
Species: *Trionyx* sp., soft-shell turtle
Material: carapace, perforated
Use: personal adornment
Number: 1
Levels: NE 10x10, ss 2-3

Artifact: ground carapace disk

Species: Emydidae
Material: carapace
Use: unknown
Number: 1
Levels: not in stratigraphic context

CATEGORY XIII: WORKED BONE FRAGMENTS

Artifact: bone "inlays"
Species: unidentified mammal
Material: unidentified bone
Use: possibly inlays
Number: 1
Levels: III*b*

Artifact: polished bone
Species: unidentified mammal, one possible porcupine
Material: unidentified mammal bone, one rib
Use: unknown
Number: 11
Levels: III*a*, III*b*, IV*a*, IV

CATEGORY XIV: SHELL ARTIFACTS

Artifact: effigy claw
Species: unidentified pelcypod
Material: portion of shell with thick nacre
Use: decorative, personal adornment
Number: 1
Levels: IV*a*
Distribution: Hopewellian of Ohio, Illinois, Michigan and elsewhere, Mississippian occupations

Artifact: spherical beads
Species: fresh water clam, unidentified
Material: umbo of valves
Use: personal adornment, grave goods
Number: 28
Levels: III*a*, III*b*, IV*a*

Artifact: cylindrical beads, columella
Species: unidentified marine gastropod
Material: columella
Use: personal adornment, grave goods
Number: 8
Levels: III*a*, IV*a*, IV*b*, IV*c*
Distribution: Archaic and Middle Woodland occupations, Northeastern states, Mississippian and Late Woodland elsewhere

Artifact: snail bead
Species: *Anculosa* sp. (distribution)
Material: ground snail
Use: personal adornment, grave goods
Number: 1
Levels: not in stratigraphic context

Artifact: cylindrical bead, elongate columella
Species: *Busycon* sp. (distribution)
Material: columella
Use: personal adornment
Number: 1
Levels: III*a*
Distribution: Middle and Late Woodland of Northeastern states

Artifact: spoons
Species: *Eliptio dilatus*
Material: notched or unmodified valve
Use: spoon or scooping implement
Number: 5
Levels: IV*a*, IV*b*, IV*c*
Distribution: Late Woodland for serrated-edge type

APPENDIX BB.

Use and Techniques of Manufacture of Antler Implements from the Schultz Site

Peter F. Murray

Antler was extensively employed by the Schultz inhabitants and warrants a more detailed discussion of the use and techniques of manufacturing implements from this versatile raw material. It is interesting to note that while antler implements are abundant in the collection, there are few types and little variation from a basic technique of manufacture. This is, as Kidder (1932: 272) points out, " . . . because the tines form, so to speak, ready made implements and there was accordingly little incentive to work them into new shapes."

Unlike many antler assemblages of European mesolithic occupations or that of the northwest coast of North America, the Woodland tool kit employed a limited number of artifacts made almost exclusively from the tines, only rarely using the main shaft.

Antler has several advantages over bone in that it lacks the hardness and brittleness which would render it difficult to work. Antler can be sawed or abraded with little effort. By soaking or boiling, it can be made pliable and soft enough to carve with ease.

A feature which attests to the popularity of antler in this assemblage is the fact that nearly half of all the nonlithic implements recovered from the Schultz site were fashioned from antler. Further, it should be noted that the proportion of antler to the remainder of all combined skeletal materials is exceedingly small.

Techniques of Manufacture

Several simple, basic techniques were employed in the manufacture of antler implements. The primary removal of the tine from the main shaft was achieved by either breaking the antler tine off with a stone, wedging it in a crevice and applying leverage, or by incising and sawing with a chipped stone tool until the cancellous bone of the core was reached. The tine could then be broken free with ease due to the weakness of the core. Many cut and broken proximal sections of the tines attest the use of these techniques.

The pieces of antler tine butts with broken proximal ends and sawed distal ends suggest that a number of tines were removed and collected at one time and saved as reserve stock. As an implement was needed, the tine could then be cut to the desired length, leaving these ringlike discards (Fig. 83).

Antler was most commonly employed as projectile points. A piece of stock was probably selected for straightness, diameter and length, then sawed to the proper size. The cancellous bone of the interior was then removed by gouging and digging with a sharp implement. Experimentation with a beaver incisor demonstrates that this tool is excellently suited for such a task. Occasionally the base of the point had been abraded smooth and thinned. One example has a partial groove around the base, presumably for the additional security of a sinew binding. The remainder of the points appear to have been simply fitted over a tapered shaft and secured with mastic.

An interesting variation of the socketed conical point is the addition of a line hole and barb to produce a toggle head har-

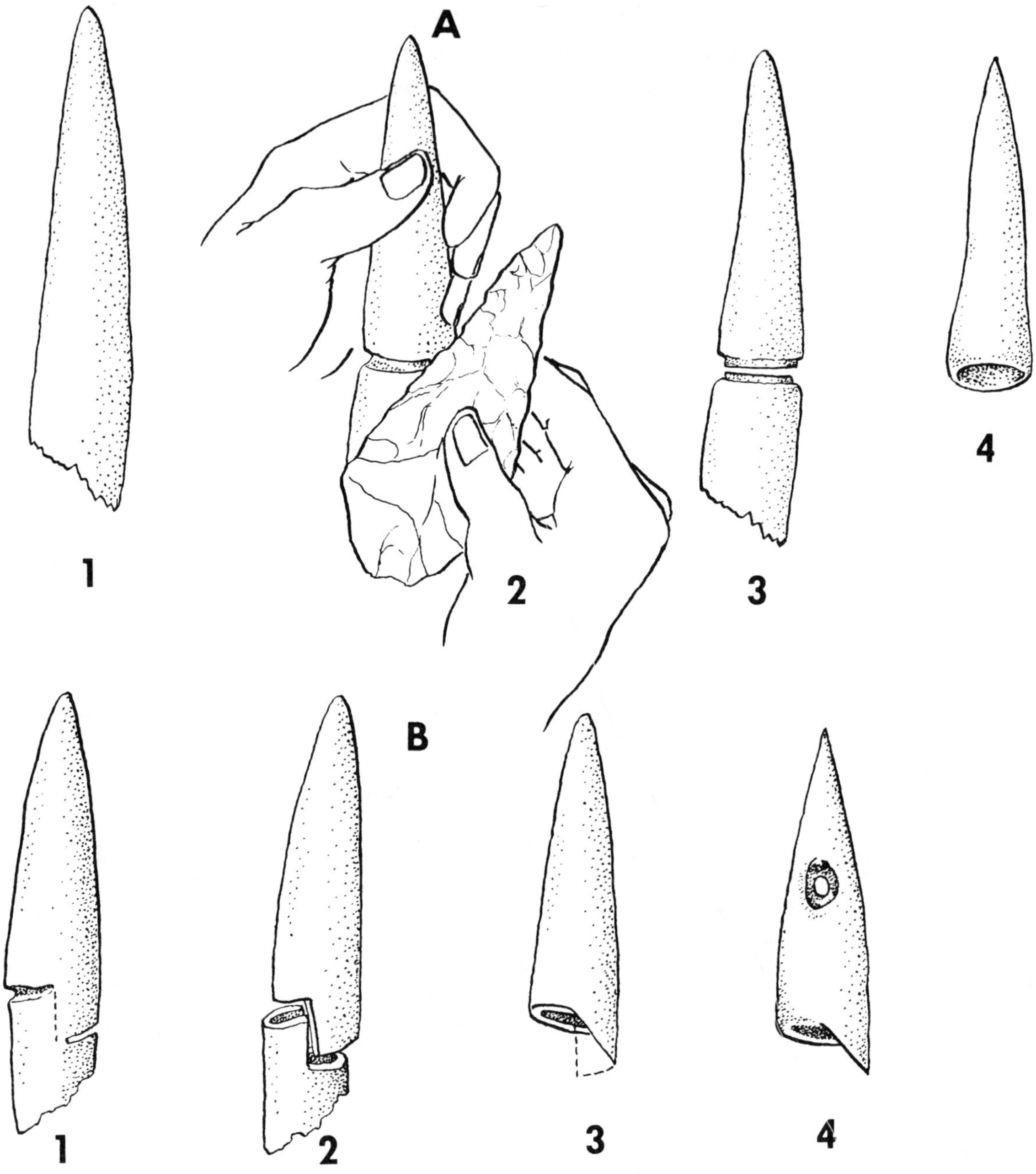

Fig. 83. A, Fashioning a socketed conical projectile point: 1, the antler tine; 2, sawing the tine to length; 3, removing the proximal end from the blank; 4, the ground and hollowed complete point. *B,* Fashioning a toggle head harpoon.

poon. The holes are conoidal or square, gouged in from each side to meet in the center. The barb was produced by removing only half of the circumference of the basal portion of the tine and sharpening the remainder to be left overhanging the shaft at an angle. Three variations of this technique are described by Maxwell (1951:103-04). Some handles were also fashioned by cutting a portion of tine to the desired length and drilling the proximal end. Occasionally, the distal end of these handles shows some usage, though the majority of this type have been rounded on the point by abrasion.

Pressure flaking implements were manufactured from curved pieces of tine or brow-tines. These were often cut at the base, suggesting that a certain length was desirable for proper handling of the tool.

Other antler tine implements were fashioned by cutting both the distal and proximal ends free, leaving a cylindrical piece and the tip free for further modification. The tip appears to have been employed as a solid conical projectile point. Some grinding of the roughened cut proximal end of the point was the only other touch of refinement. Rubbing tools and percussion flakers were derived from the unmodified tine sections. Handles with small sockets for receiving awls were drilled or the implement was simply forced into the cancellous bone until it was securely lodged.

The implements of heavy antler shafts which seem to characterize many other antler tool assemblages are not prominent in the eastern Archaic and Woodland assemblages. It is possible that, due to the abundance of versatile hardwoods in this portion of the United States, the handles of the adzes and axes were more easily fabricated with wood than with antler. On the Northwest coast and elsewhere, the soft wood of conifers would not be as efficient as antler. It is probable then, that certain environmental conditions have played a substantial part in shaping this assemblage.

Types of Wear on Tine Implements

Tine Cylinders

1. Both ends have been rounded, scratched and pitted. Striations and small nicks are present on the handle (Fig. 84).
   Interpretation: Used as a percussion flaker, scarring is due to repeated contact with a hard substance. The nicks and pits on the handle may be from retouching flakes and blades. Other marks are due to the chemical action of rootlets and fungus mycilium.
2. One end is smooth and slightly rounded. Abrasive scratches are present on the shaft. No nicks or scratches are present on the terminal portions of the tool.
   Interpretation: Tool used for rubbing or smoothing wood or leather. However, Maxwell (1951:104) believes that these are also linked to the flint working complex.

Pointed Tine Implements

1. Point polished or sharpened but no sign of wear.
   Interpretation: these appear to be projectile point fragments or pieces of awls and punches.
2. Striated flat surface on one side of point.
   Interpretation: probably a pressure flaking implement, abrasion is due to contact with stone.
3. Striated flat surfaces on two sides of point producing a chisel-like end.
   Interpretation: Flint knapper.
4. Striated scooplike surface on one side of point, one polished facet on the opposite side.

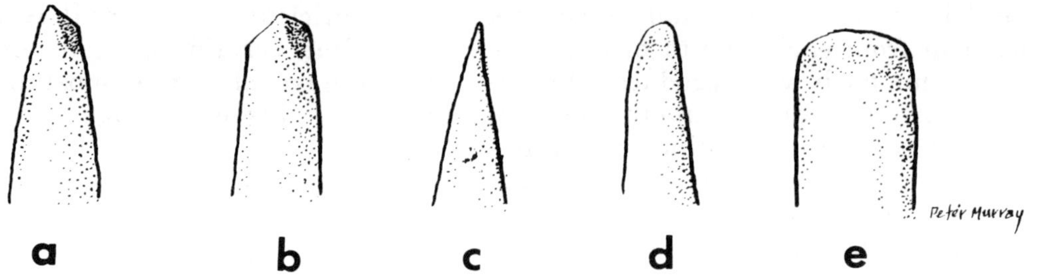

Fig. 84. Wear on tine implements.

Interpretation: indentation possibly due to rodent gnawing; facet is from abrasion applied to sharpen point. The object is probably an awl or punch.

5. Tip sharpened or unsharpened with a glossy worn surface.
   Interpretation: awl or punch, gloss due to contact with leather, wood and similar substances.

REFERENCES

Aldrich, John W. and Allen J. Duvall
1955 Distribution of American Gallinaceous Game Birds. Fish and Wildlife Service, Circular No. 34. Washington.

Allen, William Ray
1923 Studies of the Biology of Freshwater Mussels, II. Ohio Journal of Science, Vol. 23, No. 2, pp. 57-82. Columbus.

Allison, April L.
n.d. A Reconstruction of Pre-modern Vegetation in the Lower Illinois Valley. Unpublished manuscript in possession of the author.

Baerreis, David A.
1952 Pottery Type Descriptions Presented Before the Wisconsin Archeological Survey of Wisconsin, November 15, 1952. Madison.

Baerreis, David A. and Reid A. Bryson
1965 Climatic Episodes and the Dating of Mississippian Cultures. The Wisconsin Archaeologist, Vol. 46, No. 4, pp. 203-20. Lake Mills.

Baker, Frank C.
1928 The Fresh-water Mollusca of Wisconsin (2 Vols.). The University of Wisconsin Press. Madison.
1939 Fieldbook of Illinois Land Snails. State of Illinois, Natural History Survey Division, Manual No. 2. Springfield.
1941 A Study in Ethnozoology of the Prehistoric Indians of Illinois. *In:* Transactions of the American Philosophical Society, Vol. 32, Pt. 1. Philadelphia.

Baker, Frank C., James B. Griffin and Richard Morgan
1941 Contribution to the Archaeology of the Illinois River Valley. Transactions of the American Philosophical Society, Vol. 32, Pt. 1. Philadelphia.

Bigony, Bea
1970 Late Woodland Occupations of the Saginaw Valley. The Michigan Archaeologist, Vol. 16, Nos. 3, 4, pp. 115-214.

Binford, Lewis
1963*a* The Hodges Site: A Late Archaic Burial Station. Anthropological Papers, Museum of Anthropology, University of Michigan, No. 19, pp. 124-48. Ann Arbor.
1963*b* The Pomranky Site: A Late Archaic Burial Station. Anthropological Papers, Museum of Anthropology, University of Michigan, No. 19, pp. 149-92. Ann Arbor.

Binford, Lewis R. and Mark L. Papworth
1963 The Eastport Site, Antrim County, Michigan. Anthropological Papers, Museum of Anthropology, University of Michigan, No. 19, pp. 71-123. Ann Arbor.

Binford, Lewis R. and George I. Quimby
1963 Indian Sites and Chipped Stone Materials in the Northern Lake Michigan Area. Fieldiana: Anthropology, Vol. 36, No. 12, pp. 277-307. Chicago.

Black, C. A., D. D. Evans, J. L. White, L. E. Ensminger and F. E. Clark
1965 Methods of Soil Analysis: Part II. American Society of Agronomy, Agronomy Series No. 9. Madison.

Bluhm, Elaine A. and William J. Beeson
1960 The Excavation of Three Hopewell Mounds at the Caterpillar Tractor Company. Illinois Archaeological Survey, Bulletin No. 2, pp. 1-24. Urbana.

Boycott, A. E.
1929 The Oecology of British Land Mollusca, with Special Reference to those of Ill-defined Habitat. Malacological Society, Proceedings, Vol. 18, pp. 213-34. London.

Braidwood, Robert and Bruce Howe
1960 Prehistoric Investigations in Iraqi Kurdistan. Studies in Ancient Oriental Civilization, Vol. 31. Chicago.

Brainerd, George W.
1939 An Illustrated Field Key for the Identification of Mammal Bones. The Ohio Archaeological and Historical Quarterly, Vol. 48, No. 4, pp. 324-28. Columbus.

Brose, David S.
1966 The Valley Sweets Site, 20SA24, Saginaw County, Michigan. The Michigan Archaeologist, Vol. 12, No. 1, pp. 1-21. Ann Arbor.
1967 The Custer Road Dump Site: An Exercise in Victorian Archaeology. The Michigan Archaeologist, Vol. 13, No. 2, pp. 37-128. Ann Arbor.
1968 The Archaeology of Summer Island: Changing Settlement Systems in the Northern Lake Michigan Region. Ph.D. Dissertation. The University of Michigan. Ann Arbor.

Brown, James A.
1964 The Northeastern Extension of the Havana Tradition. Illinois State Museum, Scientific Papers, Vol. 12, pp. 107-22. Springfield.

Brown, Malcom, J. E. Green, T. J. Boag and E. Kuitunen-Ekbaum
1950 Parasitic Infections of the Eskimos at Islooik, N.W.T. Canadian Journal of Public Health, Vol. 41, pp. 508-12. Toronto.

Burch, John B.
1962 The Eastern Land Snails. W. Brown Co. Dubuque.

Burt, William H.
1946 The Mammals of Michigan. University of Michigan Press. Ann Arbor.

Callen, E. O. and T. W. M. Cameron
1960 A Prehistoric Diet Revealed in Coprolites. New Scientist, Vol. 8, pp. 35-40. London.

Cameron, T. W. M.
1945 Fish-carried Parasites in Canada: No. 1, Parasites Carried by Fresh Water Fish. Canadian Journal of Comparative Medicine, Vol. 9, pp. 245-54, 283-86, 302-11. Gardenuale, Quebec.

Cheatum, E. P. and D. Allen
1966 Ecological Significance of the Fossil Freshwater and Land Snails from the Domebo Mammoth Kill Site. Contributions of the Museum of the Great Plains, No. 1, pp. 36-43. Lawton.

Cleland, Charles E.
1966 The Prehistoric Animal Ecology and Ethnozoology of the Upper Great Lakes Region. Anthropological Papers, Museum of Anthropology, University of Michigan, No. 29. Ann Arbor.

Cole, Fay-Cooper and Thorne Duel
1937 Rediscovering Illinois. University of Chicago Press. Chicago.

Cole, J. L.
1878 Saginaw Notes. Michigan Pioneer and Historical Collections, Vol. 2, p. 474. Lansing.

Conant, Ruger
1958 Field Guide to Reptiles and Amphibians of Eastern North America. Houghton Miflin Company. Boston.

Cook, S. F.
1959 A Reconsideration of Shell Mounds with Respect to Population and Nutrition. American Antiquity, Vol. 12, No. 1, pp. 50-53. Salt Lake City.

Cornwall, I. W.
1956 Bones for the Archaeologist. Phoenix House. London.
1958 Soils for the Archaeologist. Phoenix House. London.

Crane, H. R. and James B. Griffin
1961 University of Michigan Radiocarbon Dates VI. Radiocarbon, Vol. 3, pp. 105-25. New Haven.
1965 University of Michigan Radiocarbon Dates X. Radiocarbon, Vol. 7, pp. 123-52. New Haven.
1966 University of Michigan Radiocarbon Dates XI. Radiocarbon, Vol. 8, pp. 256-85. New Haven.
n.d. University of Michigan Radiocarbon Dates XII. Radiocarbon. In press.

Crumley, Carole L.
1967 The Kantzler Site: A Multicomponent Manifestation of the Woodland Pattern. M.A. Dissertation. The University of Calgary.

Densmore, Frances
1926 Use of Plants by the Chippewa Indians. Bureau of American Ethnology, 44th Annual Report, pp. 277-97. Washington, D.C.

Dice, Lee R.
1943 The Biotic Provinces of North America. University of Michigan Press. Ann Arbor.

Dumond, Frank L.
1937 An Introduction to the Birds of Michigan. Michigan Audubon Society, Grand Rapids.

Dustin, Fred
1929*a* Ancient Pottery Remains in the Saginaw District, Michigan. Papers of the Michigan Academy of Science, Arts and Letters, Vol. 10, pp. 67-77. Ann Arbor.
1929*b* Some Ancient Fire-beds in Saginaw County, Michigan. Michigan History Magazine, Vol. 12, No. 4, pp. 301-07. Lansing.
1930 Some Ancient Indian Village Sites in Saginaw County, Michigan. Papers of the Michigan Academy of Science, Arts and Letters, Vol. 12, pp. 75-93. Ann Arbor.
1935 A Study of Bayport Chert. Papers of the Michigan Academy of Science, Arts and Letters, Vol. 20, pp. 465-75. Ann Arbor.
1968 Saginaw Valley Archaeology. The Michigan Archaeologist. Vol. 14, Nos. 1-2, pp. 1-130. Ann Arbor.

Faust, E. C. and P. E. Russel
1964 Clinical Parasitology. Lea and Febiger. Philadelphia.

Fitting, James E.
1965 Late Woodland Cultures of Southeastern Michigan. Anthropological Papers, Museum of Anthropology, University of Michigan, No. 24. Ann Arbor.
1968*a* Environmental Potential and the Postglacial Readaption in Eastern North America. American Antiquity. Vol. 33, No. 4, pp. 441-43. Salt Lake City.
1968*b* Northern Lake Michigan Lithic Industries. Anthropological Papers, Museum of Anthropology, University of Michigan, No. 34, pp. 116-33. Ann Arbor.
1968*c* The Spring Creek Site, 20MU3, Muskegon County, Michigan. Anthropological Papers, Museum of Anthropology, University of Michigan, No. 32, pp. 1-78. Ann Arbor.
n.d.*a* The Archaeology of Michigan. The Natural History Press. In press.
n.d.*b* The Nature and Extent of Havana Influence of the Middle Woodland Occupation of the Saginaw Valley. Paper presented at the Third Havana Conference, Springfield, Illinois, July, 1968.
n.d.*c* Unpublished Field Notes from the 1964 Excavations at the Schultz Site (20SA2) on file at the Museum of Anthropology, University of Michigan. Ann Arbor.

Fitting, James E., David S. Brose, Henry T. Wright and James Dinerstein
1969 The Goodwin-Gresham Site, 20IS8, Iosco County, Michigan. The Wisconsin Archeologist, Vol. 50, No. 1, pp. 125-83. Lake Mills.

Fitting, James E. and Charles E. Cleland
1969 Late Prehistoric Settlement Patterns in the Upper Great Lakes. Ethnohistory, Vol. 16, No. 4, pp. 289-302. Tucson.

Fitting, James E. and Susan Sassé
1969 The Hodges Site, 20SA130, Saginaw County, Michigan. The Michigan Archaeologist, Vol. 15, No. 3, pp. 57-77. Ann Arbor.

Flanders, Richard E.
1965 A Comparison of Some Middle Woodland Materials from Michigan and Illinois. Ph.D. Dissertation, University of Michigan. Ann Arbor.

Fournelle, H. J., I. L. Wallace and V. Rader
1948 A Bacteriological and Parasitological Survey of Enteric Infections in an Alaskan Eskimo Area. American Journal of Public Health, Vol. 48, No. 11, pp. 1489-97. New York.

Fowler, Melvin L.
1952 The Clear Lake Site: Hopewellian Occupation. Illinois State Museum, Scientific Papers, Vol. 5, pp. 131-76. Springfield.
1955 Ware Groupings and Decorations of Woodland Ceramics in Illinois. American Antiquity, Vol. 20, pp. 213-25. Salt Lake City.

Frostic, F. W.
1918 Floods of the Saginaw Valley: Their Cause and Effects. Papers of the Michigan Academy of Science, Arts and Letters, Vol. 20, pp. 67-81. Ann Arbor.

Goodrich, Calvin
1932 The Mollusca of Michigan. Occasional Papers, Museum of Zoology, Handbook No. 5. Ann Arbor.

Griffin, James B.
1941 Additional Hopewell Material from Illinois. Indiana Historical Society, Prehistory Research Series, Vol. 2, No. 3, pp. 165-223. Indianapolis.
1943 The Fort Ancient Aspect. The University of Michigan Press. Ann Arbor.
1945 The Ceramic Affiliations of the Ohio Valley Adena Culture. University of Kentucky Reports in Anthropology and Archaeology, Vol. 6. Lexington.
1952 Some Early and Middle Woodland Pottery Types in Illinois. Illinois State Museum, Scientific Papers, Vol. 5, pp. 93-129. Springfield.
1960 Climatic Change: A Contributary Cause of the Growth and Decline of Northern Hopewell Culture. The Wisconsin Archeologist, Vol. 41, No. 1, pp. 21-33. Lake Mills.
1961*a* Post-Glacial Ecology and Cultural Change in the Great Lakes Area of North America. Institute of Science and Technology, Great Lakes Research Division Publication No. 7, pp. 147-55. Ann Arbor.
1961*b* Some Correlations of Climatic and Culture Change in Eastern North American Prehistory. Annals of the New York Academy of Science, Vol. 95, pp. 710-17. New York.
1965 Late Quarternary Prehistory in the Northeastern Woodlands. *In;* The Quarternary of the United States edited by H. E. Wright, Jr. and David G. Frey, pp. 655-67. Princeton University Press. Princeton.

Griffin, James B. and Dan F. Morse
1961 The Short Nosed God From the Emmons Site, Illinois. American Antiquity, Vol. 26, No. 4, pp. 561-63. Salt Lake City.

Guilday, John E., Paul W. Parmalee and Donald P. Tanner
1962 Aboriginal Butchering Techniques at the Eschelman Site (36LA12), Lancaster County, Pennsylvania. Pennsylvania Archaeologist, Vol. 32, No. 2, pp. 59-83. Milton.

Guta, Margaret (translator)
1957 Journal of the Last Winter Mission of Father Henry Nouvel, Superior of the Missions of the Ottawa. The Michigan Archaeologist, Vol. 3, No. 3, pp. 13-21. Ann Arbor.

Halsey, John R.
1967 The Bussinger Site. The Saginaw Valley Archaeologist, Vol. 4, No. 2. Unpaged. Saginaw.

Hamilton, William J., Jr.
1943 The Mammals of Eastern United States. Comstock Publishing Co. Ithaca, New York.

Hankinson, Thomas L.
1932 Observations on the Breeding Behavior and Habitats of Fishes in Southern Michigan. Papers of the Michigan Academy of Science, Arts and Letters, Vol. 15, pp. 411-25. Ann Arbor.

Harrison, Sidney
1966 The Schmidt Site (20SA192), Saginaw County, Michigan. The Michigan Archaeologist, Vol. 12, No. 2, pp. 49-70. Ann Arbor.

Helman, Vernon
1950 Archaeological Survey of Owen County, Indiana. The Indiana Historical Society. Indianapolis.

Herrington, H. B.
1962 A Revision of the *Sphaeriidae* of North America (Mollusca: *Pelecypoda).* Miscellaneous Publications, Museum of Zoology, University of Michigan, No. 118. Ann Arbor.

Hough, Jack L.
1958 Geology of the Great Lakes. University of Illinois Press. Urbana.
1963 The Prehistoric Great Lakes of North America. The American Scientist, Vol. 51, No. 1, pp. 84-109. Princeton.

Hubbs, Carl L. and Reeve M. Bailey
1938 The Small-Mouthed Bass. Cranbrook Institute of Science, Bulletin No. 10. Bloomfield Hills.

Hubbs, Carl L. and Karl F. Langler
1947 Fishes of the Great Lakes Region. Cranbrook Institute of Science, Bulletin No. 26. Bloomfield Hills.

Janzen, Donald R.
1968*a* The Naomikong Point Site and the Dimensions of Laurel in the Lake Superior Region. Ph.D. Dissertation, University of Michigan.
1968*b* Survey and Excavation at Burnt Bluff in 1965. Anthropological Papers, Museum of Anthropology, University of Michigan, No. 34, pp. 61-94. Ann Arbor.

Jelinek, Arthur J. and James E. Fitting
1963 Some Studies of Natural Radioactivity in Archaeological and Paleontological Materials. Papers of the Michigan Academy of Science, Arts and Letters, Vol. 48, pp. 531-40. Ann Arbor.

Jennings, Jesse O. and Edward Norbeck (editors)
1964 Prehistoric Man in the New World. University of Chicago Press. Chicago.

Jordon, David S. and Barton W. Everman
1902 American Food and Game Fishes. Doubleday, Page and Co. New York.

Keslin, Richard O.
1958 A Preliminary Report of the Hahn (Dg 1 and Dg 2) and Horicon (Dg 5) Sites. Dodge County, Wisconsin. The Wisconsin Archeologist, Vol. 39, No. 4, pp. 191-273. Lake Mills.

Kidder, Alfred V.
1932 The Artifacts of Pecos. Phillips Academy. Andover, Massachusetts.

Krumbein, W. C. and F. J. Pettijohn
1938 Manual of Sedimentary Petrography. Appleton, Century and Crofts. New York.

Lagler, Karl F.
1949 Fish and Fishing in Michigan. Follett's. Ann Arbor.

Lambert, Robert J., Jr.
1952 Review of the Literature of Ethno-Conchology. Sterkiana, No. 2, pp. 1-8.

Leeson, Michael A.
1881 History of Saginaw County, Michigan. C. C. Chapman and Company. Michigan.

Leopold, Luna B., M. Gordon Wolman and John P. Miller
1964 Fluvial Processes in Geomorphology. W. H. Freeman. San Francisco.

McCormick, William R.
1883 Mounds and Mound Builders of the Saginaw Valley. Michigan Pioneer and Historical Collections, No. 4, pp. 379-83. Lansing.

McGregor, John C.
1952 The Havana Site. Illinois State Museum, Scientific Papers, Vol. 5, pp. 43-91. Springfield.
1958 The Pool and Irving Villages: A Study of Hopewell Occupation in the Illinois River Valley. University of Illinois Press. Urbana.

McKern, W. C.
1930 The Kletzien and Nitschke Mound Groups, Bulletin of the Public Museum of the City of Milwaukee, Vol. 3, No. 4. Milwaukee.

McPherron, Alan L.
1967 The Juntunen Site and the Late Woodland Prehistory of the Upper Great Lakes Area. Anthropological Papers, Museum of Anthropology, University of Michigan, No. 30. Ann Arbor.

Magath, Thomas B.
1954 The Importance of Syvatic Hydatic Disease. Journal of the American Veterinary Medicine Association, Vol. 125, pp. 411-14. New York.

Magath, Thomas B. and H. E. Essex
1931 Concerning the Distribution of *Diphyllobothrium latum* in North America. Journal of Preventive Medicine, Vol. 5, No. 4, pp. 227-42. Baltimore.

Mason, Ronald J.
1965 Wisconsin Middle Woodland Toggle Head Harpoons. The Michigan Archaeologist, Vol. 11, Nos. 3-4, pp. 156-64. Ann Arbor.
1966 Two Stratified Sites on the Door Peninsula of Wisconsin. Anthropological Papers, Museum of Anthropology, University of Michigan, No. 26. Ann Arbor.

1967 The North Bay Component at the Porte Des Morts Site, Door County, Wisconsin. The Wisconsin Archaeologist, Vol. 48, No. 4, pp. 267-345. Lake Mills.

n.d. Havana and Northeastern Wisconsin. Paper presented at the Third Havana Conference, Springfield, Illinois, July 1968.

Maxwell, Moreau S.
1951 Woodland Cultures of Southern Illinois. Logan Museum Publications in Anthropology, Bulletin No. 7. Beloit.

Meltzer, Herbert, L. Kovacs, T. Oxford and M. Matas
1956 *Echinococcus* in North American Indians and Eskimos. Canadian Medical Association Journal, Vol. 75, pp. 121-27. Toronto.

Miller, Albert
1888 Incidents in the Early History of the Saginaw Valley. Michigan Pioneer and Historical Collections, Vol. 13, pp. 378-80. Lansing.

Miller, Max
1953 Hydatid Infection in Canada. Canadian Medical Association Journal, Vol. 68, pp. 423-34. Toronto.

Morse, Dan F.
1963 The Steuben Village and Mounds: A Multi-component Late Hopewell Site in Illinois. Anthropological Papers, Museum of Anthropology, University of Michigan, No. 21. Ann Arbor.

1967 The Robinson Site and the Shell Mound Archaic Culture in the Middle South. Ph.D. Dissertation, The University of Michigan.

Munson, Patrick J.
1966 The Sheets Site: A Late Archaic-Early Woodland Occupation in West-Central Illinois. The Michigan Archaeologist, Vol. 12, No. 3, pp. 111-20. Ann Arbor.

Munson, Patrick J. and Robert L. Hall
1966 An Early Woodland Radiocarbon Date from Illinois. The Michigan Archaeologist, Vol. 12, No. 2, pp. 85-87. Ann Arbor.

New York State Conservation Department
1966 Aging Deer. Information leaflet.

Olsen, S. J.
1961 The Relative Value of Fragmentary Mammalian Remains. American Antiquity, Vol. 26, No. 4, pp. 538-40.

Ortmann, Arnold E.
1924 Distributional Features of Naiades in Lake Tributaries. American Midland Naturalist, Vol. 9, No. 3, pp. 101-17. Notre Dame.

Papworth, Mark L.
1967 Cultural Traditions in the Lake Forest Region During the Late High-Water Stages in the Post-Glacial Great Lakes. Ph.D. Dissertation, The University of Michigan.

Parmalee, Paul W.
1959 Animal Remains from the Modoc Rockshelter, Randolph County, Illinois. Illinois State Museum, Report of Investigations, No. 8, pp. 61-65. Springfield.

Peterson, Roger Tory
1947 A Field Guide to Birds. Houghton Mifflin. Boston.

Pike, Alan W.
1967 The Recovery of Parasite Eggs from Ancient Cesspit and Latrine Deposits: An Approach to the Study of Early Parasite Infection. *In:* Disease in Antiquity edited by Don Brothwell and A. T. Sandison, pp. 184-88. Charles C. Thomas. Springfield.

Pike, Alan W. and Martin Biddle
1966 Parasite Eggs in Medieval Winchester. Antiquity, Vol. 40, pp. 293-96. Glouchester, England.

Pilsbry, H. A.
1939 Land Mollusca of North America (North of Mexico). Monographs of the Philadelphia Academy of Natural Sciences, Vol. 1, No. 3, Pt. 1. Philadelphia.

1940 Land Molluscs of North America (North of Mexico). Monographs of the Philadelphia Academy of Natural Sciences, Vol. 1, No. 3, Pt. 2. Philadelphia.
1946 Land Molluscs of North America (North of Mexico). Monographs of the Philadelphia Academy of Natural Science, Vol. 2, No. 3, Pt. 1. Philadelphia.
1948 Land Mollusca of North America (North of Mexico). Monographs of the Philadelphia Academy of Natural Science, Vol. 2, No. 3, Pt. 2. Philadelphia.

Pi-Sunyer, Orjol
1965 The Flint Industry. *In:* The McGraw Site: A Study of Hopewell Dynamics by Olaf H. Prufer. Scientific Publications of the Cleveland Museum of Natural History (N.S.), Vol. 4, No. 1, pp. 60-89. Cleveland.

Poole, John B.
1957 *Echinococcus* Disease in North America. American Journal of Tropical Medicine and Hygiene, Vol. 6, pp. 424-29. Baltimore.

Powers, William E.
1962 Drainage and Climate. *In:* Symposium on Great Lakes Basin edited by H. J. Pincus. American Association for the Advancement of Science. Washington, D.C.

Prufer, Olaf H.
1965 The McGraw Site: A Study in Hopewellian Dynamics. The Cleveland Museum of Natural History, Scientific Publications (N.S.), Vol. 4, No. 1. Cleveland.

Prufer, Olaf H. and Douglas H. McKenzie
1965 Ceramics. *In:* The McGraw Site: A Study in Hopewellian Dynamics. The Cleveland Museum of Natural History, Scientific Publications (N.S.), Vol. 4, No. 1, pp. 18-59. Cleveland.

Quimby, George I.
1941*a* The Goodall Focus: An Analysis of Ten Hopewellian Components in Michigan and Indiana. Indiana Historical Society, Prehistory Research Series, Vol. 2, No. 2, pp. 63-181. Indianapolis.
1941*b* Hopewellian Pottery Types in Michigan. Papers of the Michigan Academy of Science, Arts and Letters, Vol. 26, pp. 489-95. Ann Arbor.
1943 The Ceramic Sequence within the Goodall Focus. Papers of the Michigan Academy of Science, Arts and Letters, Vol. 28, pp. 543-48. Ann Arbor.

Rausch, Robert
1952 Hydatid Disease in Boreal Regions. Arctic, Vol. 5, No. 3, pp. 157-74. New York.

Ritchie, William A.
1955 Recent Discoveries Suggesting an Early Woodland Burial Cult in the Northeast. New York State Museum and Science Service, Circular No. 40. Albany.
1961 Typology and Nomenclature of New York Projectile Points. New York State Museum and Science Service, Bulletin No. 384. Albany.
1965 The Archaeology of New York State. The Natural History Press. New York.

Ritchie, William A. and Richard S. MacNeish
1949 The Pre-Iroquoian Pottery of New York State. American Antiquity, Vol. 15, No. 2, pp. 97-124. Menasha.

Ritzenthaler, Robert E. and George I. Quimby
1962 The Red Ocher Culture of the Upper Great Lakes and Adjacent Areas. Fieldiana: Anthropology, Vol. 36, No. 11, pp. 243-75. Chicago.

Rostlund, Erhard
1952 Freshwater Fish and Fishing in Native North America. University of California Press. Berkeley.

A Saginaw Emigrant
1882 Michigan Pioneer and Historical Collections, Vol. 7, pp. 270-71. Lansing.

Samuels, Robert
1965 Parasitological Study of Long-dried Fecal Samples. American Antiquity, Vol. 31, No. 2, pp. 175-79. Salt Lake City.

Saunders, L. G.
1949 A Survey of Helminth and Protozoan Incidence in Man and Dogs at Fort Chipewyan, Alberta. Journal of Parasitology, Vol. 35, pp. 31-34. Urbana.

Schoenbeck, Edith
1943 Some Data on Clear Lake Village Cultural Objects. Transactions of the Illinois State Academy of Science, Vol, 36, No. 2, p. 81. Springfield.

Shane, Orrin C., III

1967*a* The Leimbach Phase and Its Position in Eastern North American Prehistory. Ph.D. Dissertation. Case Institute of Technology. Cleveland.

1967*b* The Leimbach Site: An Early Woodland Village in Lorain County, Ohio. *In:* Studies in Ohio Archaeology edited by Olaf H. Prufer and Douglas H. McKenzie, pp. 98-120. Western Reserve University Press. Cleveland.

Smith, Harlan I.

1894 Caches of the Saginaw Valley, Michigan. Proceedings of the American Association for the Advancement of Science, Vol. 42, pp. 300-03. Washington, D.C.

1901 The Saginaw Valley Collection. Supplement to the American Museum Journal, Vol. 1, No. 12, pp. 1-24. New York.

1902 The Antiquities of Michigan, Their Value and Impending Loss. Michigan Pioneer and Historical Collections, Vol. 31, pp. 230-52. Lansing.

Smith, Huron H.

1932 Ethnobotony of the Ojibwe Indians. Bulletin of the Public Museum of the City of Milwaukee, Vol. 4, No. 3, pp. 372-525. Milwaukee.

Spencer, Bernard

1968 Mississippian Influences in the Saginaw Valley. Saginaw Valley Archaeologist, Vol. 5, No. 2, unpaged. Saginaw.

Stansberry, David H.

1965 The Molluscan Fauna. *In:* The McGraw Site: A Study in Hopewellian Dynamics by Olaf H. Prufer. The Cleveland Museum of Natural History, Scientific Publications (N.S.), Vol. 4, No. 1, pp. 119-24. Cleveland.

Struever, Stuart

1964 The Hopewell Interaction Sphere in Riverine-Western Great Lakes Culture History. Illinois State Museum, Scientific Papers, Vol. 12, pp 85-106. Springfield.

1965 Middle Woodland Culture History in the Great Lakes-Riverine Area. American Antiquity, Vol. 31, No. 2, pp. 211-23. Salt Lake City.

Sweatman, G. K. and R. J. Williams

1963 Comparative Studies on the Biology and Morphology of *Echinococcus granulosus* from Domestic Livestock, Moose and Reindeer. Parasitology, Vol. 53, Nos. 3-4, pp. 339-90. New York.

Taggart, David W.

1967 Seasonal Patterns in Settlement, Subsistence, and Industries in the Saginaw Late Archaic. The Michigan Archaeologist, Vol. 13, No. 4, pp. 153-70. Ann Arbor.

n.d.*a* The Feeheley Site: A Late Archaic Site in the Saginaw Valley. Unpublished manuscript in possession of the author.

n.d.*b* Field Summary of University of Michigan Museum of Anthropology Excavations at Green Point (Schultz site, 20SA2) Saginaw County, Michigan, during the summer of 1963. Manuscript on file at the University of Michigan Museum of Anthropology. Ann Arbor.

Taylor, Walter P. (editor)

1965 The Deer of North America: Their History and Management. Stackpole Co. Harrisburg, Pennsylvania.

Tuttle, S. J., L. Clayton and W. M. Land

1964 A Comparison of Fossil Pleistocene Molluscan Fauna from North Dakota with a Recent Molluscan Fauna from Minnesota. American Midland Naturalist, Vol. 71, No. 2, pp. 344-62. Notre Dame.

Underhill, Ruth M.

1953 Redman's America. University of Chicago Press. Chicago.

U.S. Army Corps of Engineers

1957 Report on the Saginaw River Basin. Washington, D.C.

U.S. Department of Agriculture

1951 Soil Survey Manual. U.S.D.A., Handbook No. 18. Washington, D.C.

U.S. Department of Agriculture—Forest Service

1948 Woody-Plant Seed Manual. U.S.D.A., Miscellaneous Publication, No. 654. Washington D.C.

Van der Schalie, Henry

1938 The Naiade Fauna of the Huron River in Southeastern Michigan. Miscellaneous Papers, Museum of Zoology, University of Michigan, No. 40. Ann Arbor.

1947 The Ecology of Molluscs for the Biology Teacher. The American Biology Teacher, Vol. 9, No. 6, pp. 174-76.

1948 The Commercially Valuable Mussels of the Grand River in Michigan. Michigan Department of Conservation, Miscellaneous Publications, No. 4, Ann Arbor.

1960 Pearls, Food and Buttons: Practical Uses of Michigan Mussels. Michigan Department of Conservation, Fish Division, Pamphlet No. 32. Lansing.

Verger, T.
1929 The Dog: A Reservoir of the Broad Tapeworm. Journal of the American Medical Association, Vol. 92, pp. 607-08. Chicago.
1930 Causes Underlying Increased Incidence of Broad Tapeworm in Man in North America. Journal of the American Medical Association, Vol. 95, pp. 1579-81. Chicago.
Vik, R.
1964 The Genus *Diphyllobothrium*. Experimental Parasitology, Vol. 15, pp. 361-80. New York.
Walker, Winslow M.
1952 The Dickison Mound Group, Peoria County, Illinois. Illinois State Museum, Scientific Papers, Vol. 5, pp. 13-41. Springfield.
Wardle, R.
1935 The Fish Tape Worm. Biological Board of Canada, Bulletin 45. Ottawa.
Wayne, William J. and James H. Zumberge
1965 Pleistocene Geology of Indiana and Michigan. *In:* The Quarternary of the United States edited by H. E. Wright, Jr. and David G. Frey, pp. 63-84. Princeton University Press. Princeton.
White, Anta M.
1963 Analytical Description of the Chipped Stone Industry from Snyders Site, Calhoun County, Illinois. Anthropological Papers, Museum of Anthropology, University of Michigan, No. 19, pp. 1-70. Ann Arbor.
White, Theodore
1953 A Method of Calculating Dietary Percentages of Various Food Animals Utilized by Aboriginal Peoples. American Antiquity, Vol. 18, No. 4, pp. 396-98. Salt Lake City.
Wedel, Waldo R.
1961 Prehistoric Man on the Great Plains. University of Oklahoma Press. Norman.
Wells, Mrs. Edward
1964 Another Toggle Head Harpoon From Door County, Wisconsin. The Wisconsin Archaeologist, Vol. 45, No. 2, pp. 99-100. Lake Mills.
Winters, Howard D.
1961 The Adler Mound Group. Illinois Archaeological Survey Bulletin No. 3, pp. 57-88. Urbana.
1963 An Archaeological Survey of the Wabash Valley in Illinois. Illinois State Museum, Report of Investigations, No. 10. Springfield.
Wobst, Martin H.
1968 The Butterfeld Site, 20BY29, Bay County, Michigan. Anthropological Papers, Museum of Anthropology, University of Michigan, No. 32, pp. 173-275. Ann Arbor.
Wolfgang, R. W.
1954 Indian and Eskimo Diphyllobothriasis. Canadian Medical Association Journal, Vol. 70, pp. 536-39. Toronto.
Wolman, M. Gordon and Luna B. Leopold
1957 River Flood Plains: Some Observations on Their Formation. U.S.G.S. Professional Paper 282-C. Washington, D.C.
Wray, Donald E. and Richard S. MacNeish
1961 The Hopewellian and Weaver Occupations of the Weaver Site, Fulton County, Illinois. Illinois State Museum, Scientific Papers, Vol. 7, No. 2. Springfield.
Wright, Gary A.
1967 Some Aspects of Early and Mid-Seventeenth Century Exchange Networks in the Western Great Lakes. The Michigan Archaeologist, Vol. 13, No. 4, pp. 181-97. Ann Arbor.
1968 A Further Note on Friendship and Gift Giving in the Western Great Lakes. The Michigan Archaeologist, Vol. 14, Nos. 3-4, pp. 145-47. Ann Arbor.
Wright, Henry T.
1964 A Transitional Archaic Campsite at Green Point (20SA1). The Michigan Archaeologist, Vol. 10, No. 1, pp. 17-22. Ann Arbor.
n.d. The Geological Sequence of the Schultz Site, Saginaw County, Michigan. Unpublished paper on file at the Museum of Anthropology, University of Michigan. Ann Arbor.
Wright, Henry T. and Richard E. Morlan
1964 The Hart Site: A Dustin Fishing Camp on the Shiawassee Embayment. The Michigan Archaeologist, Vol. 10, No. 3, pp. 49-53. Ann Arbor.
Wright, J. V.
1965 A Regional Examination of Ojibway Culture History. Anthropologica, Vol. 7, No. 2., pp. 189-227. Montreal.
Yarnell, Richard Asa
1964 Aboriginal Relationships Between Culture and Plant Life in the Upper Great Lakes Region. Anthropological Papers, Museum of Anthropology, University of Michigan, No. 23. Ann Arbor.